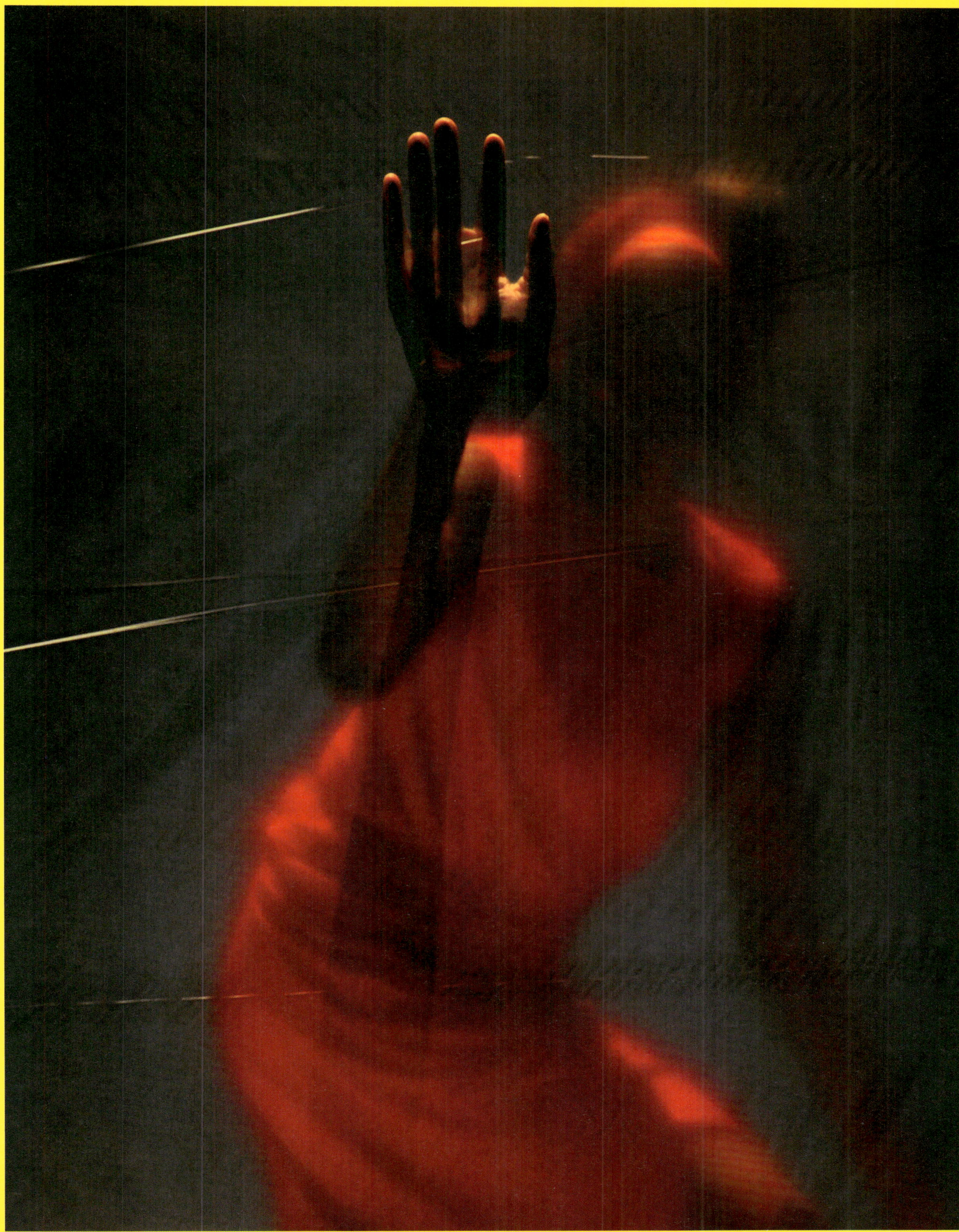

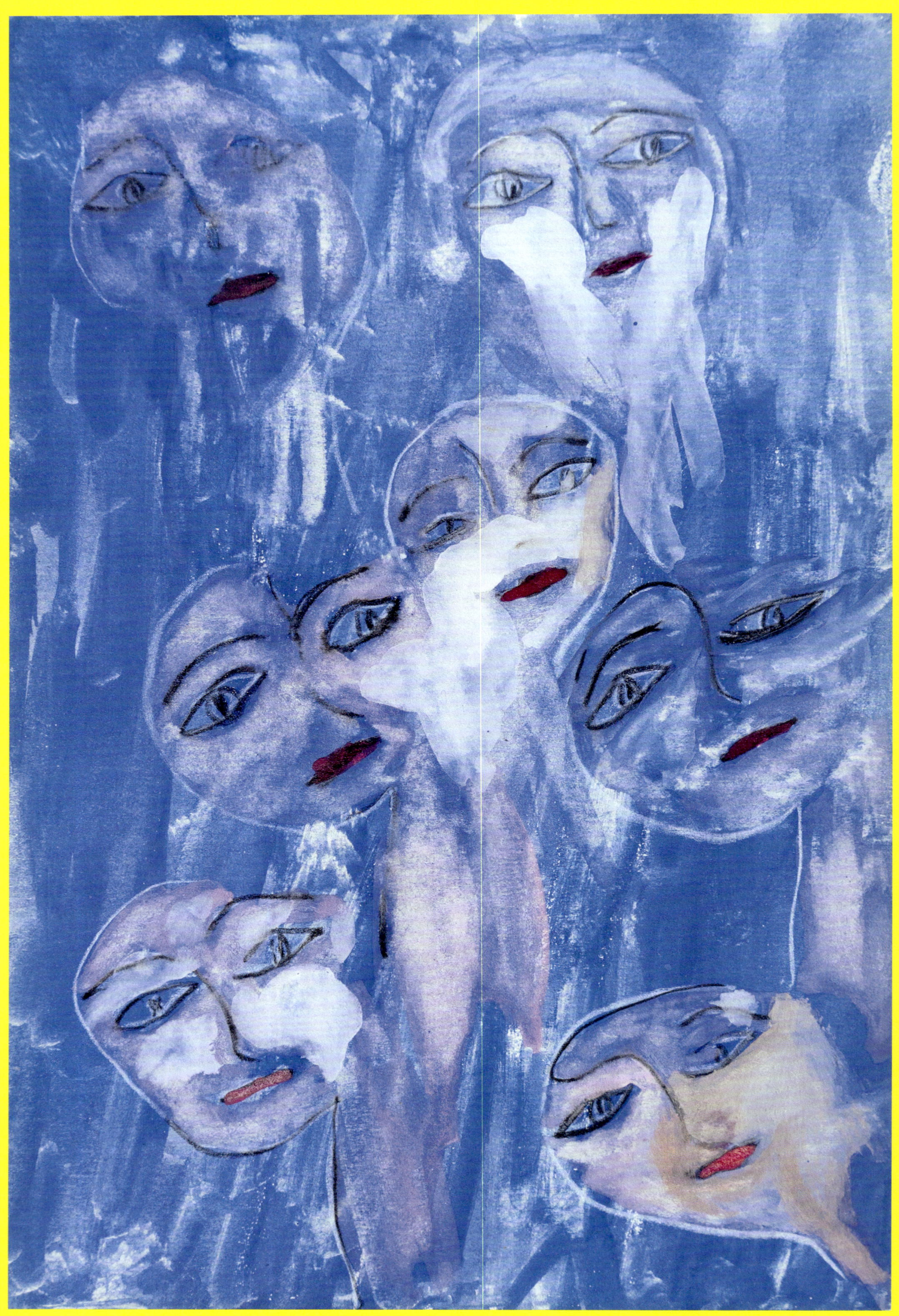

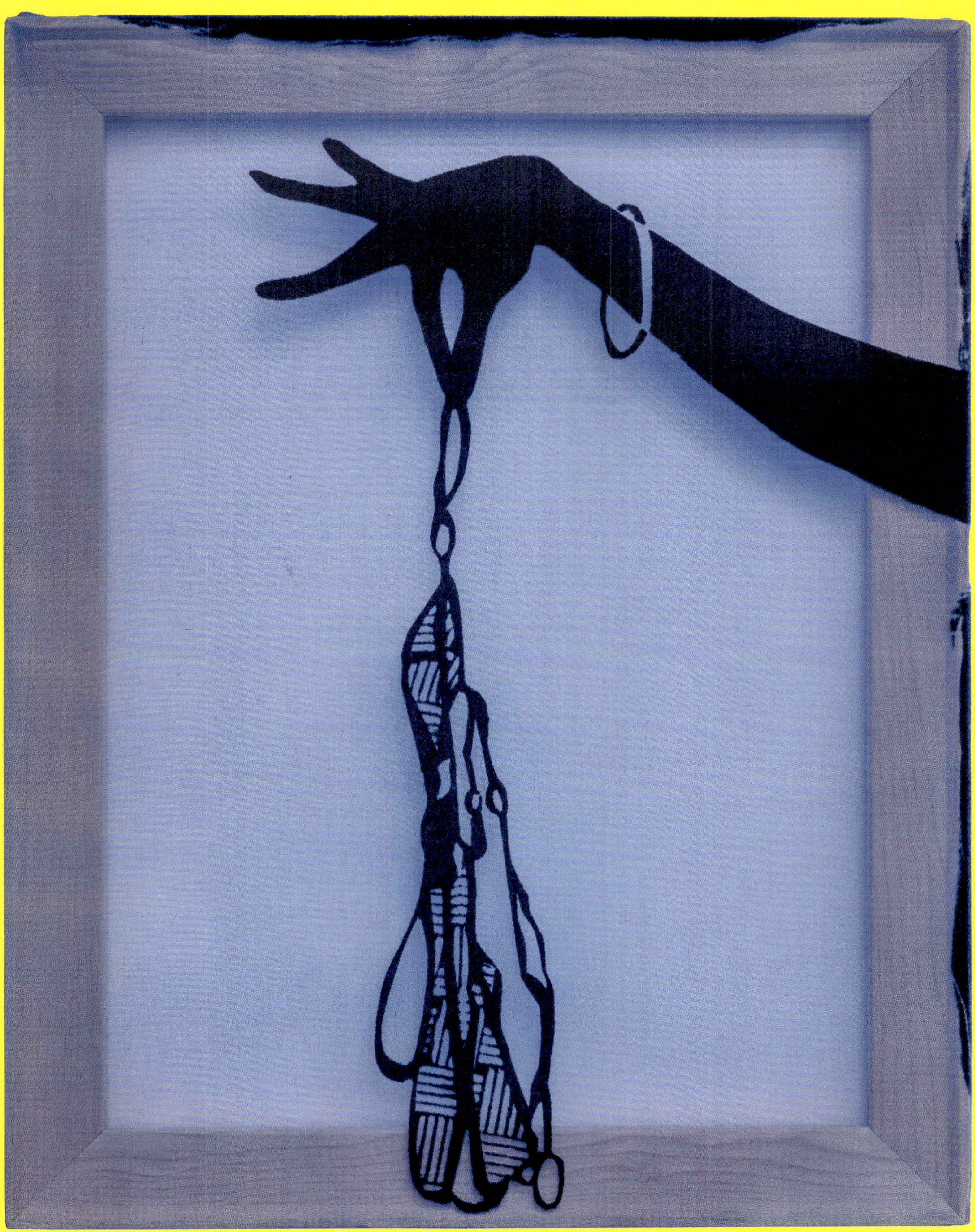

WOMEN OF MONTMARTRE.

THE illustration on this page is from a sketch of a band of women who were marching to Montmartre, during the second siege of Paris, to defend a barricade which they had erected there. These are the Amazons of the Commune, and womanly qualities which we admire, forgetting that it may be the very want of those attributes which has induced them to quit the conventional mode of life. The *vivandière* of our imagination is always young and pretty and innocent, a gay young creature amidst the regiment of rough, kindly men, and our feelings receive a shock sinew, ferocity such as the weaker vessel, man, can not hope to rival, and such a love of riot—always appearing in the van when Paris rises—that we might almost say that if revolutions are not produced by them, they are produced by the revolutions, and are imbued with their very spirit. These are some of the antagonists the Ver-

An eye-witness of this march to Montmartre writes: "I met a company of female Federals bearing two great red flags, and shouting the 'Marseillaise' and 'Vive la Commune.' I fancied I recognized at the head of the company one of the favorite orators of the club at the Boule Noire, who seemed to take the place of

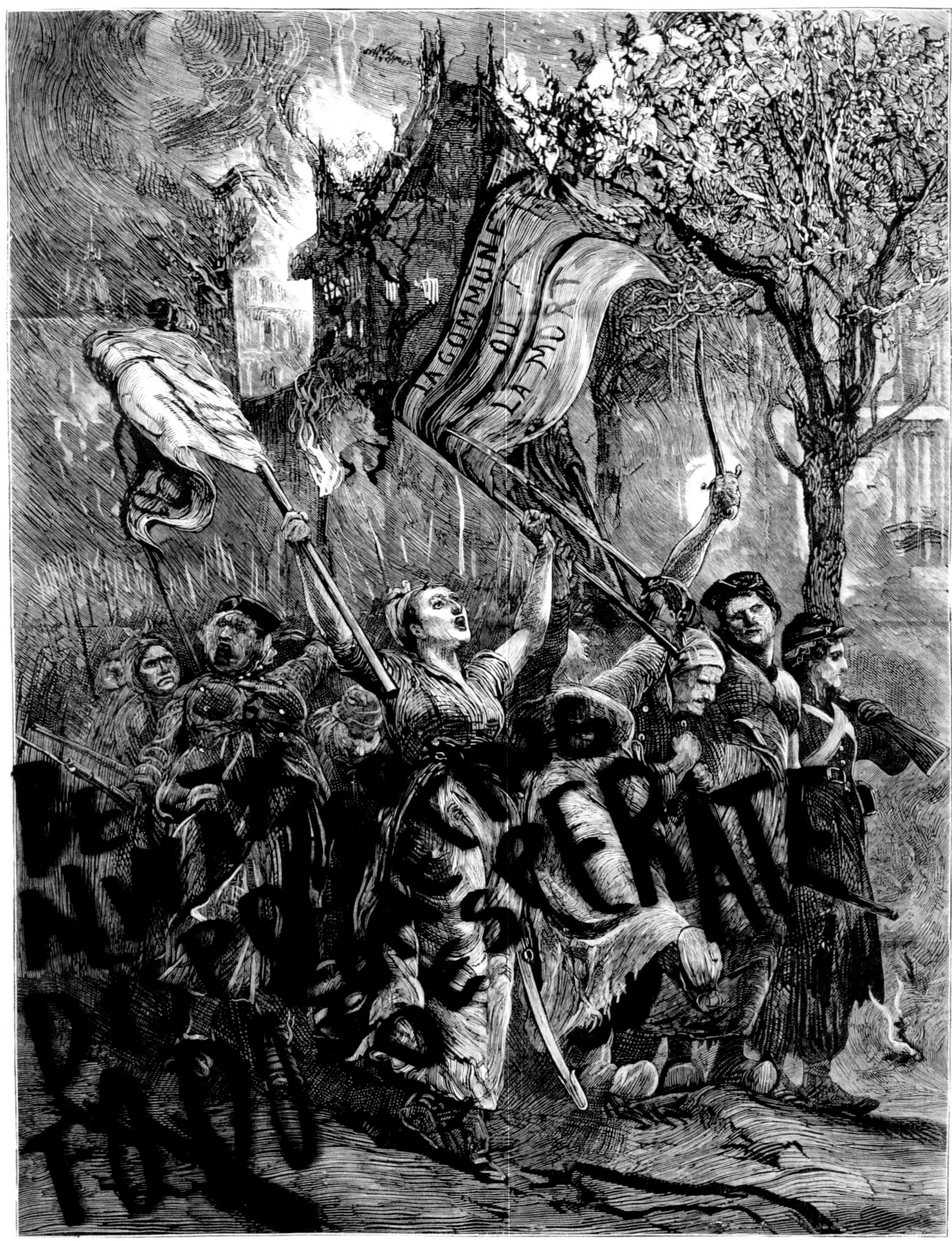

"THE COMMUNE OR DEATH!"—WOMEN OF MONTMARTRE.

give us an idea of what the warrior-woman really is—coarse, brawny, unwomanly, and degraded; picturesque certainly, but by no means pleasing. When women appear in exceptional situations we always picture them as we wish them to be, and mostly find them something very different. We generally endow them with those when we see the reality. The Amazon of romance is always beautiful and stately as Diana; but, if such a race ever existed, we should discover there was not much of woman's beauty about them, perhaps no more than we find in these fighting women of the Commune. They are fitted for their work; they have muscle and sailles troops had to conquer before they could call Paris their own, and in the accounts given of the long trains of prisoners, the most melancholy features are these women—defiant, jeering, and shameless—on their way to the hulks or the scaffold, or the trench, where the firing party awaited them.

an officer. Each woman had a Chassepôt slung across her shoulders, and a belt and cartouch box, amply supplied with cartridges, round her waist. The by-standers signified their disgust, but took care not to speak too loud, as it was evident these women were disposed to do something desperate."

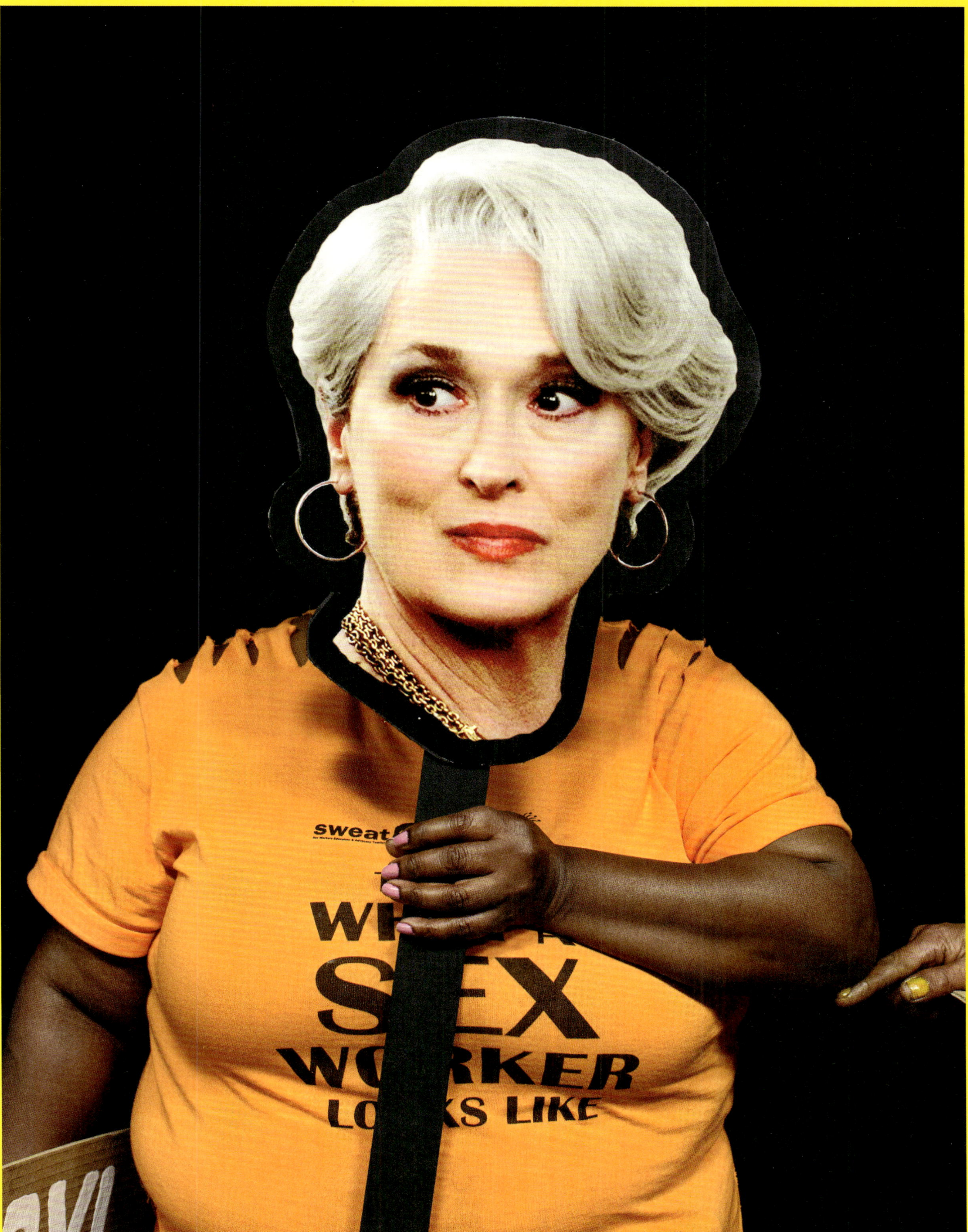

sweat
WH__ __
SEX
WO__KER
LO__KS LIKE

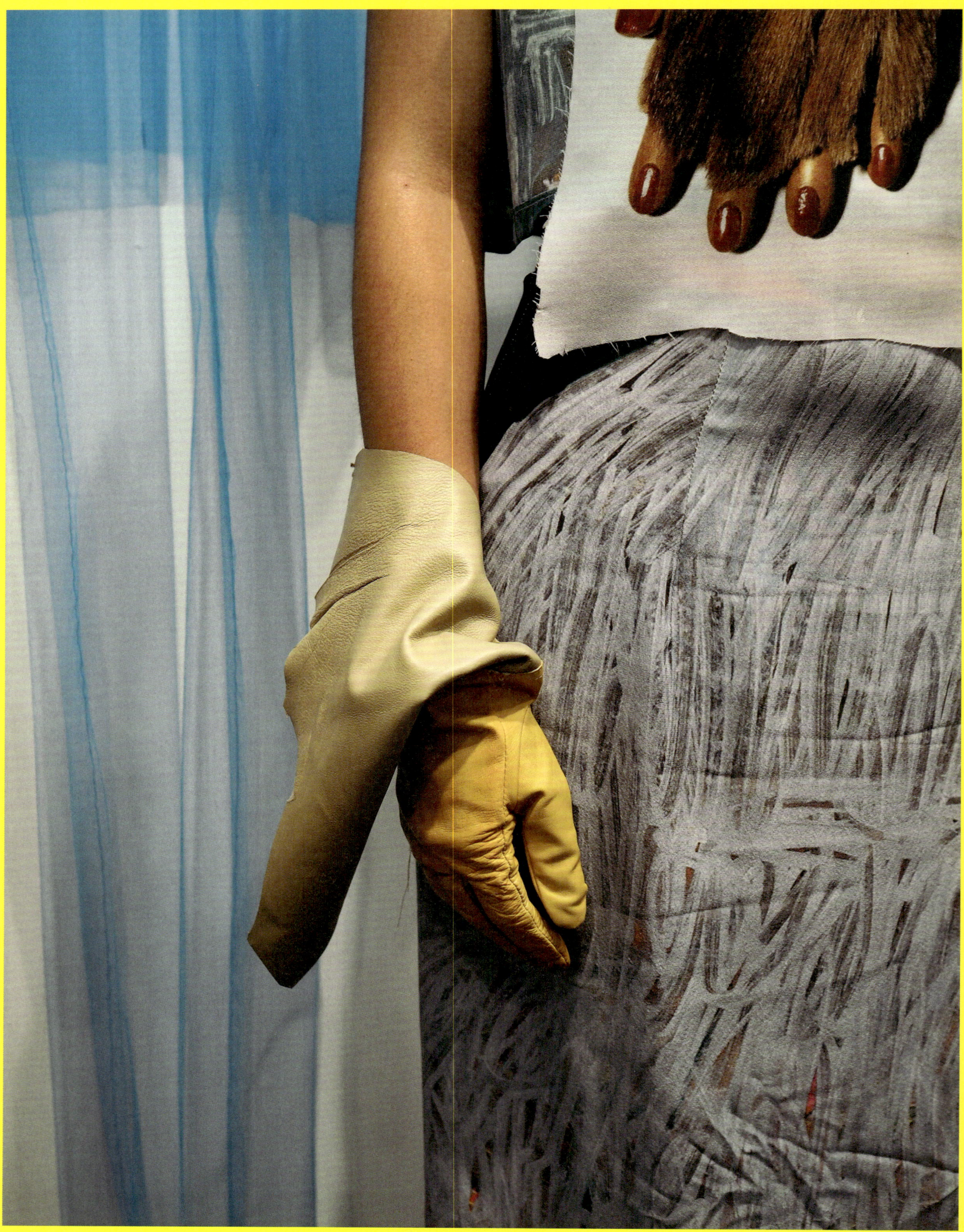

Witch Hunt

Leonor Antunes

b. 1972, Portugal. Lives and works in Berlin, Germany, and Lisbon, Portugal.

Leonor Antunes uses sculpture to explore history, memory, and placemaking in ways that are tied to the specific locales where her work is shown. Her materials and formal references are inspired by extensive research into craft traditions from Europe and South America, and into the work of underrecognized twentieth-century artists and designers—figures who are mostly, though not exclusively, women. Embodying a politics of remembrance and radical care, Antunes's work centers on highlighting the relationship between bodies and architectural space, teasing out a collective memory that unfolds across cultural, geographic, and temporal borders.

Each of Antunes's projects begins with the artist's collecting of personal accounts and aesthetic references related to the architecture of a particular exhibition site. Details and measurements from banisters, staircases, and windows are translated into delicate geometric sculptures made of wood, rope, leather, cork, and brass, materials that in turn refer to other artists and artisans. Antunes's 2017–18 exhibition *the frisson of the togetherness* at London's Whitechapel Gallery brought together her interest in the museum's history—namely, in the 1956 British Constructivism exhibition *This Is Tomorrow*—with her desire to highlight women artists whose contributions to modern art and architecture have been marginalized. In addition to original works by Antunes herself, the exhibition included wire jewelry by Brazilian artist Lucia Nogueira, vitrines by Danish designer Nanna Ditzel, and a rug by British artist Mary Martin, who herself appeared in *This Is Tomorrow*. Works with titles such as *Nanna* (2017) and *Discrepancies with M. M.* (2017) make explicit these hidden protagonists of Antunes's project. The smell of hanging horse bridles—sculptures from the random intersections series (2007–), crafted in the leather-braiding tradition of Antunes's native Portugal and inspired by the designs of Italian artist Carlo Mollino—conjured the stables that once stood where the Whitechapel now resides.

In Antunes's hands, every sculpture and exhibition becomes an archive of its own, bringing physical form to the lives of its subjects. *The last days in chimalistac*, held at Kunsthalle Basel in 2013, took its title from the life of Cuban-born designer Clara Porset. Having protested two governments in her home country, Porset fled to Mexico in 1935 and spent the rest of her life in the cobblestoned neighborhood of Chimalistac. The exhibition featured wood-and-rope sculptures inspired by Porset's furniture designs, as well as other works referencing Eileen Gray and Porset's lifelong friend Anni Albers, whom she met while studying at Black Mountain College in North Carolina. Porset was cited again in Antunes's exhibition *discrepancias con C. P.* (discrepancies with C. P., 2018).

Memory, for Antunes, is thus inextricably linked to the tactile and psychic qualities of materials. To engage in the vernacular traditions of a region—to handle wood, glass, and rope with a certain care—is to bear witness against the disappearance of ancestral legacies. In an era of vast industrialization and dehumanized production, Antunes claims the maintenance of craft as a political stance. The artists she cites also frequently upheld the language of craft themselves; consider Albers's extensive writing on textile history, or Porset's fondness for the agave fibers of indigenous Mexican traditions. Rather than mere duplication, however, Antunes's engagement with the legacies of modernism is akin to a call-and-response that allows her to deviate from her predecessors' practices when necessary. In *Anni #19* (2018), for example, Antunes adapts the design of Albers's linen-and-cotton tapestries into a delicate construction of threaded brass and steel. Like Ariadne, whose gift of red thread allowed Theseus to navigate Minos's Labyrinth toward freedom, Antunes uses material to trace a genealogy of radical artistic practice.

In her 1995 essay "Black Vernacular: Architecture as Cultural Practice," bell hooks writes, "Subversive historiography connects oppositional practices from the past with forms of resistance in the present, thus creating spaces of possibility where the future can be imagined differently—imagined in such a way that we can witness ourselves dreaming, moving forward and beyond the limits and confines of fixed locations." Antunes's move toward this aspirational place—a place embracing histories that have existed silently underneath other, more visible narratives—is just such a subversive historiography. Collapsing a complex and densely layered network of seemingly disparate memories onto a single plane, Antunes argues for the creation of alternative temporalities that defy a contemporary culture of forgetting.

—Vanessa Arizmendi

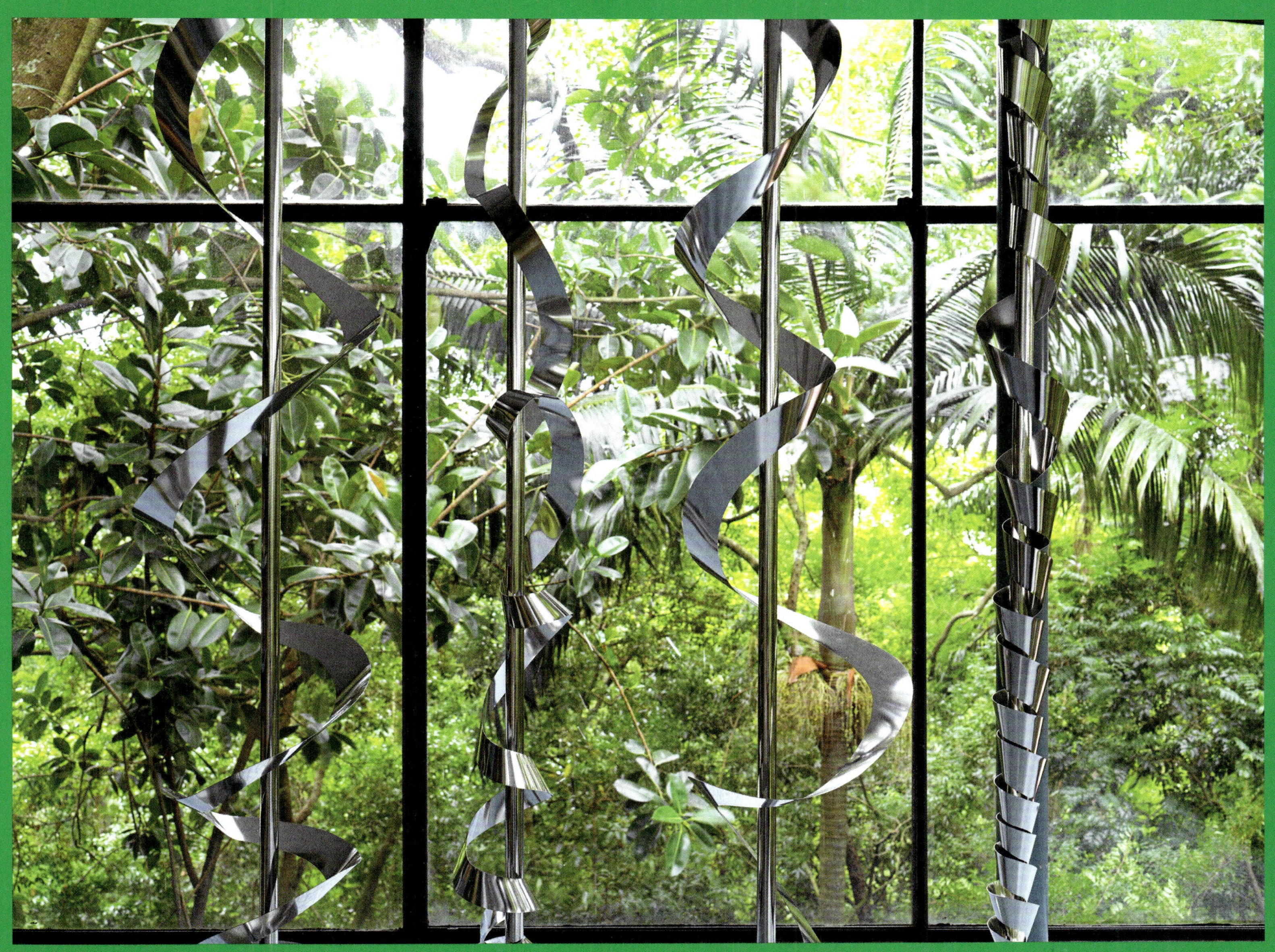

Lygia #1, #2, #3, #4, 2019

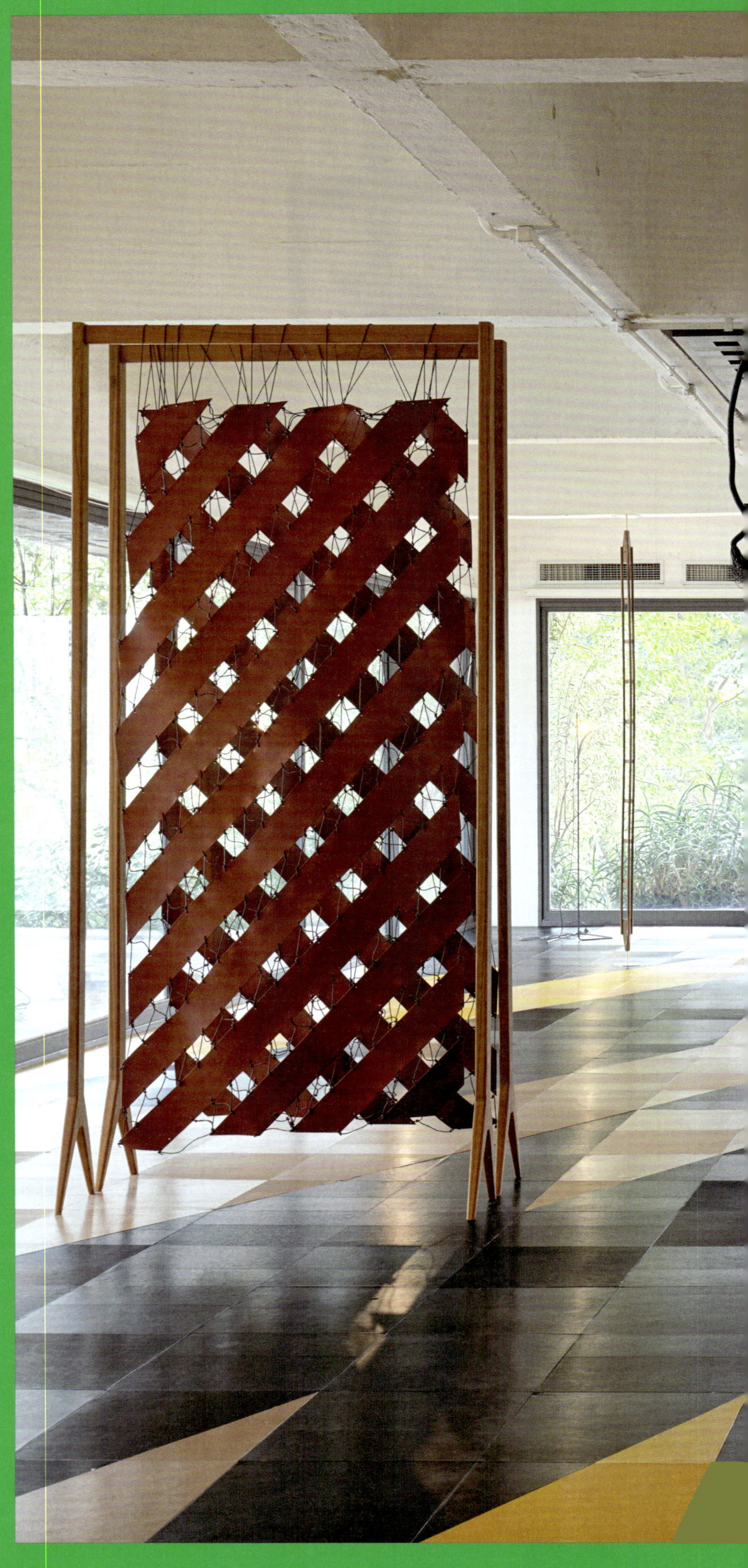

joints, voids and gaps, 2019

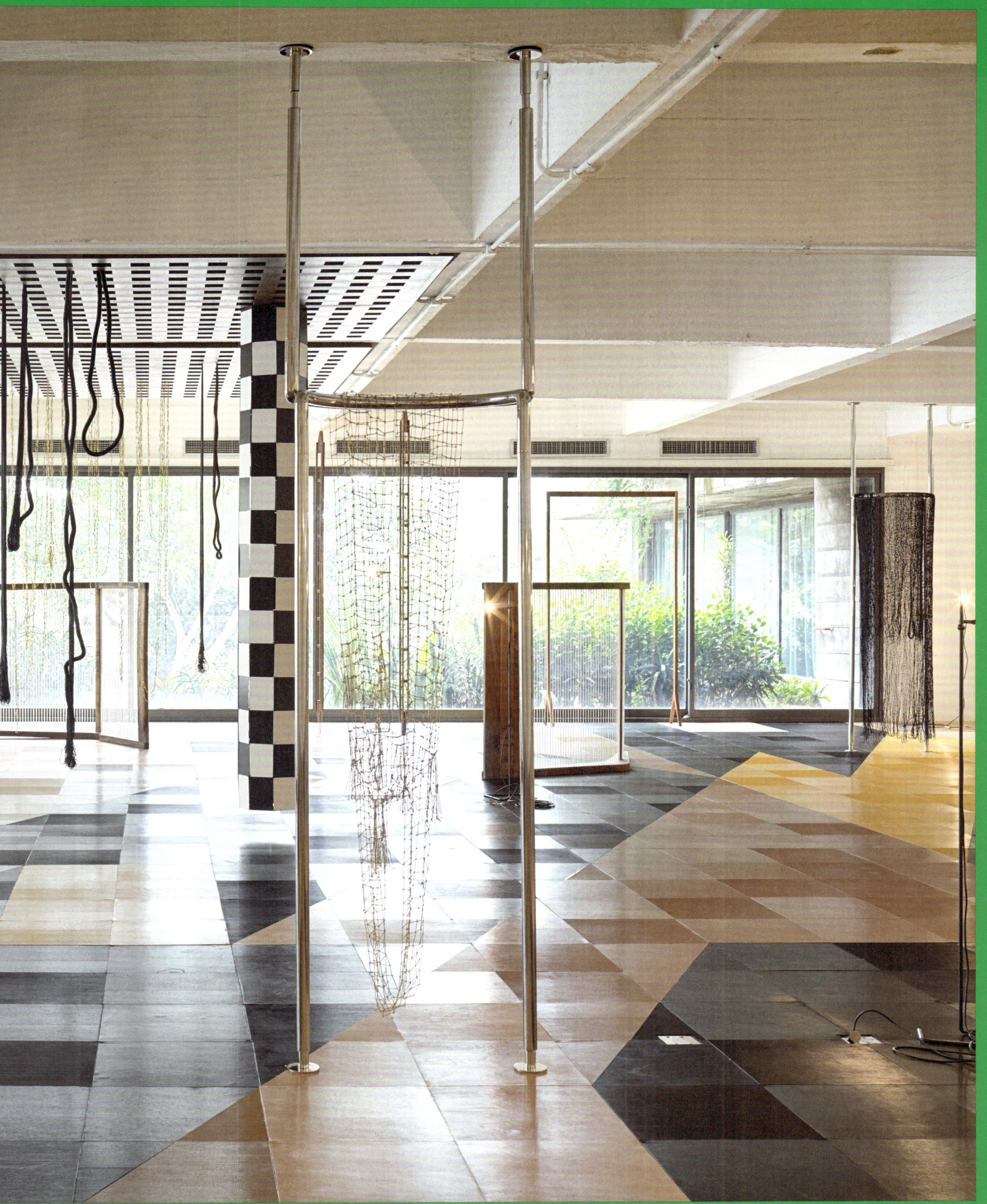

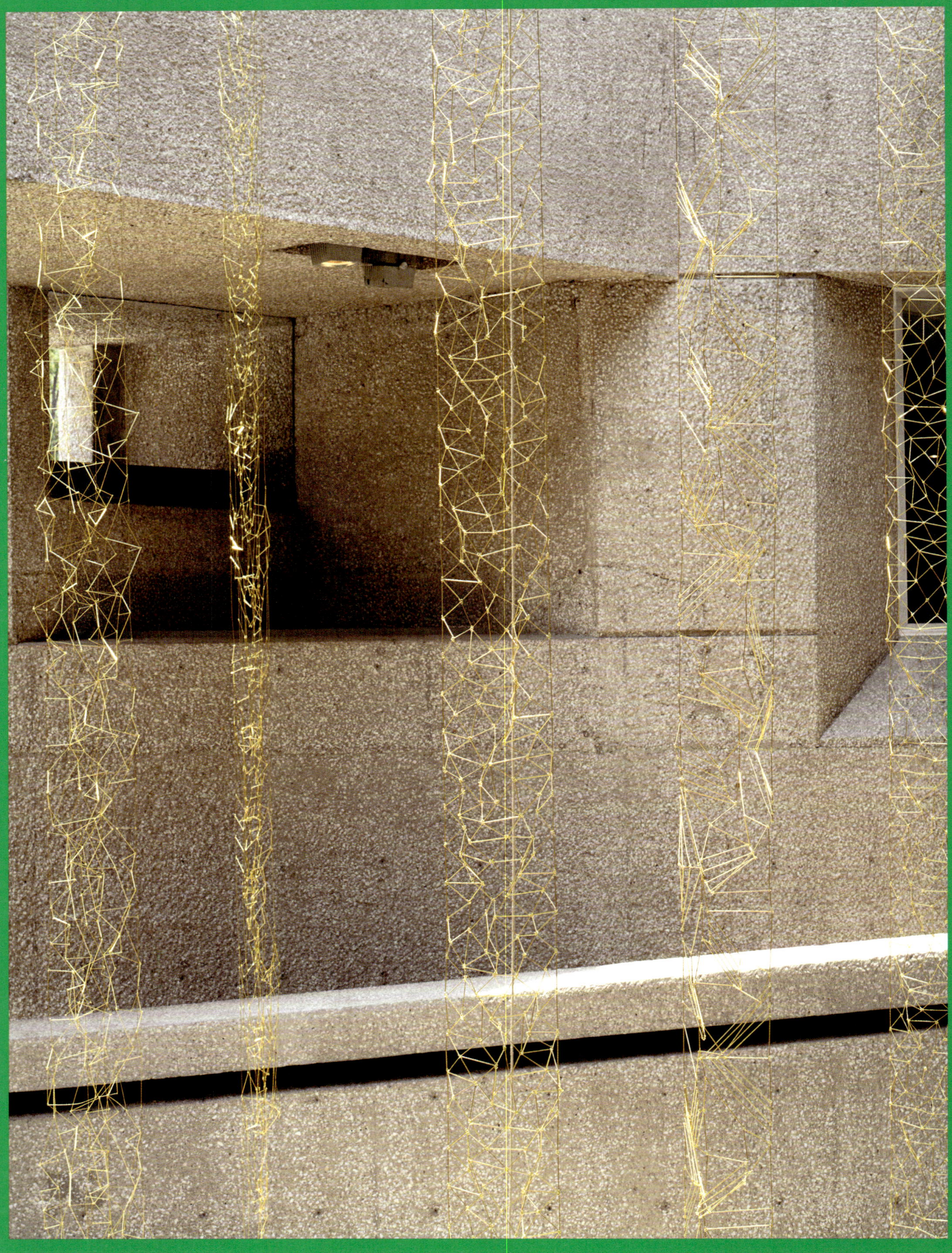

Oaxacan textile I + II, 2018

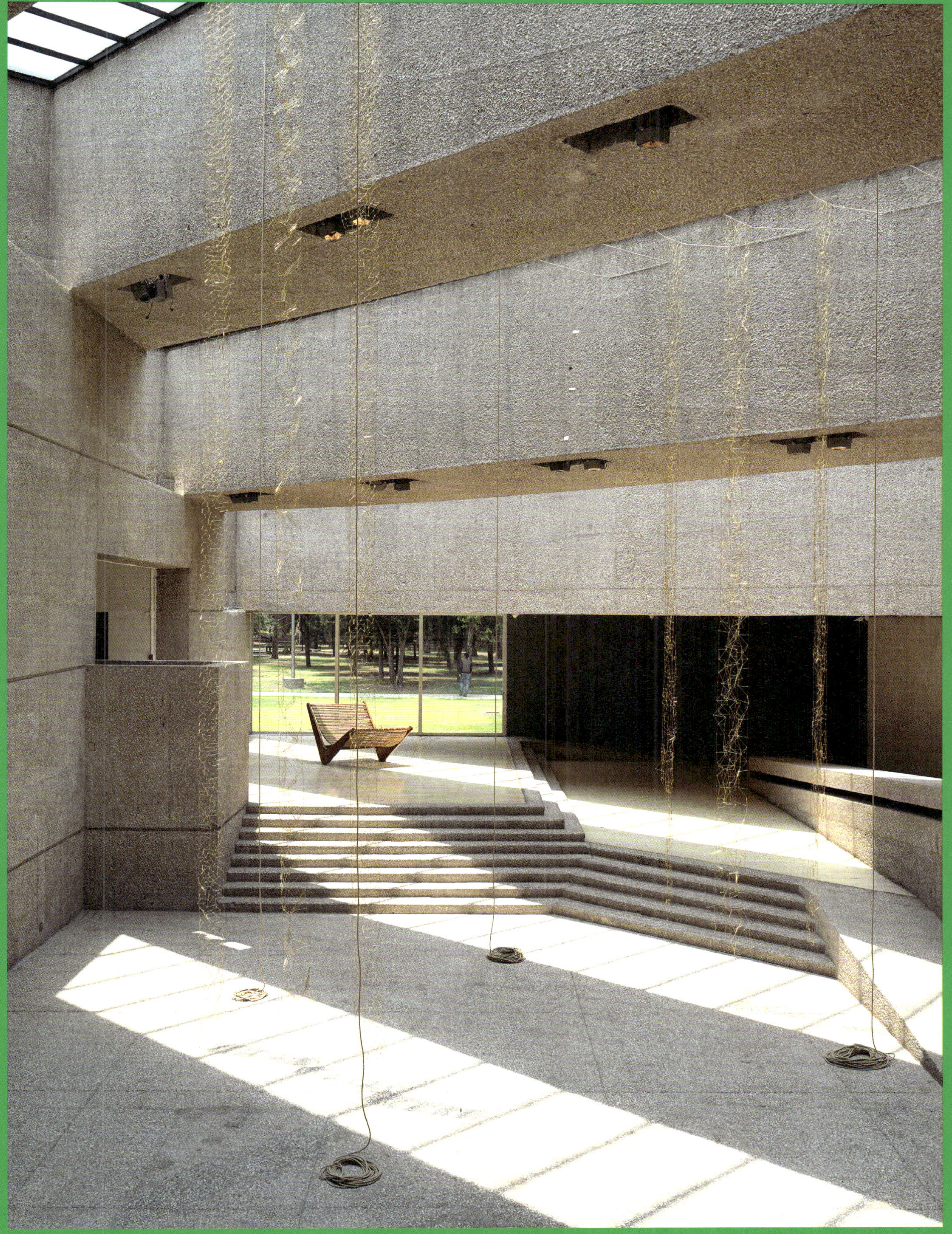

discrepancias con C. P. (discrepancies with C. P.), 2018

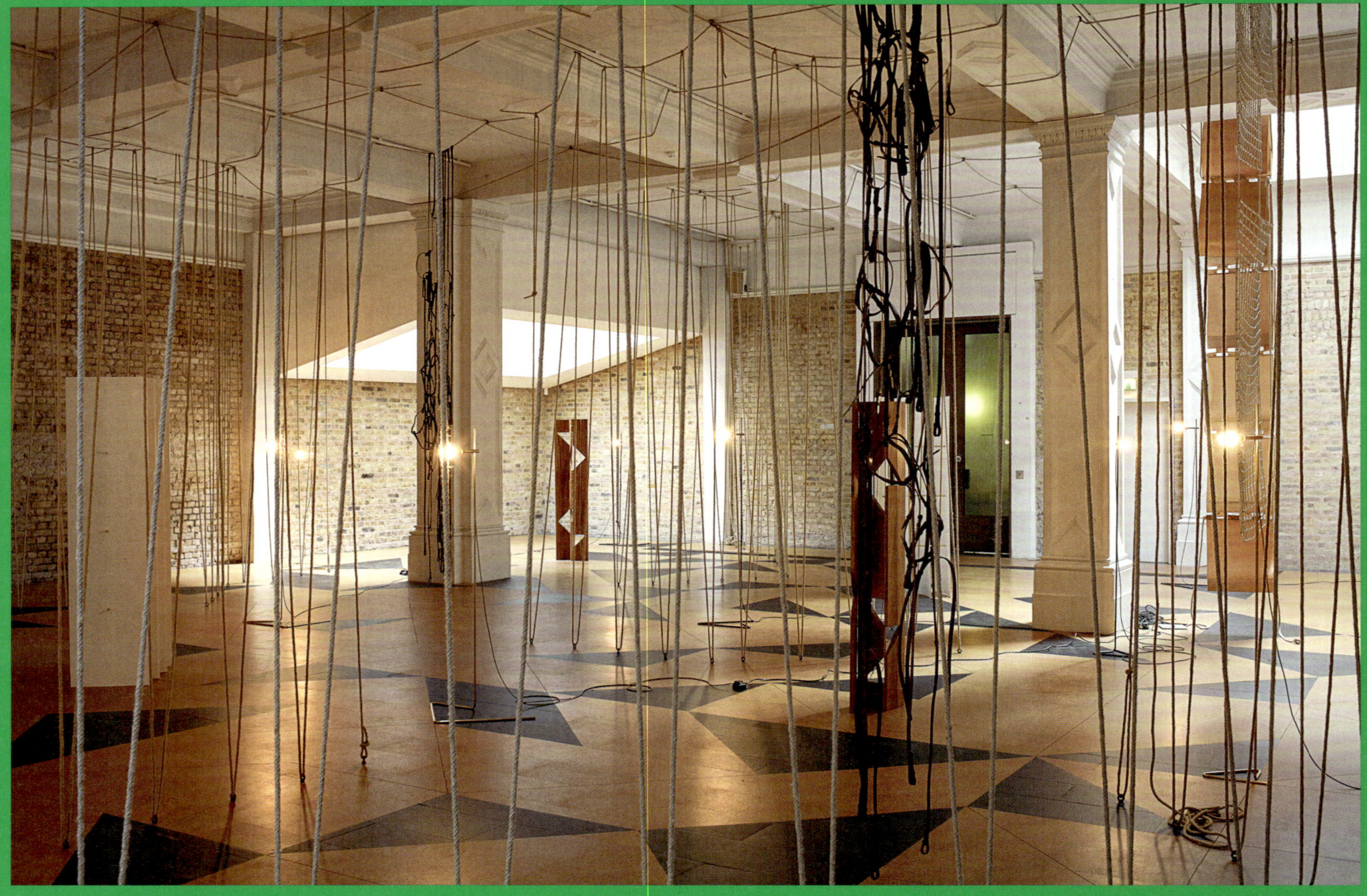

the frisson of the togetherness, 2017–18

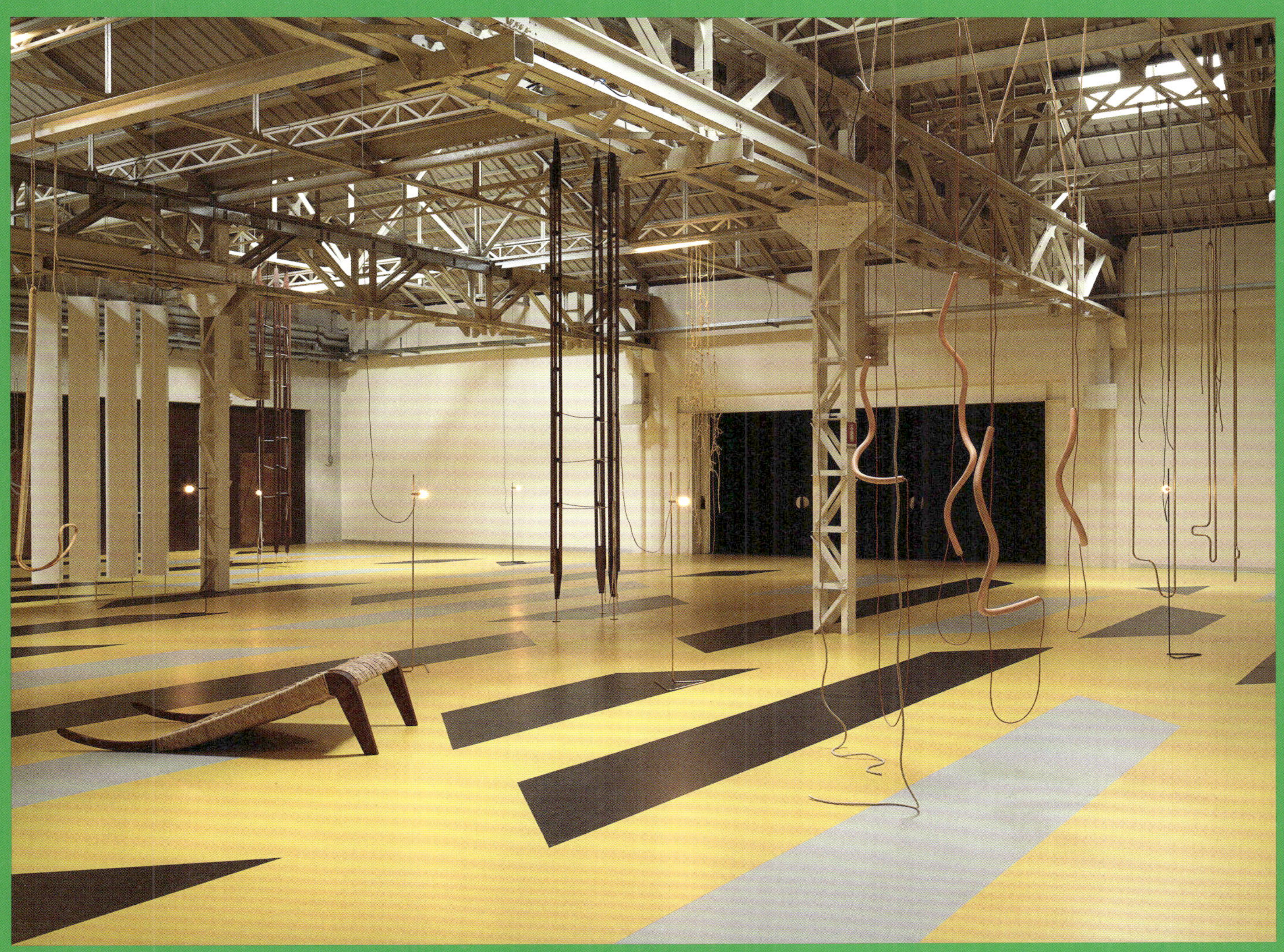

the last days in Galliate, 2018–19

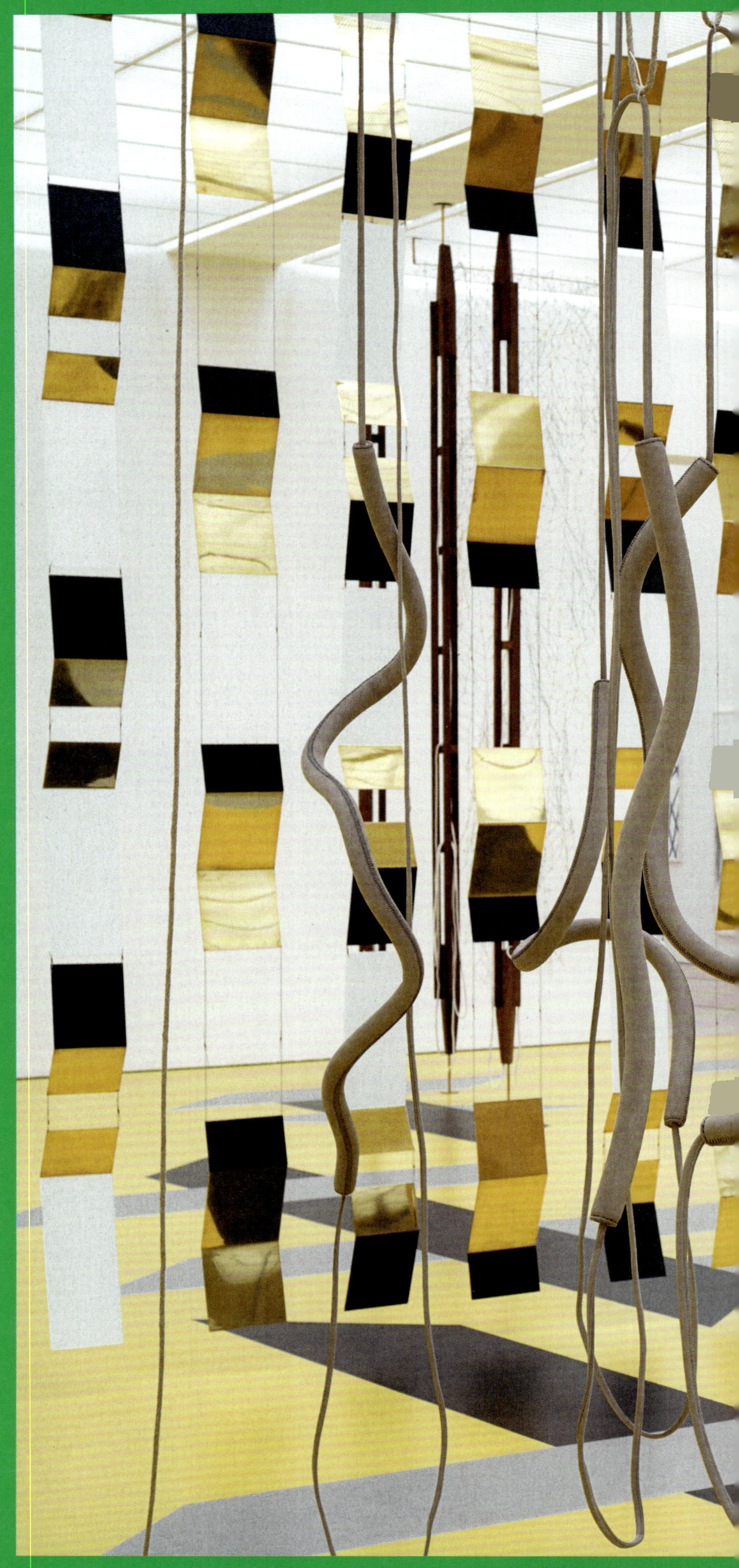

Resonating Spaces, 2019–20

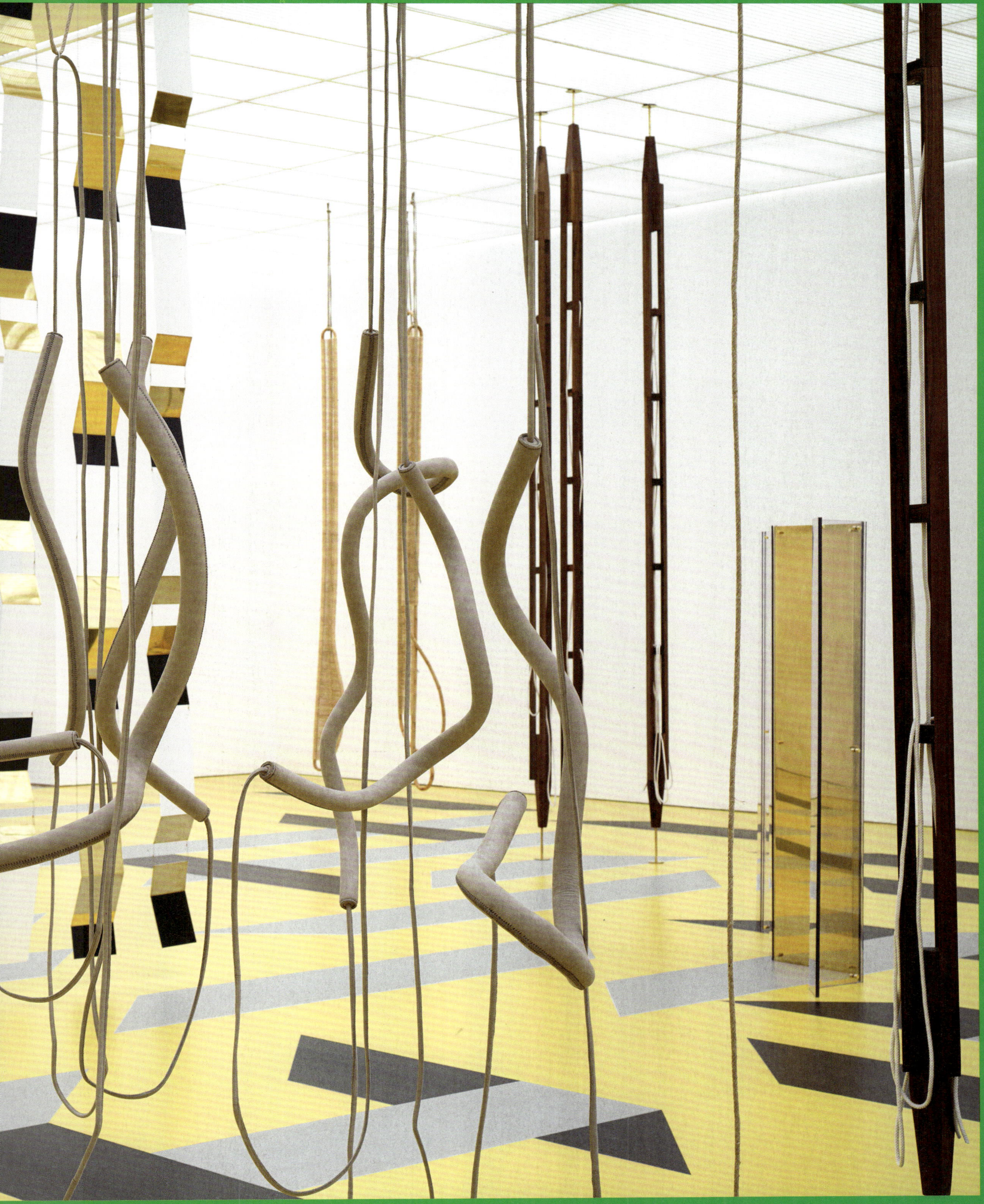

Yael Bartana

b. 1970, Israel. Lives and works in Amsterdam, Netherlands, and Berlin, Germany.

In Yael Bartana's work, histories collapse on themselves and political imagination becomes a stage for expansive landscapes of untold realities, collective desires, and societal fears. Bartana's practice involves extensive research into the strategies used to uphold different systems of power—particularly those found in political and religious propaganda—which the artist transforms into experimental film, installation, performance, and photography. The almost mythological style of Bartana's work blurs distinctions between prophecy and history, between truth and fiction, to undermine the seeming inevitability of historical narratives and reflect on issues of political and religious identity.

In *Wild Seeds* (2005), Bartana uses political reenactment as a tool for exploring the painful reality of Israel's militarized occupation of Palestine. The video documents a game played by young Israeli pacifists (based on a violent 2002 incident involving the extraction of Jewish settlers from the Occupied Territories) that allows them to share knowledge and develop collective strategies for resistance. Bartana captures the activists as they take turns acting as police while others interlace their bodies to avoid being removed. Tight, grainy shots of arms forcefully gripped, clenched teeth, and jerking limbs jostle between wider frames that reveal a sizable mass of young adults joyously wrestling on a green hillside. Bartana distorts the laughter and shouting captured by the camera, mixing it with the distant voice of a female cantor singing of God's love. The impressionistic editing and sound in *Wild Seeds* gives the work emotional tones that gesture toward the convoluted and painful realities that surround this playful staging of historical trauma.

Bartana's style of historical assemblage takes on a more linear, narrative quality in the feature-length, three-part video *And Europe Will Be Stunned* (2007–11). The triptych tells the story of a fictional political movement that demands that the Jewish population of Poland be returned to its pre-Holocaust level of 3.3 million. The movement's leader is played by a real-life journalist and political activist with whom Bartana collaborated to create the character, endowing the work with real-world political fantasies. The artist shot the film to be in stylistic communication with the work of Nazi filmmaker Leni Riefenstahl, and Bartana uses tropes and symbols of German filmmaking to reframe the sites of Jewish trauma and their reception. She also uses symbols from Zionist and Soviet propaganda, and references to the Palestinian Occupation, all part of her strategy of stylistic and historical anachronism to connect disparate histories. Bartana employs a historiographic understanding of images in the collaging of political propaganda, while remaining sensitive to them as powerful sites of human longing. By recasting them outside a linear understanding of history, she lays bare their power; they exist in a liminal space where desires meet the shared fantasies of religious and political ideologies.

In the more recent performance work *What if Women Ruled the World?* (2017), Bartana again turns to a discursive space between fiction and reality as she takes up the gendered power structures of international political relations. The partially improvised performance takes place within a re-creation of the war room depicted in Stanley Kubrick's classic 1964 film *Dr. Strangelove*. In Kubrick's satire, Cold War tensions, male hysteria, miscommunication, racist ideologies, and bellicose patriarchal values allow a rogue US general to order an attack on the Soviet Union without the president's approval, starting a nuclear war. In Bartana's reimagined "peace room," what's under siege is the gendered nature of politics and its effect on international relations. In the piece, officials of a female-led country with a pacifist constitution meet to discuss a breach in an international nuclear agreement and their possible response. In each iteration of the work, the cast is joined by five real-world female experts from a range of fields—defense advisers, human-rights activists, politicians, soldiers, strategists. The president and her advisers then consult with the invitees to shape a consensus. Bartana's feminist gesture is focused more on process than on outcome, on the dramatic shift in values and communication styles that takes place when women run a room. The work, like much of Bartana's output, dramatizes a fictionalized staging of history told through layered temporalities. It's a method that the artist calls "historical pre-enactment," a way of manifesting parallel realities and potential futures.

—Nika Chilewich

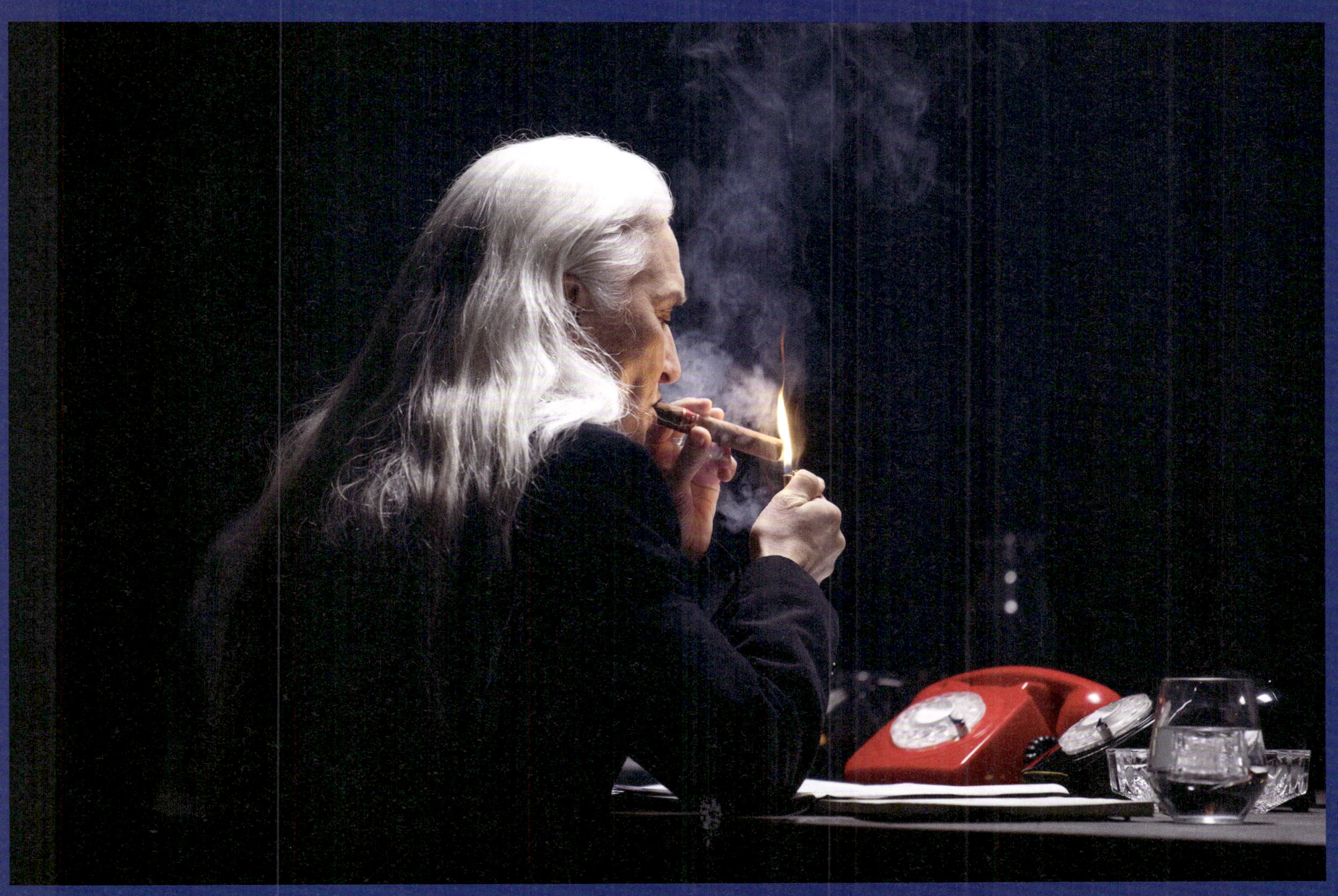

What if Women Ruled the World?, 2017

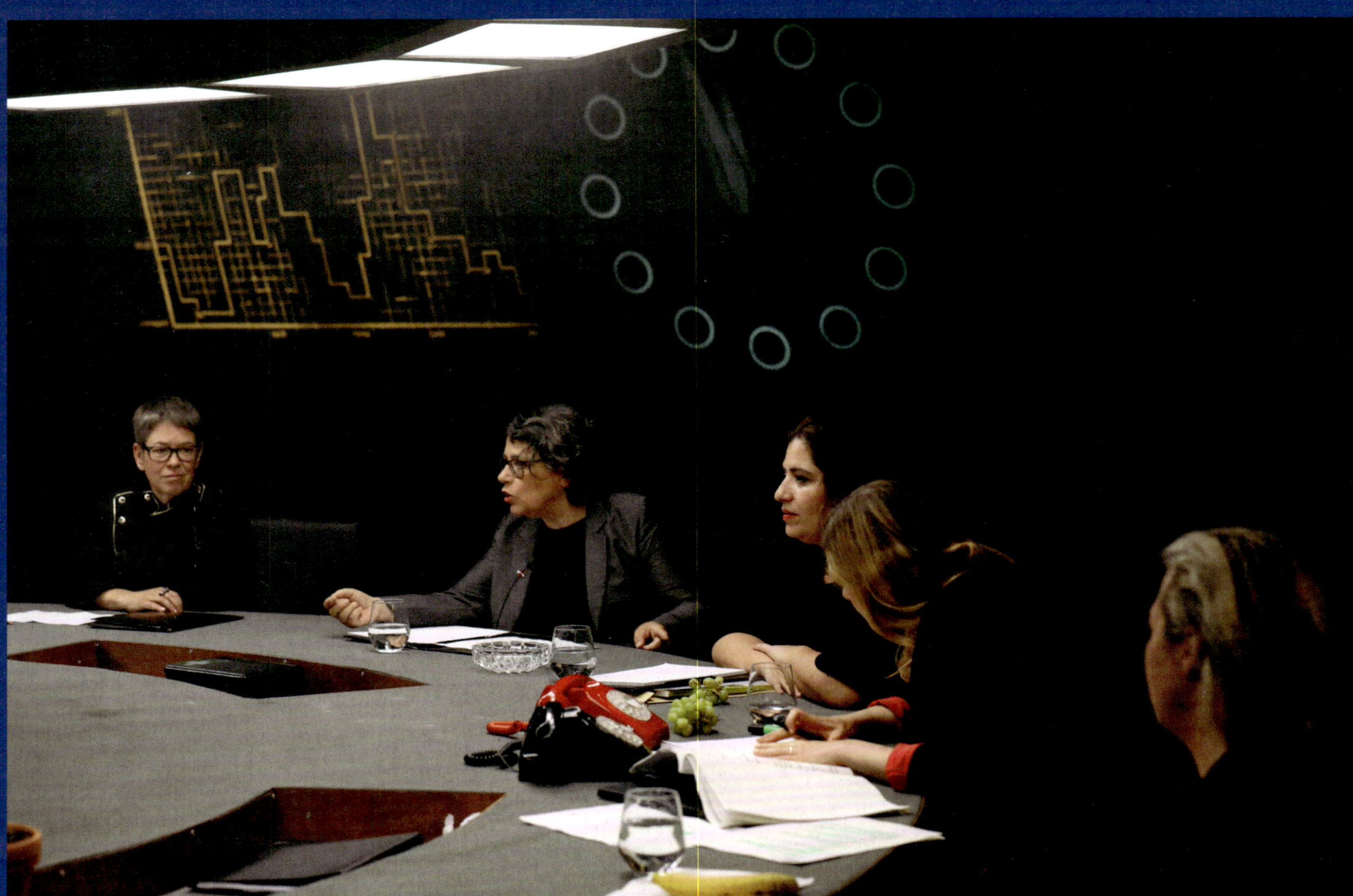

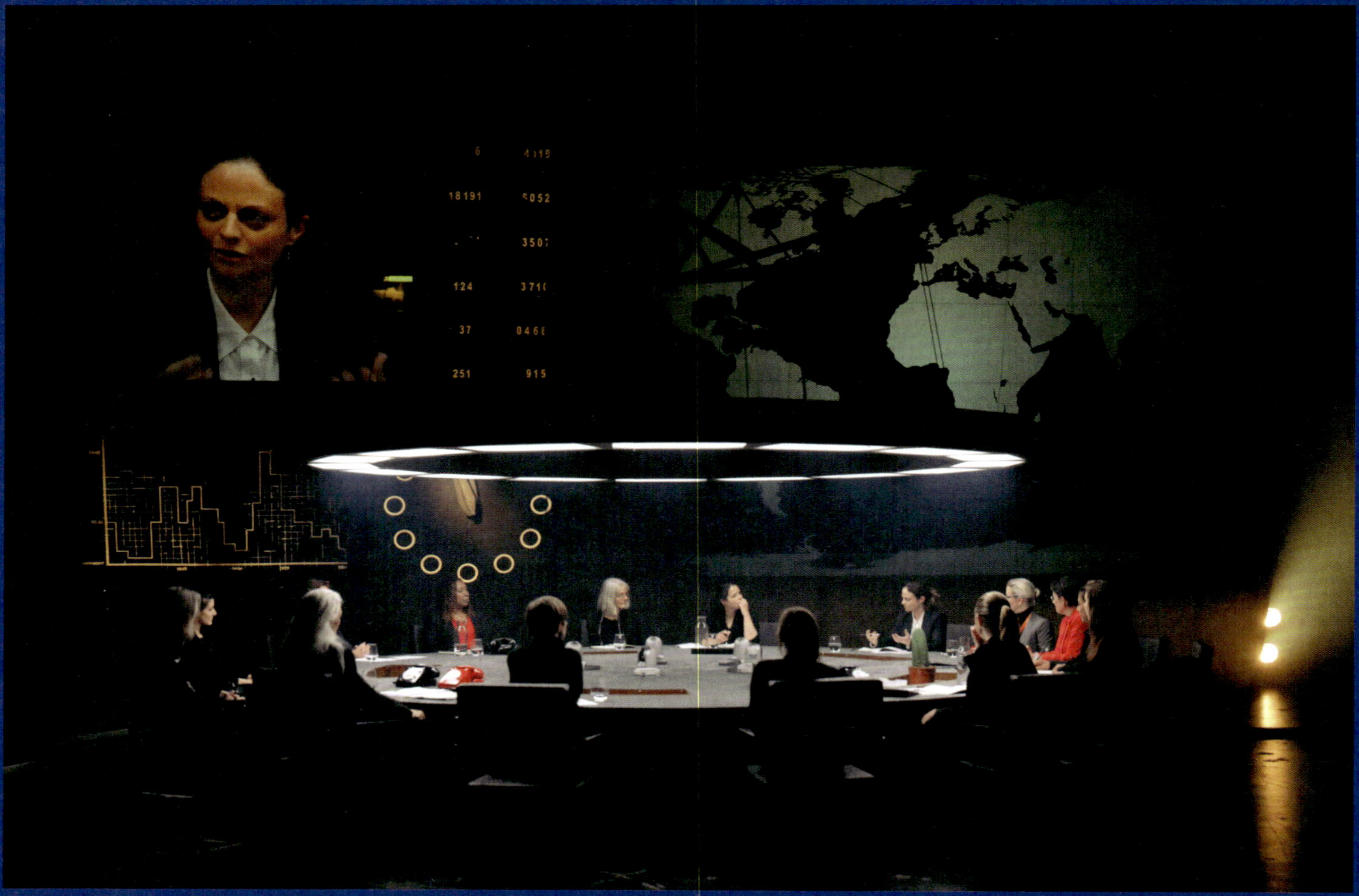

What if Women Ruled the World?, 2017

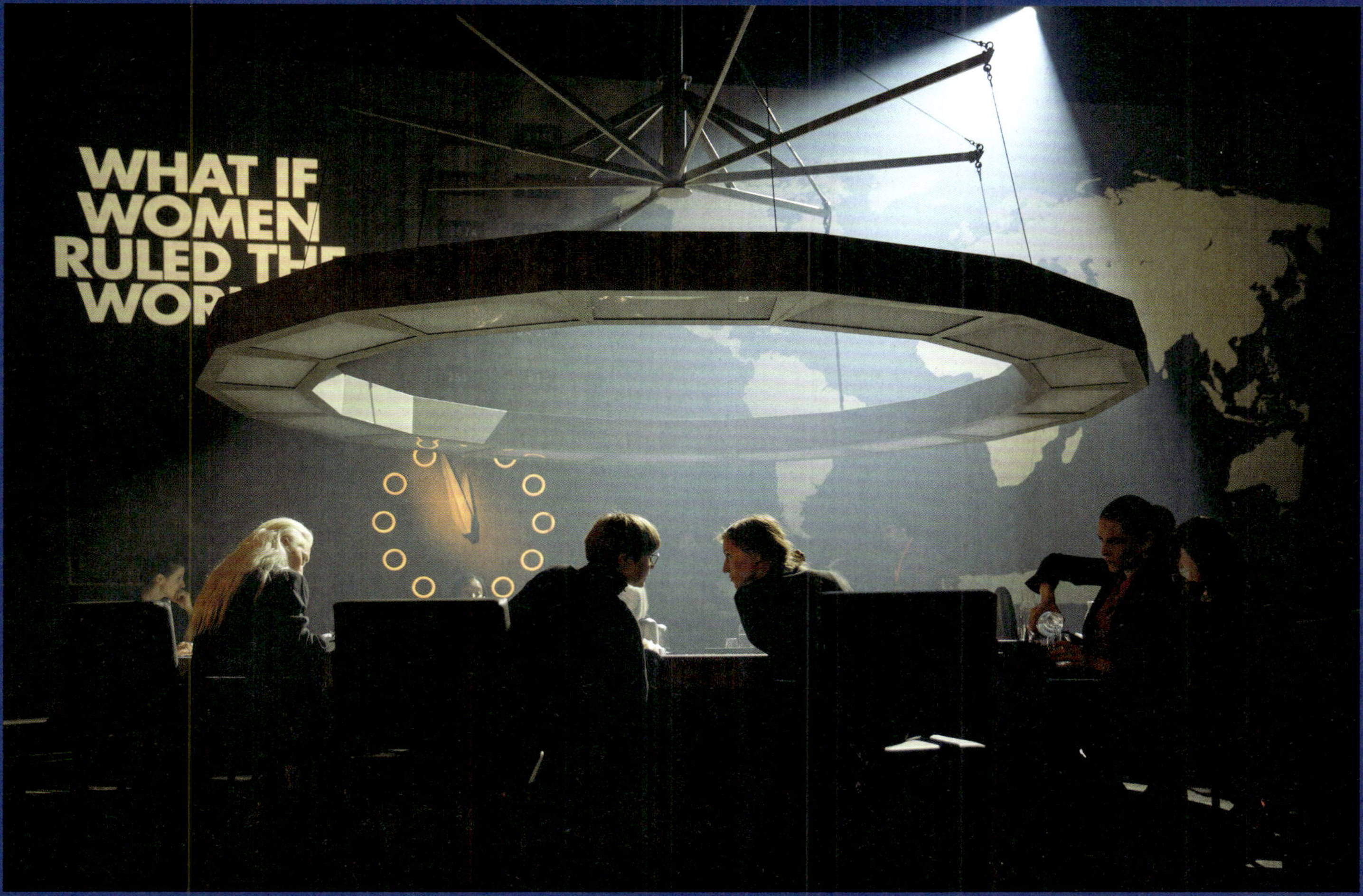

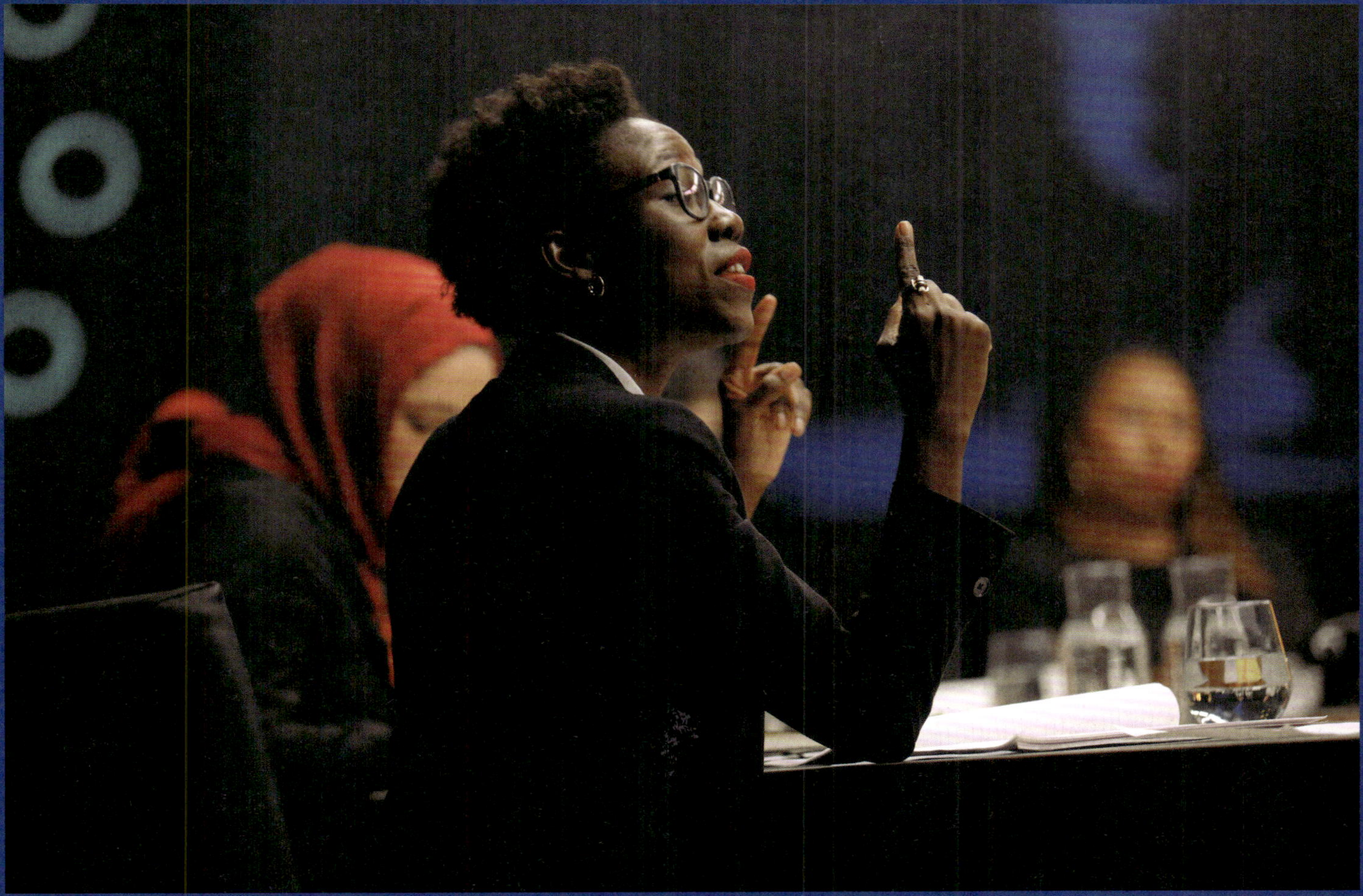

What if Women Ruled the World?, 2017

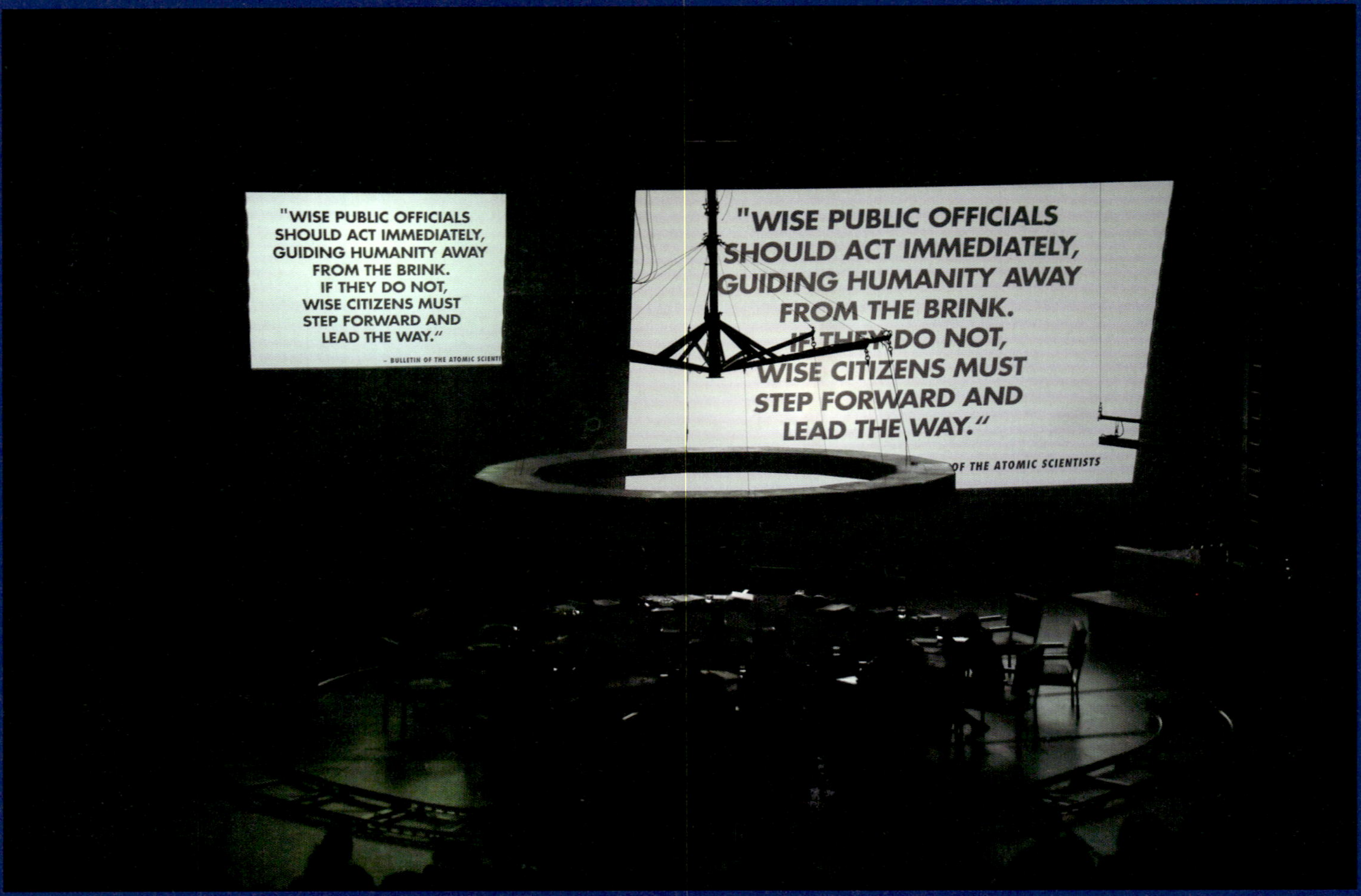

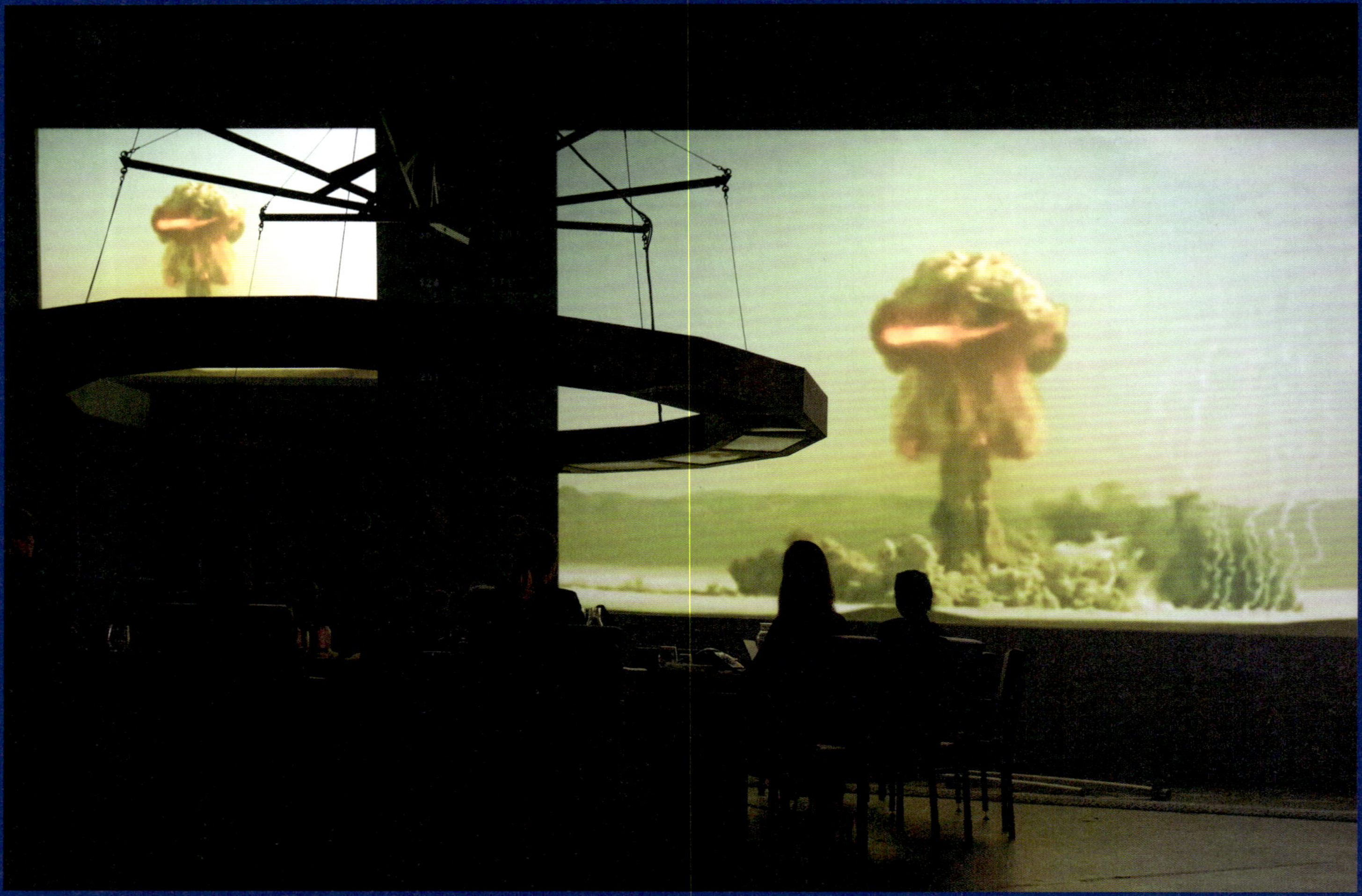

What if Women Ruled the World?, 2017

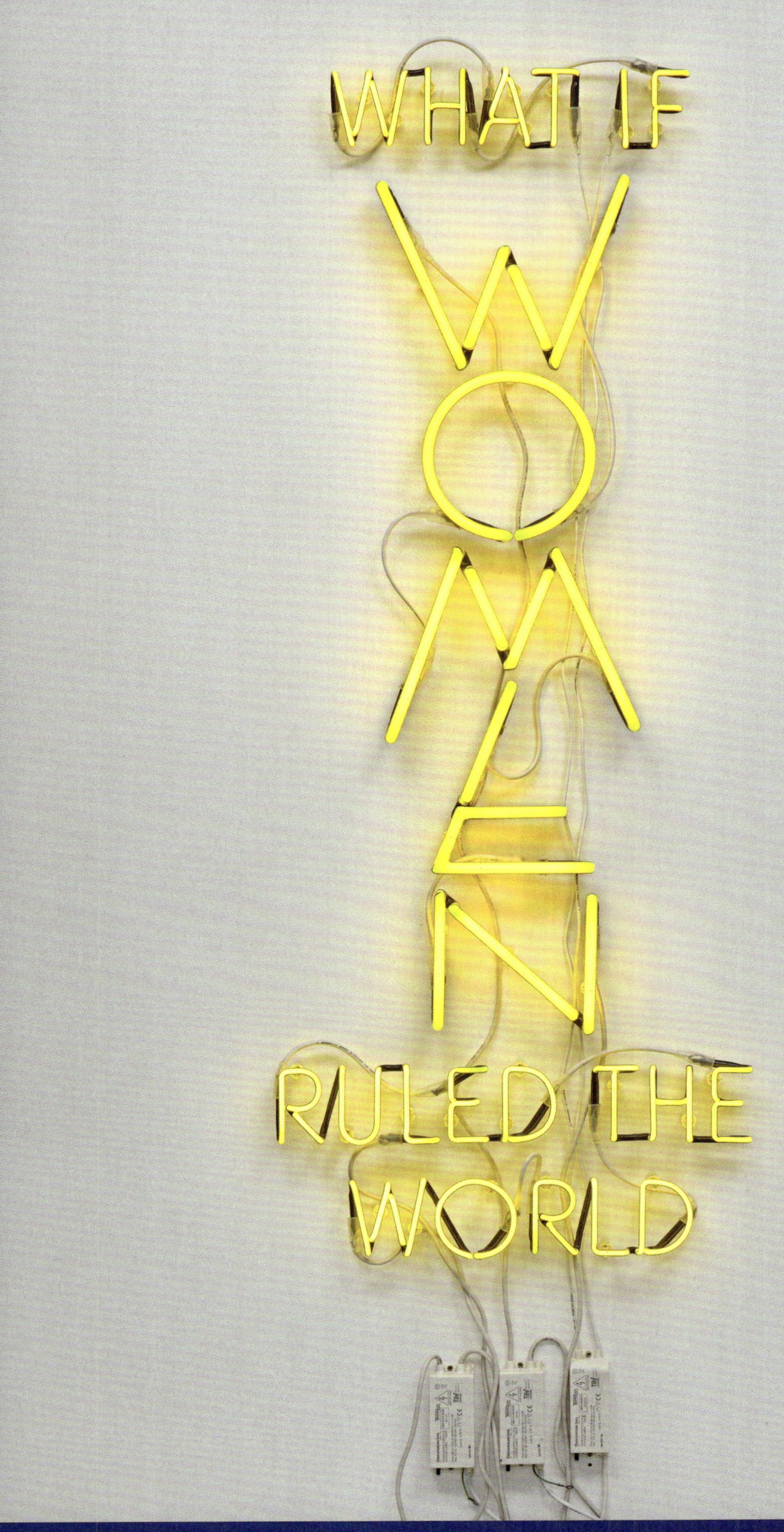

What if Women Ruled the World?, 2016

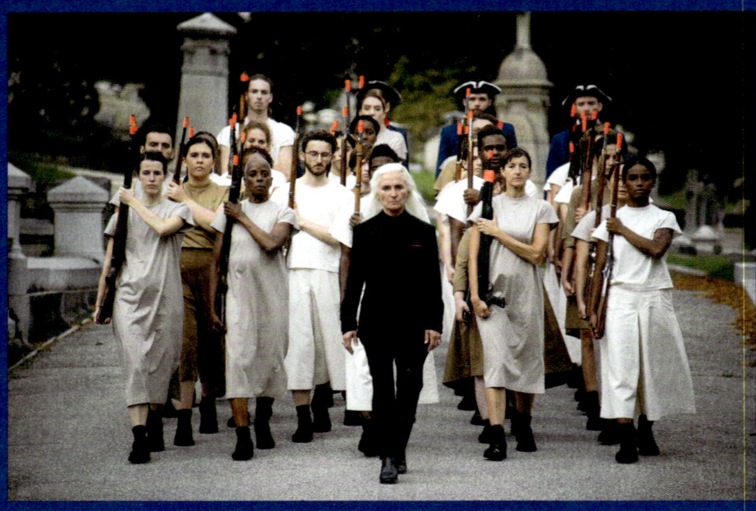
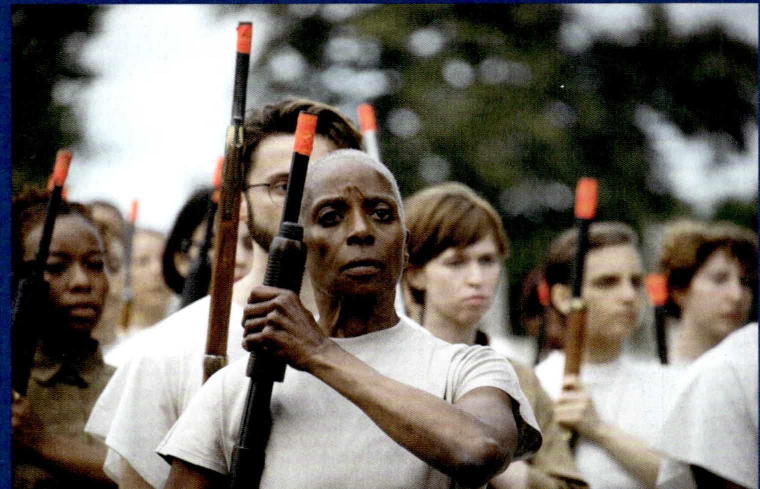
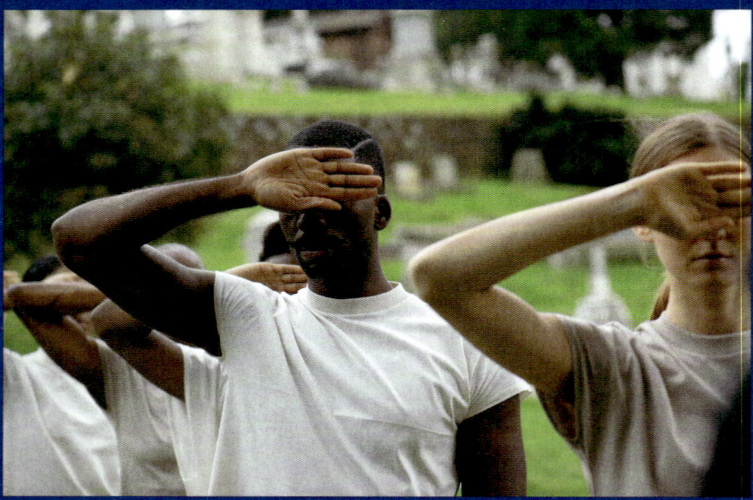
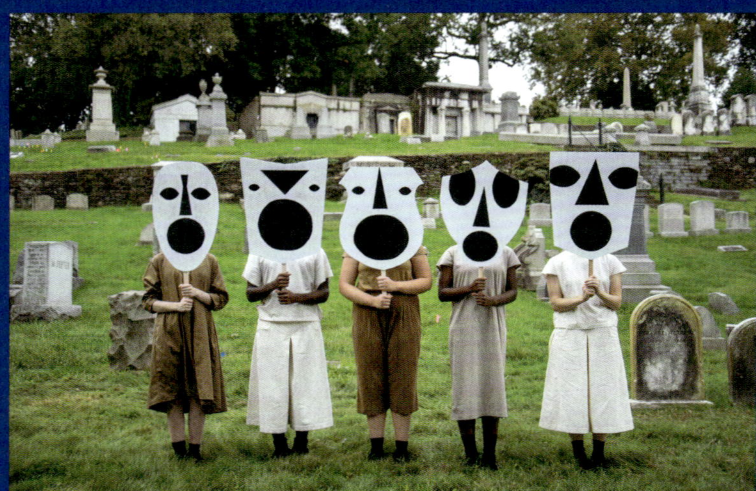

Bury Our Weapons, Not Our Bodies!, 2018

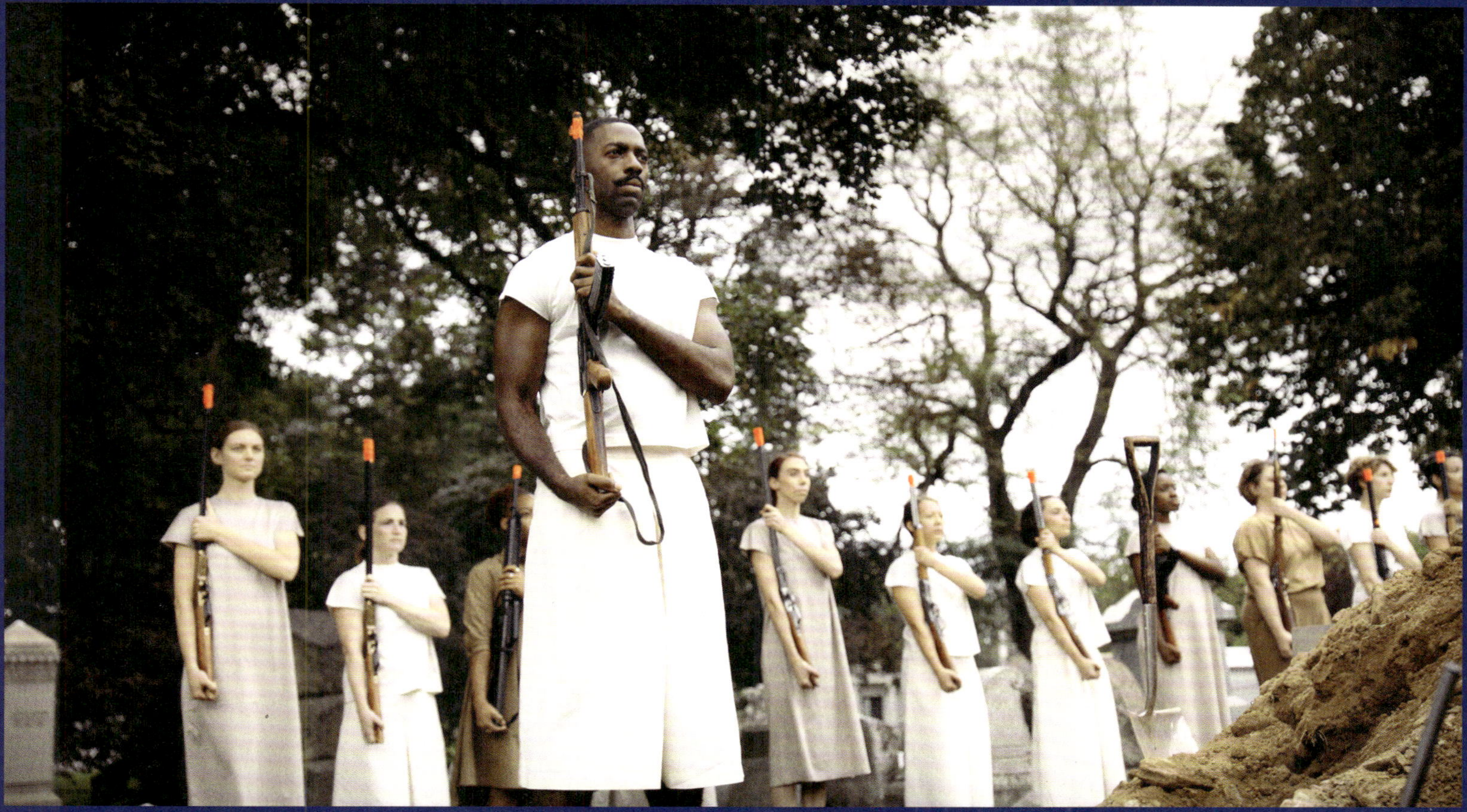

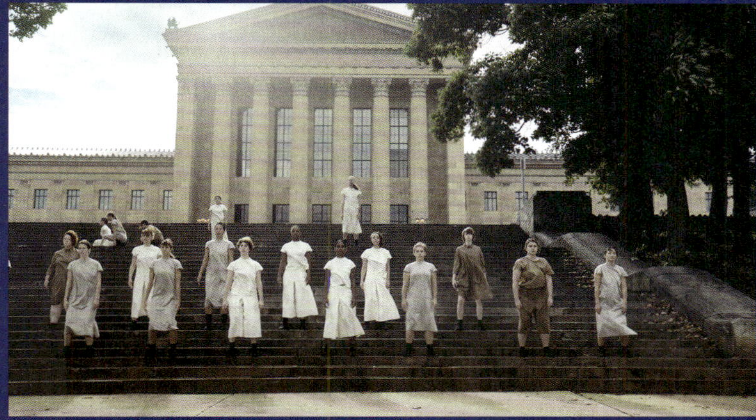

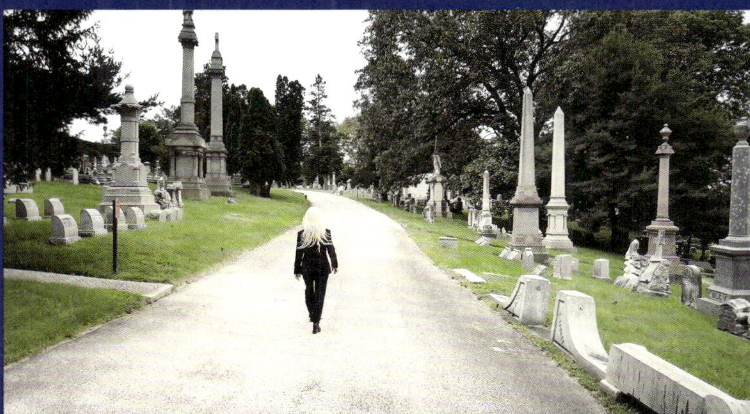

Bury Our Weapons, Not Our Bodies!, 2018

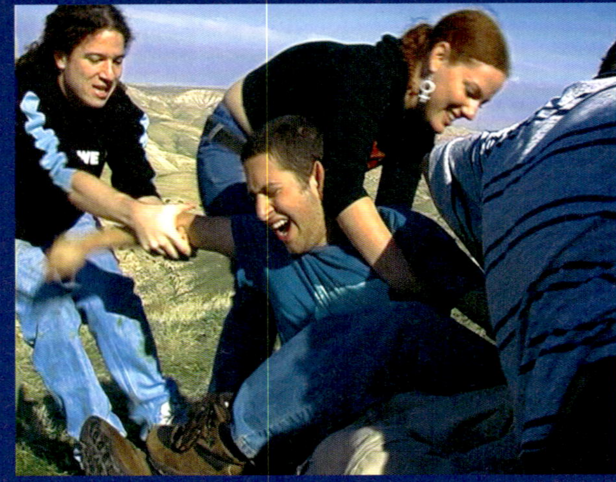

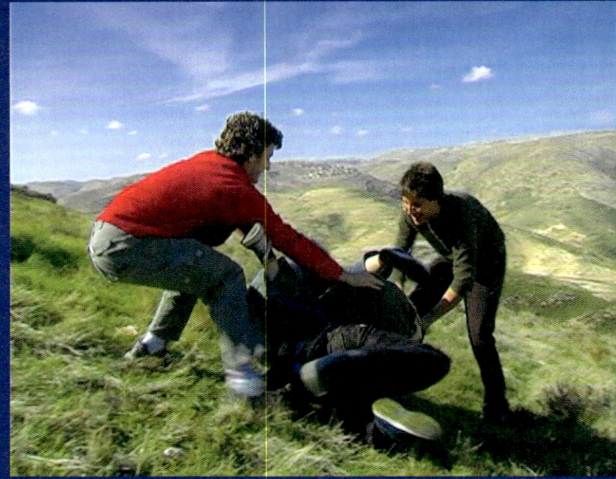

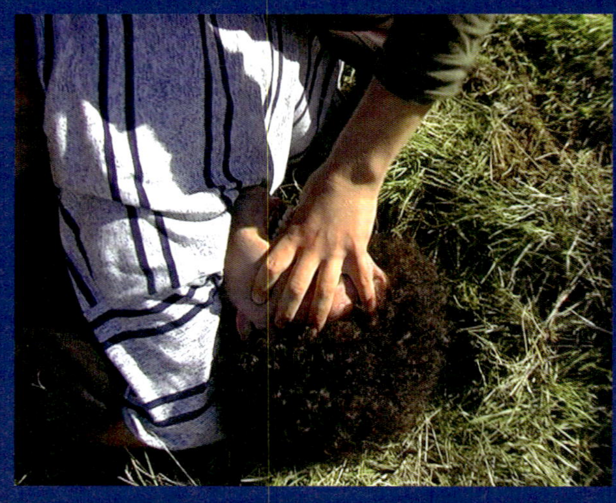

Wild Seeds, 2005

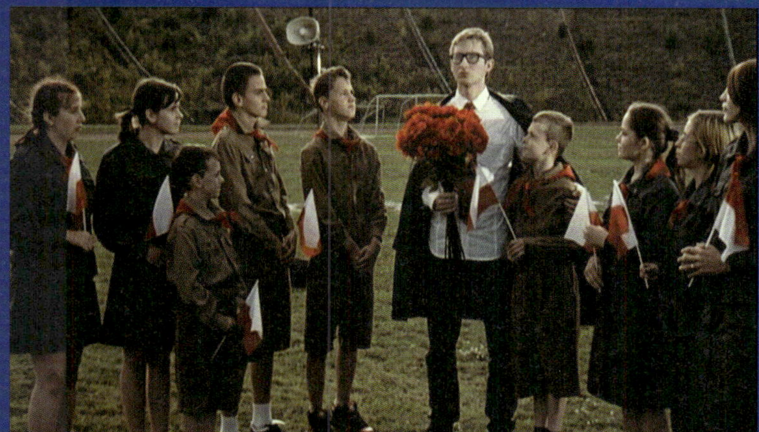

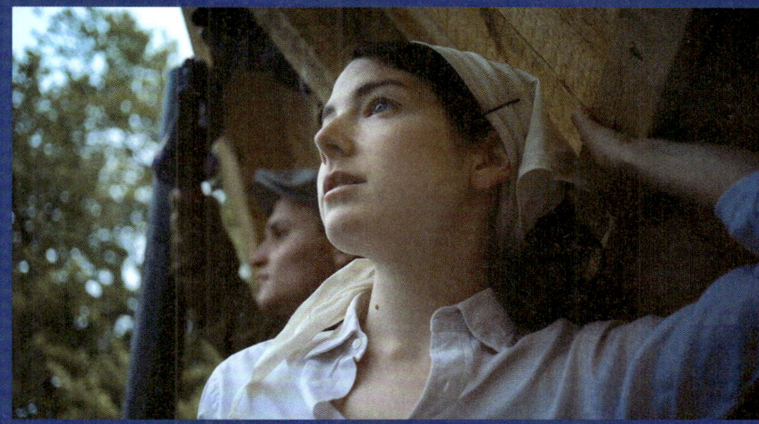

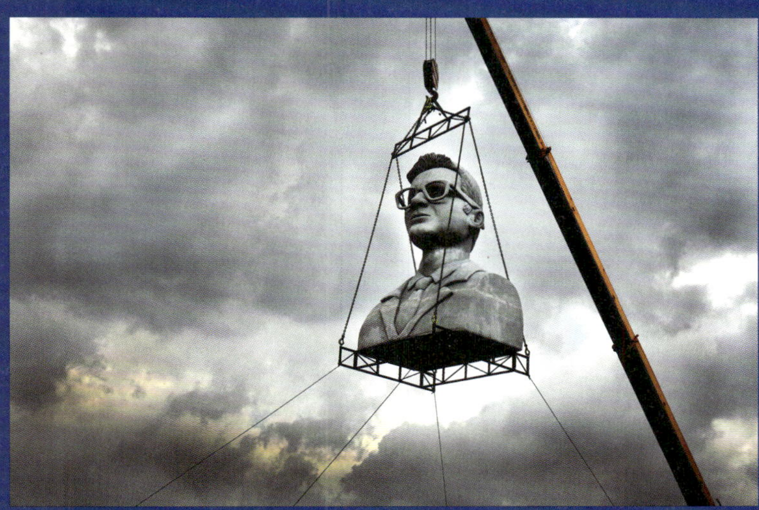

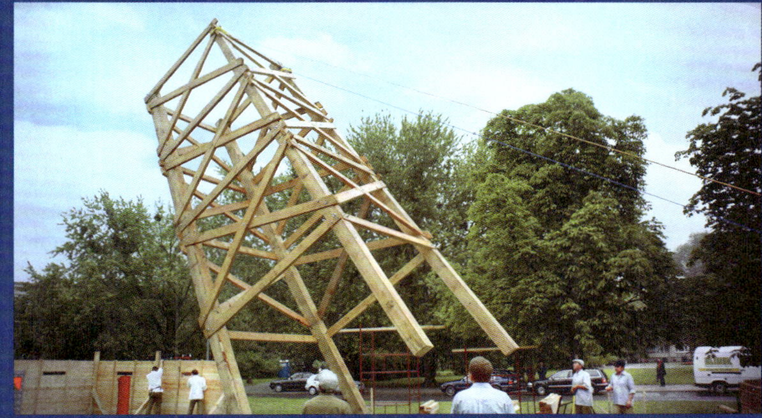

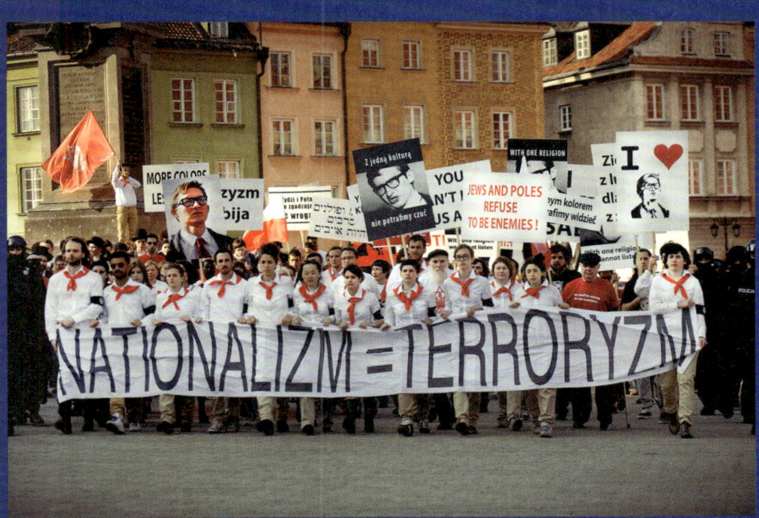

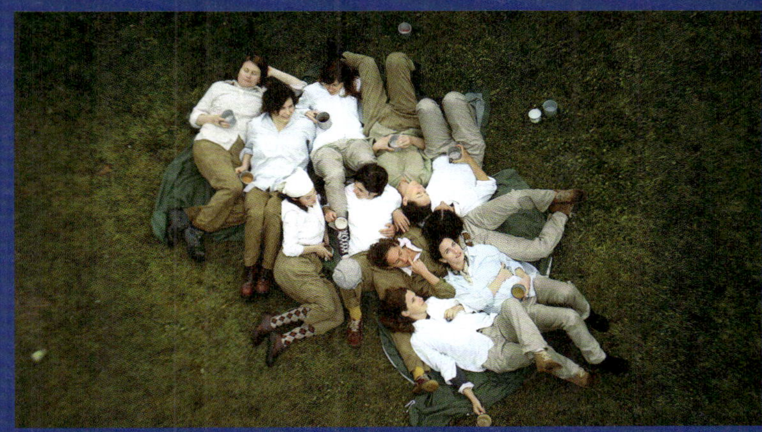

top: *Mary Koszmary* (Nightmares), 2008
middle and bottom: *Zamach* (Assassination), 2011

Mur i wieża (Wall and tower), 2009

Pauline Boudry /
Renate Lorenz

Collaborating since 2007. Live and work in Berlin, Germany.

A key influence on Berlin-based artists Pauline Boudry / Renate Lorenz is the work of composer and electronic-music pioneer Pauline Oliveros. Her open, nonhierarchical reorientation of the relationship between artist/composer, audience, and work provides a blueprint for the duo's collaborations on film, installation, sculpture, and writing since the mid-2000s. Boudry/Lorenz examine the inherent artifice of images and sound as well as the construction of histories and subjectivities, re-presenting received information from across time to complicate the source materials—and, perhaps, bring these sources back to life. Their strategies of mimicry, repetition, theatricality, and revealing the apparatus of production use the past to find new approaches to the present. Queer histories serve as points of extended meditation; Boudry/Lorenz's works have referenced Gertrude Stein, Jack Smith, and Yvonne Rainer. *I Want* (2015) involves the artist Sharon Hayes interchangeably performing texts from radical feminist writer Kathy Acker and antiwar activist Chelsea Manning, leaving it unclear to viewers who is actually speaking and when. Jean Genet serves as a point of reference in two works that feature the pair's frequent collaborators Ginger Brooks Takahashi and Werner Hirsch speaking as Genet, first in his words from a 1985 interview (*Toxic*, 2012) and then through a speech based on his untitled 1970 essay written in support of the Black Power movement, later published in his volume *L'ennemi déclaré* in 1991 (*Opaque*, 2014).

Such works foreground the artists' ongoing use of a decentered voice in their work, allowing their performers to embody the speech of other figures from across time and disciplines. One such figure is Oliveros herself, to whom Boudry/Lorenz pay direct homage in the 2017 work *Telepathic Improvisation*. In 1974, Oliveros prepared a twenty-five-part text-based score titled *Sonic Meditations*. In the written introduction to the piece, Oliveros outlines its aim: "to erase the subject/object or performer/audience relationship by returning to ancient forms which preclude spectators," instantiating an interest in "communication among all life forms." One of the score's movements, "Telepathic Improvisation," asks the audience to mentally send sounds to the musicians, and for those performing to be open to collaborating with the audience in this way.

As with its namesake, the notion of receptivity is central to Boudry/Lorenz's *Telepathic Improvisation*. The piece comprises an installation of a video projected amid various props and sculptural elements that are also present on-screen—white, geometric, mobile platforms; stage lighting; grouped microphone stands with fuzzy windscreens; and an oversize pair of handcuffs that hangs suspended in the air. The performers in the video, artists Marwa Arsanios, Takahashi, Hirsch, and MPA, move about a black-box setting in striking white and red outfits, reciting fragments of text from Oliveros's score alongside excerpts from an essay by German radical Ulrike Meinhof: "Protest is when I say I don't like this. Resistance is when I see to it that the things that I don't like no longer occur." These words, channeled by MPA, were written by Meinhof, who paraphrased them from a speech by Fred Hampton of the Black Panther Party. An act of doubled ventriloquism, the utterance calls forward these figures from the past and pays homage to histories of radical action while simultaneously creating something distinct and embodied, breaching the fourth wall of the screen to directly address the viewer. Light and sound elements appear on and off throughout the film, and plumes of white smoke act as transition points, temporarily obscuring the action, almost taking on the role of a character itself.

The array of performers, objects, sounds, and language of *Telepathic Improvisation* reveals Boudry/Lorenz's overall discursive approach to representing time and history and their rejection of the hierarchies of artistic authorship. They encourage a dynamic exchange between audience and performer that causes viewers to recognize their roles as active participants in the production of the work and its meaning, and as agents well beyond the work. The artists' resistance to centering a specific authorial voice, focusing instead on the voices of Oliveros, Meinhof, Hampton, et al., is rooted in deep generosity toward others past and present. Every choice by the artists and their collaborators offers a new way forward, a different way of looking, listening, and being in the world.

—Jamillah James

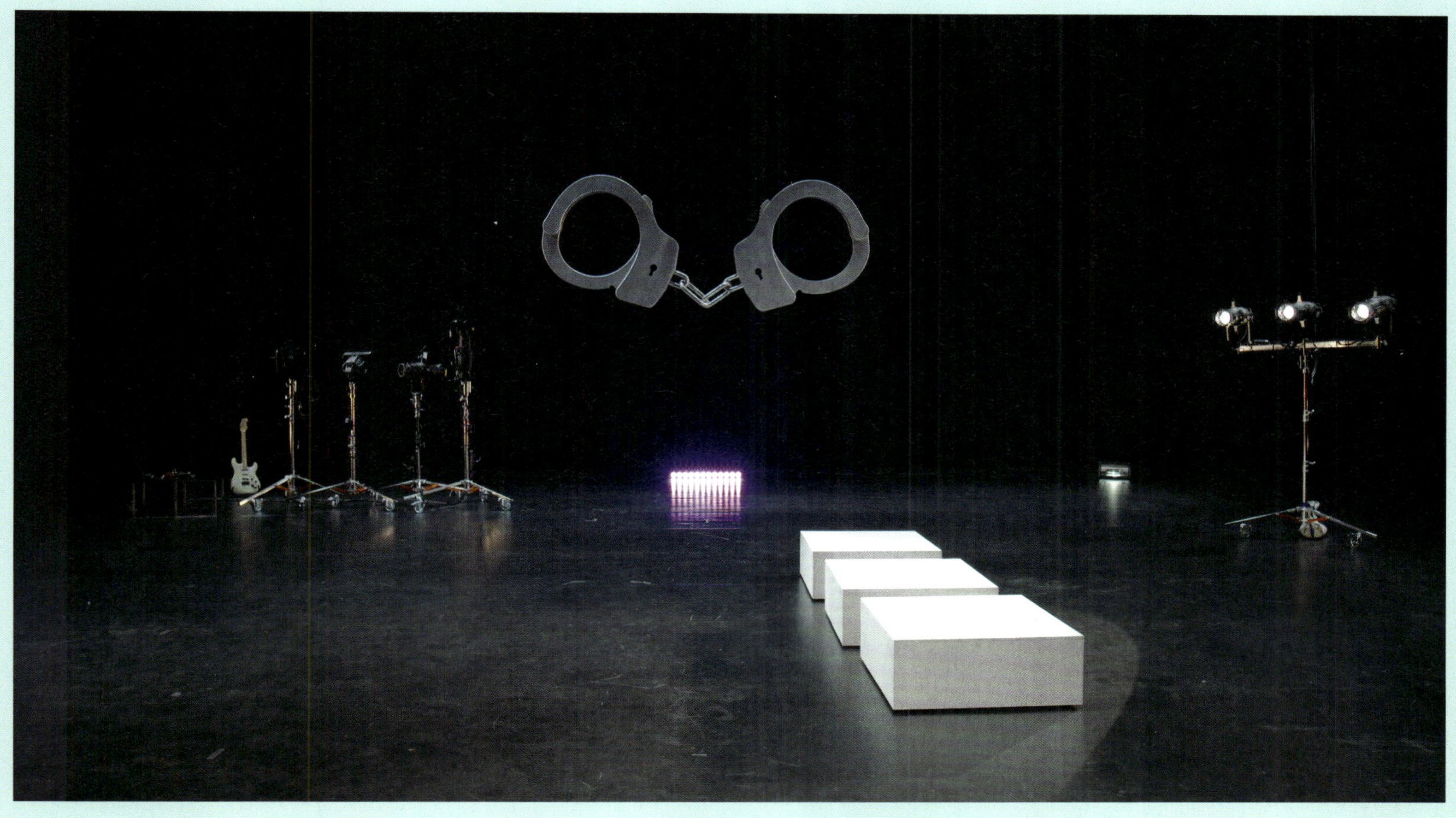

Telepathic Improvisation, 2017

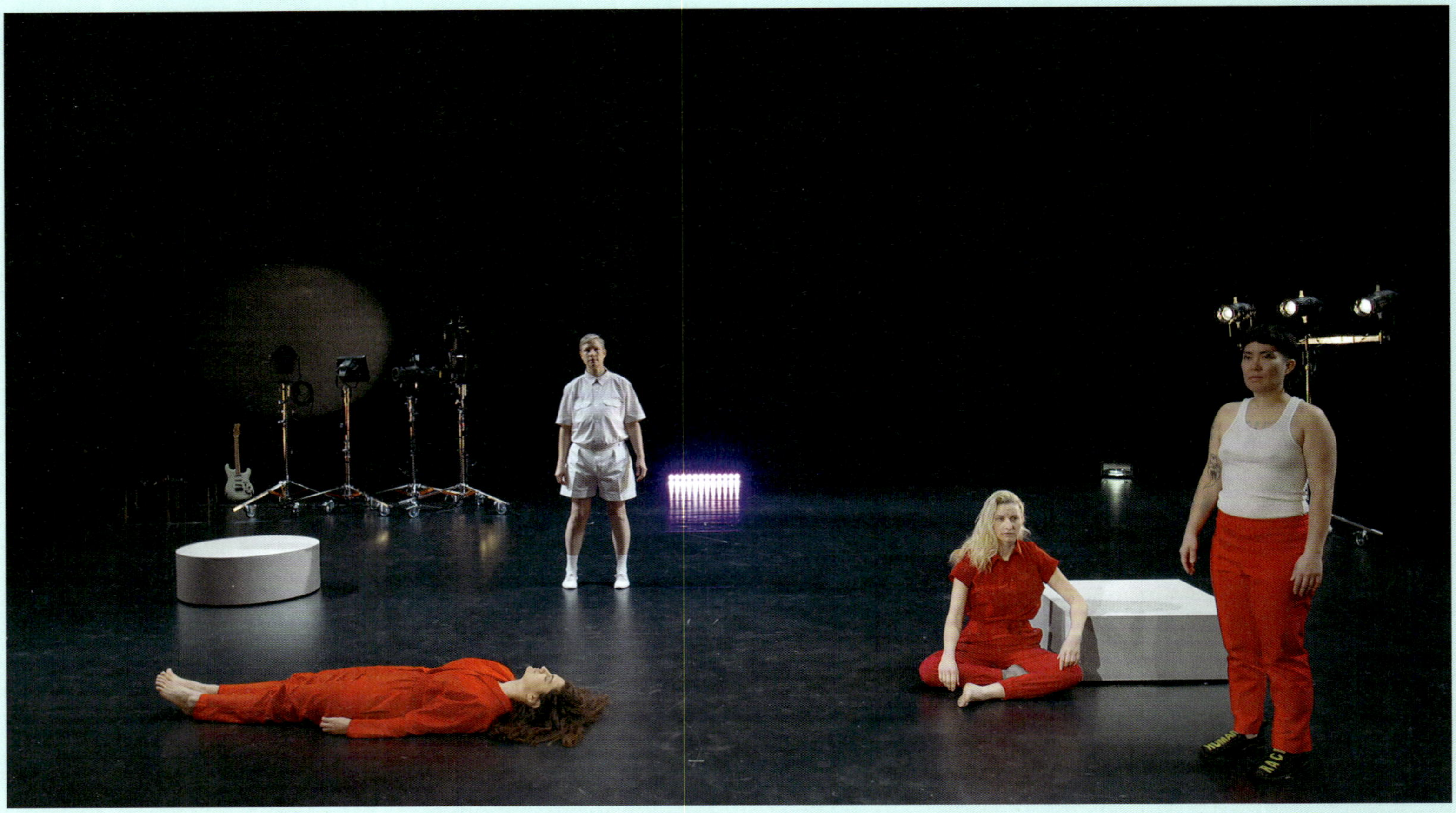

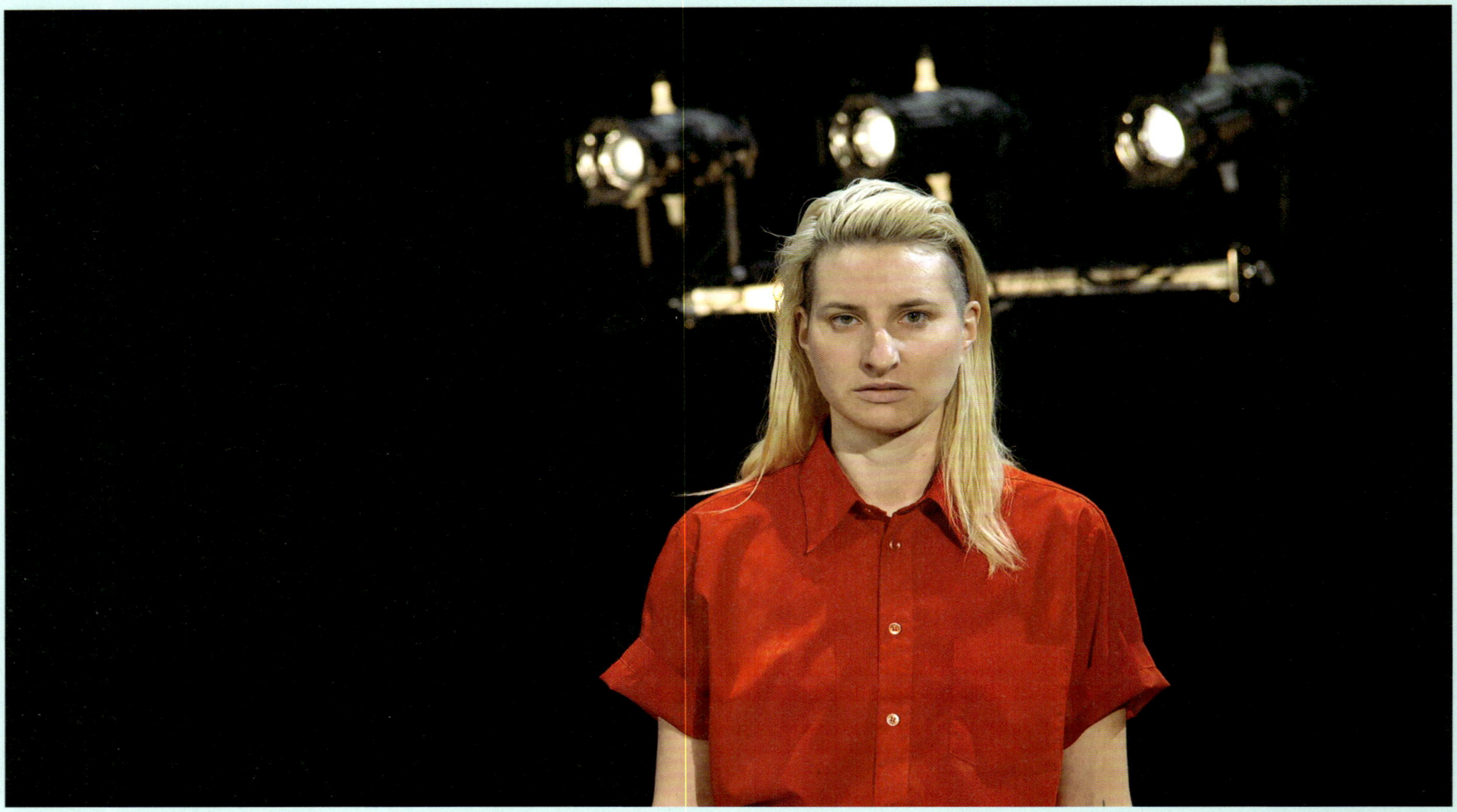

Telepathic Improvisation, 2017

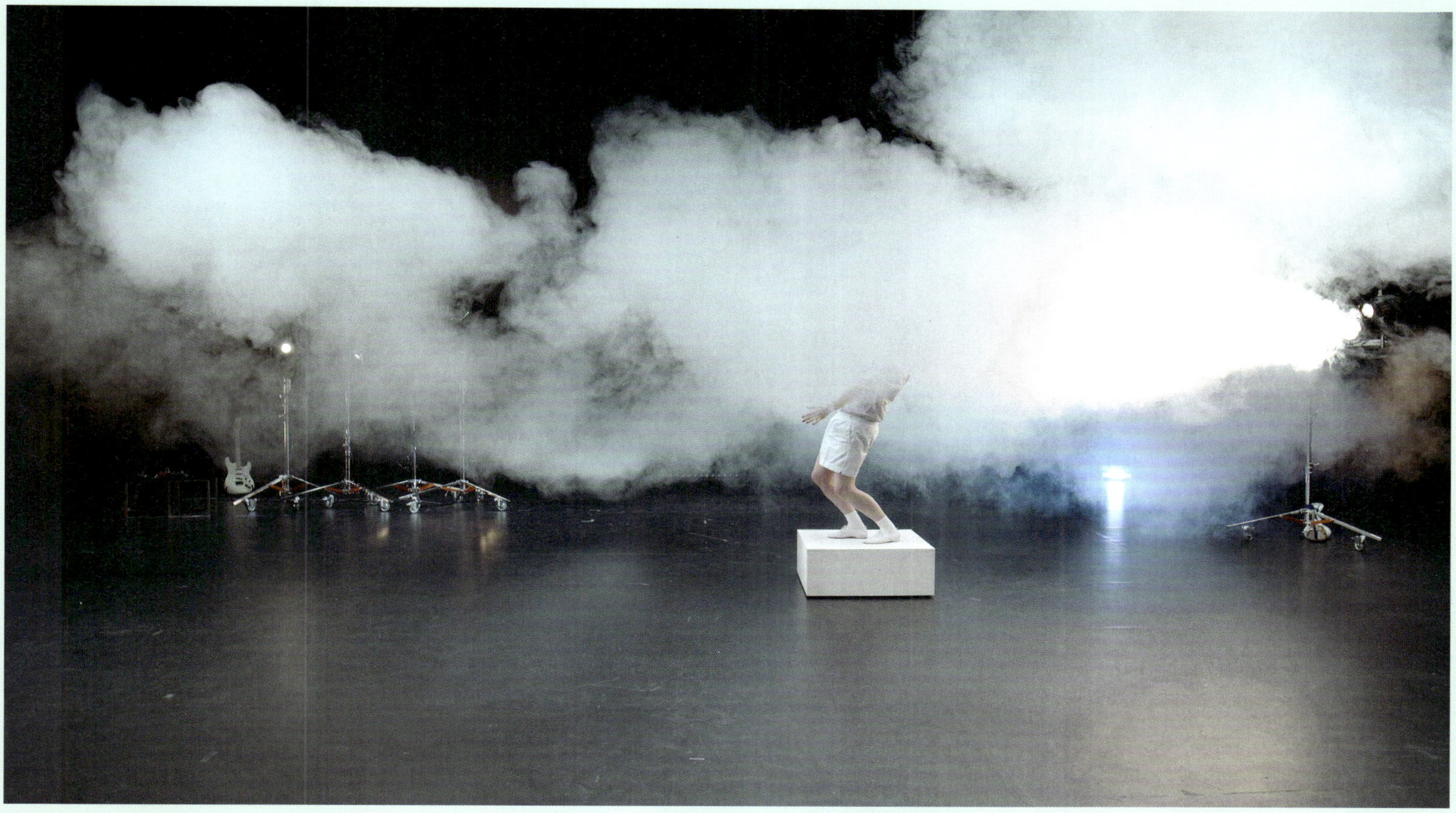

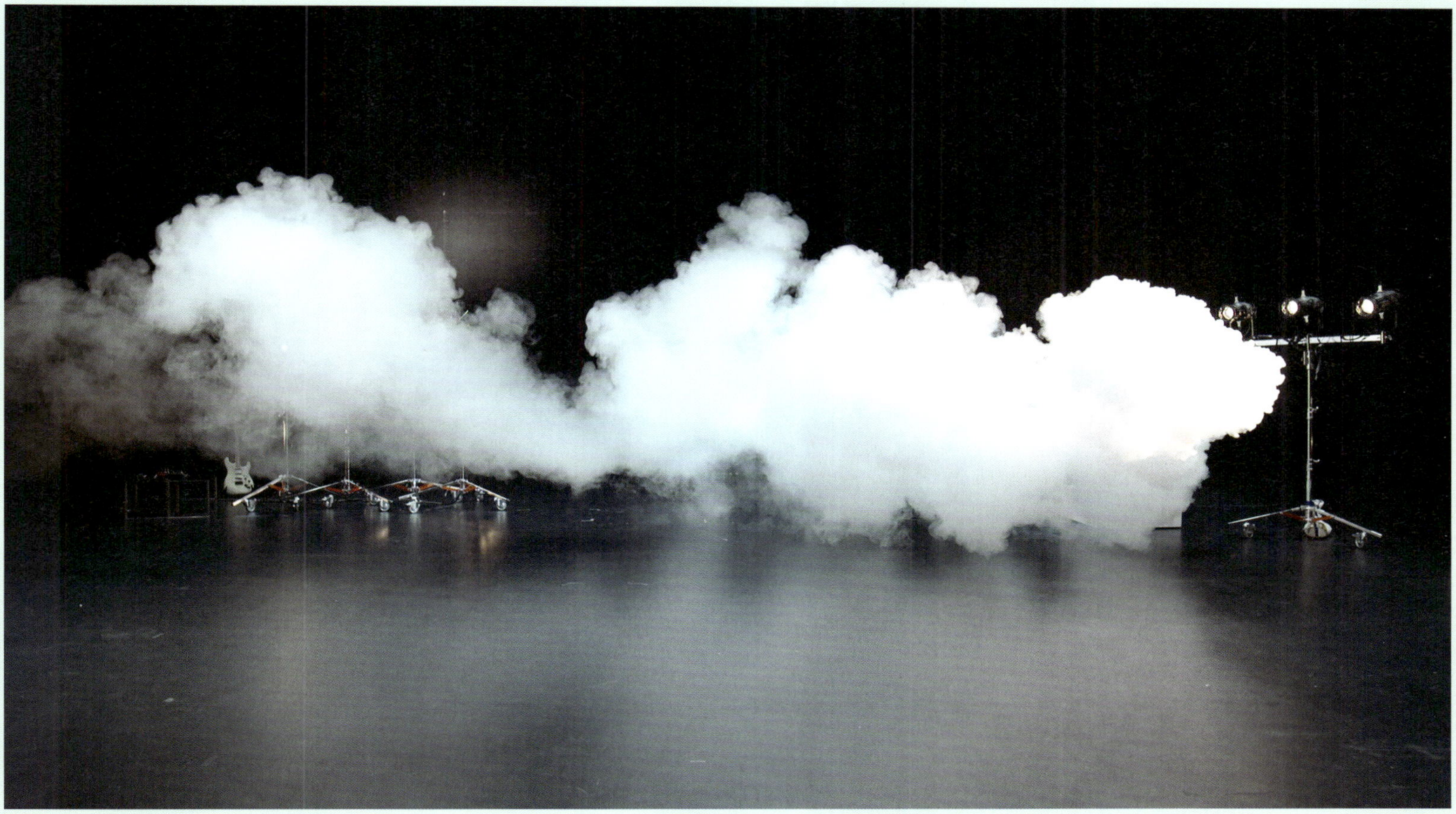

Telepathic Improvisation, 2017

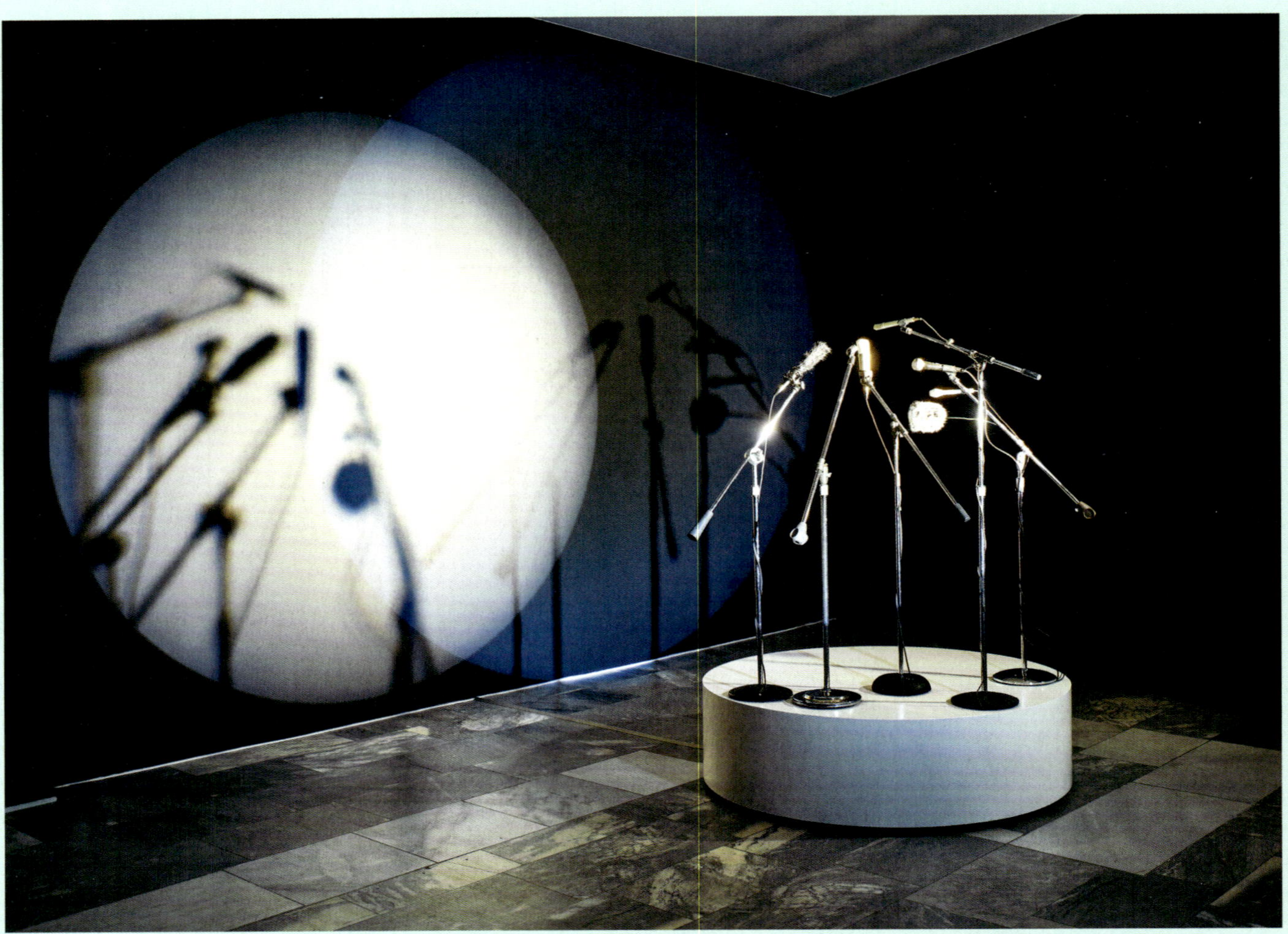

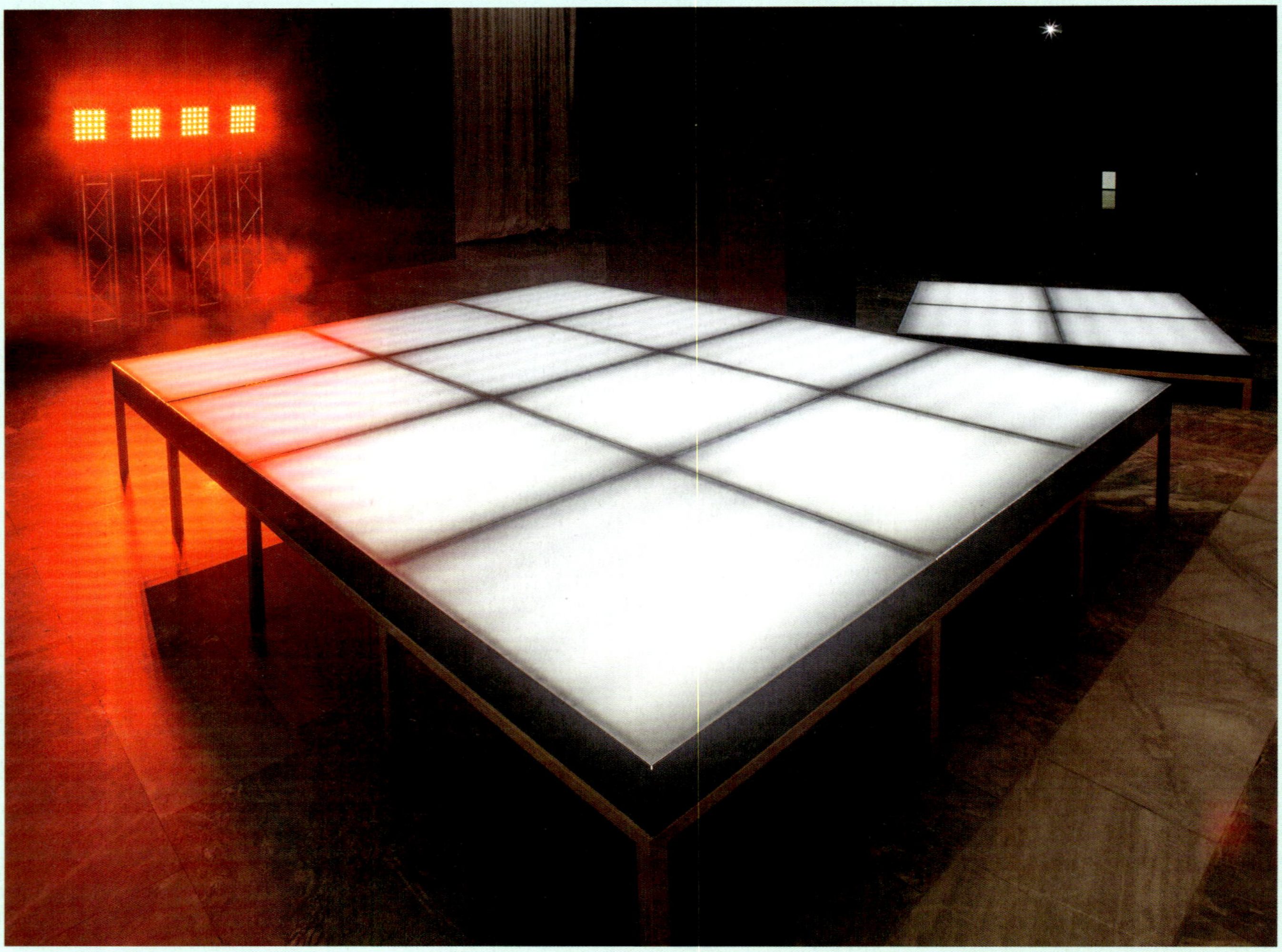

HE EAR R, 2016
Stage Piece (Untimely Collaboration), 2018

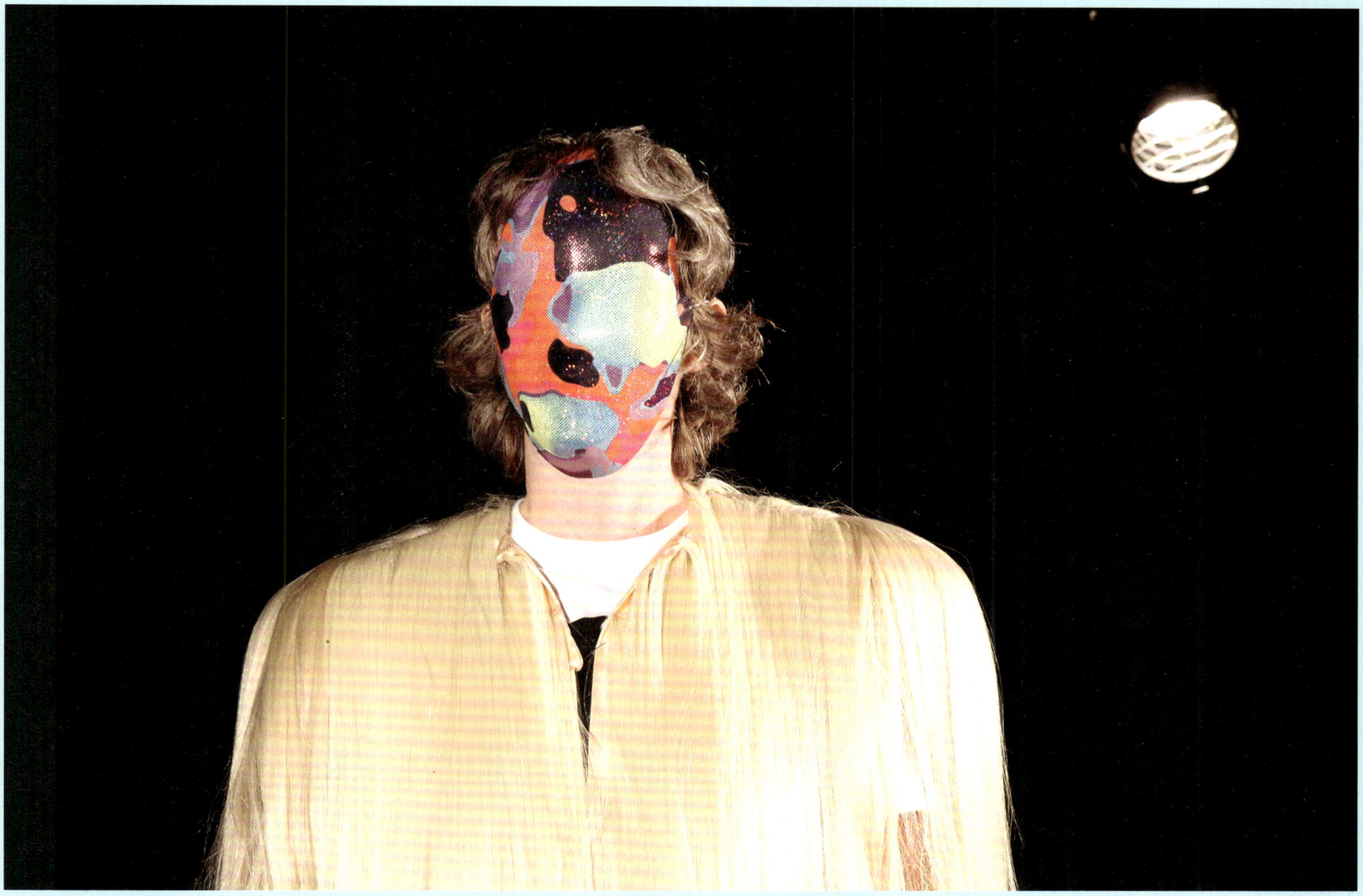

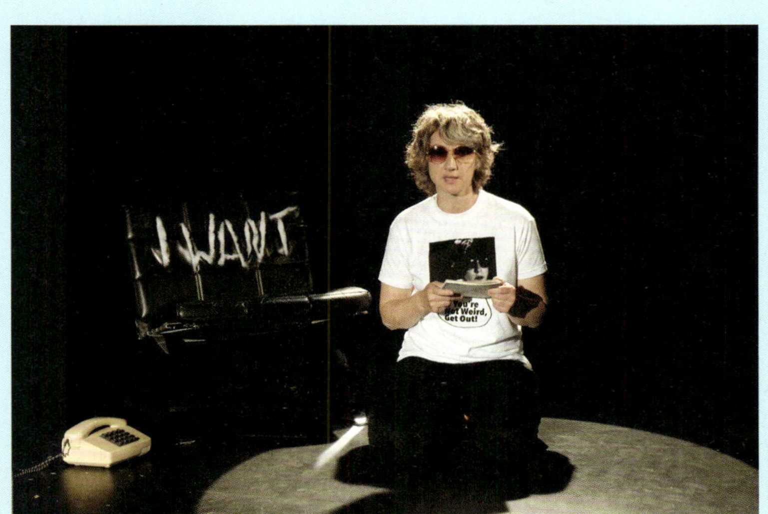

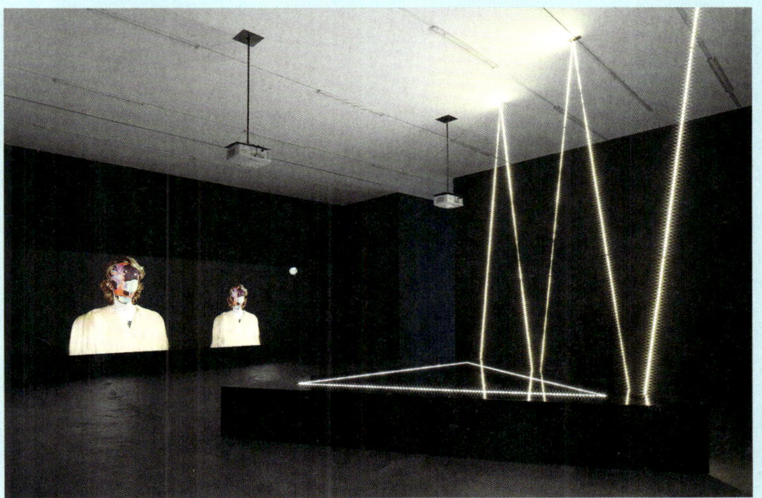

I Want, 2015

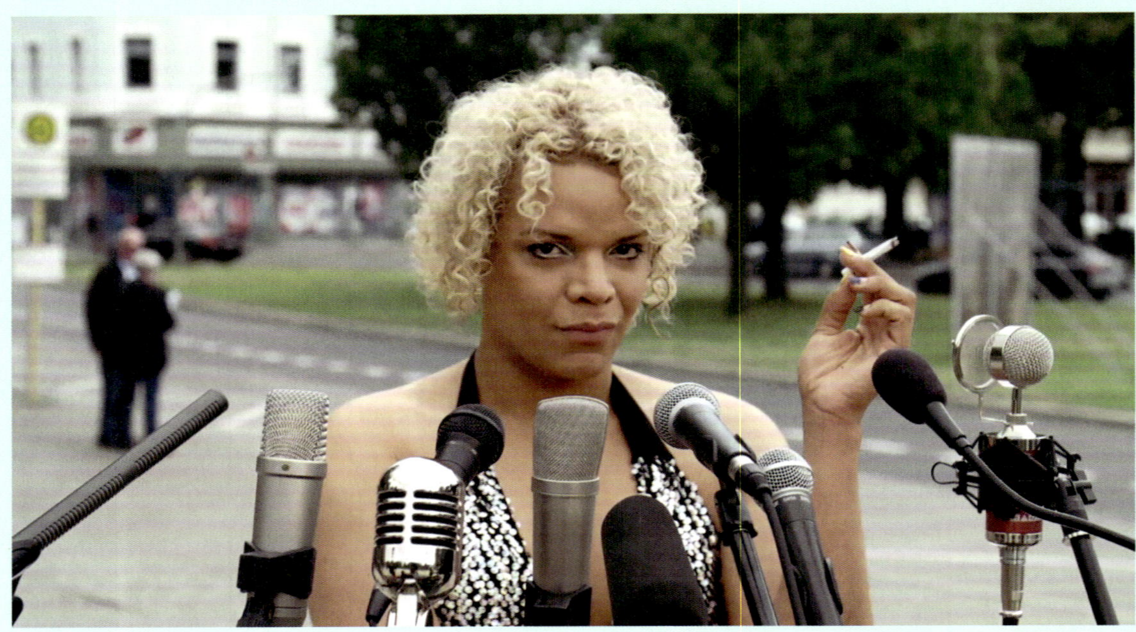

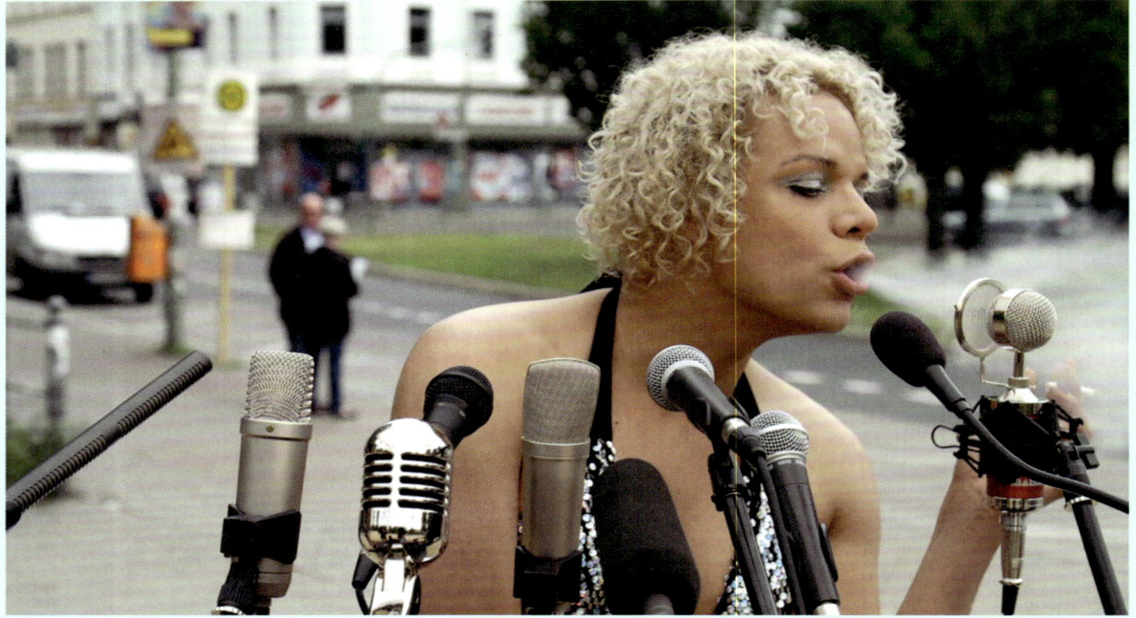

Silent, 2016

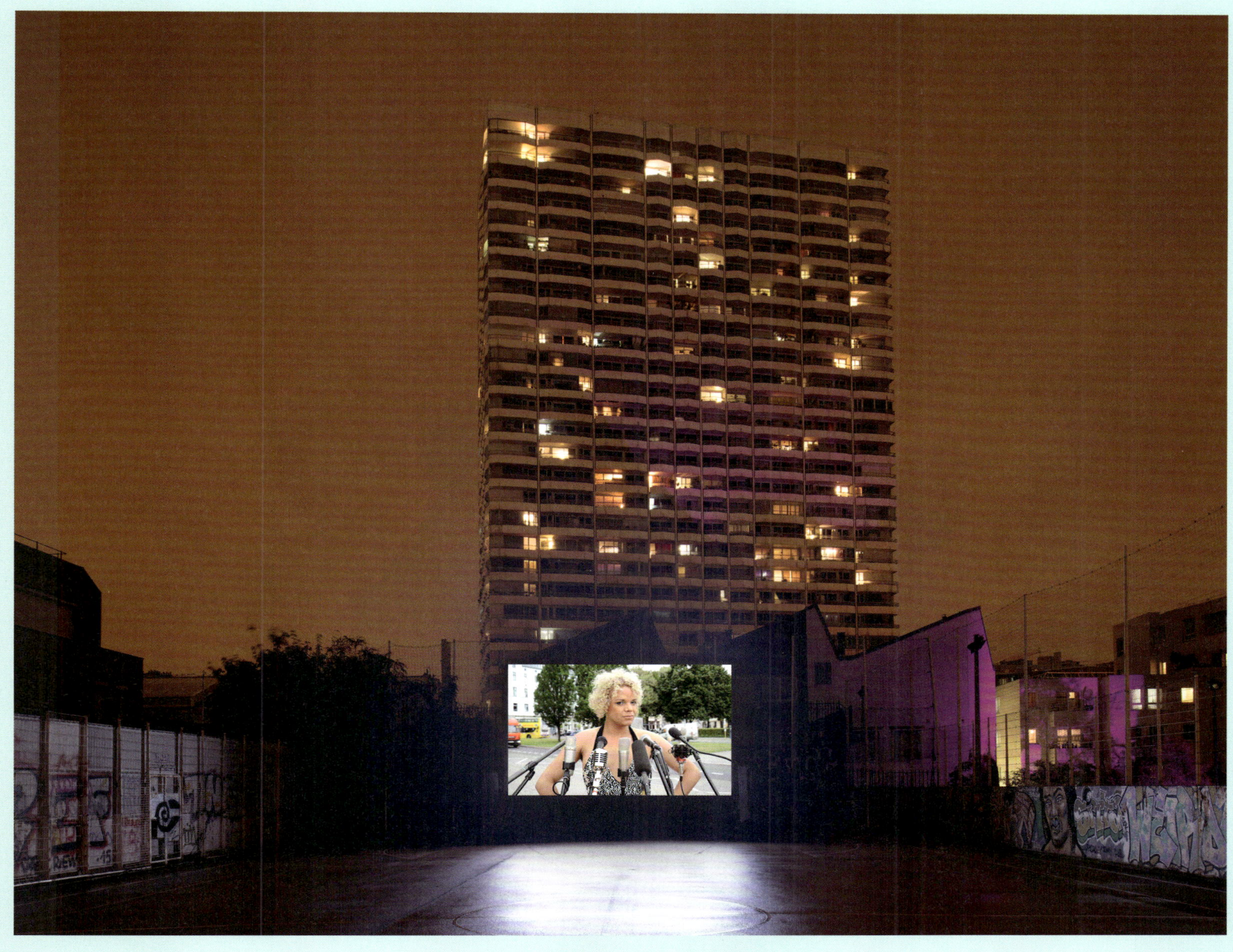

Silent, 2016

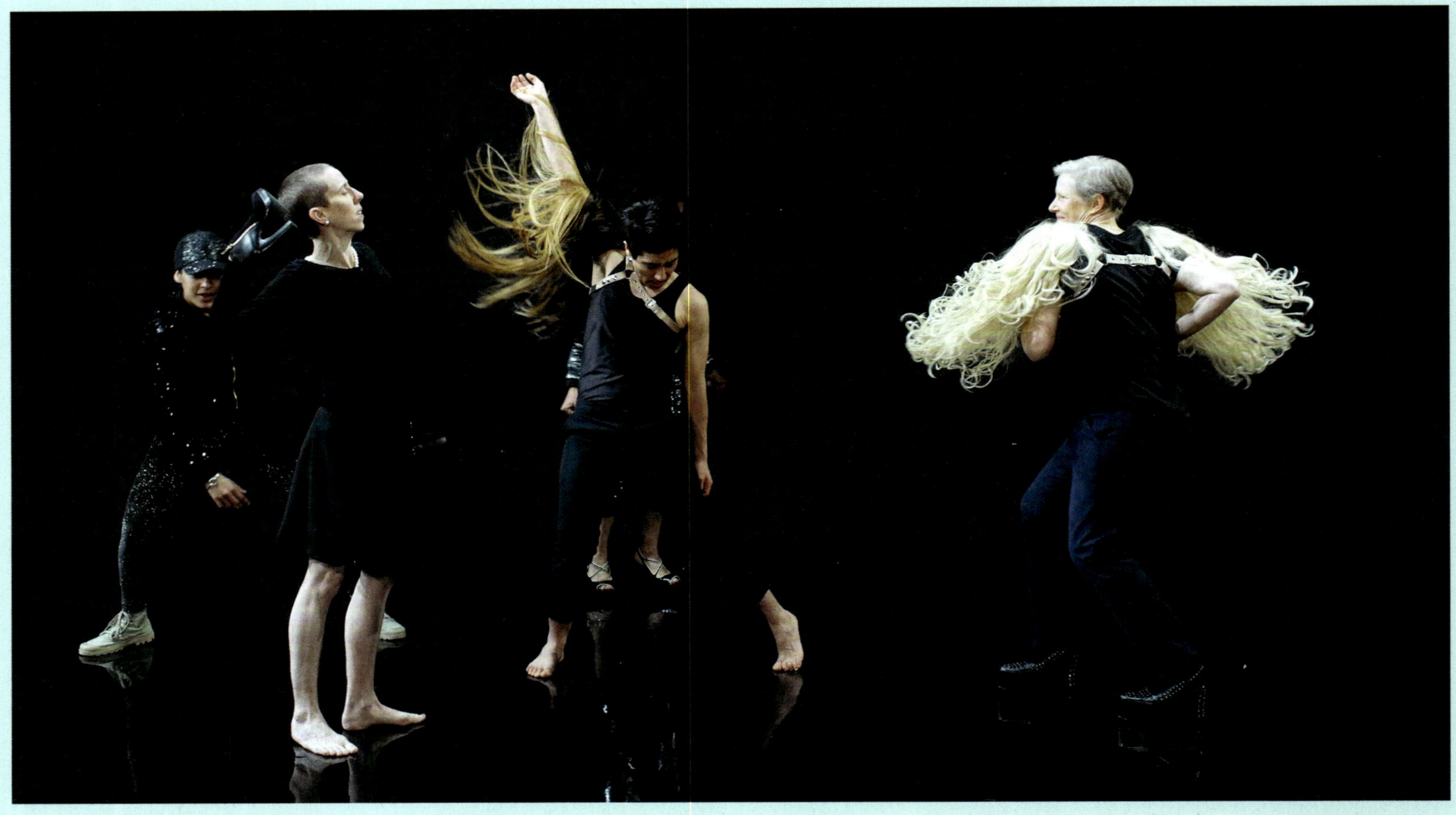

Moving Backwards, 2019

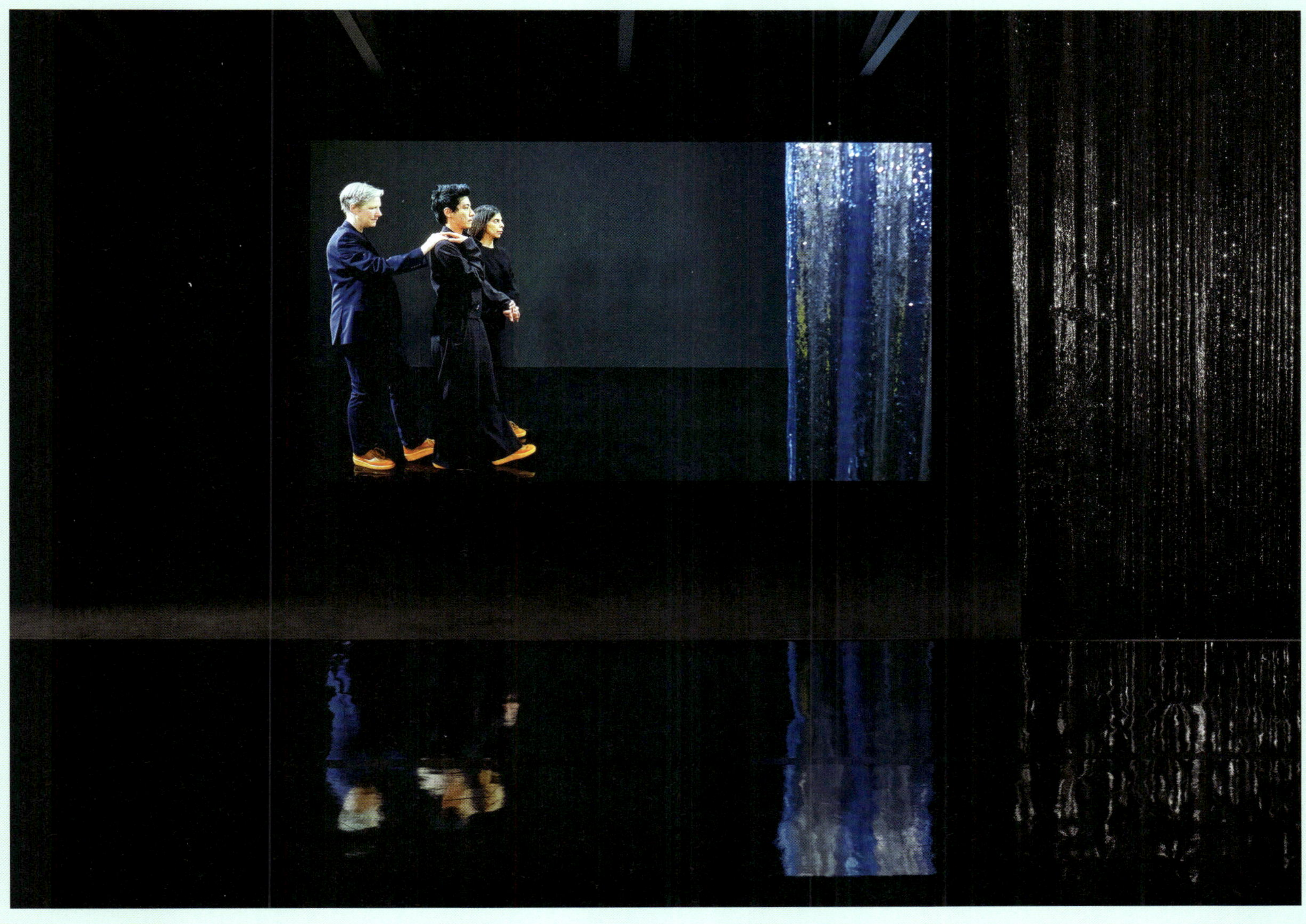

Moving Backwards, 2019

Candice Breitz

b. 1972, South Africa. Lives and works in Berlin, Germany.

Candice Breitz's practice zooms in on real and imagined communities, examining identities that are shaped not only by questions of national belonging, race, gender, and religion but also by the undeniable influences of television, cinema, and social media. From video portraits of devout fan communities—such as *King (A Portrait of Michael Jackson)* and *Queen (A Portrait of Madonna)*, both from 2005—to the polyphonic montages of film clips featuring Jack Nicholson and Meryl Streep entitled *Him* (1968–2008) and *Her* (1978–2008), Breitz's work has long considered the impact of media culture on the formation of the self. More recently, she has addressed the entanglement of individuals within complex political circumstances, reflecting explicitly on the callousness of an entertainment-saturated mediascape in which identification with fictional characters and celebrity figures runs parallel to widespread indifference to the plight of those facing sociopolitical and economic adversity.

In *Love Story* (2016), the first chapter of a trilogy of video installations, Breitz asks viewers to reflect on the kinds of stories that we are not only willing to hear but that move us to tears. Why are the tales that capture our attention so often blockbuster fictions, yet in the face of actual human suffering many of us remain unmoved? The two-room installation opens with a cinematic montage in which actors Alec Baldwin and Julianne Moore perform spoken fragments from the personal histories of six refugees fleeing violence and persecution in Syria, Angola, the Democratic Republic of the Congo, India, Venezuela, and Somalia. The stories of Shabeena Saveri, Mamy Maloba Langa, Sarah Mardini, Farah Abdi Mohamed, José Maria João, and Luis Nava Molero are urgent yet in a way familiar, and all too easily ignored in the contemporary media environment. As Baldwin and Moore recite their lines, the experience is disorienting—the stories they recount clearly are not their own— yet what they are sharing is so personal and heartbreaking that we watch, mesmerized equally by tragedy and by stardom. In the second part of *Love Story*, each tale is given a face and voice as the individuals themselves appear on-screen to speak in their own right. In a world dominated by a fast-moving attention economy, Breitz succeeds at getting viewers to take note of six true stories of personal strife. Does it matter that we were baited by a familiar face?

The second chapter of Breitz's trilogy, a thirteen-channel installation titled *TLDR* (2017), appears in *Witch Hunt*. Titled after the internet acronym for "Too Long; Didn't Read," the work likewise addresses the dynamics of the attention economy while focusing on a heated ongoing debate among feminists around sex work. Made in dialogue with the South African organization SWEAT (Sex Workers Education and Advocacy Taskforce), *TLDR* includes a three-channel projection narrated by Xanny "The Future" Stevens. Delivered with the frankness of a child, the dramatic tale underscores the high stakes motivating the struggle of sex workers for basic human rights and the decriminalization of their labor, all the while dissecting a particular mode of white saviorism. Stevens is flanked by a Greek chorus comprising eleven sex workers who punctuate their words with protest slogans as Breitz's fast-paced edits are soundtracked with music ranging from Zulu and Xhosa protest songs to Rihanna's hit "Work." In the second room of the installation, visitors are invited to spend time with the same sex workers in more than eleven hours of intimate interviews with Zoe Black, Connie, Duduzile Dlamini, Emmah, Gabbi, Regina High, Jenny, Jowi, Tenderlove, and Nosipho "Provocative" Vidima. Picking up where *Love Story* left off, *TLDR* reflects on the relationship between whiteness, privilege, and visibility vis-à-vis the role of celebrity and the pressures of the contemporary mediascape.

—Ana Briz

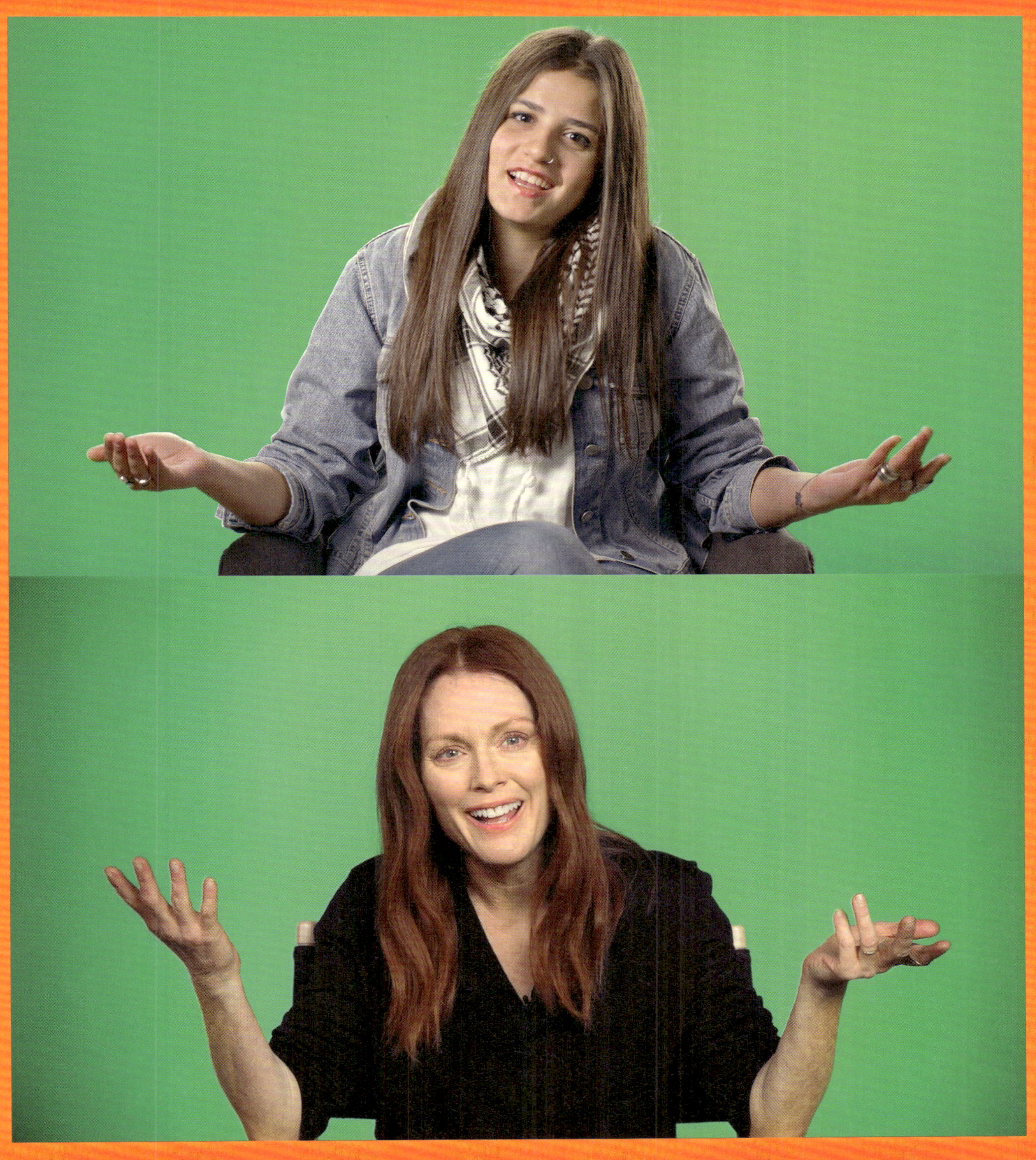

Love Story, 2016

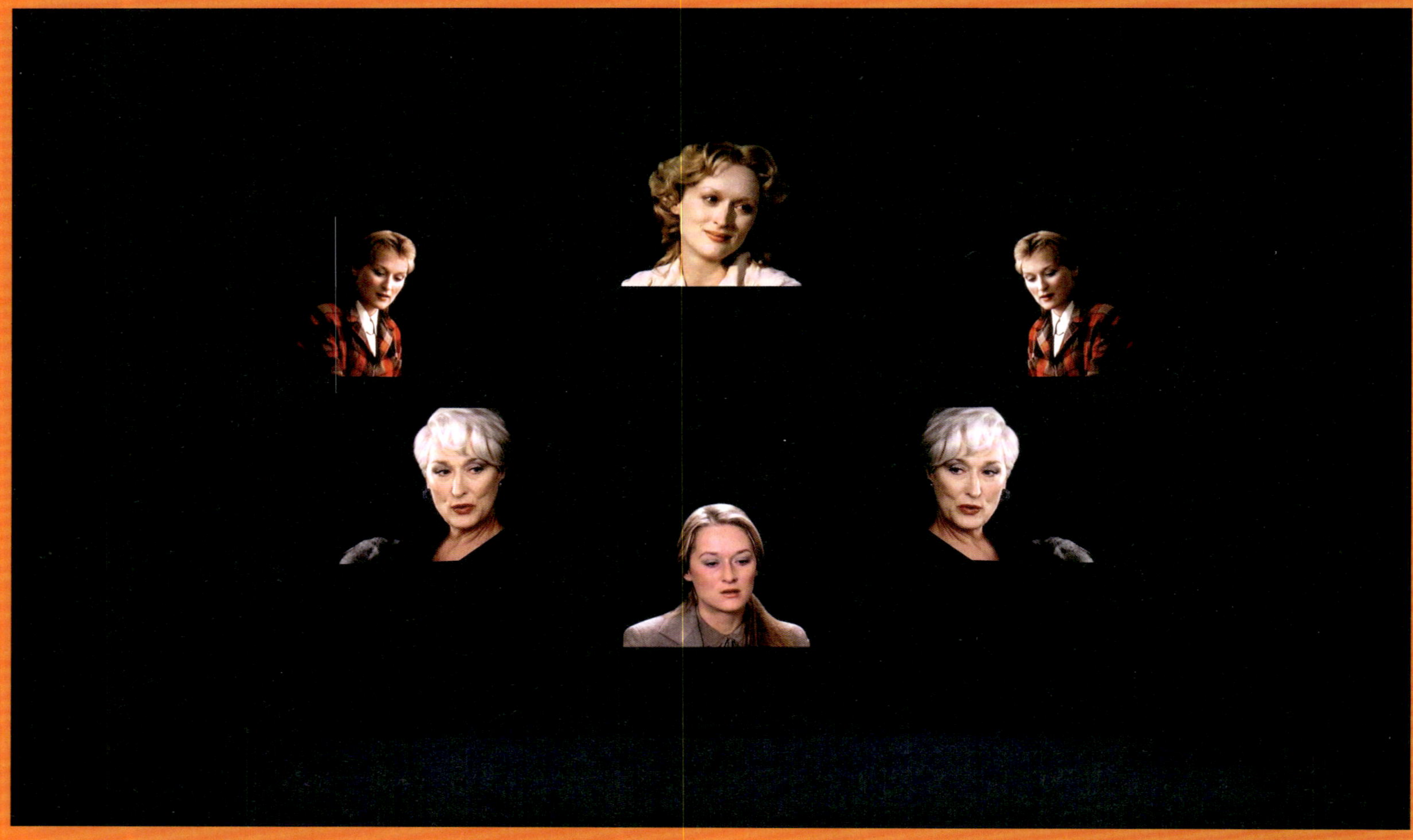

Her, 1978–2008

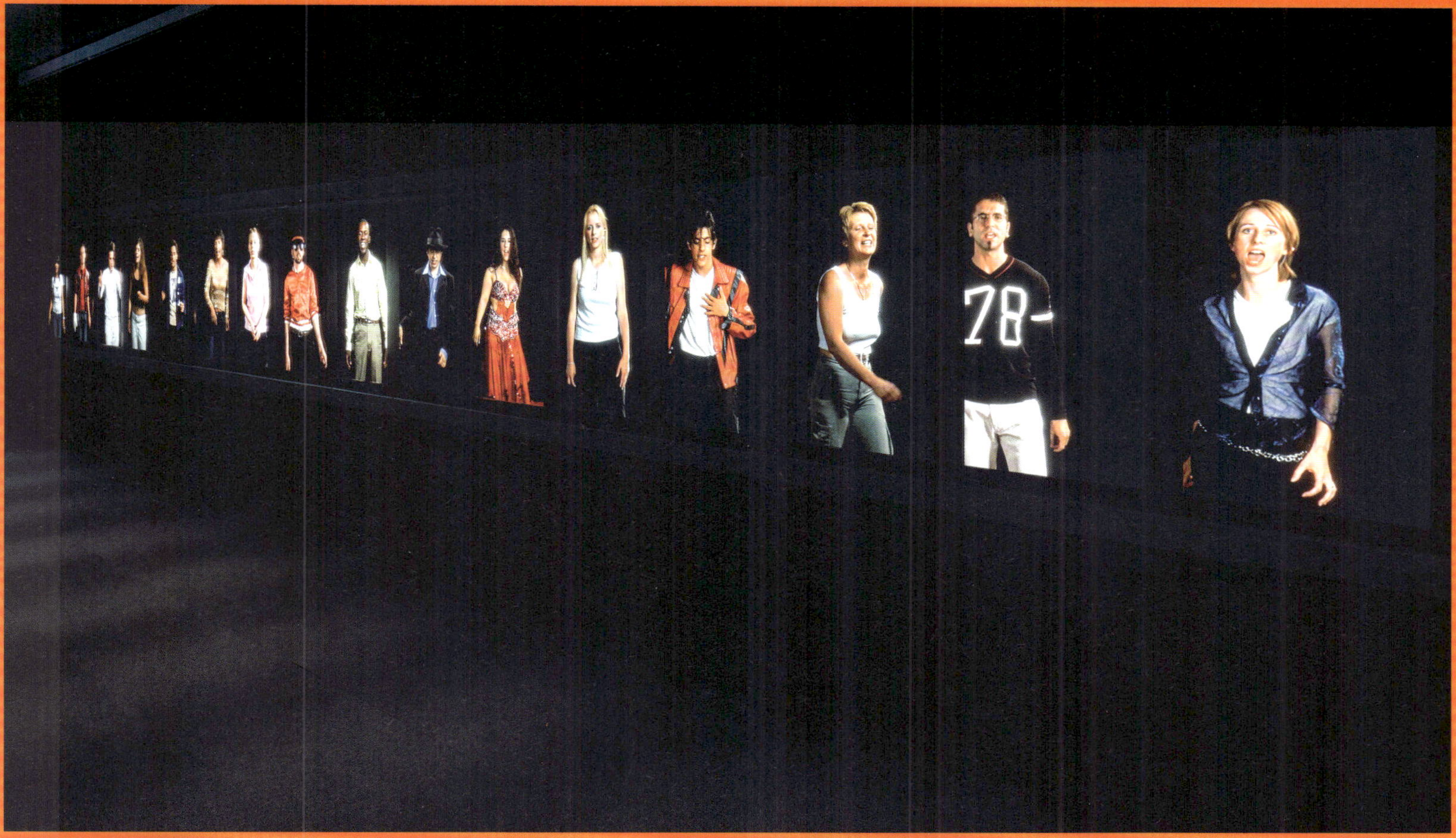

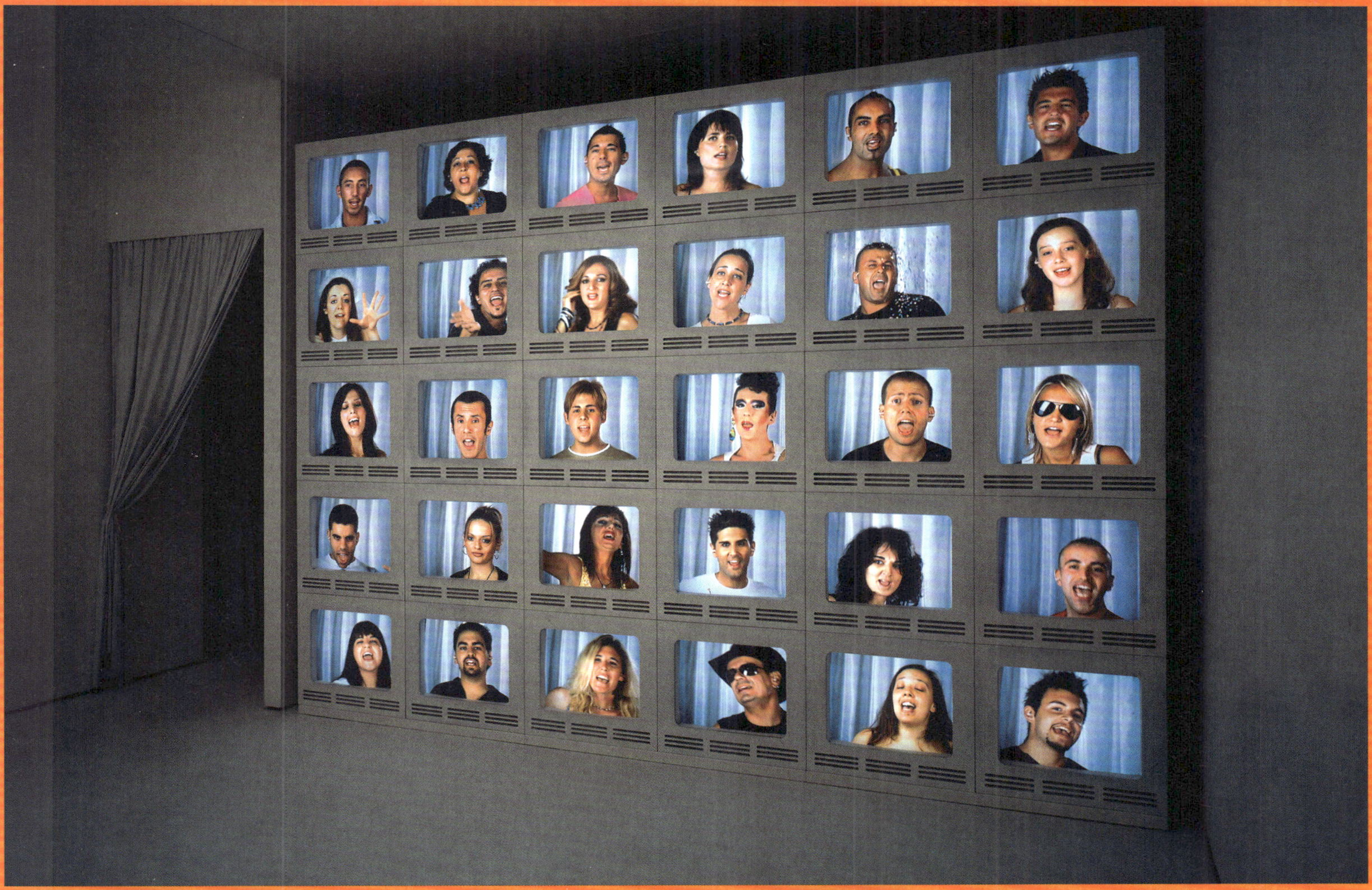

King (A Portrait of Michael Jackson), 2005
Queen (A Portrait of Madonna), 2005

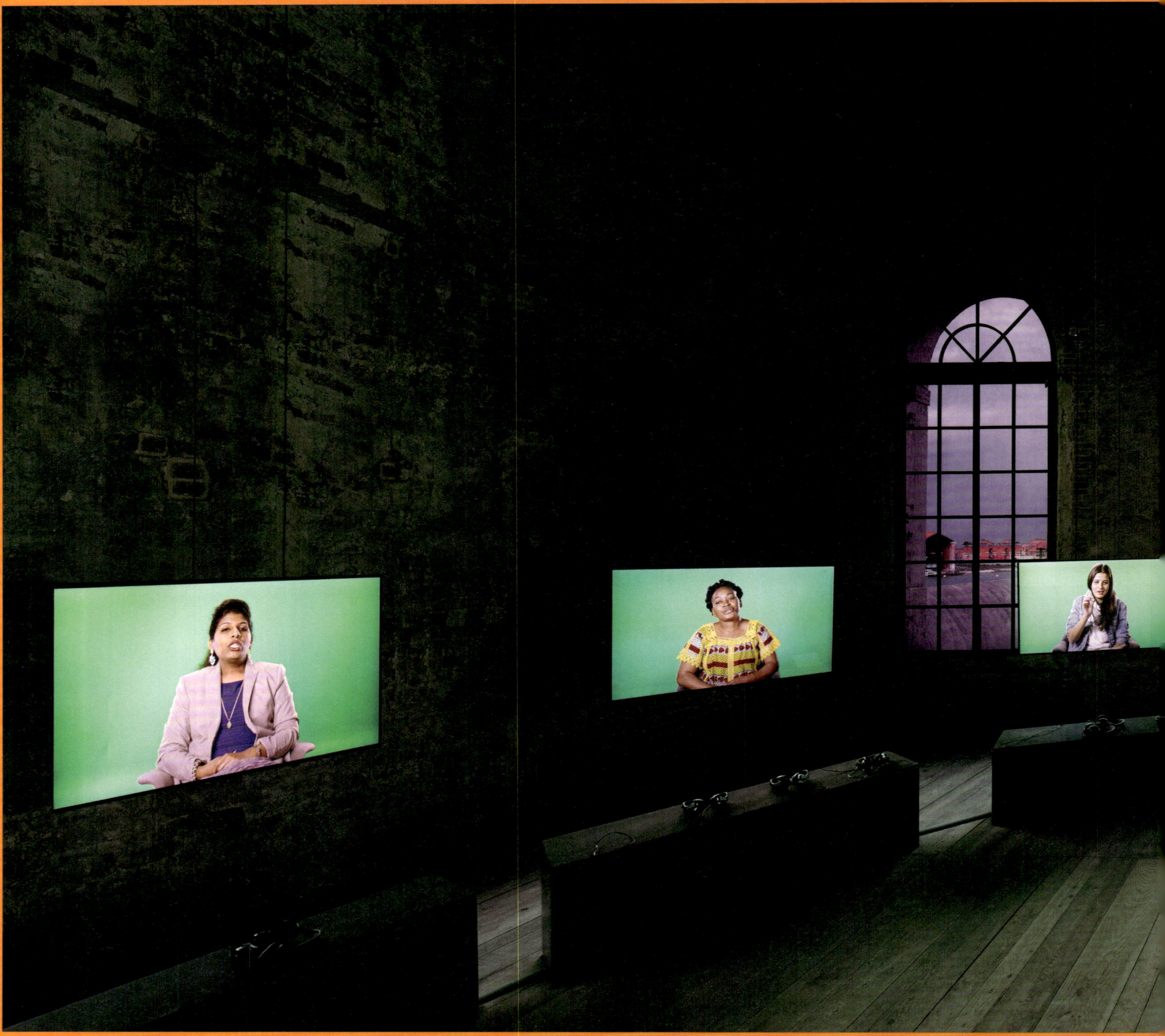

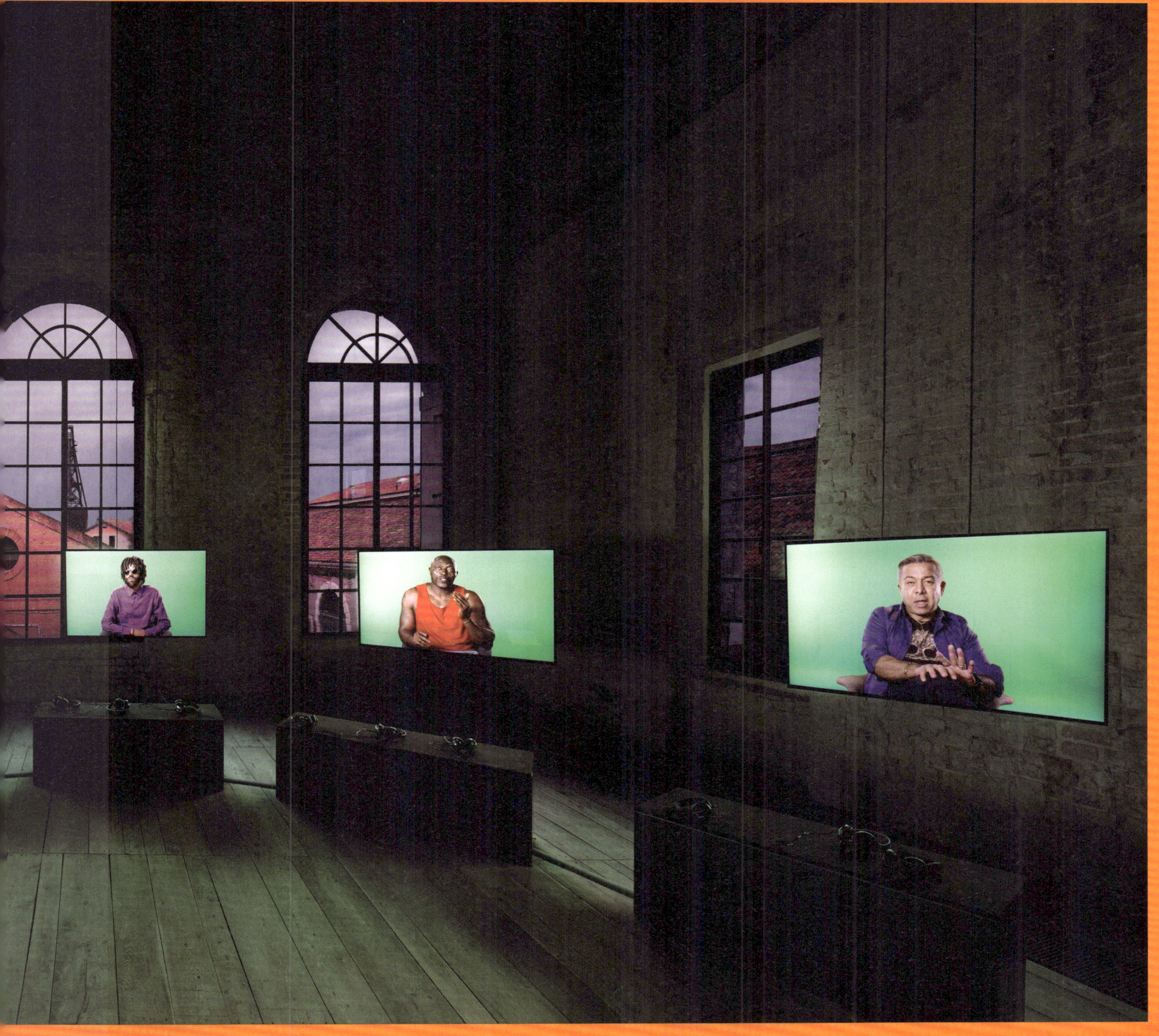

Love Story, 2016

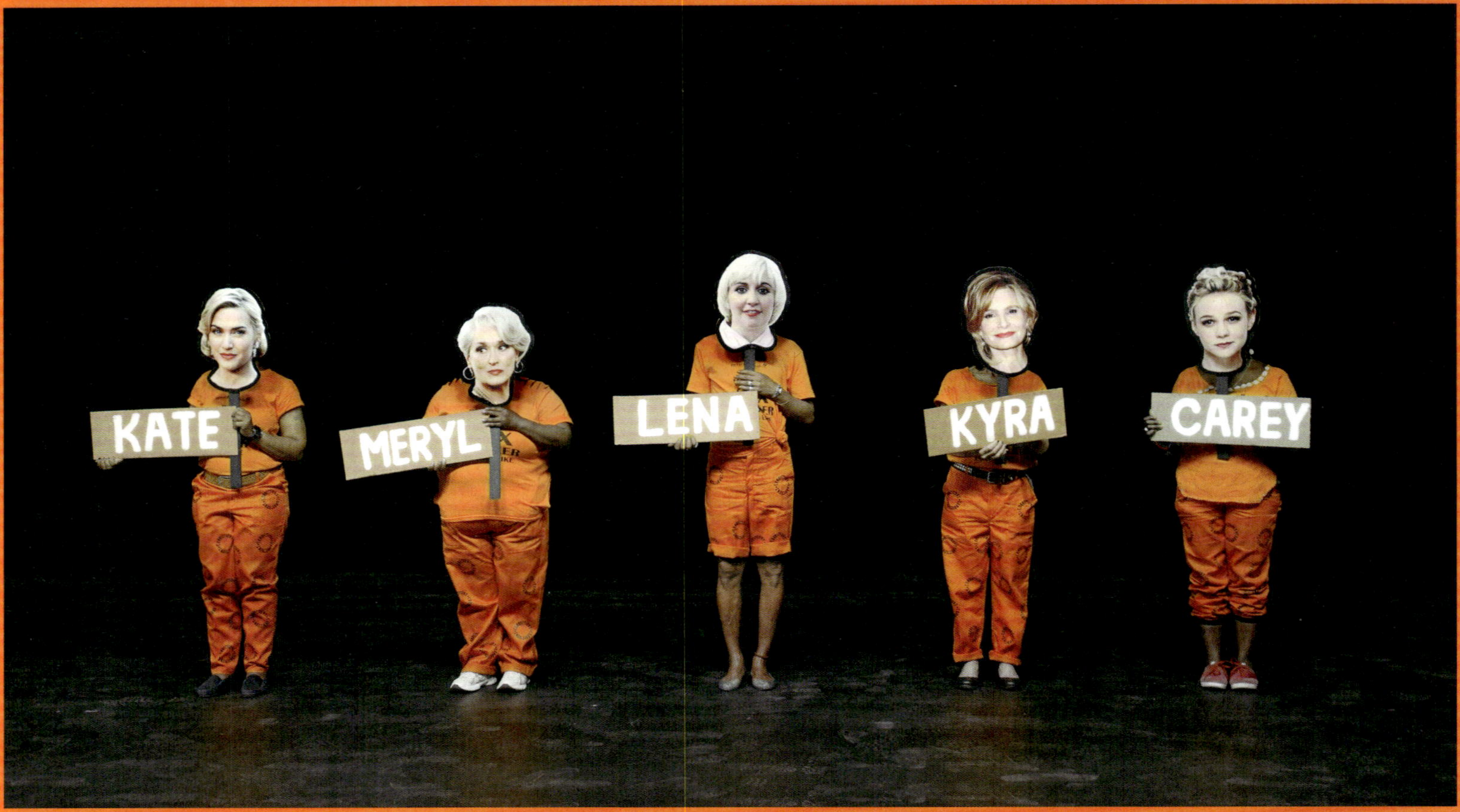

KATE
MERYL
LENA
KYRA
CAREY 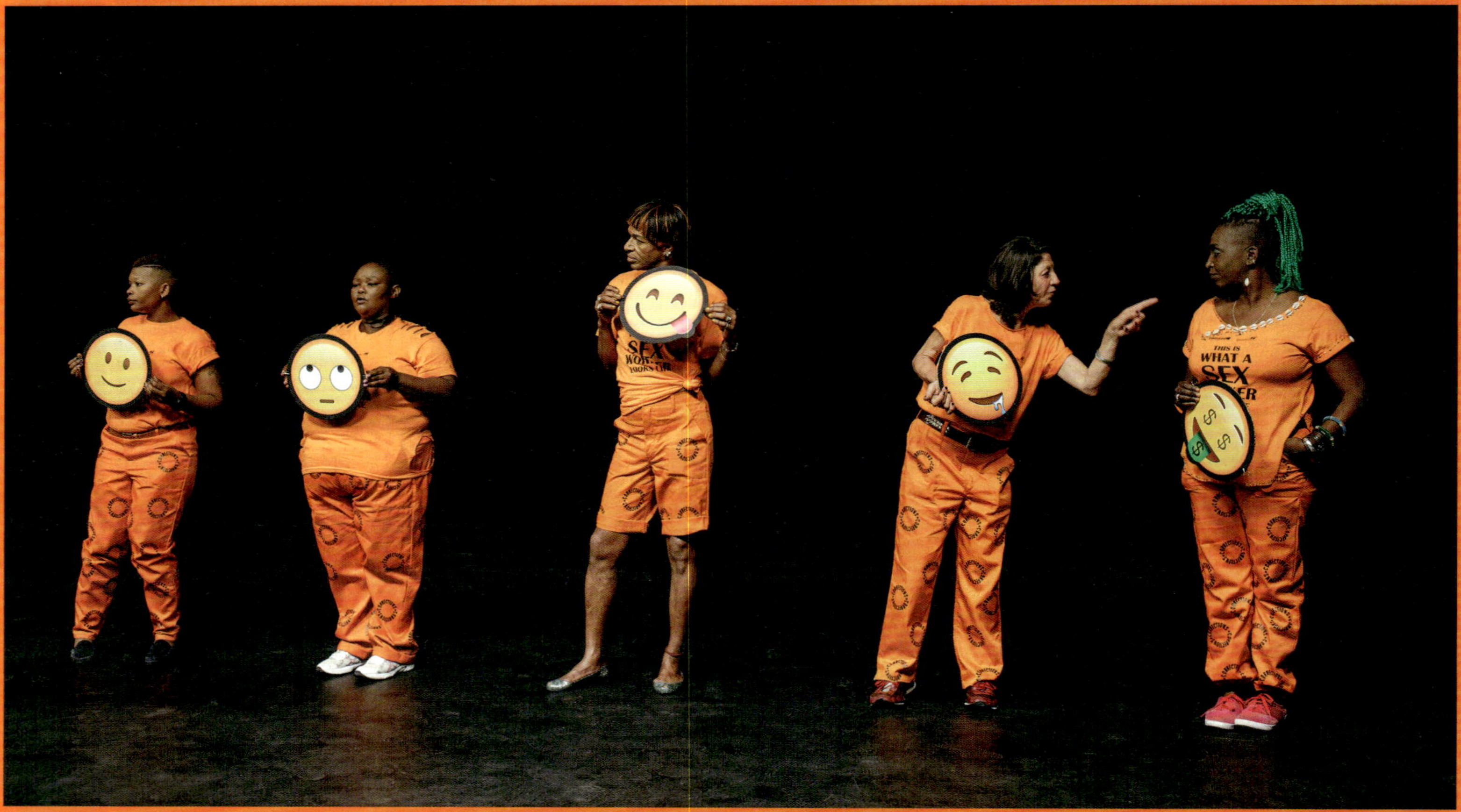
SEX WORKER
THIS IS WHAT A SEX WORKER

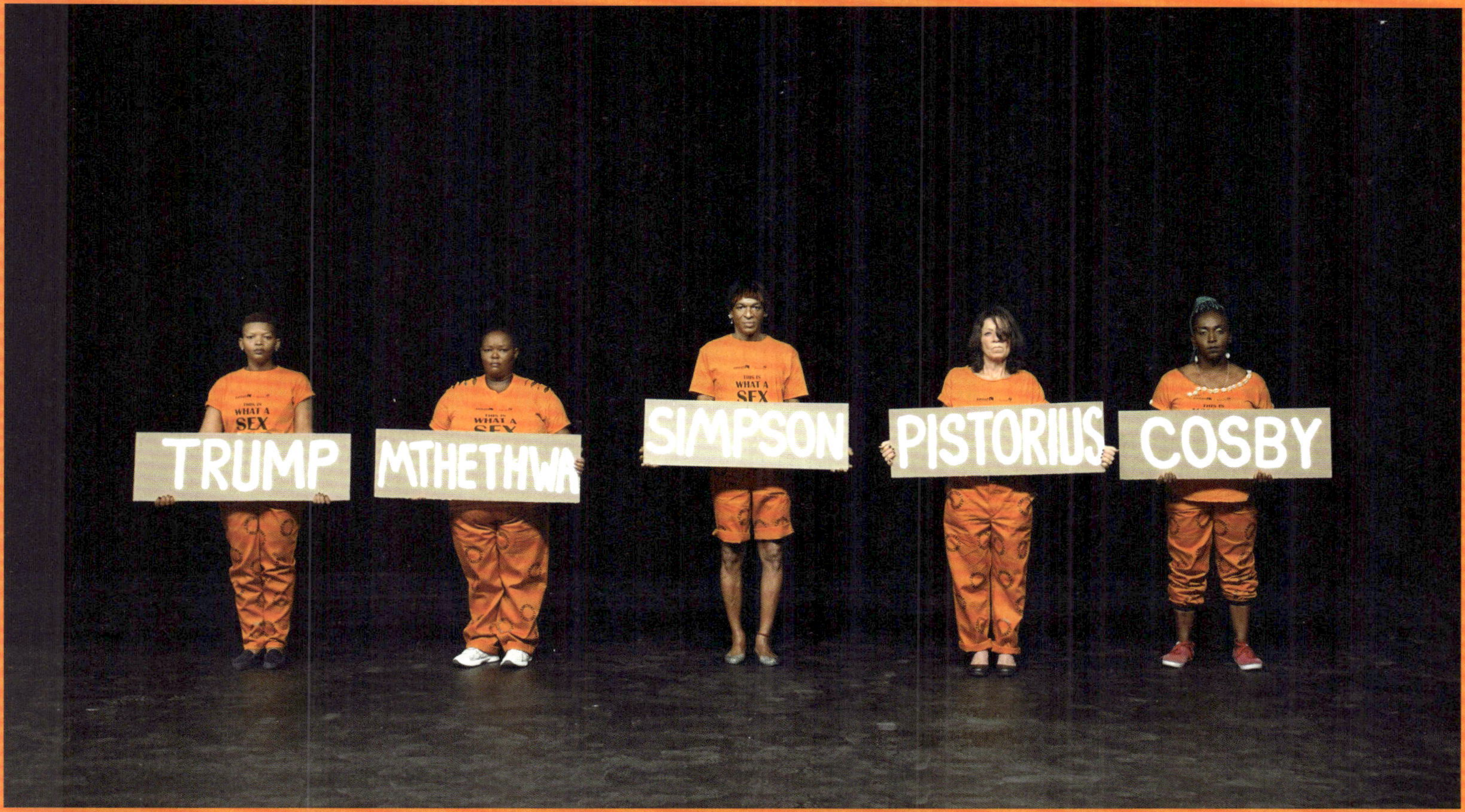

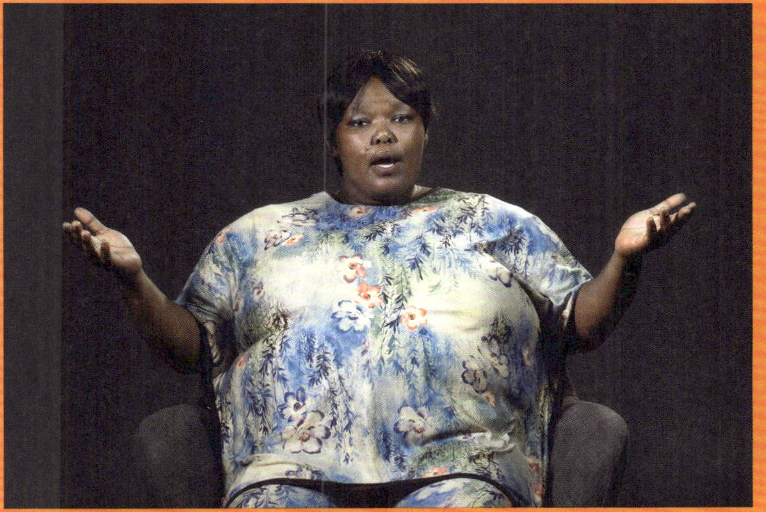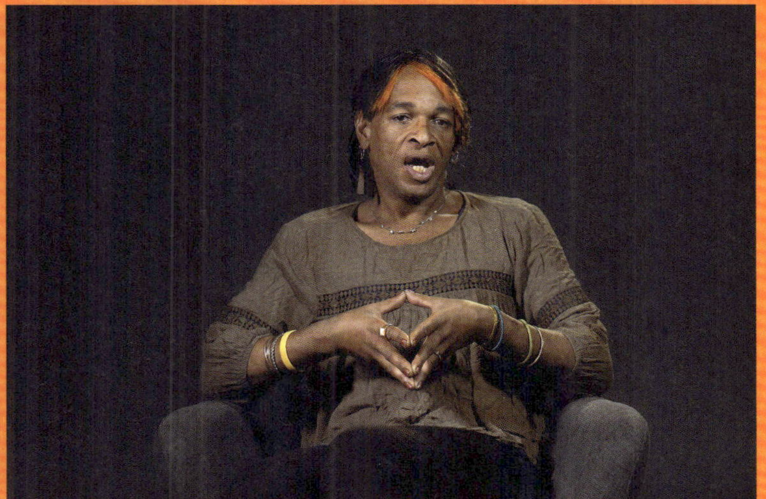

TLDR, 2017

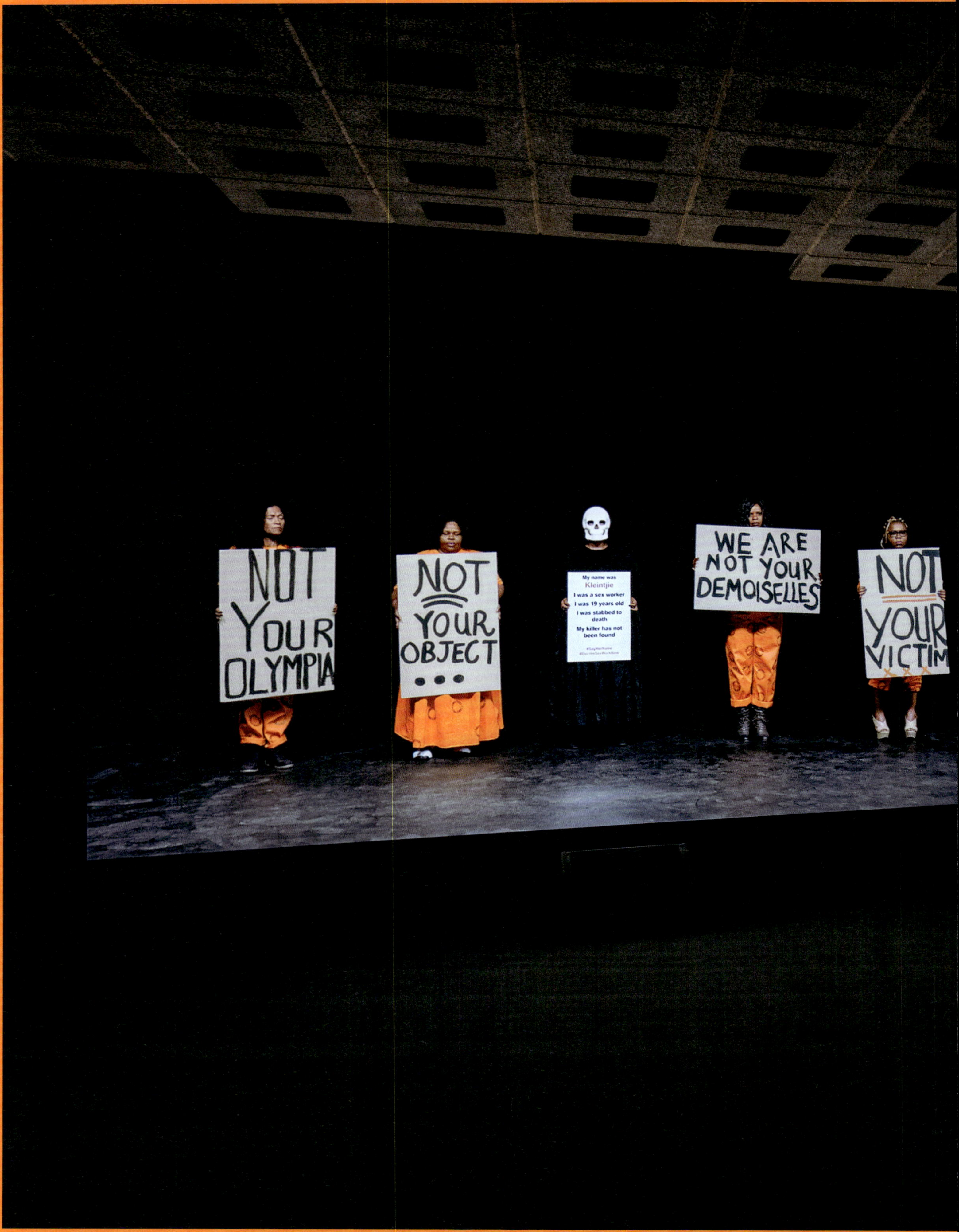

NOT YOUR OLYMPIA
NOT YOUR OBJECT ...
My name was
Kleintjie
I was a sex worker
I was 19 years old
I was stabbed to death
My killer has not been found
WE ARE NOT YOUR DEMOISELLES
NOT YOUR VICTIM

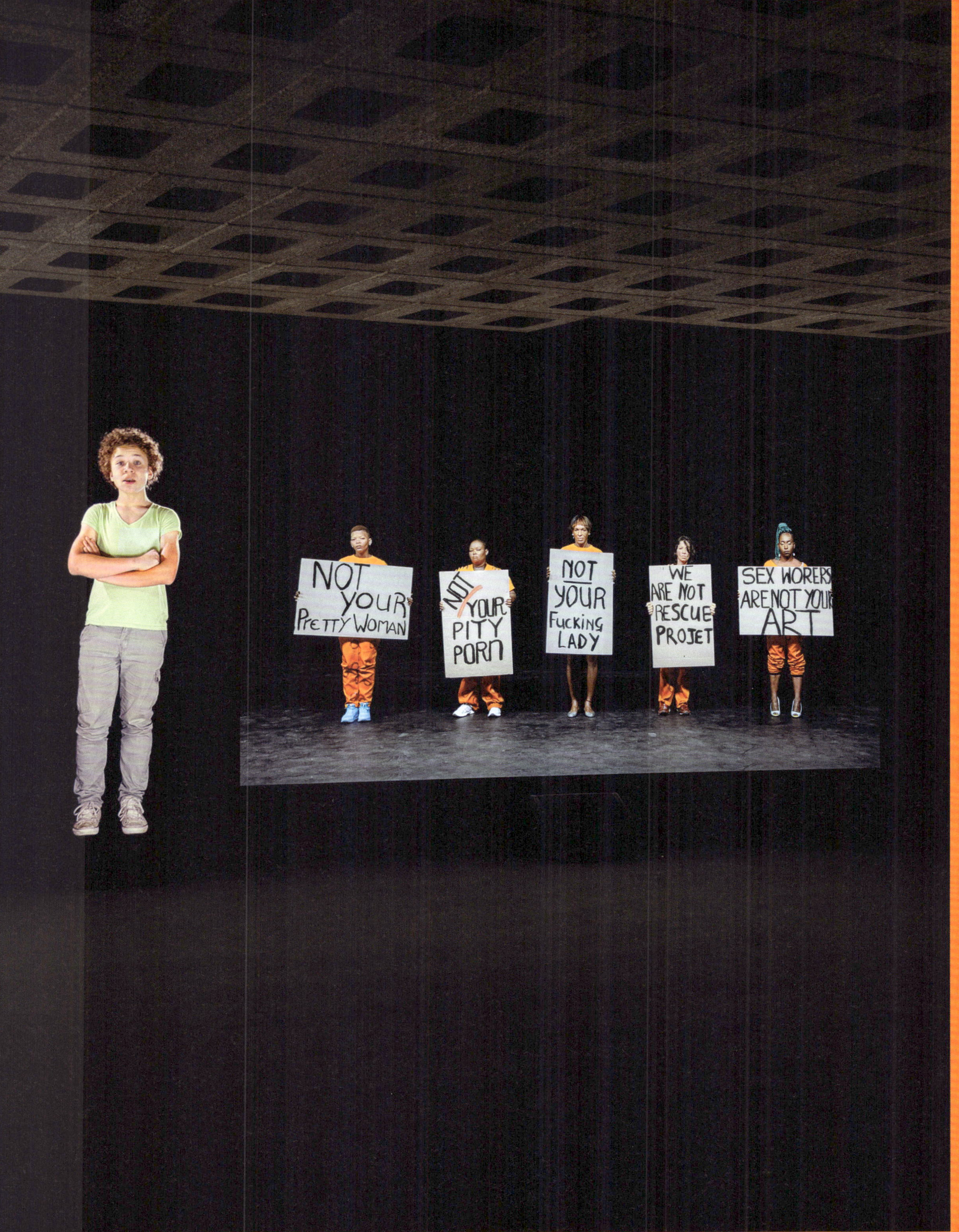
NOT YOUR Pretty WOMAN
NOT YOUR PITY PORN
NOT YOUR Fucking LADY
WE ARE NOT RESCUE PROJET
SEX WORERS ARE NOT YOUR ART

TLDR, 2017

Shu Lea Cheang

b. 1954, Taiwan. Lives and works in Paris, France.

Shu Lea Cheang is an artist and filmmaker whose work explores the nature of sociopolitical control in the digital age. Cheang's immersive technological landscapes invite publics to engage with the constructs of gendered, racial, and sexual characterizations that exist across virtual, textual, and biomedical technologies. Her projects employ a combination of film, sculpture, and interactive web design in works that mimic collective digital spaces and the inhabitants of contemporary informational ecosystems. A self-identified activist, she invites viewers to collaborate in the virtual and representational space of her work, consciously undermining the singularity of normative social discourse. Cheang's ambitious scope and cinematic narrative style repurpose heterarchical networks of digital surveillance and control, transforming them into mechanisms for visualizing connections between cyber, social, and biological space in which viewers both knowingly and unknowingly participate.

The artist developed her first large-scale cybernetic installation in 1995 at the Walker Art Center in Minneapolis. Titled *Bowling Alley,* this web-based interface connected the museum to the city's historic Bryant Lake Bowling Alley. Cheang collaborated with ten women in the local creative community and asked them to reflect on themes of desire, mobility, access, and agency within patriarchal structures. Projected as part of an installation at the Walker, the website followed an algorithm in which hyperlinks guided the viewer through evolving combinations of layered images and text. Sensors installed at the bowling alley triggered a "scrambling" effect that disrupted and reconfigured the site's information each time someone bowled a strike or spare. The installation functioned as an instrument for visualizing the nature of public space.

In *Brandon: A One-Year Narrative Project in Installments* (1998–99), Cheang designed a platform that delved into issues of gender fusion and technocorporeality in both public and cyber space. The first web-based artwork commissioned by the Guggenhein Museum, *Brandon* was named after Brandon Teena, a transgender person who was raped and murdered in Nebraska in 1993 after his biological sex was revealed. The universe of *Brandon* mimicked the discursive unfolding of online space, in that the individual voices that over time inhabited the piece collectively defined it. Over the course of a year the site became a repository for images, newspaper clippings, and legal documents that traced the contours of the gendered body.

In 2019 for Taiwan in Venice, Cheang premiered her installation *3×3×6*. In it, she reimagined the classic architecture of surveillance, the panopticon, in a time when digital technologies have become increasingly sophisticated and their mechanisms of control normalized within our digital landscape. In *3×3×6*, Cheang used facial-recognition technology to design a 3D-camera surveillance system that captured the faces of visitors and disguised them with a morphing program. The work centered around ten videos, each containing a fictionalized narration of cases throughout history in which individuals have been persecuted and imprisoned for their sexual and gendered behavior—including those of historical figures like the Marquis de Sade and the panopticon's archanalyst, Michel Foucault. The scripts for the videos were cowritten with curator and writer Paul B. Preciado, whose work has both influenced and been influenced by Cheang. Loosely informed by Preciado's work on subjugation and on the psychopharmaceutical, the layered narrations in *3x3x6* became a collective roadmap for resisting normativity by finding glitches in the system.

Witch Hunt features *UKI Virus Rising* (2018), a three-channel video installation that forms part of the sequel to Cheang's cyperpunk film *I.K.U.* (2000). In the more recent work, the viewer is thrust into a dystopic, infected technological universe to explore themes of transparency, anonymity, and technocorporeal identity. In the installation, floor-to-ceiling projections envelop the viewer in a chamber of floating red blood cells, creating a sensation of being inside a cardiovascular system. Here the viewer encounters Reiko—a coder and political insurgent in the postapocalyptic digital universe Cheang has created. Viewers follow Reiko through the electronic wastescape E-trashville where she attempts to reboot herself into existence and regain control of her body. In this process of reprogramming, Reiko is infected and transformed into the virus. The work serves as a conceptual sketch for the feature-length film *UKI* that Cheang is currently developing.

—Nika Chilewich

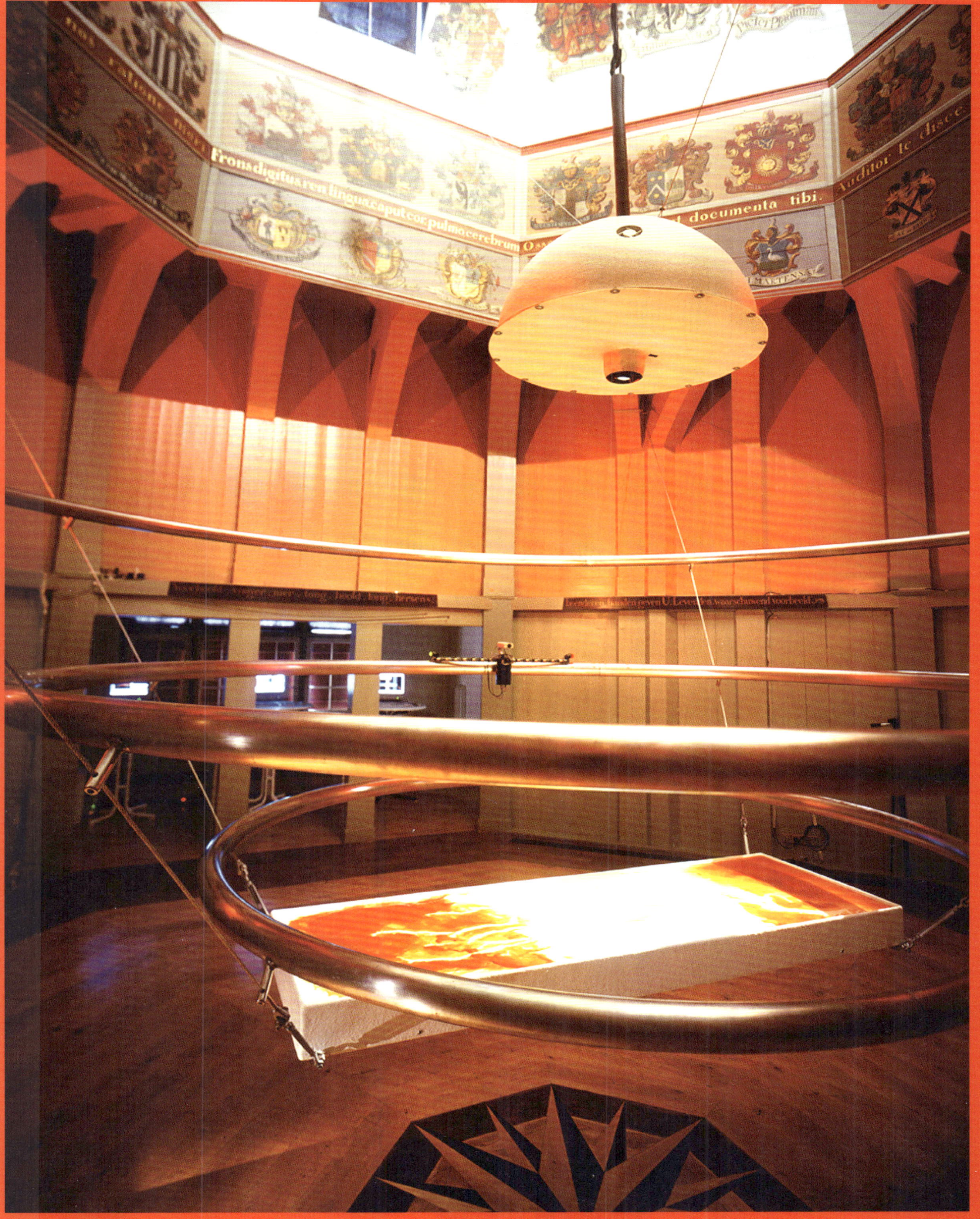

Brandon: A One-Year Narrative Project in Installments, 1998–99

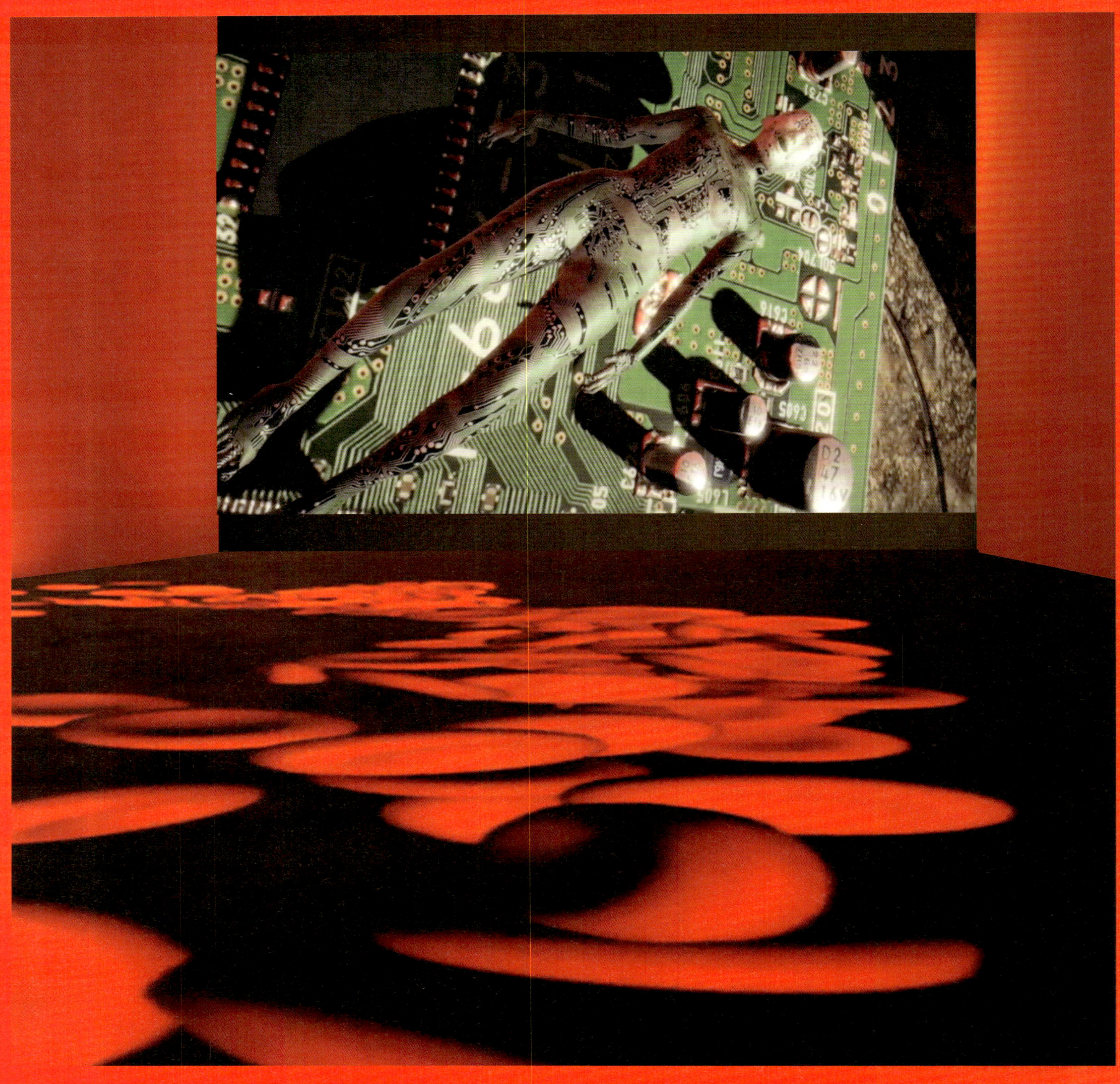

UKI Virus Rising, 2018

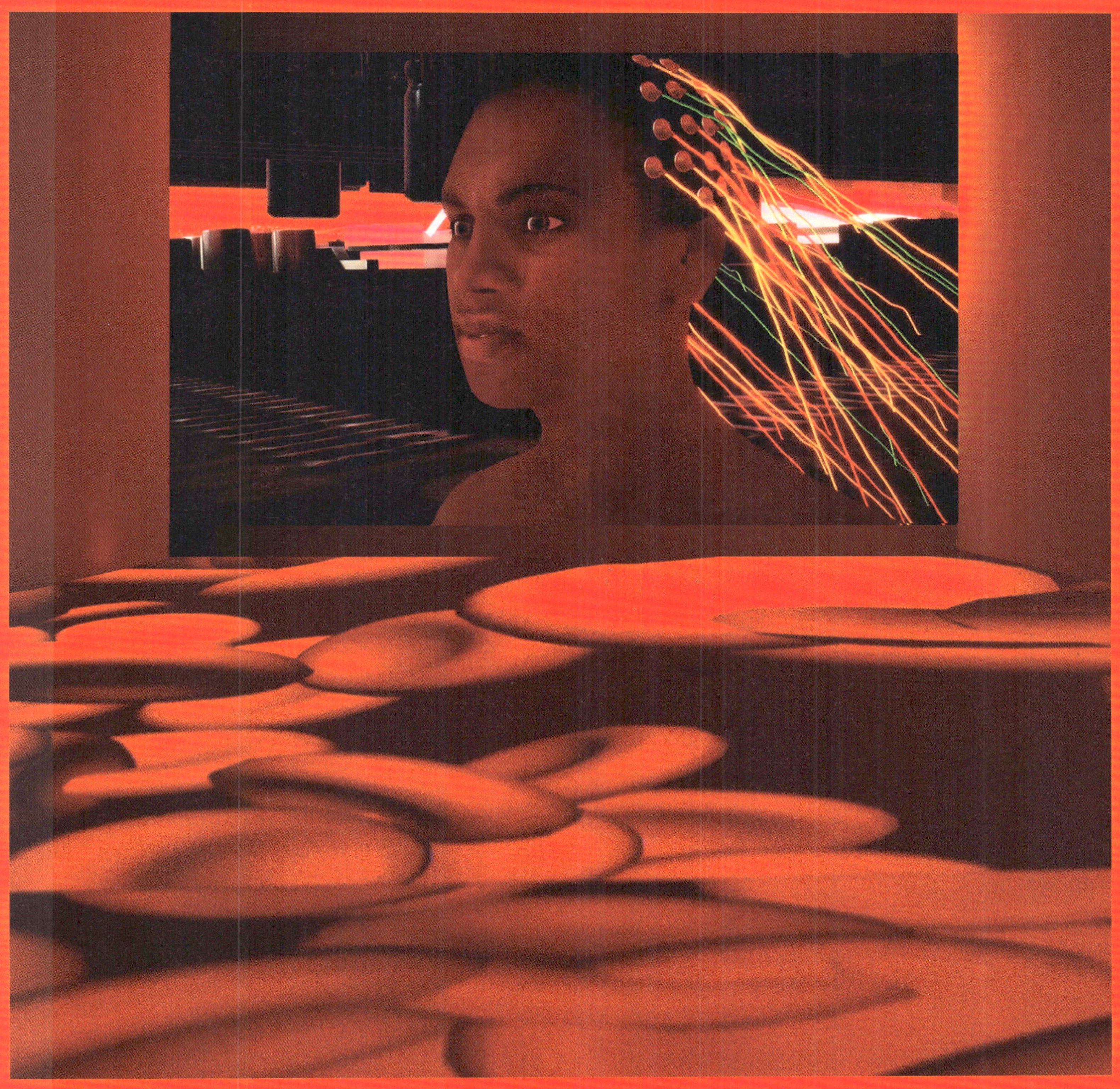

UKI Virus Rising, 2018

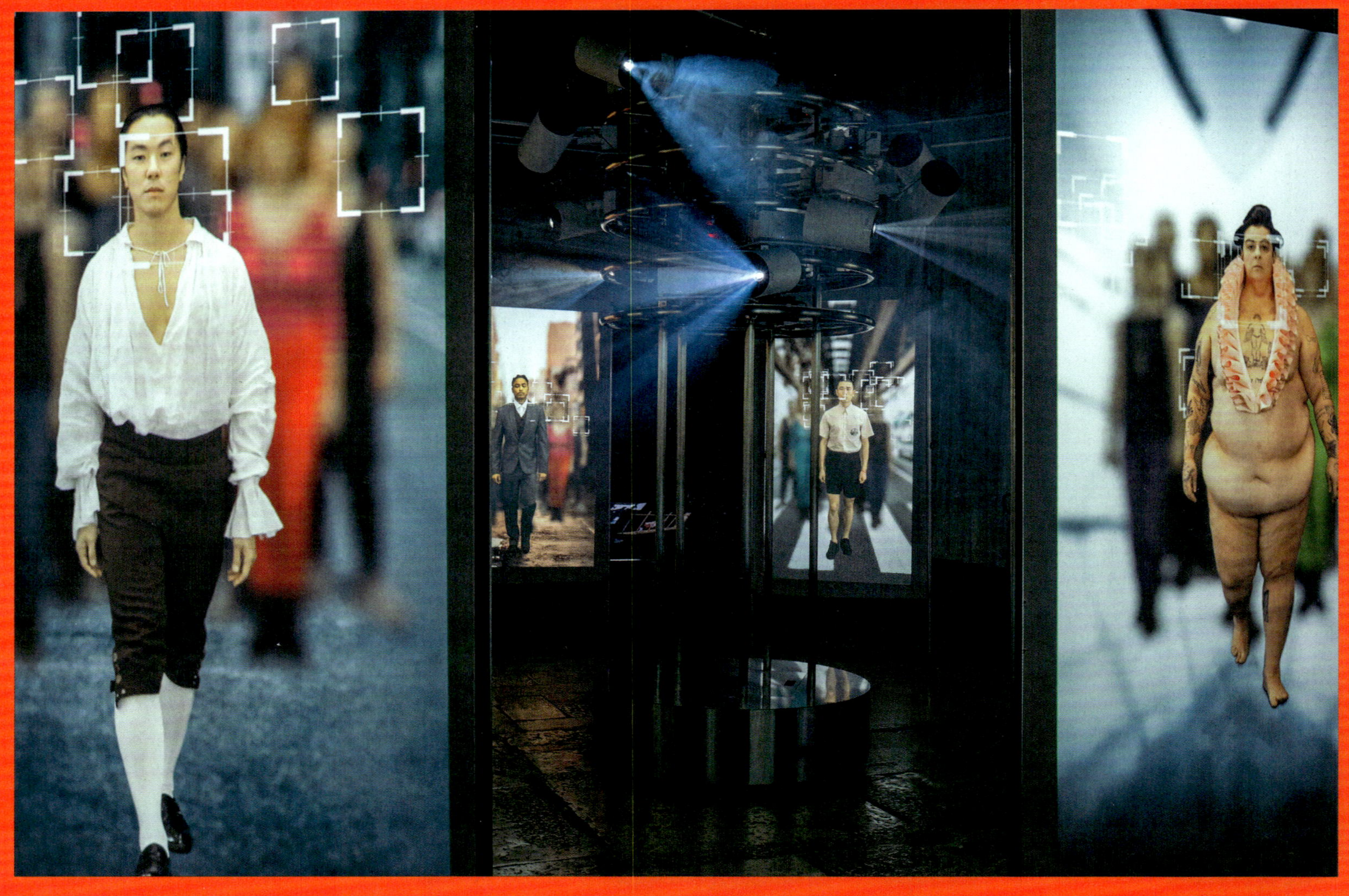

3×3×6, 2019

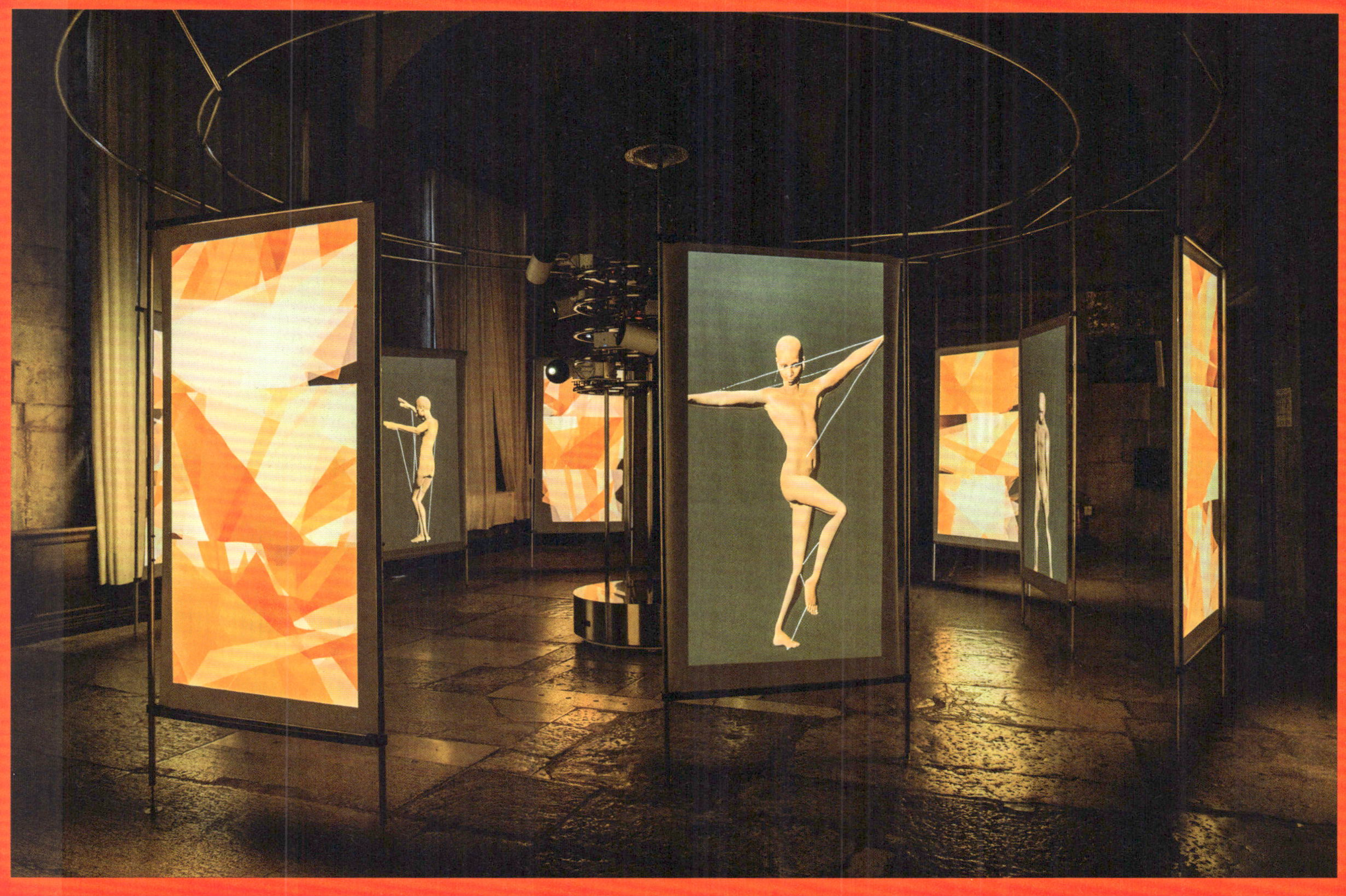

3×3×6, 2019

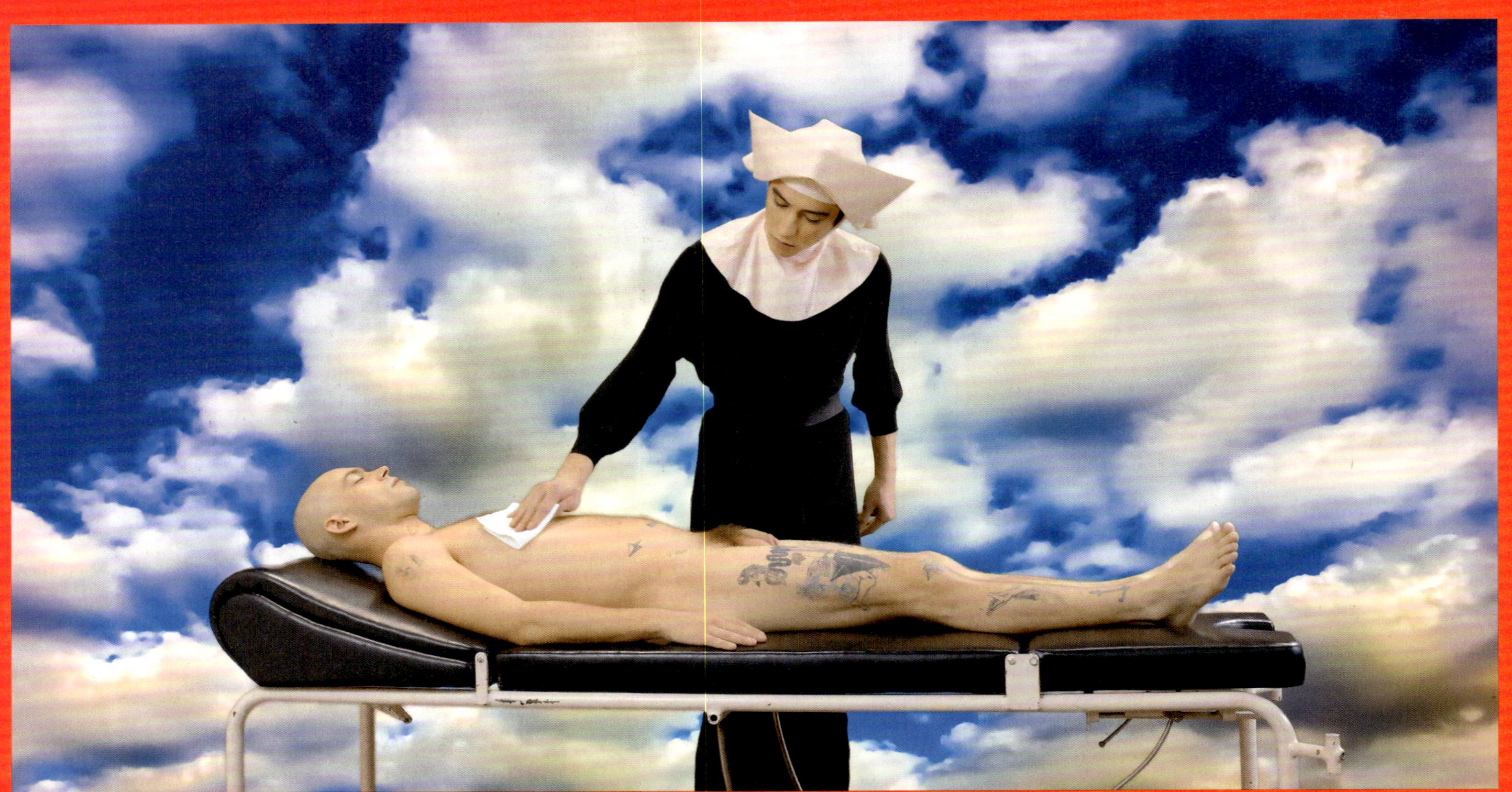

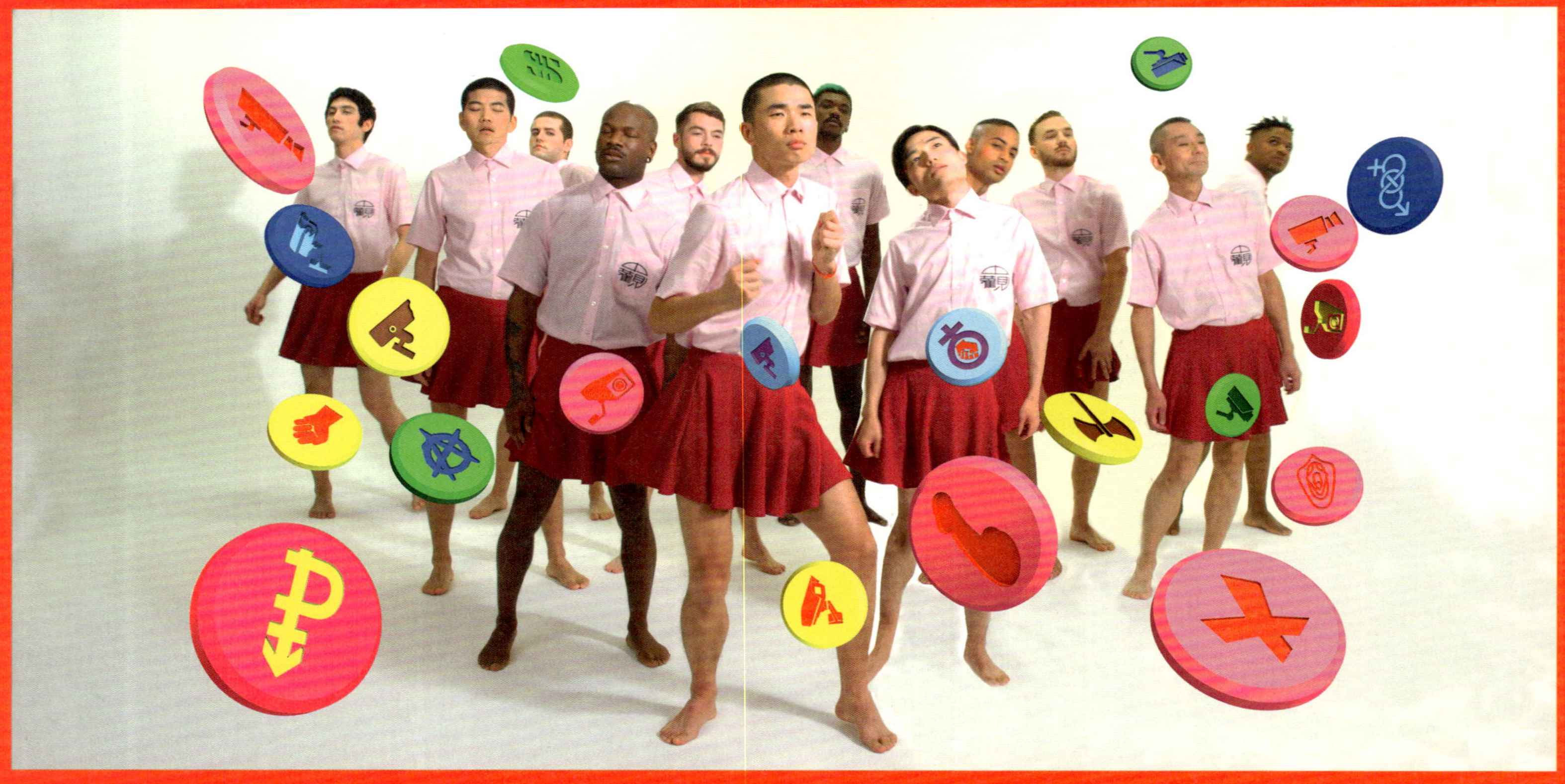

Faucault X, from 3×3×6, 2019
OOX, from 3×3×6, 2019

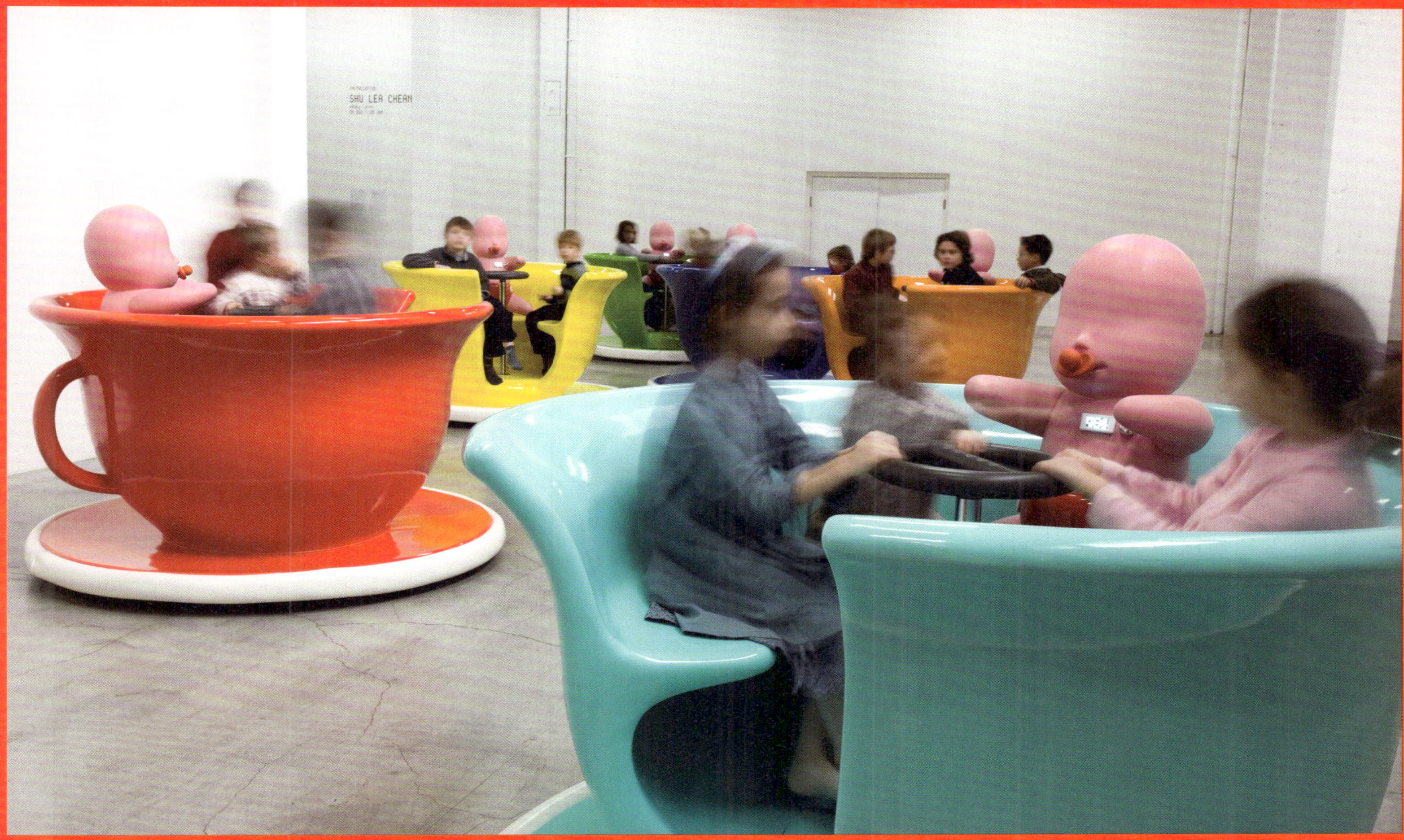

Baby Love, 2005

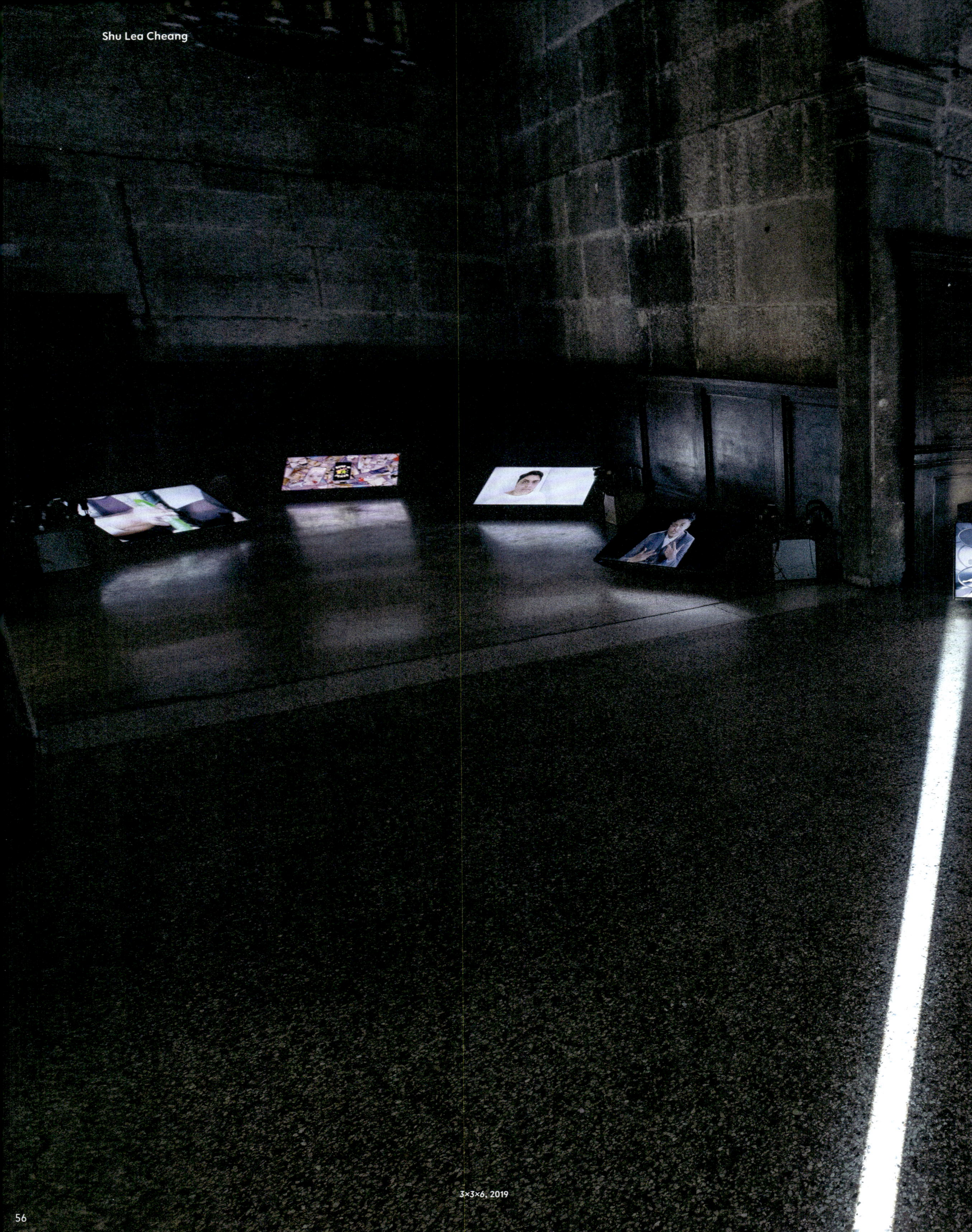

3×3×6, 2019

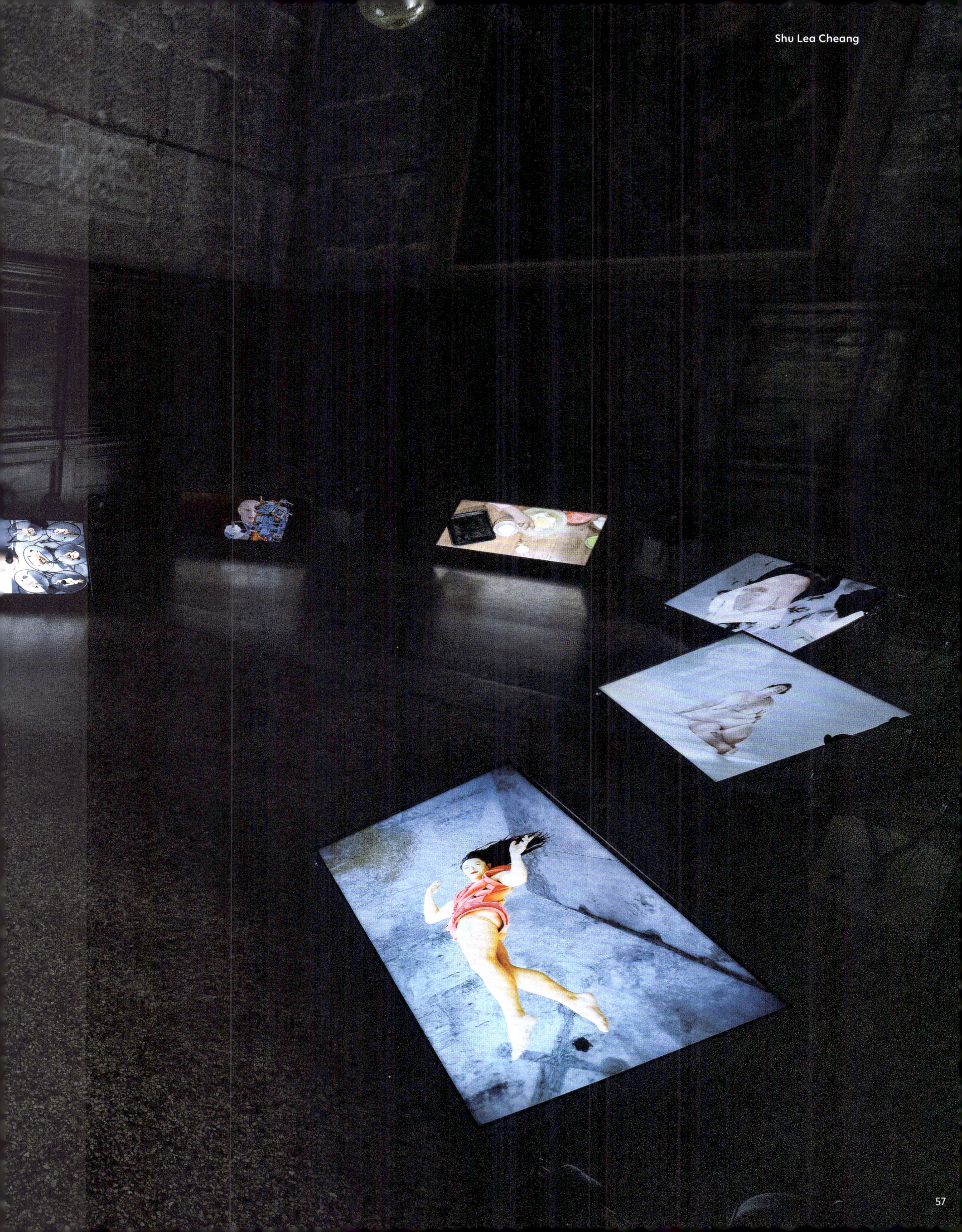

Minerva Cuevas

b. 1975, Mexico. Lives and works in Mexico City, Mexico.

Minerva Cuevas mines the symbolic languages of capitalism to comment on colonial power structures latent in contemporary societies. She appropriates a disembodied institutional voice, doctoring the logos of corporations in conceptual projects that address the exploitative treatment of natural and human resources as commodities. Rooted in extensive research into international political and economic histories, her projects often manifest in iterative, site-specific installations that evolve over time. With acerbic wit, Cuevas distorts corporate culture to create unexpected associations drawn from collective visual memory.

In Mexico City in 1998, Cuevas founded *Mejor Vida Corp.* (Better Life Corp.), a nonprofit corporation whose mission is to intervene in daily urban societal rites to enhance the political agency of citizens. For example, Cuevas traveled the city providing free goods, such as subway tickets, stamps, student ID cards, lottery tickets, and barcode stickers that could be used to reduce the cost of produce. Over more than two decades, *MVC* has been activated in cultural venues around the world, offering a variety of services, including assistance with recommendation letters and cleaning cities' subway stations.

Cuevas's a appropriative gestures are both playful and subversive, mimicking the alluring forms of branded content. For *Causa y efecto* (Cause and effect, 2007), Cuevas placed the eagle from the logo of Mexico's state-owned petroleum company, Pemex, in oil fields to comment on the hundreds of thousands of birds killed every year by industrial oil drilling. In *Melate* (2000), one of her first mural paintings and poster campaigns, she reproduced the symbol of the eponymous Mexican lottery, whose proceeds are supposedly used for public assistance, and replaced the prize amount with statistics on poverty in the country. One of her most ambitious interventions involved a reconfiguration of Del Monte's product branding to include historical references to the United Fruit Company using the slogan "Pure Murder." First featured in *Del Montte: Bananeras* (2003), the double *t* in Cuevas's reimagined logo refers to Guatemala's violent dictator in the 1980s, José Efraín Ríos Montt, and serves as commentary on the corporation's collusion with militarized histories of genocide and displacement, the degradation of Central America's natural resources, and the erasure of endemic farming traditions. In *Égalité* (2004), Cuevas alters the logo of the French bottled water brand Evian to read "Égalité: Une Condition Naturelle" (Equality: A Natural Condition). The phrase, a reference to France's revolutionary motto *Liberté, égalité, fraternit*é, invokes the European Enlightenment and its ushering in of modernity through violent oppression. The utopian messaging of equality coupled with the familiar ethereal landscape of Evian's logo points to the entwining of political enterprises with the damage caused by extractive global industries.

For *Witch Hunt,* Cuevas has reconfigured her installation *Feast and Famine* (2015). Described by the artist as a singular "essay," it employs the rhetorical conventions of ethnographic and natural history museums alongside the allure of contemporary imagery to explore the colonial legacies of international trade. The work takes up the history of cacao in Mexico, probing the tension between its religious, political, and social roles and its transformation into an international cash crop. Vitrines display fictional archeological objects, while found advertisements for Pleasure Island Chocolates, Hershey's, and Toblerone conceal messages of violence, conquest, and consumption. Signs created by silk-screening liquid chocolate display slogans derived from Carlos Jáuregui's 2008 book *Canibalia.* Each one refers to the figure of the "savage Indian," pointing to practices of othering, exoticizing, and demonizing indigenous peoples in the Americas to justify violent conquest—the heart of colonialism's "civilizing" enterprise. *Famine 3.6* (2015), a small machine attached to the ceiling, drips chocolate every six seconds, a reference to the global rate of deaths from starvation. A material representation of this alarming statistic, the work creates an ephemeral memorial that grows over the course of the exhibition. The metal and wood tables deployed recall the sterile environment of a scientific laboratory or industrial kitchen, a visual reference Cuevas invokes to explore how individuals are trapped within capitalist cultural regimes. *Feast and Famine* points to disturbing correlations between abuses of the body inherent to a colonial project intent on dispossession and estrangement and the exploitative labor practices of large-scale industrial cacao production. Yet Cuevas's work always holds the latent possibility of revolt and revolution.

—Nika Chilewich

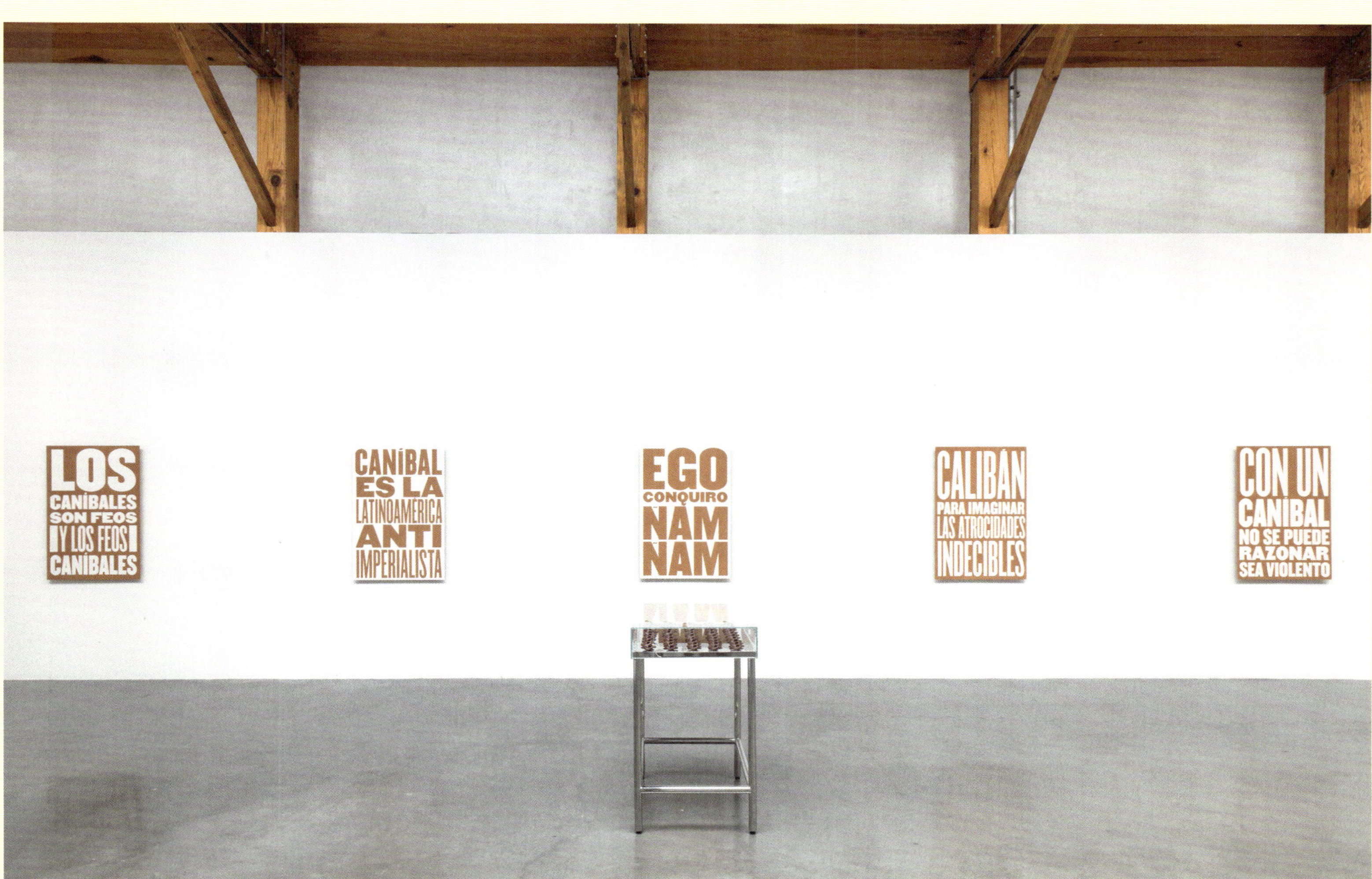

De la serie Caníbal, 2015

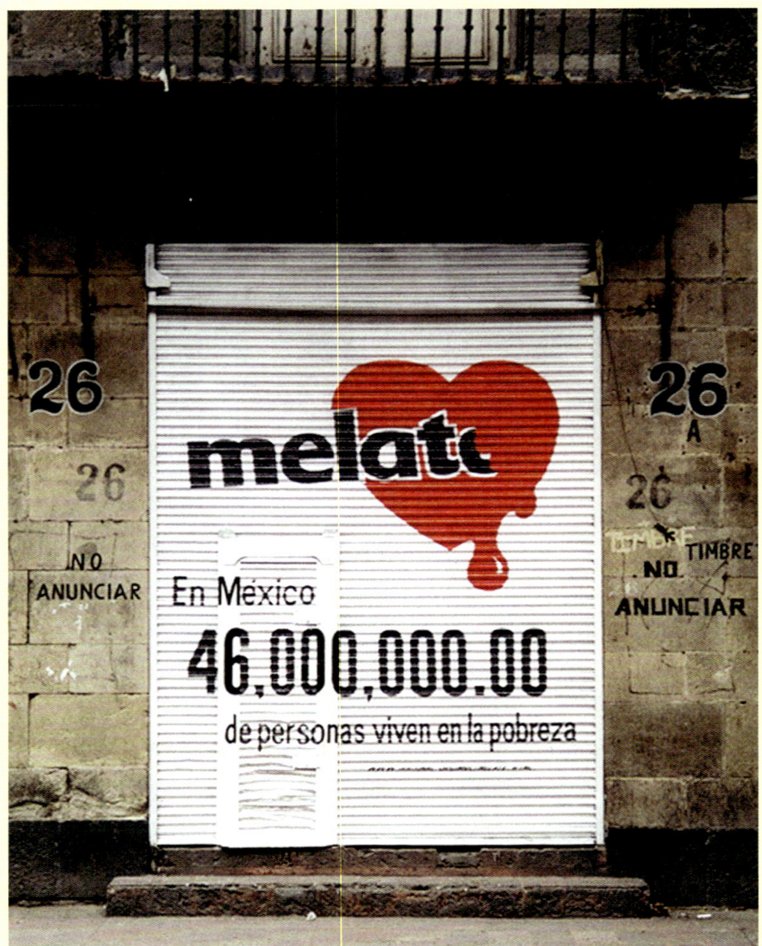

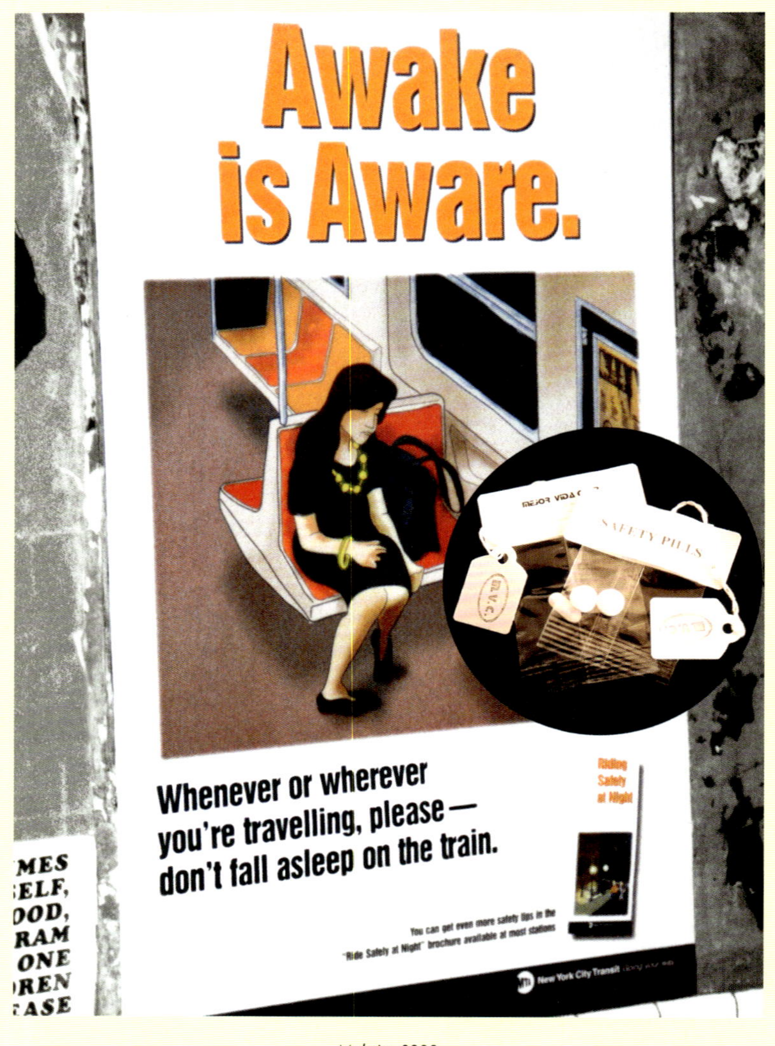

Melate, 2000
Awake Is Aware, 2000

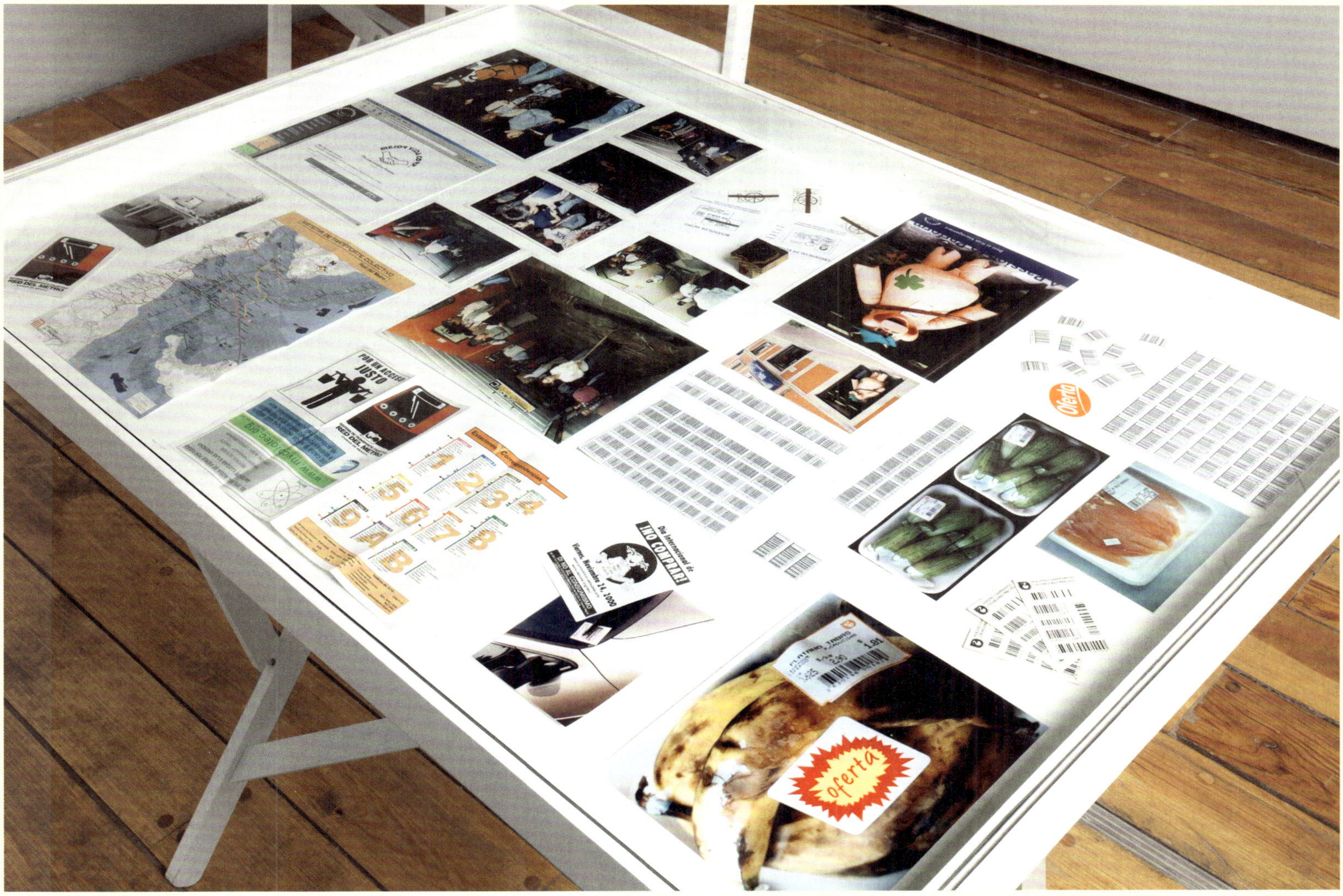

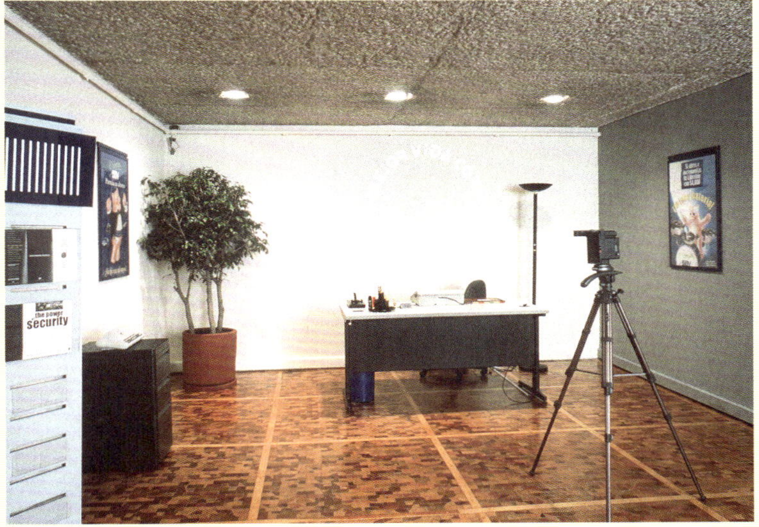

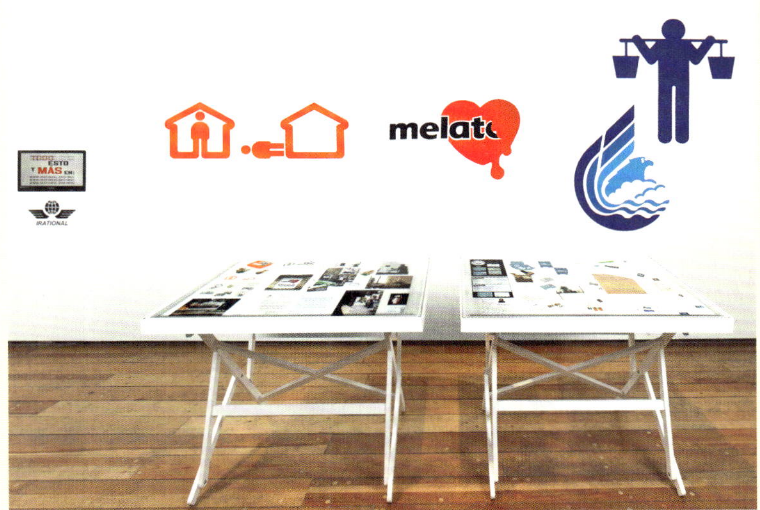

Mejor Vida Corp., 1998–

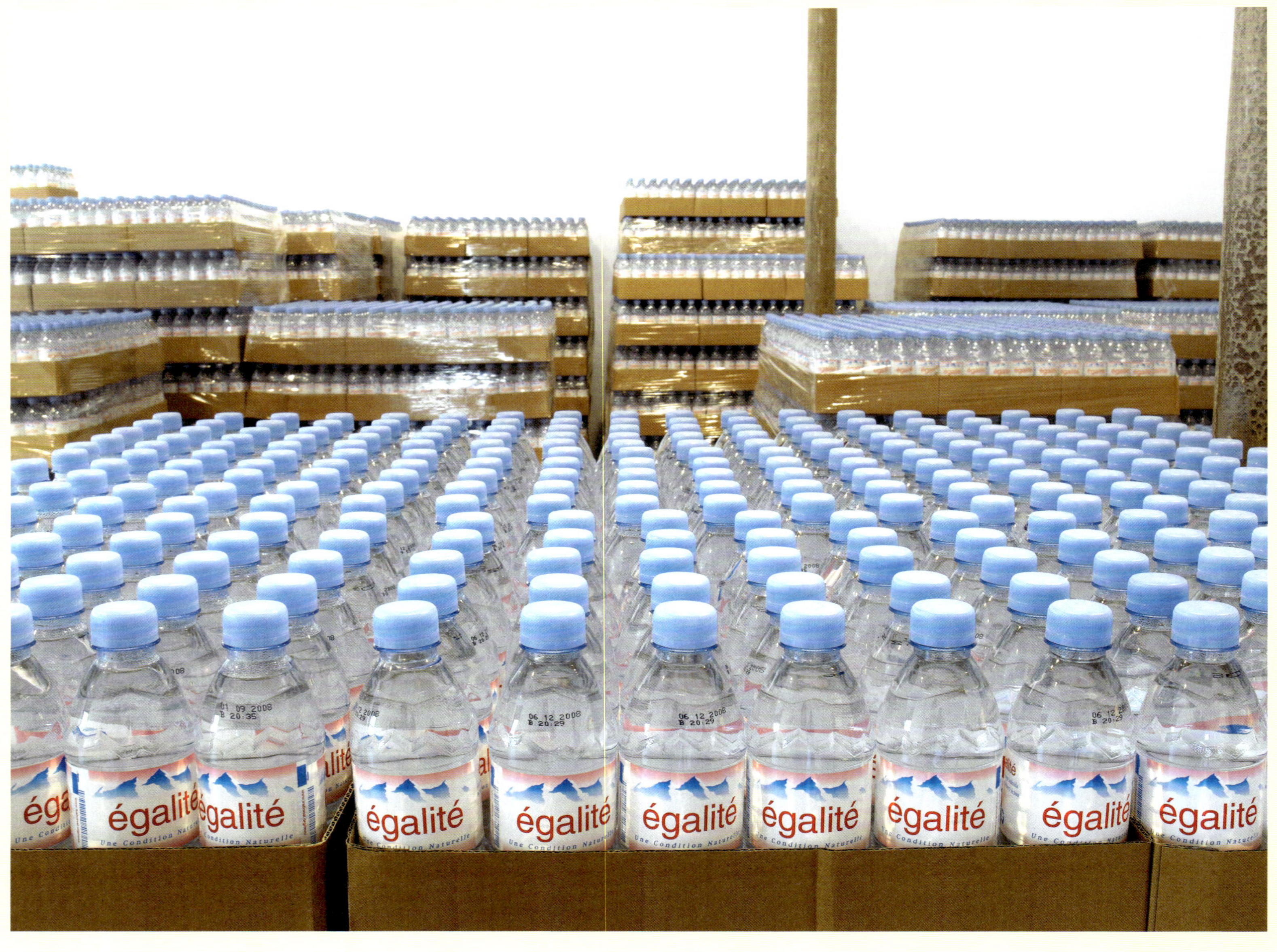

Égalité, 2004

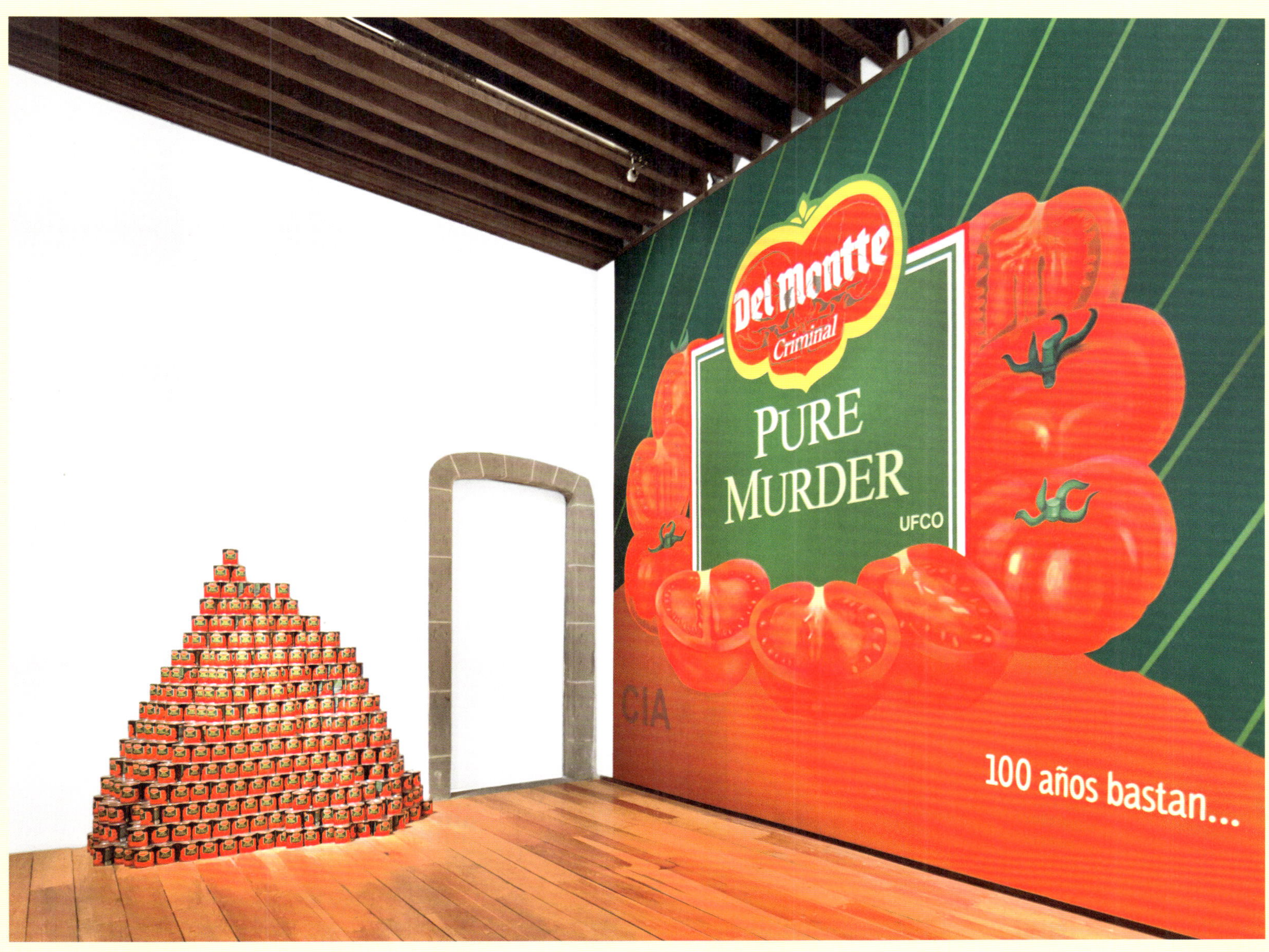

Del Montte: Bananeras, 2003

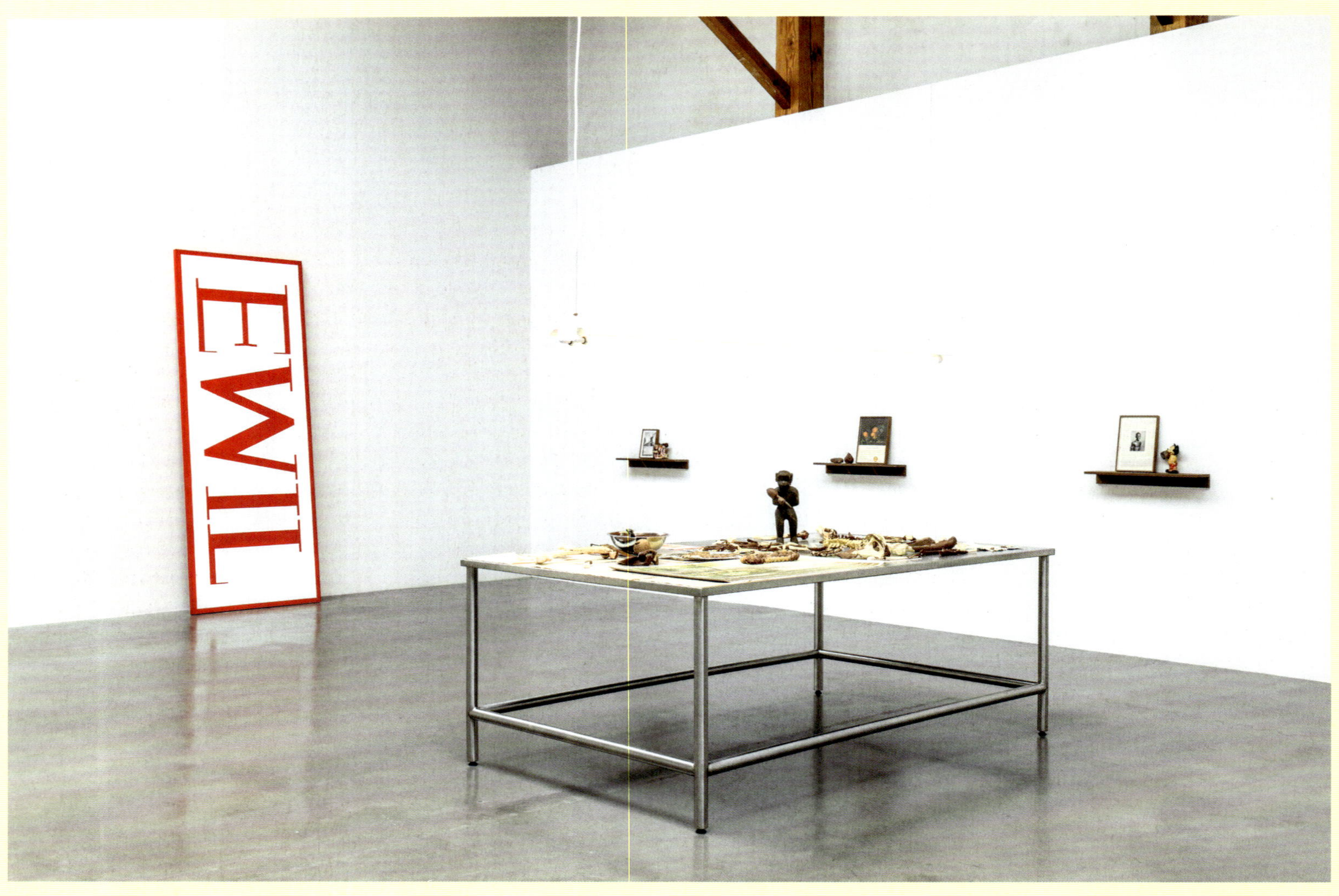

Feast and Famine, 2015

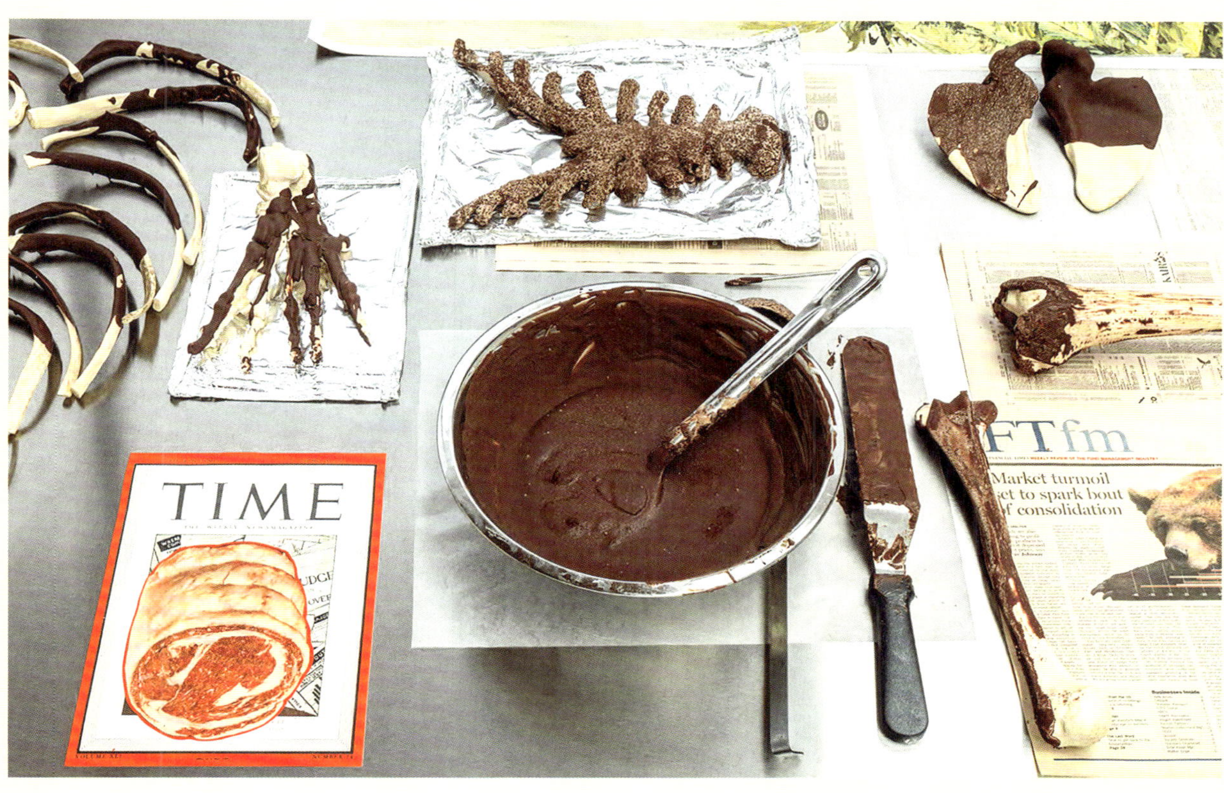

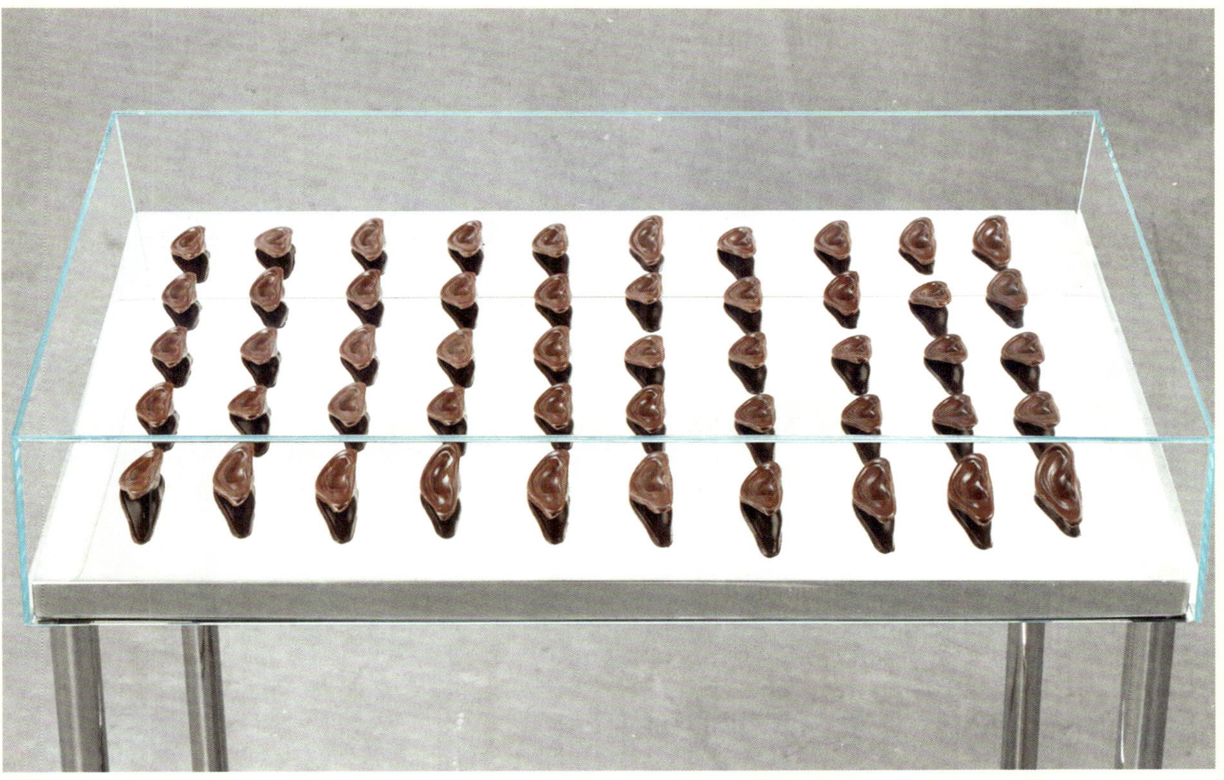

Feast, 2015
Like a Tzompantli, 2015

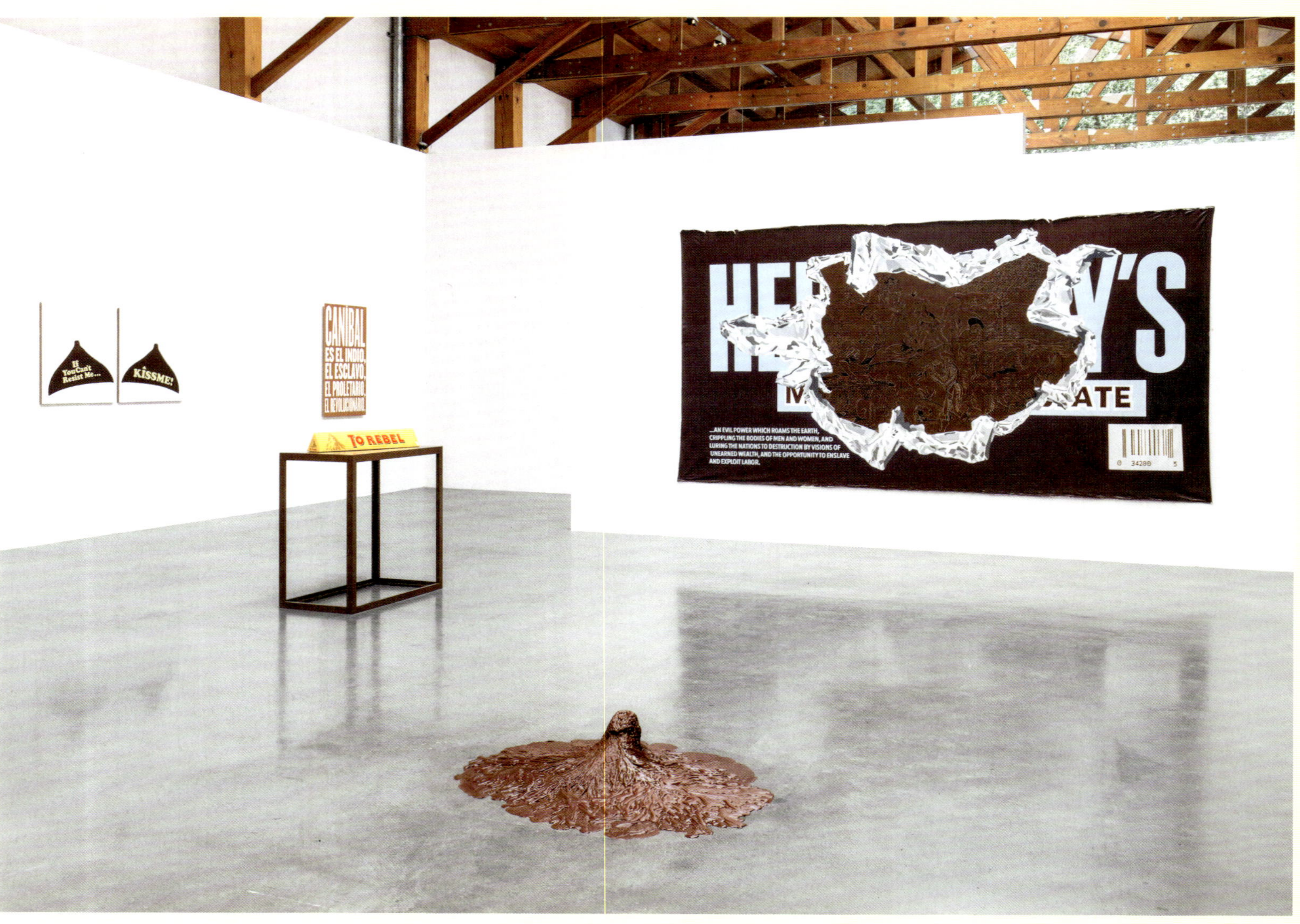

Feast and Famine, 2015

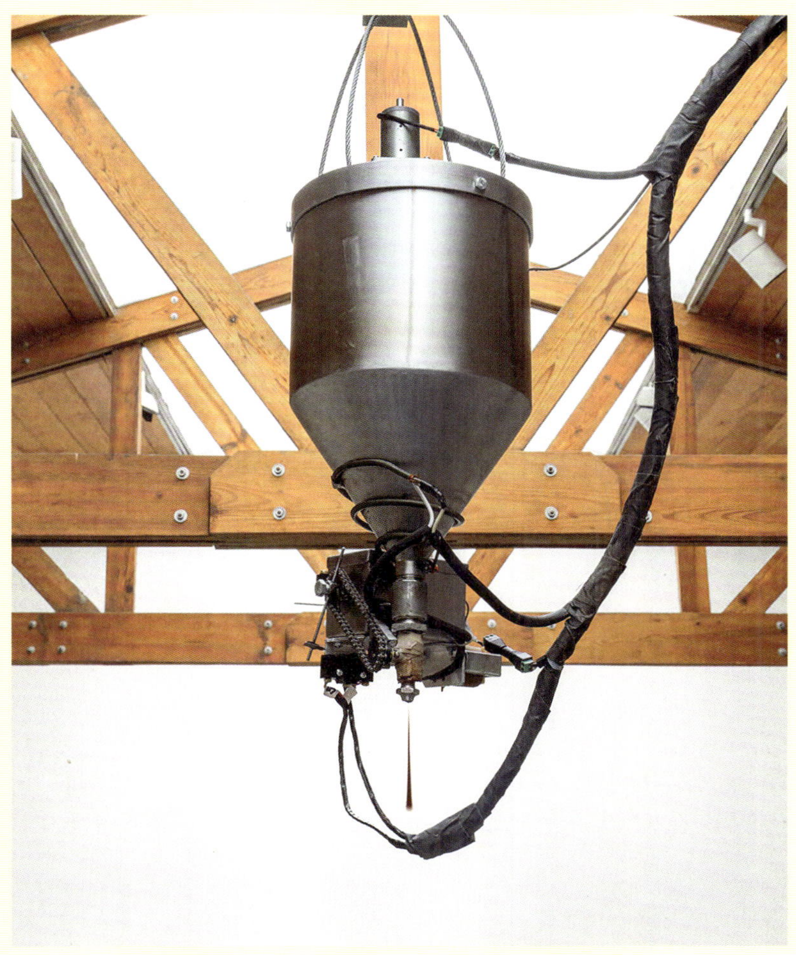

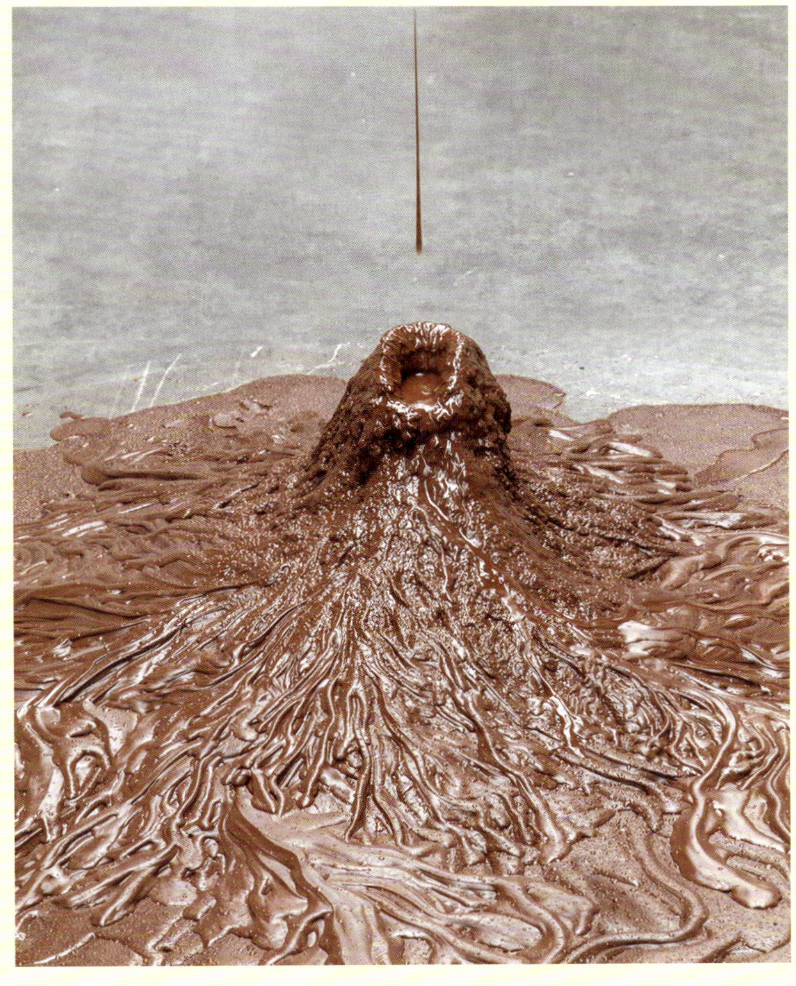

Famine 3.6, 2015

Vaginal Davis

b. United States. Lives and works in Berlin, Germany.

Vaginal Davis is an artist and cultural figure whose work, rooted in performance, adopts notions of freakiness to dismantle cultural norms around gender, sexuality, and race. A key figure in the Los Angeles homocore punk movements of the 1980s and '90s, Davis employs an anticorporate aesthetic and ethos of irreverence to examine some of society's most taboo subjects.

In the 1970s and '80s, Davis established a varied practice that was centered on embodying a range of incendiary and refreshingly bizarre personas. Averse to the elitism of mainstream gay culture, which at the time lacked feminist and queer voices, she performed within the punk community. She began her artistic career as a founding member of the collective the Afro Sisters (1978), and when the group began performing music in the 1980s, the 6'6" artist starred as its towering frontwoman, publicly taking on the name Vaginal Davis. Other bands cofounded by Davis include the feminist Chicanx group ¡Cholita!, the Female Menudo, a sassy pop band (1987); Pedro, Muriel, and Esther, or PME (1989); and black fag (1992). In each of these groups, Davis incorporated aspects of her personal history, and of her African American, Choctaw, Mexican, and intersex identities. The punk scene allowed Davis to use an anti-entertainment perspective as a critical tool. Throughout her work, the artist would pursue a type of drag outside the homage to traditional representations of femininity performed in drag bars and bring a queer agenda to the often-misogynist punk scene.

For Davis, drag functions as a conceptual framework founded on a diverse set of evolving principles like obscenity, hyperbole, community, and chaos. Her approach—dubbed "aesthetic terrorism" by scholar José Esteban Muñoz in his essay "'The White to Be Angry': Vaginal Davis's Terrorist Drag"—critiques cultural norms by personifying racial, sexual, and gendered obsessions and phobias, and involves a total merging between the artist's lived identity and her characters. Davis's personas—the most well known of whom is Vaginal Davis herself—make recurring appearances throughout her oeuvre, which includes records, zines, writing, performance, and short films, which she began writing and directing in the 1980s. In one of the artist's first films, *That Fertile Feeling* (1982), she takes up the issue of queer parenting, as her friend Fertile La Toyah Jackson becomes the first woman to give birth to eleven-tuplets. In *The White to Be Angry* (1999), Davis explores an eroticism of racial terror through the character of a neo-Nazi, whom we first see watching television while his mother spouts white-supremacist rhetoric. Later, while walking his dog, he encounters a lean, muscular, queer Black man in mini shorts. They cruise one another, creating a scandalous moment of mutual objectification and desire for the very thing that most threatens each character's racial, sexual, and gendered identities.

Davis perpetuates the communitarian bent of both queer and punk cultures in her dedication to radical pedagogy. Since 2010, she has taught iterations of a performance workshop called "Framing the Freakazoid: Perverse Assemblages," and in 2015, she collaborated with artists and students at New York University to stage a reworking of Mozart's *The Magic Flute*. In 2012, the artist had her first solo show of paintings and sculptures, which she has been making since the 1980s—small devotional portraits and busts made from makeup and other beauty products she has lying around her house. Delicately layering color and texture, the raw, gestural works provide an intimate counterpart to Davis's incendiary performances.

For *Witch Hunt*, Davis has taken up the subject of her mother, a Black Creole lesbian who moved to Los Angeles from Louisiana as part of the Great Migration of Blacks from the Southern states. A feminist ahead of her time, she also possessed supernatural powers, according to the artist, and became increasingly radicalized as part of her involvement in a female separatist society. For the exhibition, Davis has created a sound installation and a series of paintings and objects that weave together childhood memories and impressions of her mother—sewing dresses for Vaginal and surrounding her with lesbian uncles, "old school proper butches," with archival research that Davis has conducted.

—Nika Chilewich

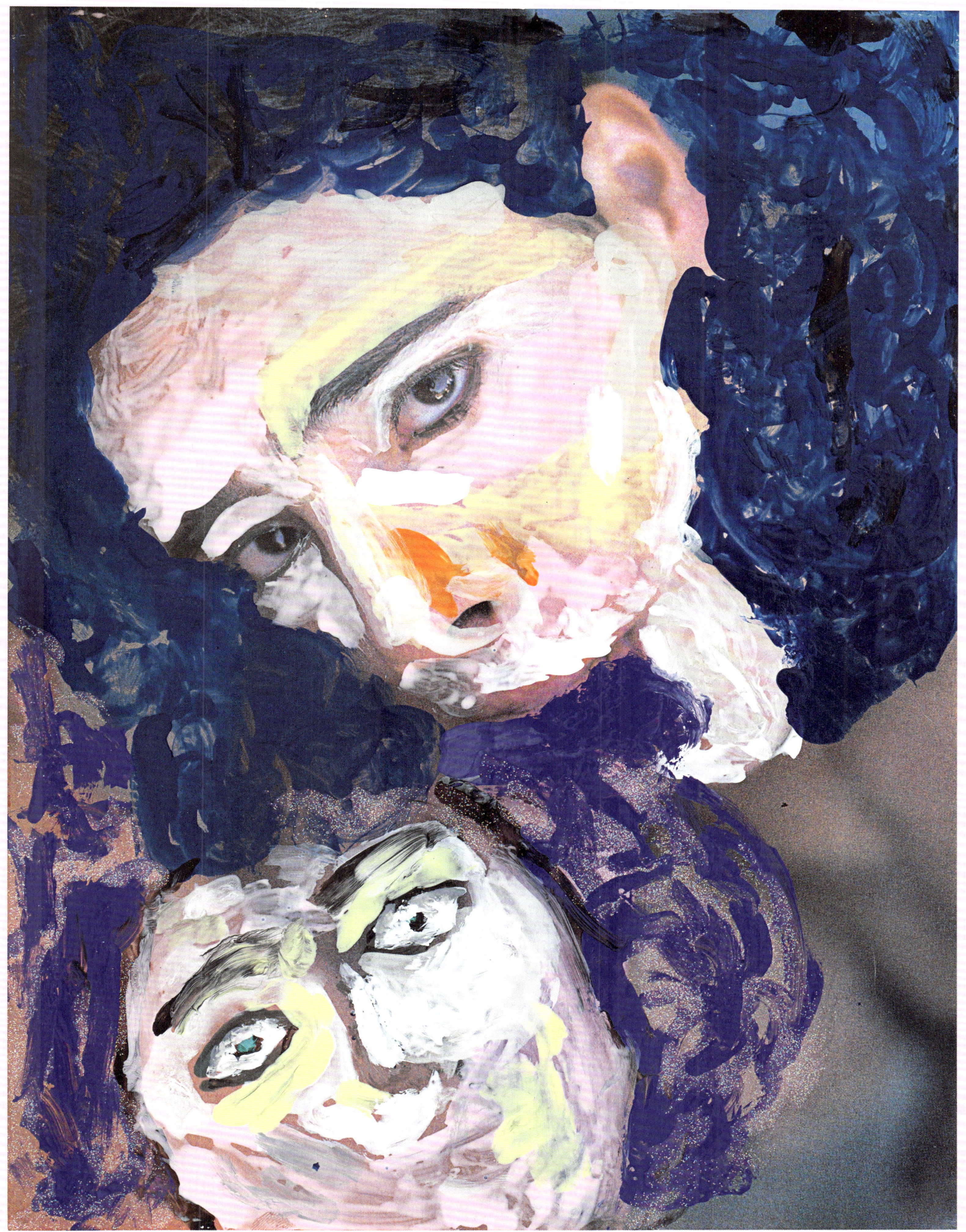

Book of Salma and Suvad, 2017

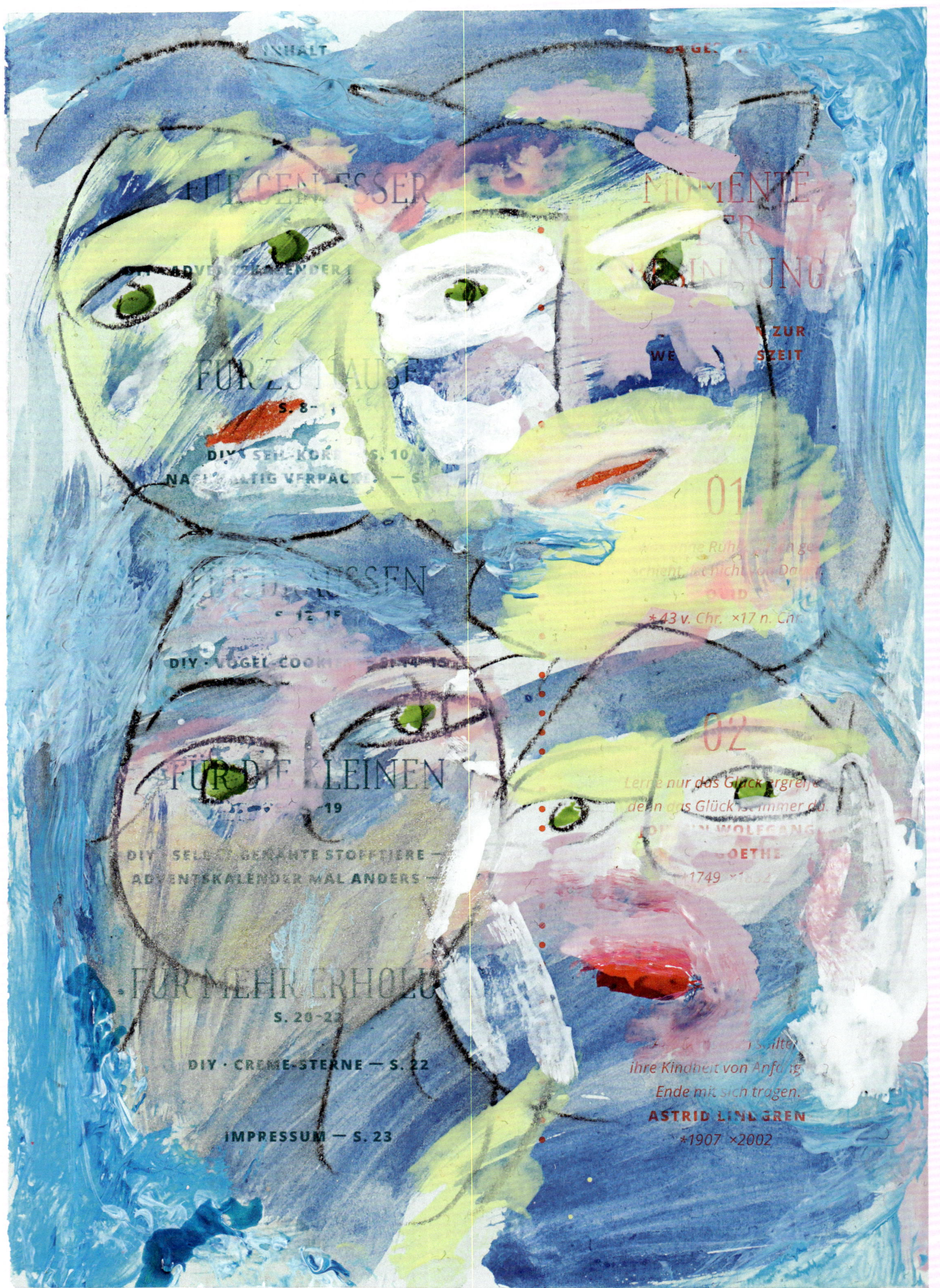

Book of Sawab and Suvur, 2018

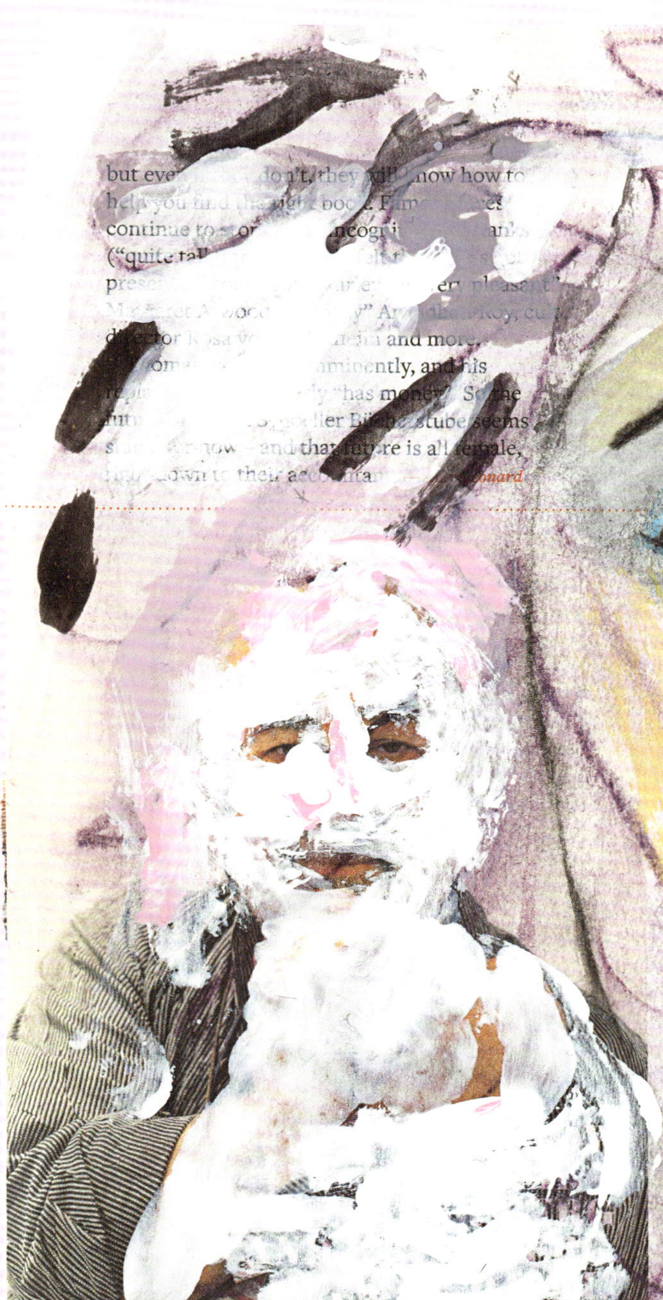

Heart and Sparks, 2018

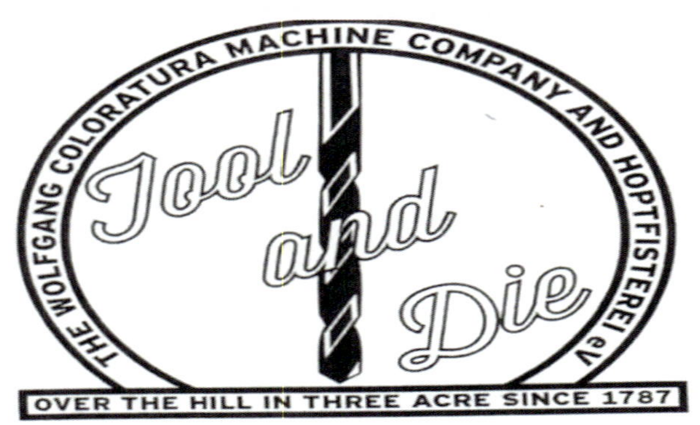

the entire capitalist system is
based in coercion; a form of
Slavery

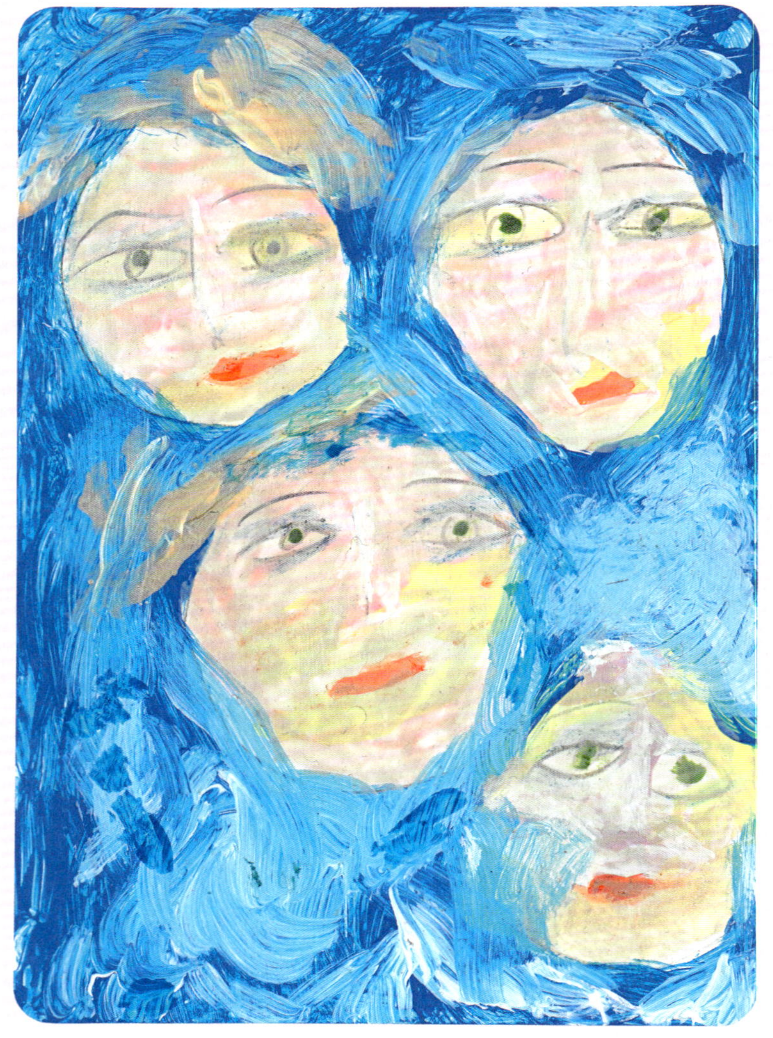

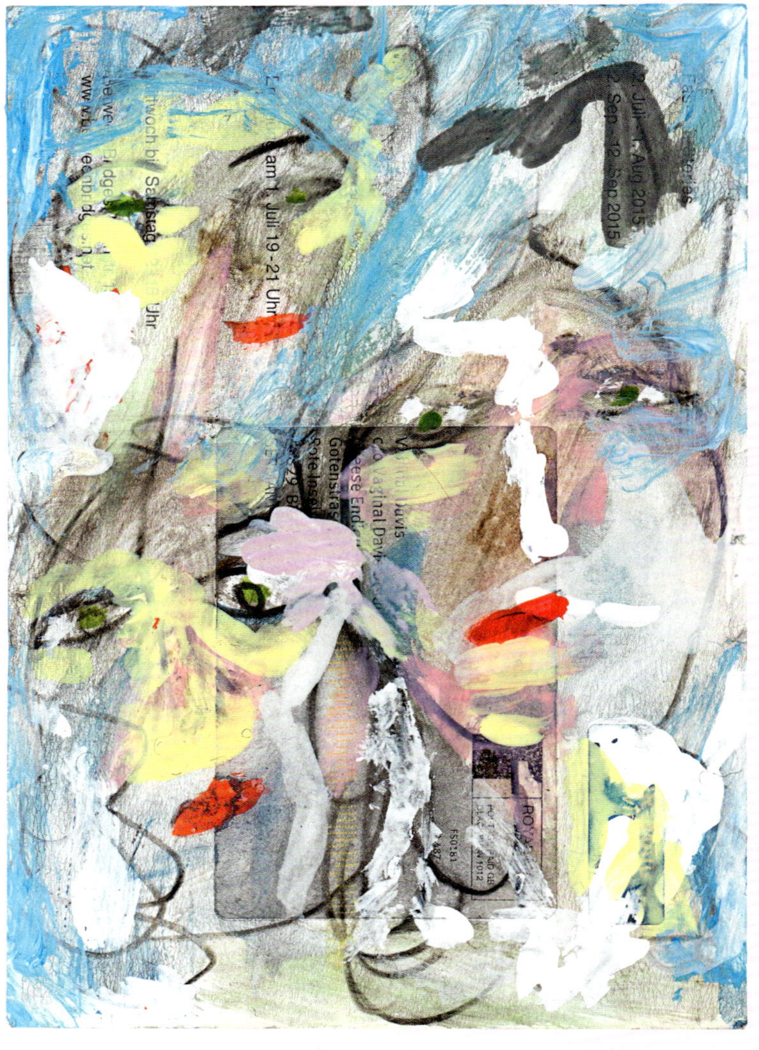

trailer for *Mary Mary*, 2020
Le Spectre Vert, 2018; *This for Zahed*, 2018

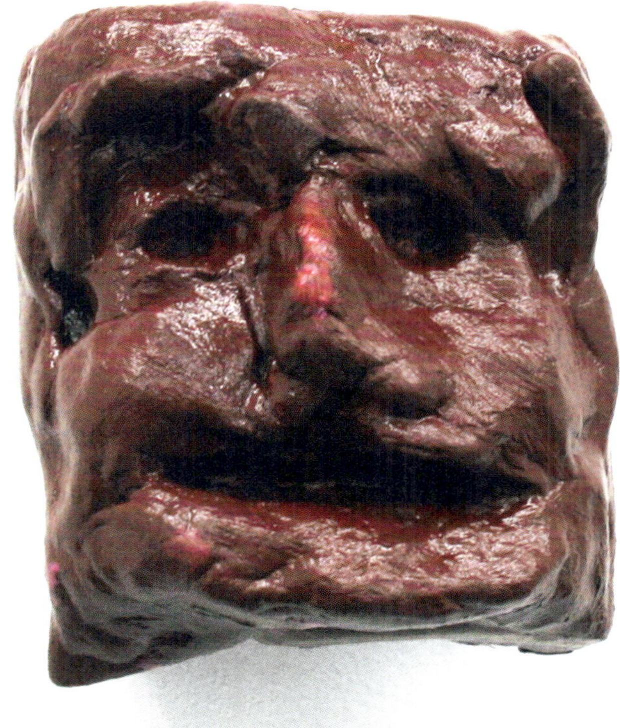

Proper Butch Goddess Freya, 2015

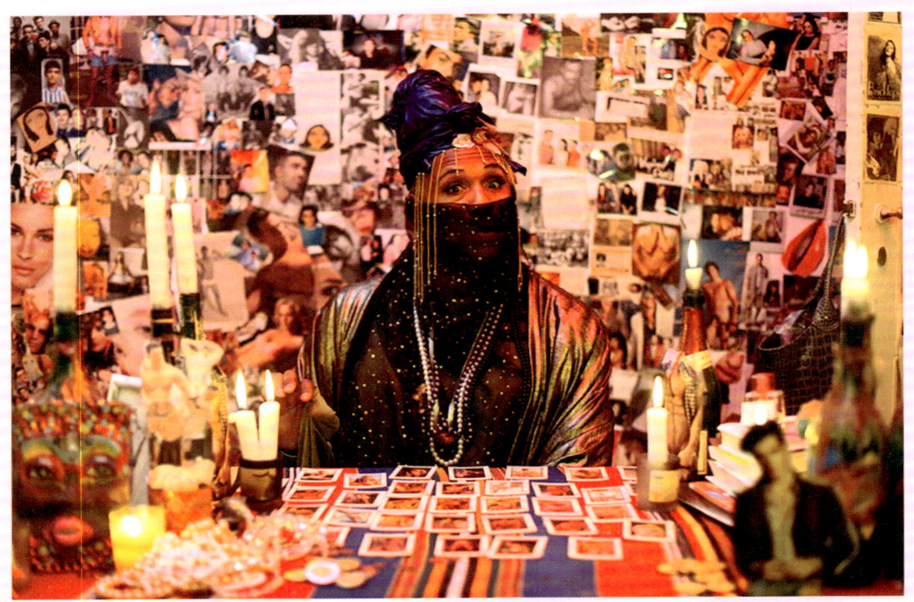

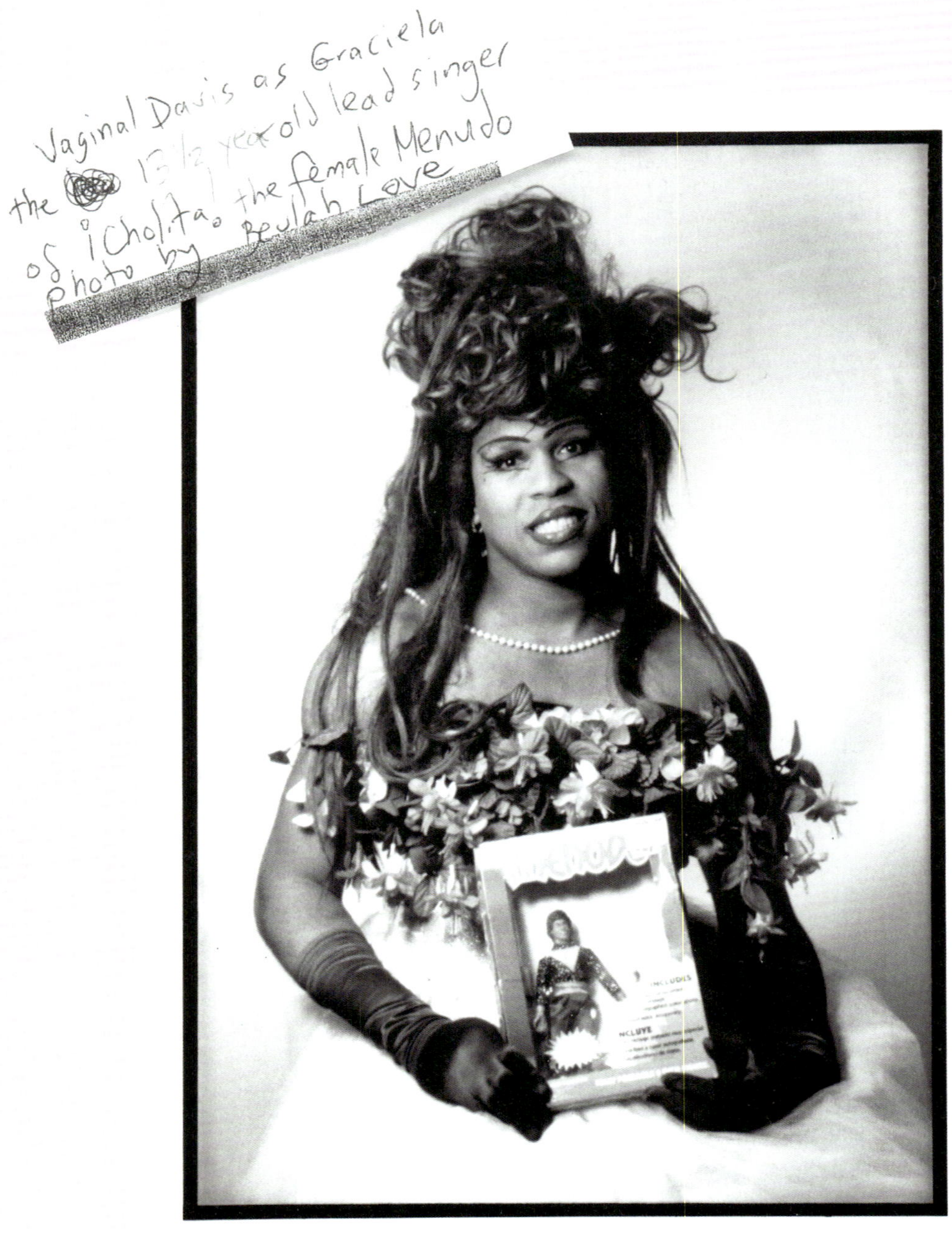

Vaginal Davis in Zackary Drucker and Rhys Ernst, *She Gone Rogue*, 2012
Vaginal Davis in a promotional still for ¡Cholita!, the Female Menudo, 1990

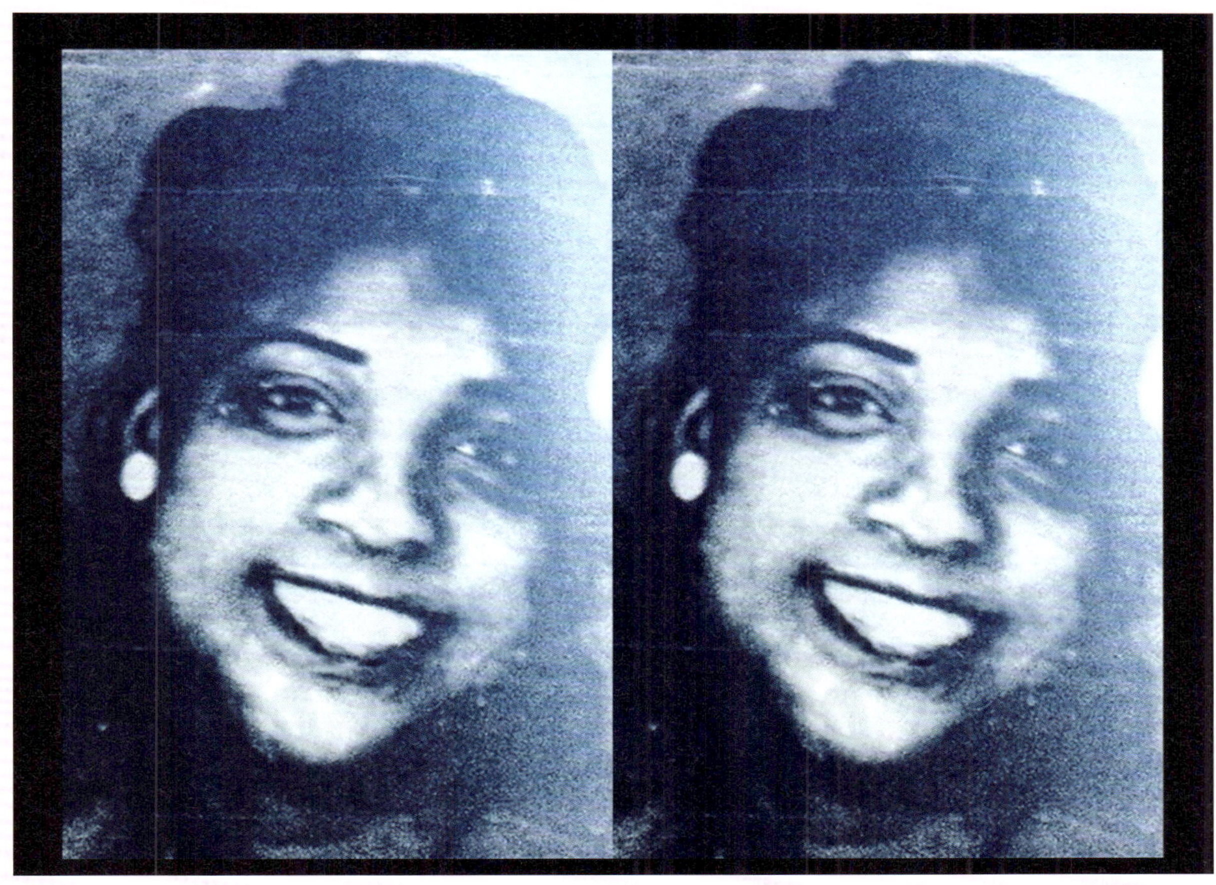

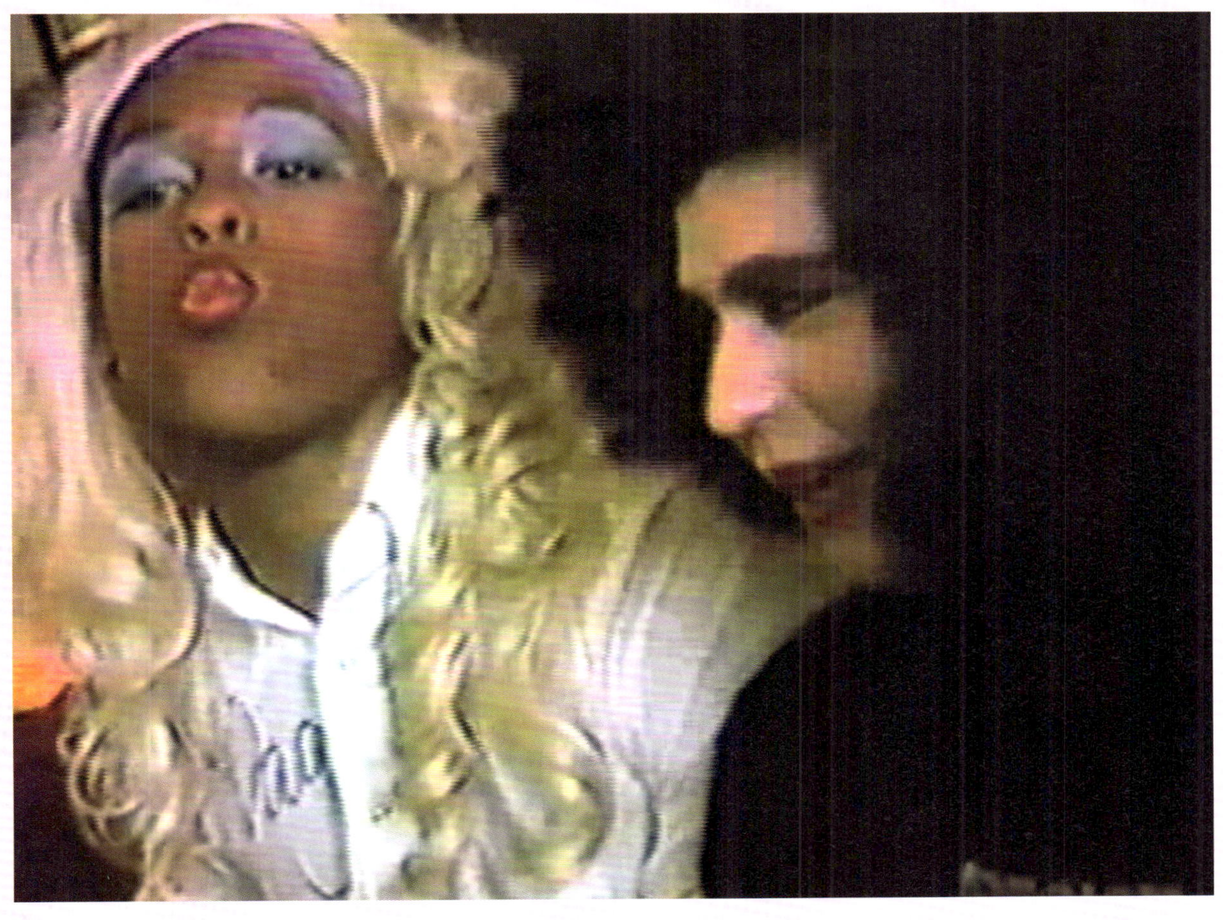

trailer for *Mary Mary*, 2020
That Fertile Feeling, 1982

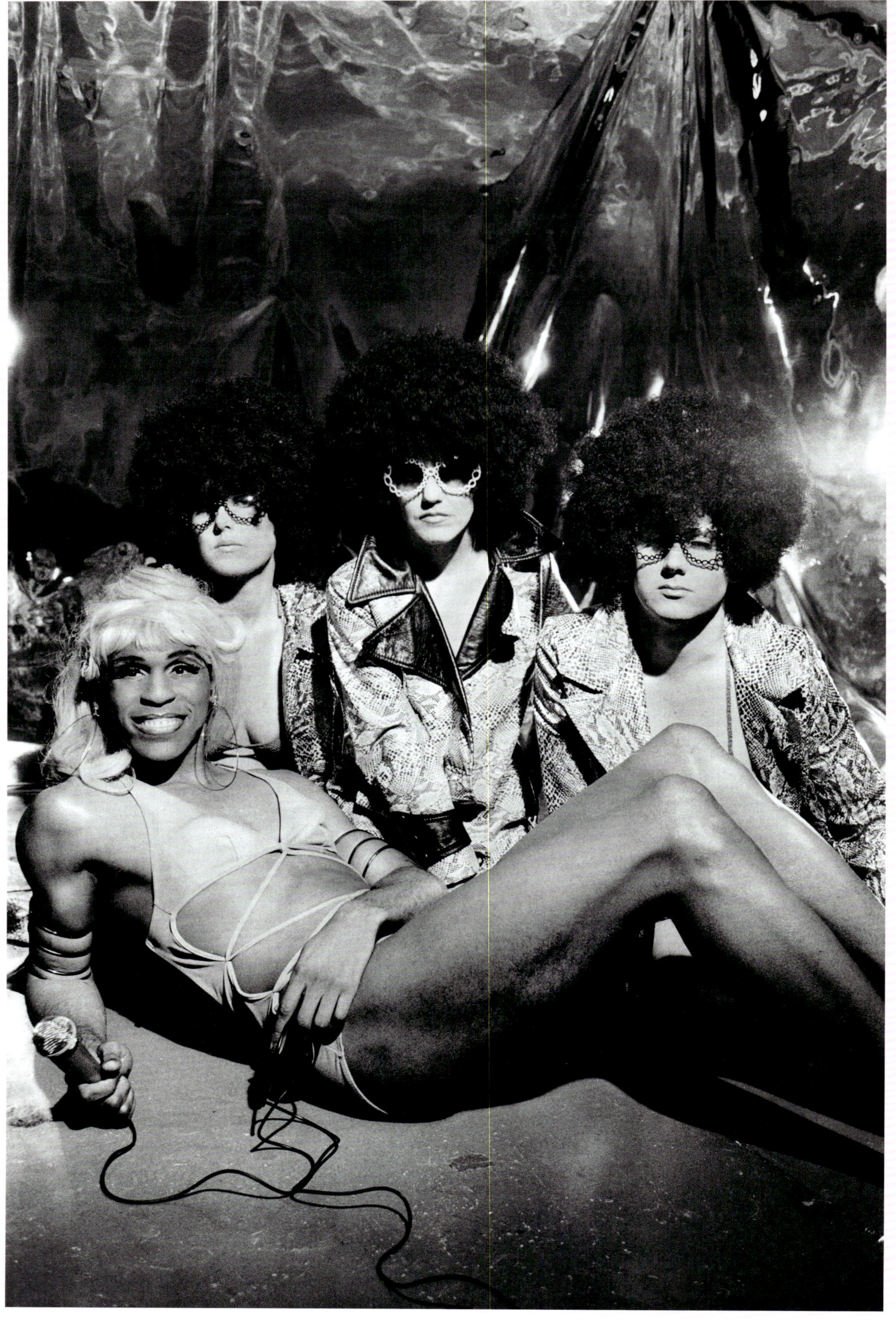

Vaginal Davis and the Afro Sisters in *Interview* magazine, 1986

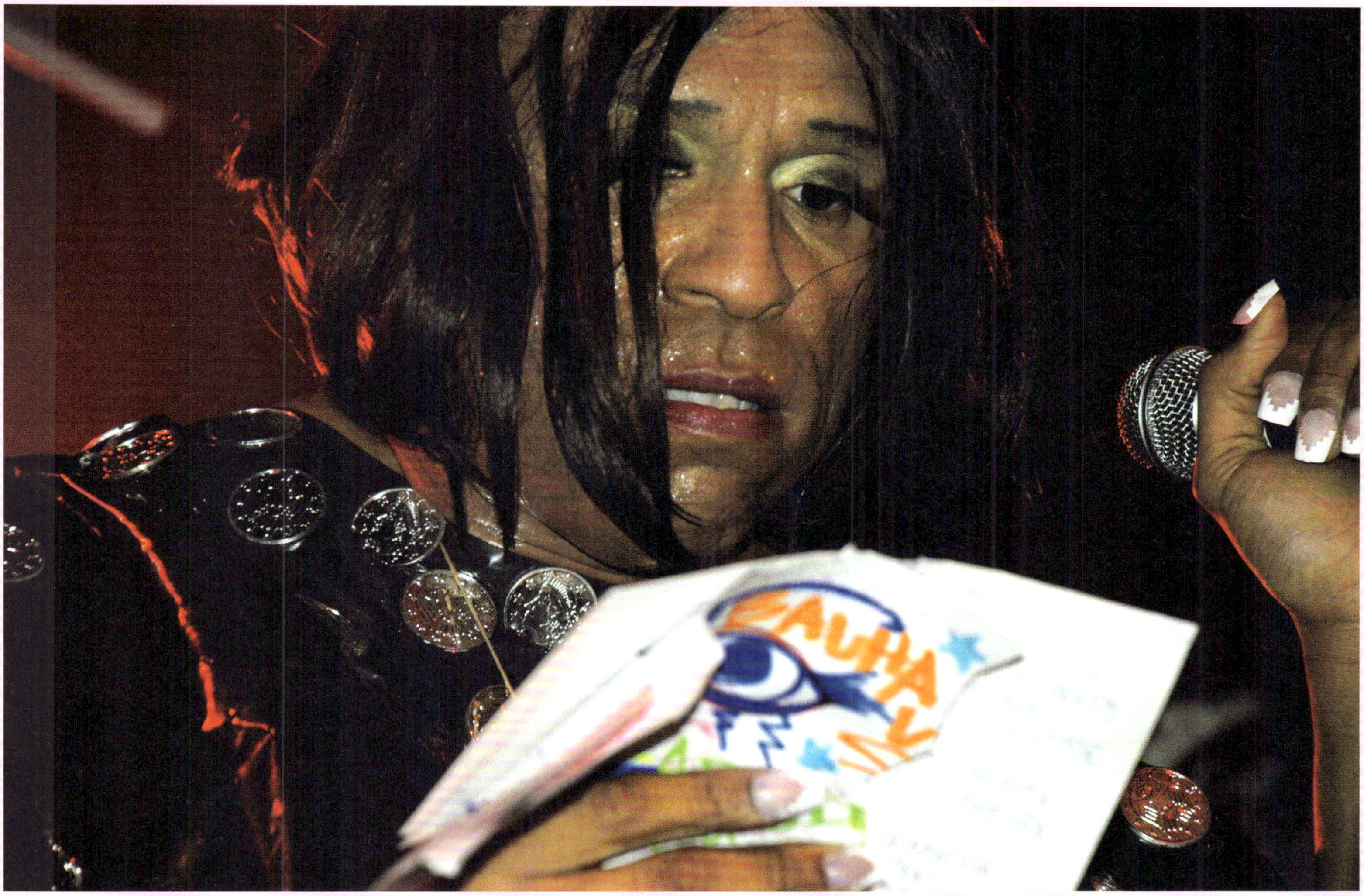

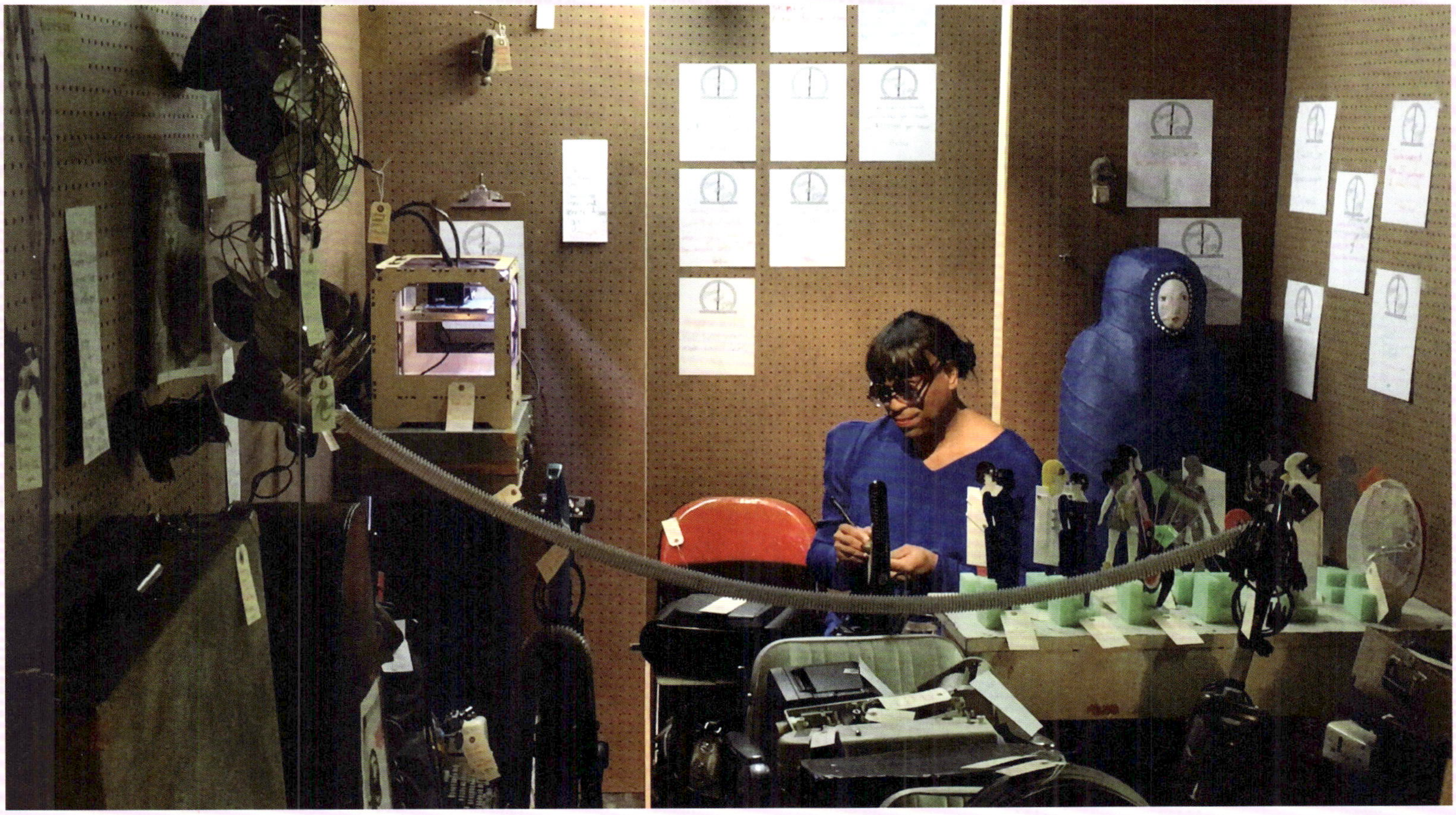

Vaginal Davis in Pedro, Muriel, and Esther (PME)'s *Advanced Capitalism Reunion: Reparations and Retardations*, 2009
Vaginal Davis as Heike in *Overture Machine Shop*, 2015

Every Ocean Hughes

b. 1977, United States. Lives and works in Stockholm, Sweden.

Every Ocean Hughes is a transdisciplinary artist whose work focuses on forms of social space as they relate to queer histories and identities. Throughout her practice, writing functions as a through line, a means for circulating ideas and developing new vocabularies. In projects that move between photography, printmaking, installation, and curating, EOH approaches art as a method for questioning how identity is both collectively and individually shaped.

EOH's early career was marked by her involvement in the collaborative queer journal *LTTR* (2002–06) and the associated collective, which the artist, then known as Emily Roysdon, founded with artists K8 Hardy and Ginger Brooks Takahashi. EOH declared her intentions for the project in its first issue: "to perform our symptoms for each other and create the space to question our development as artists, workers, and thinkers." A nod to feminist art publications of the past and the work that emerged from the AIDS activism of the 1980s and '90s, the annual brought together feminist and queer artists of all genders to share their processes and explore possibilities for a collective language. *LTTR* set a precedent for the type of iterative, conversational voice that EOH would develop, gentle yet persistent, a ceaseless closing in on something that had before seemed unnamable.

The artist's early writing helped establish a particular discursive method for articulating a queer experience that is immensely candid, deeply humorous, and graceful. Throughout EOH's work, the body functions as both site and script, performance as both form and metaphor. For the installation *Comedy of Margin Theatre* (2015), the artist built a kind of stage set for an indefinite, unmarked character, a colorful and disorienting mise-en-scène including props and a costume. In *Scenic, Say* (2017), photographic murals of staged performances and cinematic landscapes hung on the walls, while excerpts of the artist's writings stood on lecternlike pedestals to be read (or performed) by the viewer.

From 2012 to 2015, EOH worked on a twenty-three-part piece of writing titled *Uncounted*, which explores themes of time, movement, and transgression—what the artist has called the "politics of transitions," or all that happens beyond documented experience. The text yielded a series of performances in the United States and Europe (2014–17) engaging local artists and performers who were invited to reflect on one of the essay's fragments. In *Uncounted*, language functions as a social and political architecture, something concrete through which we define and are defined, which EOH turns on itself to undermine the official horizons of representation. In closing, she writes, "If we do—do revel in the uncounted, do wave, do transition, do trespass, do make due. If we do, then we live in the experience of uncounted futures. A commitment to the unseen in time. Beyond the will to measure."

For *Witch Hunt*, EOH will show the video *One Big Bag* (2021), the second piece in a recent series based on the artist's experiences with death and grief, which prompted an extensive period of research that coincided with the artist changing her name. The video contains themes of corpses, care, and mutual aid and focuses on a mobile corpse kit with everything one needs to tend to a death. The work deals with questions of materiality and loss, and is based on workshops, trainings, and interviews conducted by the artist. In it, EOH plays with sound to re-create an affective space that captures feelings of defamiliarization and estrangement, which occur when one is confronted with the loss that attends death. *Help the Dead* (2019) is a theatrical and musical experience in which two performers pose a series of thoughts and questions to the audience: "What is dead? What do we let die? Who do we let die? Who do we actively harm? What do we actively extinguish?" In the course of five acts, the duo sings songs written by the artist and shares technical information related to the practice of being a death doula in a form that, for EOH, represents a queering of death. "Being kind was queer," she writes. "Helping someone you love die is queer. Changing my name is a kind of queer death. I got out of my own way."

—Nika Chilewich

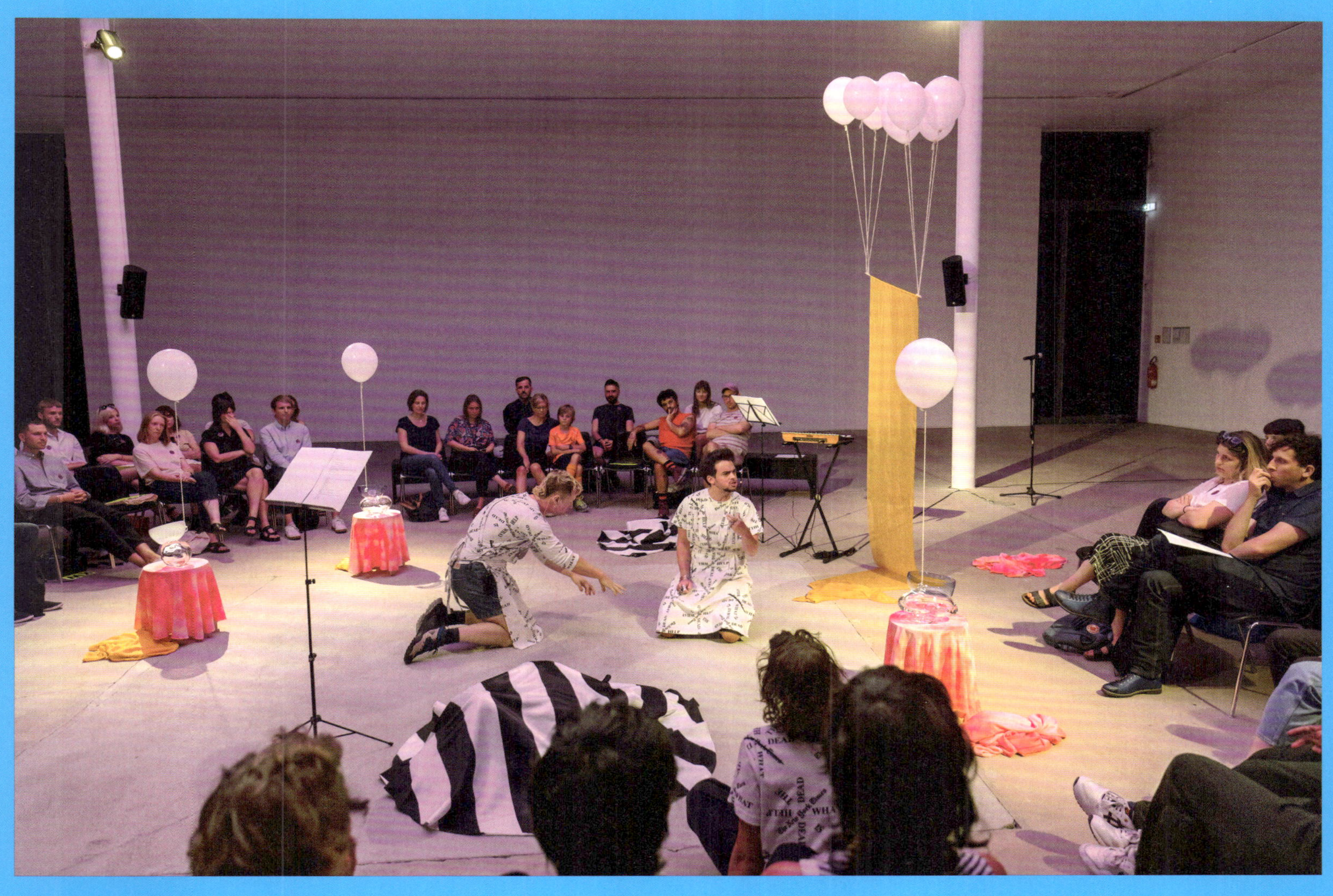

Help the Dead, 2019

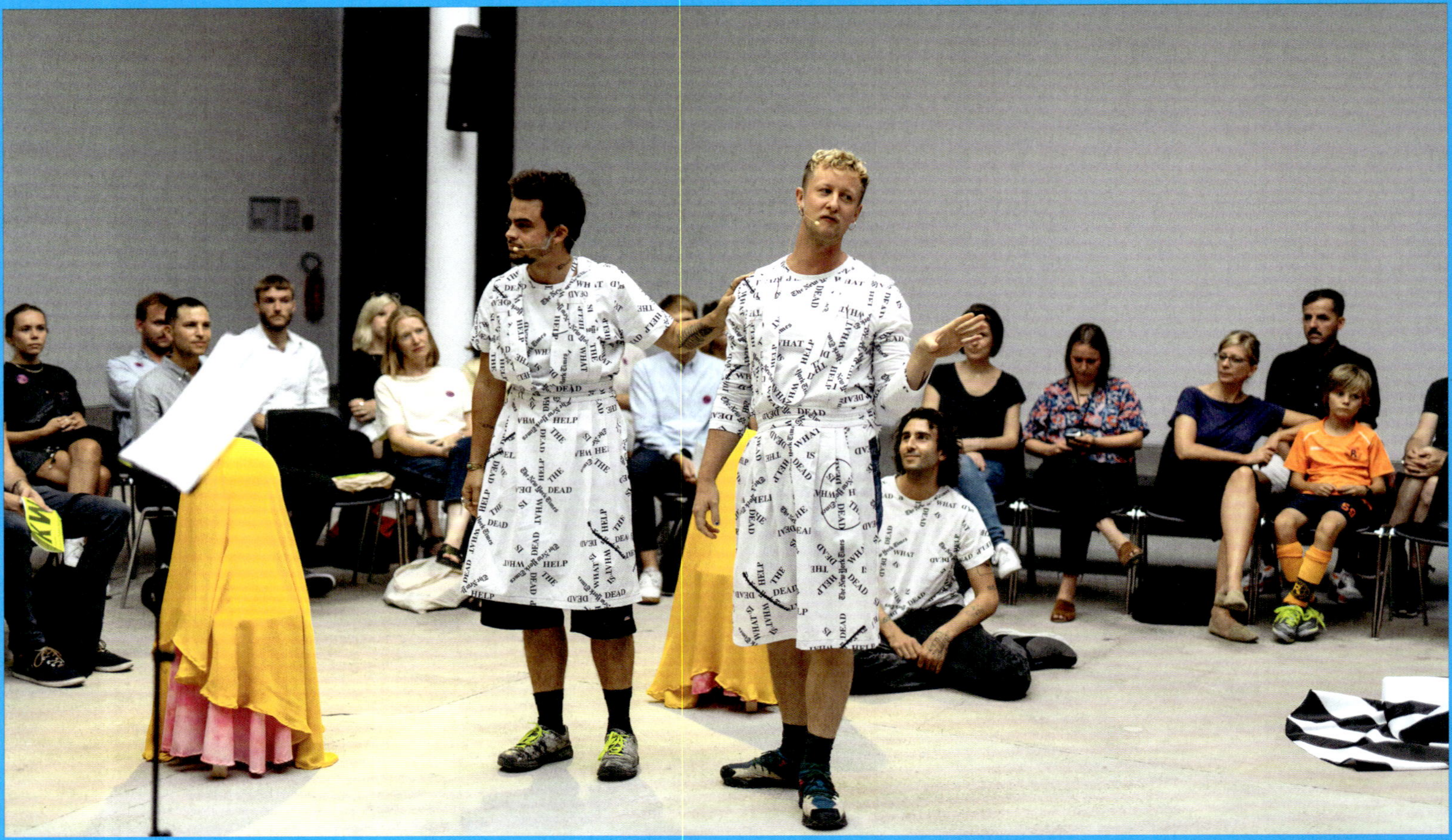

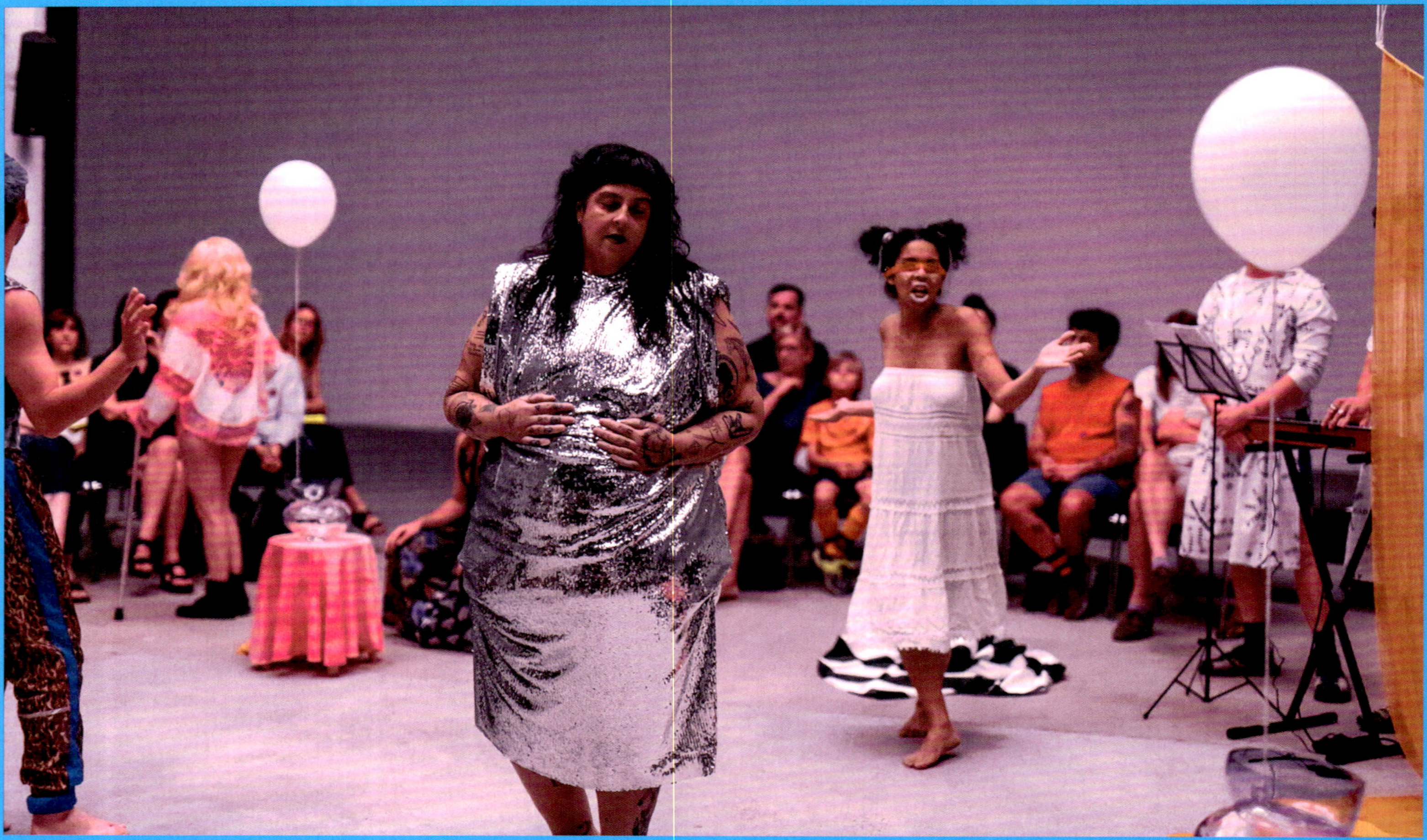

Help the Dead, 2019

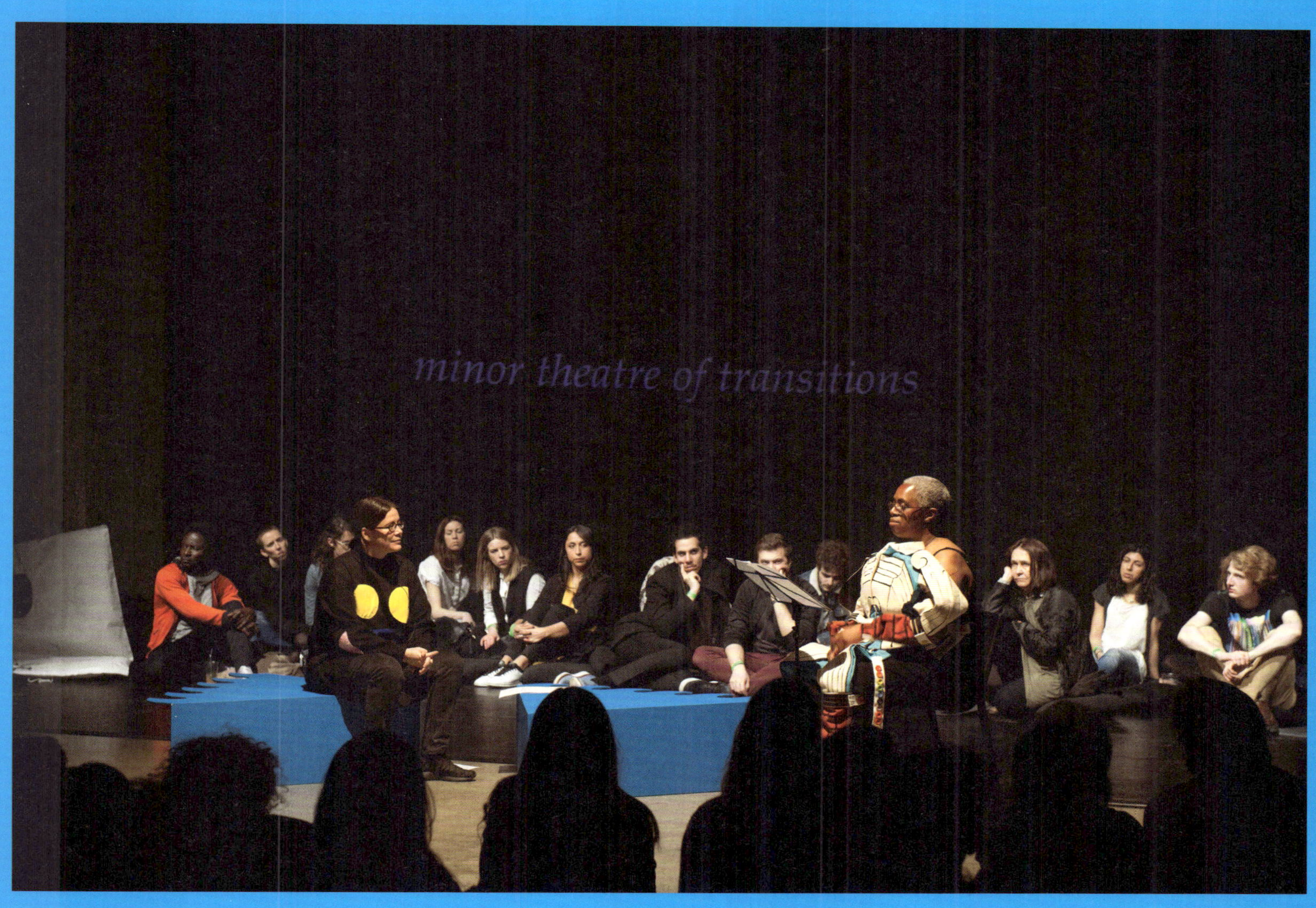

Uncounted (performance 9), 2017

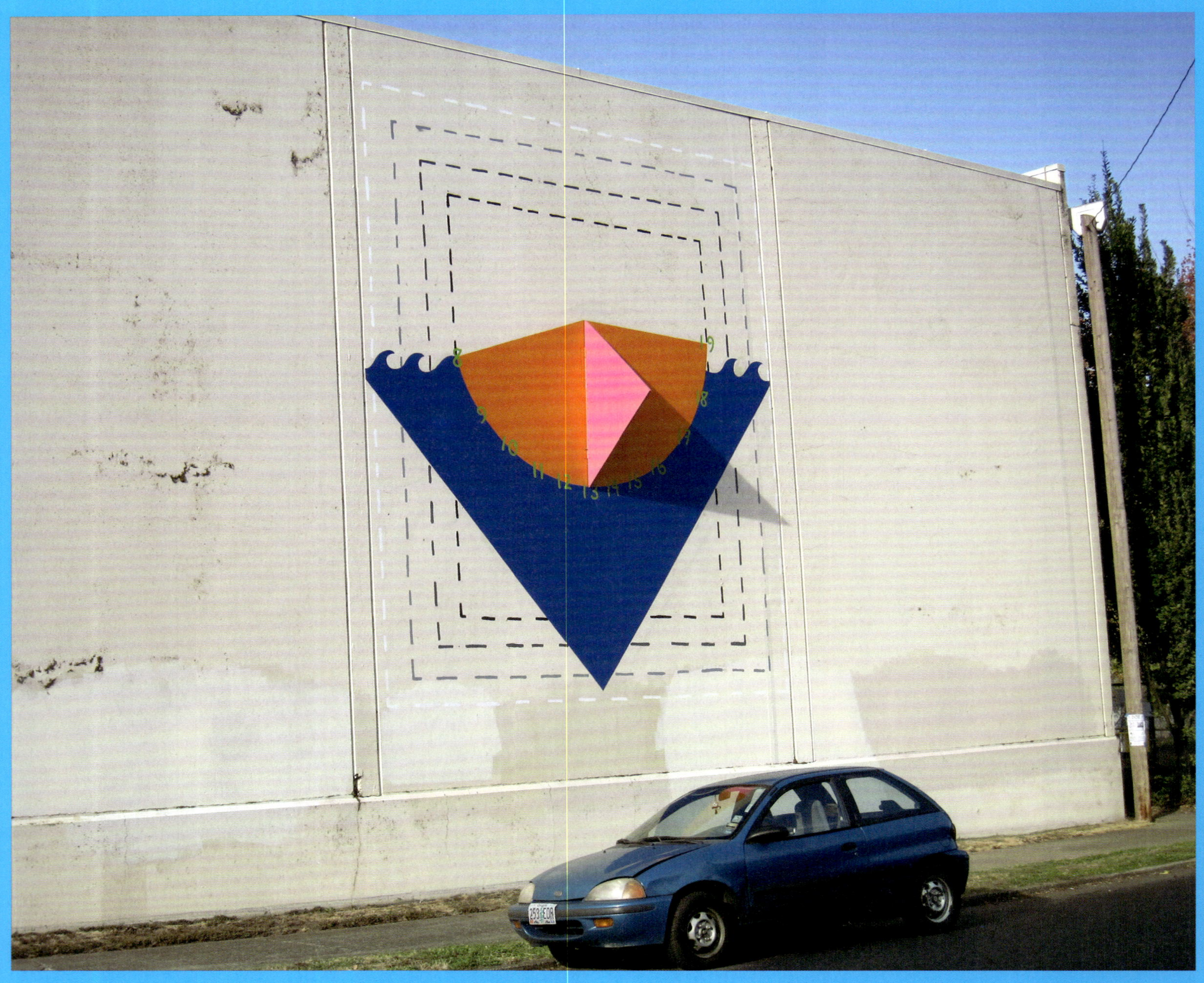

Reading the Shade of a Pink Triangle, 2013

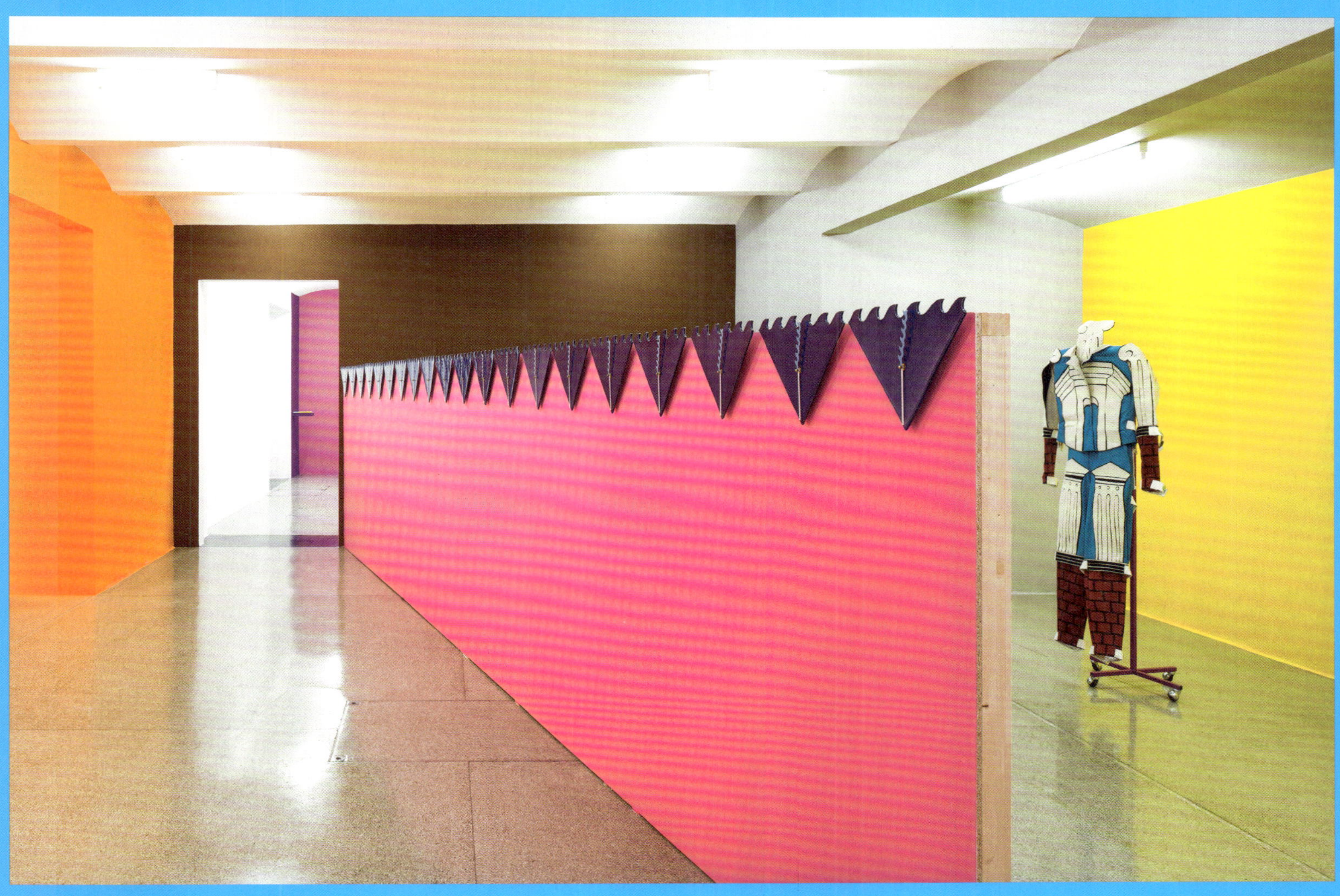

Comedy of Margin Theatre, 2015

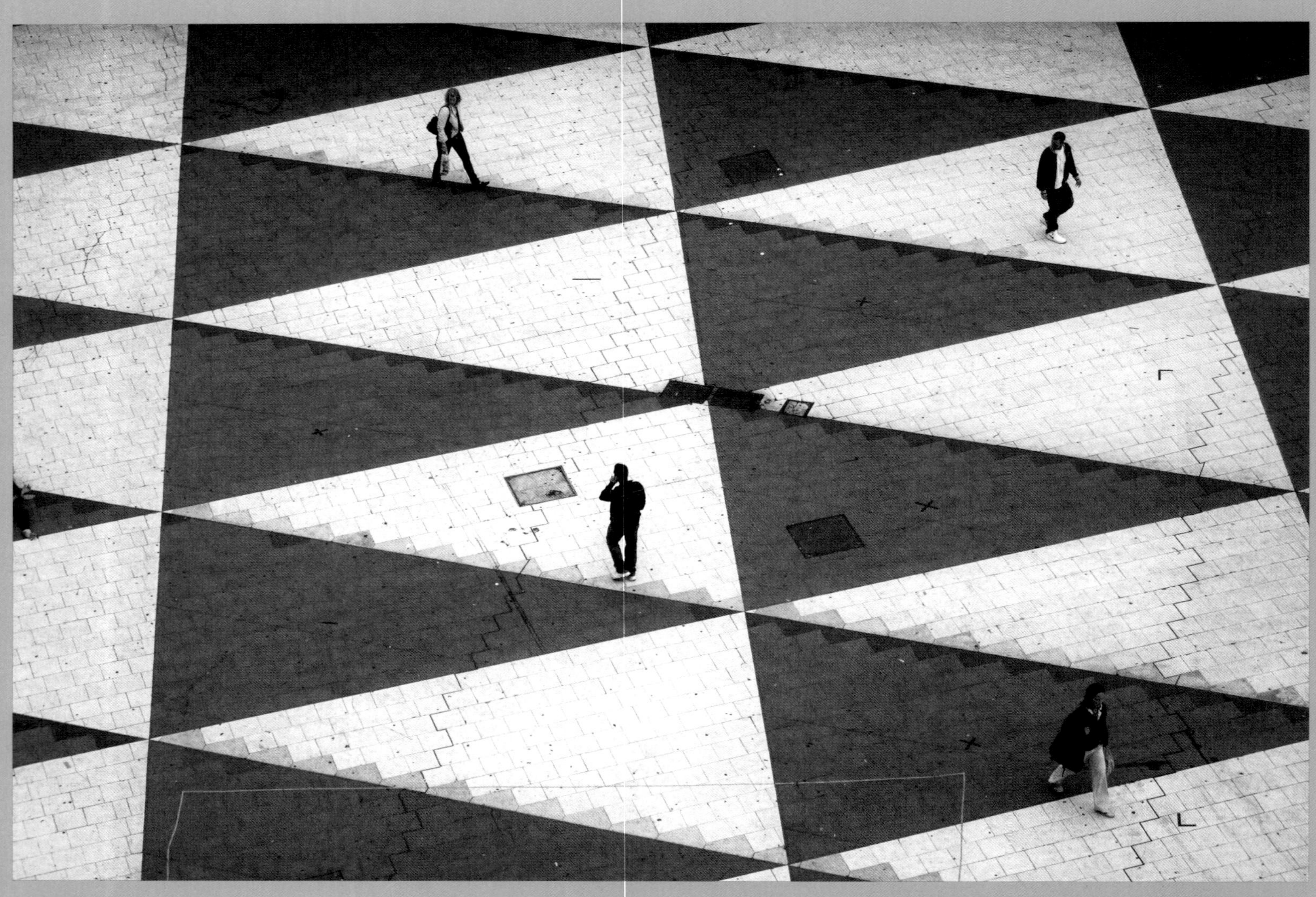

Sense and Sense, 2010

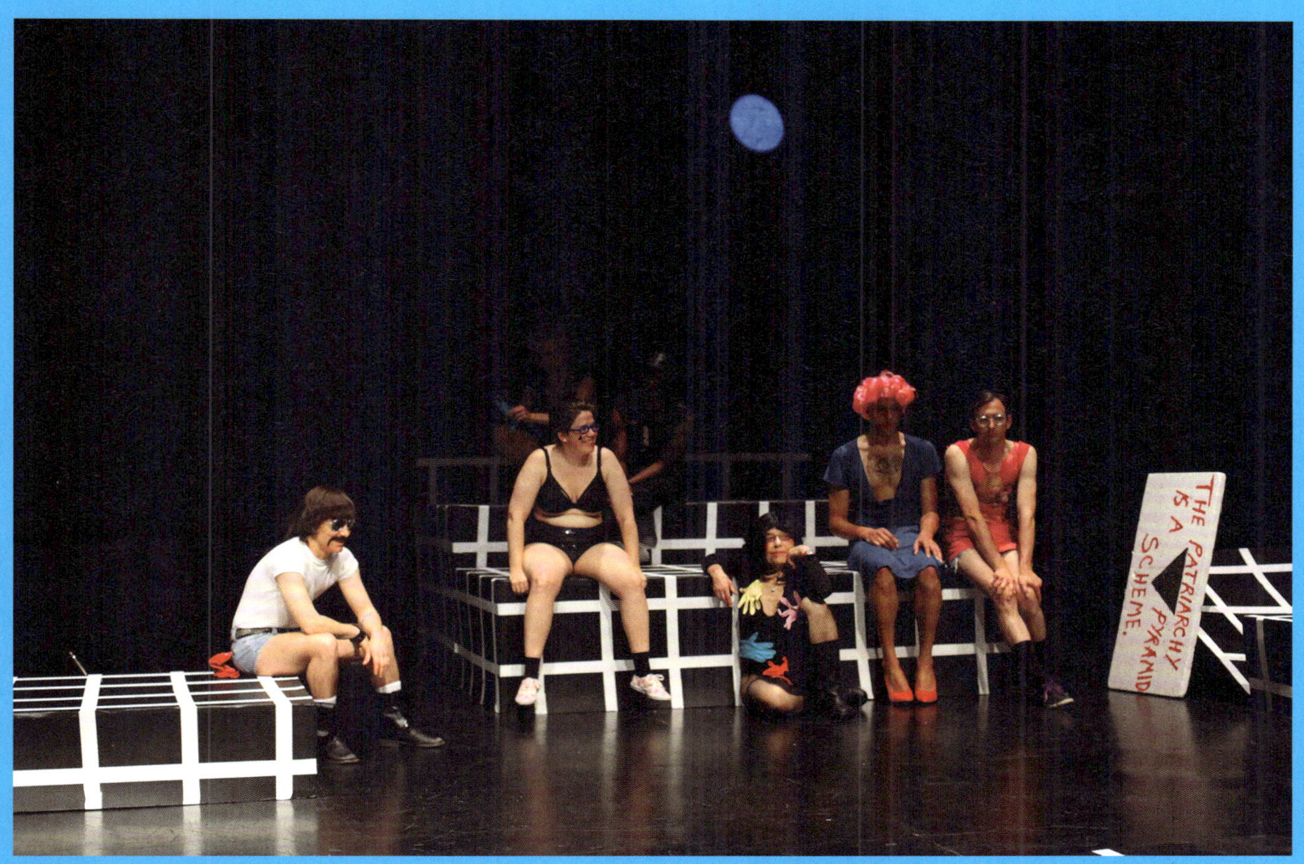

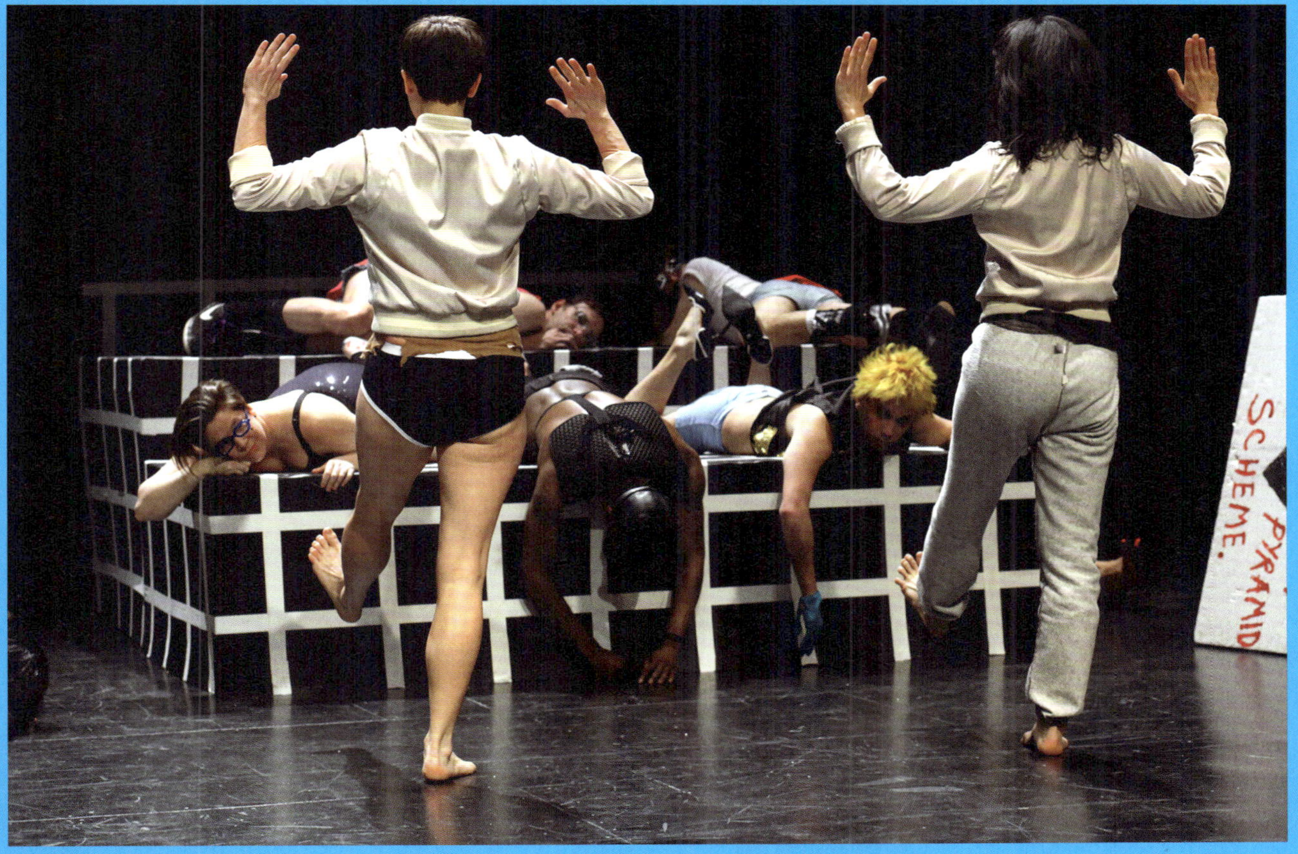

A Gay Bar Called Everywhere (With Costumes and No Practice), 2011

1.

I believe in an alchemy of time. That a certain combination of words, a length of inaction, a discomposed room, or with some such cipher, I believe we can make time.

2.

In a memorial poem to Yeats, W.H. Auden wrote "poetry makes nothing happen."[1]

Nothing is the realm of uncounted experience.

3.

Uncounted experience, unseen in time. If only a wave in proximity to other waves. If only a wave that made a texture of a surface of a top of the line. If only a wave expressing the contour of a bottom, its bottom, the under. If only a wave a rhythm. All potential to break. Crash. hit. rock. wander. If only a night wave, peaking. If only a wave never counted. Measured if a threat.

4.

In the same poem Auden repeated but one refrain, "what instruments we have agree" "what instruments we have agree."

What instruments have we?

5. Beyond the will to measure.

6.

Gertrude Stein said: "The only thing that is different from one time to another is what is seen and what is seen depends upon how everybody is doing everything."[2] what is seen. How everybody is doing everything. In 1926 Stein wrote "Composition as Explanation" to talk about *time-sense, distribution, using everything,* and a *continuous present.* In her elliptical statement on epochal thinking, imaging and representation (what is seen, difference) are aligned with the ability, potential, and mechanics of the body and technology (how everybody is doing everything). To which I add: How everybody is doing everything is what is different, and how difference is seen. *What is seen depends upon how everybody is doing.*

7. What is time if not activism?

8.

I've been thinking about the word "to discompose" for about two years now, and I can barely use it in a sentence. In some ways I have taken this as a good sign, and in others, the failure has felt constitutive of the idea itself—a focus on the frame, a limit. My pleasure in holding on to it was to work with something open-ended and hard to harden, a word that eschews form and opens to the queerly formed. That, as a horizon of thought, I could not see the end of its line.

Now as I write this I am noticing something.

A scene I have been seeing and not saying that has gone unnamed.

Behind the eyelids. I realize that I am someplace when I see this word. When I hold this word, to discompose, there is a particular wall in the Museum of Modern Art that I feel like I am walking past. It is a blank wall, taller than I, whiter than I. There are other people in the room, gazes in all directions. It is no coincidence that it is one of the atrium walls used in MoMA's performance program. I'm looking in the direction of this wall and walking by.

. . . And now moments pass in writing and I can examine the "scene of my thought," it is in fact still, a still picture. I have the gesture of a stride, but I am still. The people around me are fixed points.

To discompose, I have always resisted conjugating it. The infinitive form is part of the proposition, an integral part of the dramaturgy of the idea. That it's in motion. But the action I cling to in the word, is stilled by the scene of its thinking. My struggle to understand it has been in this contradiction—that the movement became an image, fixed and framed out of time.

And I could not use it in a sentence.

9.

What if the museum becomes the authority on alive time? How does an organization, built to historicize and exhibit, work in aliveness? Practically, everybody's asking, practically. Institutions discipline live time within an architecture of power, so how now, thinking through movement, what is an ethical way to authorize alive time?

10.

I look to Lucinda Childs's masterpiece *Dance,* a collaboration with Phillip Glass and Sol LeWitt. About this work Childs has said, "The conflict in *Dance* between the image and the dancer is very much intended." I know that here she is referring to LeWitt's projection onto the dancers. I know this is formal and that *Dance* is the title of the work. But what if we extended the metaphor into all elements of this collaboration . . . Glass's monumental repetition with variation. LeWitt's perspective- and scale-altering projection. Childs's rigorous epic continuous movement. Some of these elements, adjectives, are of the house already built. For is not traditional exhibition making "monumental repetition with variation?" And then some of the elements are strategies for how to recognize conflict in that house—rigorous, continuous, scale-altering, movement. Could Childs's intentional conflict be a script for liveness in institutions?

I look to Jack Smith, who was obsessed with what he called "landlordism" and made work that started seven hours late and lasted five hours long. Undisciplined time to counter the culture of owning and renting.

I listen to David Hammons when he says "nothing fits, but everything works."[4]

11.

How to be alive in a museum? Any living thing becomes queer in the museological. Queer in the museological.

Aliveness trespasses. It doesn't know it's marginal.
Aliveness as marginalia, genitalia, queer in the museological.

How to be alive in a museum? Labor and leaving.

How to be alive in a museum? Use everything.

How to be alive in a museum? I once saw MPA hump, mount, and destroy a Carl Andre sculpture at the Hessel. Living for a few moments in the thought that it might be real and really happening.[5]

How to be alive in a museum? "Make nothing happen" and revel in the uncounted.

12.

Collectivities instead of collections. Is this a question? Can we support collectivities instead of collections?

13.

Does naming time generate time? Rehearsal is a great name for time, solitude another. Clock into darkness. Clock into leave. Falling, a time. What if we all agreed to live a year on moon time shunning the sun. Name it. Your period is a great name for time. Now another.

Alive time, name it, now another, is there anything else? Alive time, call and response. There is the right time and punctum. And the unstable value of kairos and around, the end in the beginning. Now another.

14.

For the past while I've been thinking about transitions. The shifting of weight, changing of direction. Genders and governments. Choreographic and interpersonal. Transitions, no matter the context, are a political moment. A chance to detach from weighted positions, a chance to be moved.

What is a transition that is not a solution?

What's a transition that is not a solution?[6]

15.

With every passing, any awareness of time, the choreographic discomposes the space around us, asking how we arrange our bodies in response.

16.

Virginia Woolf opens *A Room of One's Own* with a disclaimer, "I have shirked the duty of coming to a conclusion upon these two questions—women and fiction remain, so far as I am concerned, unsolved problems." Woolf resists the call to a conclusion and instead performs as an unsolved problem—she thinks. She writes a scene of thinking.

Thought—to call it by a prouder name than it deserved—had let its line down into the stream. It swayed, minute after minute, hither and thither among the reflections and the weeds, letting the water lift it and sink it until—you know the little tug—the sudden conglomeration of an idea at the end of one's line: and then the cautious hauling of it in, and the careful laying of it out? Alas, laid on the grass how small, how insignificant this thought of mine looked; the sort of fish that a good fisherman puts back into the water so that it may grow fatter and be one day worth cooking and eating. I will not trouble you with that thought now, though if you look carefully you may find it for yourselves in the course of what I am going to say.

But however small it was, it had, nevertheless, the mysterious property of its kind—put back into the mind, it became at once very exciting, and important; and as it darted and sank, and flashed hither and thither, set up such a wash and tumult of ideas that it was impossible to sit still. It was thus that I found myself walking with extreme rapidity across a grass plot. Instantly a man's figure rose to intercept me. Nor did I at first understand that the gesticulations of a curious-looking object, in a cut-away coat and evening shirt, were aimed at me. His face expressed horror and indignation. Instinct rather than reason came to my help, he was a Beadle; I was a woman. This was the turf; there was the path. Only the Fellows and Scholars are allowed here; the gravel is the place for me. Such thoughts were the work of a moment. As I regained the path the arms of the Beadle sank, his face assumed its usual repose, and though turf is better walking than gravel, no very great harm was done. The only charge I could bring against the Fellows and Scholars of whatever college might happen to be was that in protection of their turf, which had been rolled for 300 years in succession they had sent my little fish into hiding.

What idea it had been that had sent me so audaciously trespassing I could not now remember.[7]

Thinking as trespass.

She hopped up, Virginia Woolf popped up and sprang about. Her thought had her alight and the territory fell away. That she was minor, and should be mindful escaped her. That she was minor and should be mindful and un-thinking escaped her. That she was minor and should be mindful and un-thinking and un-passionate and not un-bound escaped her.

There were bushes aflame in autumn light and soon proud thoughts hither and thither. So there was no territory. There was a stream and a line down. So there was no territory. So there was no, so there was. Was territory.

The thinker, call her by any name you please, had trespassed where there was no, where there was.

17.

How can we build a structure to be alive inside?

To to to-wards a building of space and commons that privileges movement and margins.[8]

18. Not to be the thing itself.

I was in a workshop with Miguel Gutierrez, he asked us twenty-six questions and this was one of my answers. Life, permission, conditions. When I build something—a project, phrase, collaboration—there are little holes everywhere. I encourage the space between 0—0 Little gaps of intention that life fills up with conditions, with proximities. Little holes everywhere 0—0 little holes.
Permission.
Not to be the thing itself. It's also a way of saying "with" 0—0 entanglement and alignment. Honoring a margin from a movement.
Not to be the thing itself is a transition that is not a solution.
Is this the queer form?

19.

On April 4th of last year I had the idea to write a play where "something fantastic is discovered, something that debunks the white supremacy ideology of the ruling patriarchy."

This lost thing would let loose the ordering energies, shift the paradigm. You could find it under water. Or it could be in a major collection's closet. Underwater, that would be theatrically productive. Gravity would shift. The audience could be weightless. Blue. Shouldn't we be constantly surprised, a politics of surprise.[9]

20.

This year it was suggested that humans had the capacity to conceptualize time 5,000 years before previously believed. Stone Age holes filled by the light of the moon. The will to measure. The moon the method. The ordering energies of day and night. Hanging our narrative on breakfast lunch and dinner.[10] The construction of time and history itself. What is under the water after the moon? A minor planet dragging through the galaxy? Scale-altering temporal drag.[11] Something to slip through.

21.

The most crucial and most queer thing I can say is that these thoughts are all about that which is *unseen in time.* All that exists and goes unnamed, uncounted, disregarded. In a queer life you use and mis-use shards of time, search out references, create your own constellation and pull small threads forward.

You dig and discover all that was, in its time, against the continuity of its time.

That which stepped out to a different speed and didn't reproduce itself in the pendulum's binary.

Can we grab the discontinuous untimely and name it in the future it didn't know?

Where is the permission to name? To use, to materialize, to make due.

22.

If yes, if we do—
do revel in the uncounted,
do wave, do transition,
do trespass, do make due.
If we do, then we live in the experience of uncounted futures.

A commitment to the unseen in time.

Beyond the will to measure.

23. What instruments have we?

UNCOUNTED
Emily Roysdon

I dedicate this text to Ian White. I had the pleasure to discuss some of these thoughts with Ian in our last conversation, his fierce mind a reflection. Ian was a beloved friend and inspiration, and I dedicate these uncounted futures to him.

1. While reading and researching around the idea of "uncounted futures" I found a book called *Open Secret* by Anne-Lise François where she discusses uncounted experience. I first found the Auden quoted there. The poem, "In Memory of W. B. Yeats," was published in Auden's 1940 anthology *Another Time.* François, *Open Secret: The Literature of Uncounted Experience* (Redwood City: Stanford University Press, 2007) and Auden, *Another Time* (New York: Random House, 1940), pp. 93–96.

2. Gertrude Stein, "Composition as Explanation," in Ulla E. Dydo, ed., *A Stein Reader* (Evanston: Northwestern University, 1993), p. 497.

3. As Robin Bernstein says in her text "Dances with Things: Material Culture and the Performance of Race," "the term script denotes not a rigid dictation of performed action but, rather, a necessary openness to resistance, interpretation, and improvisation." Bernstein, "Dances with Things," *Social Text* 27, no. 4 (Winter 2009): 68.

4. Hammons quoted in Peter Schjeldahl, "The Walker," *The New Yorker,* December 23, 2002, p. 156. The full quote, as it was published in a 1986 interview with Hammons by Kellie Jones: "I just love the houses in the South, the way they built them. That Negritude architecture. I really love to watch the way Black people make things, houses, or magazine stands in Harlem for instance. Just the way we use carpentry. Nothing fits, but everything works. The door closes, it keeps things from coming through. But it doesn't have that neatness about it, the way white people put things together, everything is a 32nd of an inch off." Kellie Jones, "David Hammons," *Real Life Magazine,* no. 16 (1986): 8.

5. MPA performed *Untitled Response to Works in the Hessel Collection* on May 1, 2011, as part of the exhibition *What's past is prologue* curated by Julia Paoli at the Hessel Museum, Bard College.

6. This question was developed in conversation with Eleanor Bauer.

7. Virginia Woolf, *A Room of One's Own* [1929] (Orlando: Harcourt, 1989), pp. 5–6. A beadle is "a minor official who carries various civil, educational, or ceremonial duties."

8. Three quotes below the line:
"Act so that there is no use in a center." Gertrude Stein, *Tender Buttons* [1914] (Mineola: Dover Publications, 1997), p. 43.
"The place in which I'll fit will not exist until I make it." James Baldwin, 1957 letter. See James Baldwin and Sol Stein, *Native Sons* (New York: One World Books, Random House, 2005), pp. 96–97.
"How we define public space is intimately connected with ideas about what it means to be human, the nature of society, and the kind of political community we want." Rosalyn Deutsche, "Agoraphobia," in *Evictions: Art and Spatial Politics* (Cambridge, Mass. and London: MIT Press, 1996), p. 269.

9. In the introduction to *Time Travels: Feminism, Nature, Power,* Elizabeth Grosz writes about a "politics of surprise." Grosz, *Time Travels: Feminism, Nature, Power* (Cross Nest: Allen & Unwin, 2005), p. 2.

10. A story through Sara Jaffe about Lynne Tillman realizing her time structure could be meal time.

11. *Temporal drag* was coined by Elizabeth Freeman in *Time Binds: Queer Temporalities, Queer Histories* (Durham: Duke University Press, 2010).

I wrote this inconsistently between 2012 and 2014, accumulating questions and phrases and sometimes presenting them along the way, notably at three performance conferences: "How Are We Performing Today?" at MoMA, New York, in November 2012; "Dancing With the Art World" at the Hammer Museum, Los Angeles, in April 2013; and "Is the Living Body the Last Thing Left Alive?" The new performance turn, its histories and its institutions" at Para Site Hong Kong in April 2014. Simultaneously were year-long commissions from Portland Institute of Contemporary Art's TBA Festival and a partnership between If I Can't Dance and the Stedelijk Museum, Amsterdam, which encouraged these questions in textual, material, and performative ways. Grand Arts, Kansas City, supported the writing of this text. Poster designed with Carl Williamson.

poster for *Uncounted,* 2015

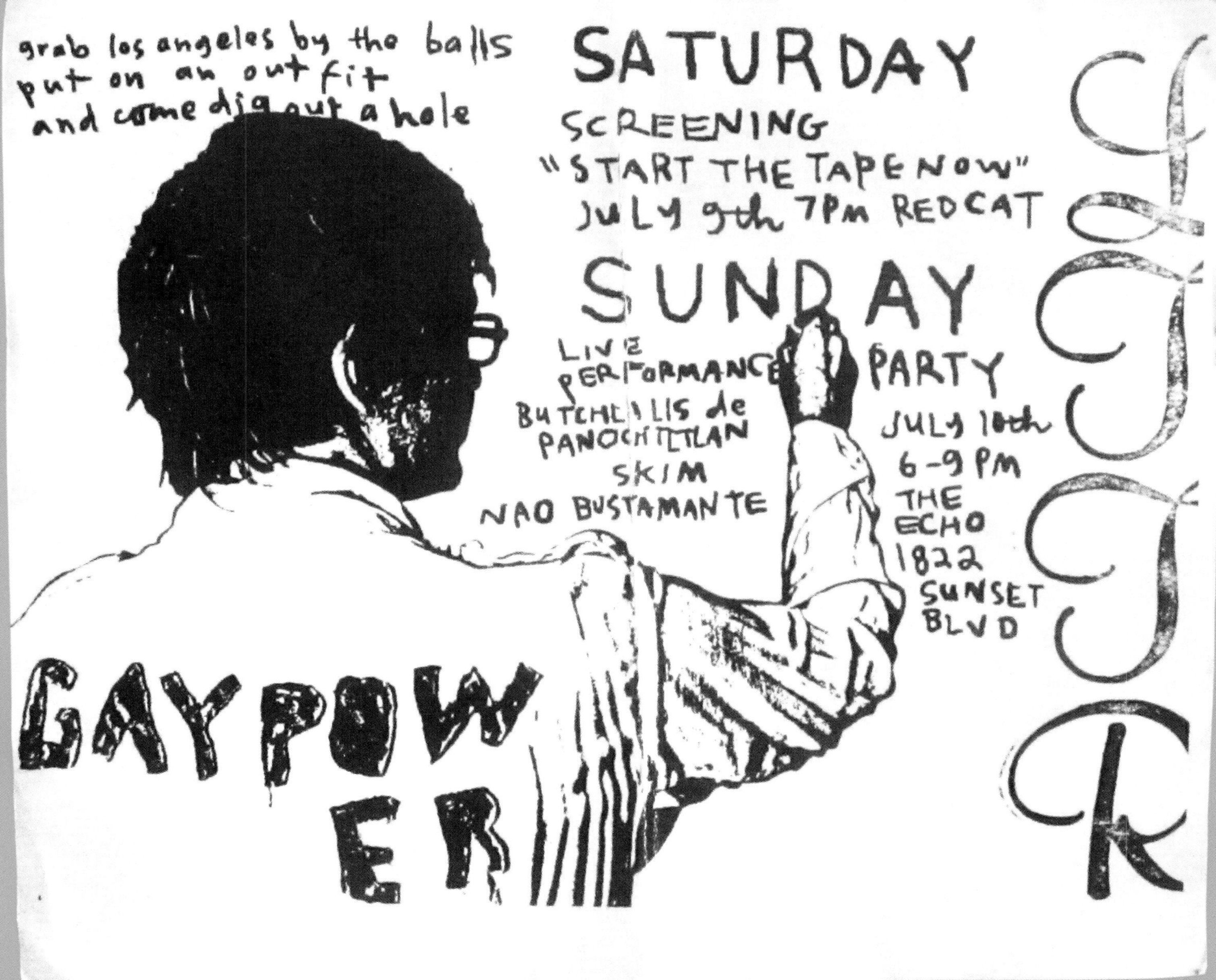

LTTR event flyer, 2006

Witch

Organized by the Hammer Museum, Los Angeles,
and the Institute of Contemporary Art, Los Angeles

Connie Butler and Anne Ellegood

Hunt

Hammer Museum   University of California, Los Angeles
DelMonico Books • D.A.P.   New York

Contents

Director's Foreword

2020 will surely go down as one of the most significant years in our history. Some eighteen months into the pandemic, the coronavirus has forever changed how we live our lives, do our work, and think about our institutions. Originally planned for fall 2020, *Witch Hunt* now opens a year later. In the interim, the country experienced a momentous, contentious American presidential election and enormous protests for racial justice. Museums that shuttered their doors for in some cases more than a year have reopened to a changed world. It is my strong belief that everything we do in our exhibitions and programs at the Hammer is deeply tied to our mission to highlight how art and artists inspire us to make a more just world, and *Witch Hunt* exemplifies this aspirational goal. Each of the artists in this exhibition—all of whom the curators have long wanted to work with—has spent a career devoted to feminist issues, which are, of course, human issues. I can think of no better moment to turn our attention to artists to help us navigate the complex times in which we live and to help us rethink, through the lens of gender, what it means to be human.

The American election of 2020 made it once again regrettably clear that the US is still not ready for a woman president, but we have seen that many of the countries—New Zealand, Finland, Denmark, and others—that have been the most successful in dealing with the virus are, in fact, led by women. As we absorb the implications of this fact and consider female leadership and the impact of feminist agendas on cultures across the globe, we and many of our colleague institutions have organized projects that are hopeful, inspiring, and provocative. Under the umbrella of a national initiative called the Feminist Art Coalition, *Witch Hunt* is one project among many others that grapples with what feminism means today, and how artists consider its many impacts. Connie Butler and Anne Ellegood began working on *Witch Hunt* several years ago, prompted by the Women's March in early 2017 and the outpouring of anger at the results of the 2016 election. Each of them has, for many years, been devoted to feminist causes both in their curatorial work and within the institutions to which they are committed. Although Anne has since left the Hammer to assume the role of Good Works Executive Director at the Institute of Contemporary Art, Los Angeles (ICA LA), she and Connie wanted to fully realize their partnership by sharing the exhibition between our two institutions. I thank Anne and Connie for their spirit of collaboration and for their fortitude in organizing such a strong exhibition of powerful projects by an incredible, international group of woman-identified artists.

We are excited to be partnering with ICA LA on the presentation of *Witch Hunt*. A project of this scale requires the entire museum to contribute at every level. The outstanding staffs at both the Hammer and ICA LA have supported this exhibition through a pandemic and a number of postponements, and I am grateful for their work, enthusiasm, and commitment. I want to thank the Hammer's deputy directors, Cynthia Burlingham, deputy director of curatorial affairs, Michael Harrison, deputy director of finance, operations, and administration, and Fred Yeries, deputy director of external affairs, who advise me and have helped enormously during this difficult time. Additionally, I am deeply grateful to the Hammer's Board of Directors, who support our mission unconditionally and have sustained our staff during the pandemic. I want to acknowledge our board Chair Marcy Carsey in particular for being our most avid champion. Our Board of Advisors provides critical support to our Hammer Contemporary Collection and are active ambassadors on behalf of the museum and our exhibition program.

I am grateful to all those who funded the exhibition at a time when support of our programs and exhibitions is even more meaningful and necessary. *Witch Hunt* is made possible by lead funding from the Kaleta A. Doolin Foundation. Major support is provided by Kelsey Lee Offield, with generous funding from Darren Star, Jill and Peter Kraus and from Hope Warschaw and John Law. The exhibition is also supported by Bill Hair, Emily and Teddy Greenspan, and by Étant donnés Contemporary Art, a program developed by FACE Foundation and the Cultural Services of the French Embassy in the United States, with lead funding from the French Ministry of Culture and Institut Français-Paris, the Florence Gould Foundation, the Ford Foundation, the Helen Frankenthaler Foundation, Chanel USA, the ADAGP, and the CPGA. Additional support is provided by Artis and Betty Duker. At ICA LA, major support for the exhibition is provided by the Vera R. Campbell Foundation and the Younes and Soraya Nazarian Family Foundation. The exhibition is also generously funded by grants from the Pasadena Art Alliance, the Art Dealers Association of America Foundation, and the Henry Moore Foundation, as well as contributions from Christine Meleo Bernstein and Armyan Bernstein, Alice and Nahum Lainer, Marla and Jeffrey Michaels, and members of the Curator's Council.

Finally, I thank the artists in *Witch Hunt* whose work I have personally been eager to see in our galleries and downtown at ICA LA: Leonor Antunes, Yael Bartana, Pauline Boudry / Renate Lorenz, Candice Breitz, Shu Lea Cheang, Minerva Cuevas, Vaginal Davis, Every Ocean Hughes, Bouchra Khalili, Laura Lima, Teresa Margolles, Otobong Nkanga, Okwui Okpokwasili, Lara Schnitger, and Beverly Semmes. Each of their practices is conceptually focused, visually rich, and fiercely human. In spite of politics, or because of it, the work of the artists gathered here has resonated for many years and will continue to do so, and we are honored to support and show their work at the Hammer and ICA LA.

Ann Philbin
Director, Hammer Museum

Curatorial Acknowledgments

> This book is an action, a political action where revolution is the goal. It has no other purpose. It is not cerebral wisdom, or academic horseshit, or ideas carved in granite or destined for immortality. It is part of a process and its context is change. It is part of a planetary movement to restructure community forms and human consciousness so that people have power over their own lives, participate fully in community, live in dignity and freedom.
> —Andrea Dworkin, *Woman Hating*

In 1974, Andrea Dworkin characterized her book *Woman Hating* less as the analysis of oppression that it was and more as something deliberately political and kinetic. In many ways, *Witch Hunt* is likewise an action, with the intention of supporting revolution and the demands for racial justice and gender equity that are echoing loudly in the streets of our cities worldwide. While no single exhibition or work of art can reverse the deep cultural misogyny and histories of violence experienced by women, it feels important, and particularly timely, to put a project into the culture with the goal of inspiring dialogue, encouraging participation in community, and arguing for the dignity of all people. Indeed, we hope it may incite and nurture outrage as a productive tool toward change.

The exhibition *Witch Hunt* has been in the works for a long time. As curators, we are both committed to the goals and ideologies of feminism and to presenting and writing about the work of woman-identified artists. As early as 2013, working together at the Hammer, we noticed how many artists of a younger generation were reexamining the legacies of second-generation feminist practices and reinventing them, making work that addressed the new specificities of lives and identities that were under attack. At that time—which now feels like a distant and more hopeful past—it seemed to us that curating a group exhibition about feminist practices might somehow diminish the many incredible artists who, in fact, deserve solo presentations and the full attention of scholarship and critical writing about their work. Why make another group show if we could imagine a long line of solo projects that would satisfy our feminist desires—political, curatorial, aesthetic—into the foreseeable future? Notably, the Hammer Museum does have a commendable history of solo exhibitions devoted to women artists, from emerging to historically overlooked, including Lee Bontecou, Zarina Hashmi, Sarah Lucas, Marisa Merz, Adrian Piper, Alina Szapocznikow, and many others, not to mention numerous Hammer Projects that have featured women artists usually early in their careers.

But after the US presidential election in 2016, everything changed. The political and cultural environment required an urgent response. We had what could undeniably be called "a situation"—not only in the vernacular sense but, as feminist and cultural theorist Lauren Berlant defines it, "a state of things in which something that will perhaps matter is unfolding amidst the usual activity of life." The election of a man who was visibly and provably a misogynist, a self-admitted serial sexual predator, and a white nationalist meant that the work of feminism as we knew it was not only far from complete but redefined seemingly overnight. As Berlant explores in her 2011 book *Cruel Optimism*, we live in a time of great precarity in which a crisis mode has become commonplace, a far too frequent facet of our everyday lives. This has been made only more evident during the COVID-19 pandemic in which structural racism has been made evident at every level of our society.

We began with a question: What does it mean to be feminist in the age of Donald Trump? As painful as it is to name him, this project would likely not have happened without the reactionary populist backlash that ushered him, and others like him around the world, into power. *Witch Hunt* is a way of processing our rage against a government and a country that feel utterly indifferent to our safety and well-being. And it is a form of articulating resistance. We often consider our work, and that of our compatriots in feminism, to be living and producing in a state of resistance, doing our work in plain sight in a nation that doesn't always want what we have to offer or listen seriously to our opinions.

In any political movement, feminist ones in particular, there is strength in mutual aid—in connecting individuals who have been working in their personal contexts and with their communities to increase awareness and enact change. We hope that, as an exhibition, *Witch Hunt* begins to outline certain formal, methodological, and conceptual trends spanning the past several decades with the ambition of tracing a transnational genealogy where there was none. Ours is an exhibition of fierce cis and trans women artists who are refreshingly clear about their courses of research and how they manifest their ideas. They refute the historical trope of the midcareer female artist who recedes into the black hole of critical lack of attention, market devaluation, and invisibility. They have managed to avoid the pitfalls of a fickle art world that has looked in other directions for decades. Instead, the artists in *Witch Hunt* have been working for years to consistently produce insightful, meaningful, and truly powerful works of art. They are in demand and unafraid. Indeed, their work gets more bold and more radical over time as they gain wider recognition. It is our great pleasure and honor to work with each of them. While their shared commitment to feminist perspectives and the subjects they choose to address are highlighted within the contours of this thematic group show, we simultaneously think of *Witch Hunt* as a gathering of individual projects, wherein each artist is given sufficient space to present a significant installation.

We began our research for *Witch Hunt* several years ago with a small roundtable at the Hammer, which brought together a group of peers to discuss how museums might address the imperatives of various forms of feminism. We are grateful to the colleagues who participated in the conversation that day: UC Irvine associate professor Rhea Anastas; director of the Wexner Center for the Arts Johanna Burton; Erin Christovale, who was then an independent curator and is now our valued colleague and associate curator at the Hammer Museum; Ivet Curlin of the What, How and For Whom (WHW) curatorial collective; head of contemporary art at the Los Angeles County Museum of Art Rita Gonzalez; and artist Sharon Hayes.

The ideas generated that day led us to form an initiative at the Hammer we dubbed the Bureau of Feminism. An homage to Gran Fury's graphic design collective Bureau—and a tongue-in-cheek suggestion that perhaps institutions should have such a brick-and-mortar division to bring down the gavel on issues of gender inequity—the Bureau of Feminism became the overarching moniker we used for a range of programs at the museum, from small-scale exhibitions to film screenings to panel discussions, that took up questions and positions related to feminist actions, scholarship, and cultural production. The point of establishing a name for an ongoing, evolving series of programs was to underscore the museum's commitment to feminist ideas through a range of institutional imperatives. Over time, conversations among ourselves and with respected peers in the field also made us confident that the time had come for a larger-scale exhibition that aimed to take up the complexities and possibilities for feminisms articulated by an international roster of artists.

As we committed to the idea that would become *Witch Hunt*, we also began in early 2017 to participate in conversations about what would later come to be called the Feminist Art Coalition (FAC). Similarly catalyzed by the increasing hostility toward women and transgender people so evident in politics and cultural contexts, the FAC is a platform for institutions across the United States to stage projects informed by feminisms. The original intention was for projects to occur simultaneously in the fall of 2020 to coincide with the presidential election season, but the coronavirus pandemic resulted in the necessary shifting of many schedules, resulting in FAC projects taking place across the country in late 2020 and throughout 2021. Established to encourage institutions and individuals to commit to social justice and structural change, the FAC seeks to raise awareness of feminist thought, experience, and actions. Given that our nascent idea for an exhibition was starting to take hold at the time the FAC was taking shape, we agreed it would be an ideal project to fall under this larger umbrella. The exhibition was originally slated for the Hammer Museum, but once longtime Hammer senior curator Anne Ellegood left to become Good Works Executive Director at the Institute of Contemporary Art, Los Angeles (ICA LA), we decided the exhibition should be a partnership, taking place at both museums.

In 2019, Nika Chilewich joined the Hammer staff as curatorial assistant and became our primary partner on the curatorial team for *Witch Hunt*. She has worked on every aspect of the exhibition, and we are grateful for her energy, her commitment, and her thoughtful contributions to the project, including her illuminating artist entries in this catalogue. This project has touched every department at the Hammer and ICA LA. At the Hammer, we are grateful to director Ann Philbin for her immediate enthusiasm for the subject and her unwavering support. As one of the most respected and visionary female leaders of a major cultural institution, she is a role model and an inspiration. We thank our curatorial colleagues associate curator Erin Christovale and curator Aram Moshayedi at the Hammer and senior curator Jamillah James at ICA LA, who responded to the idea of the exhibition with wonderful suggestions of artists to consider and rigorous feedback about the conceptual framework. Deputy director of curatorial affairs Cynthia Burlingham and director of exhibitions and publications Melanie Crader were both generous with their time and energy as they oversaw the administrative coordination of the exhibition.

Witch Hunt is accompanied by this beautiful catalogue, which has been a complex labor of love. We are indebted to project manager of exhibitions and publications Claire Dilworth, who expertly guided and coordinated all aspects of the book. Hammer curatorial assistant Vanessa Arizmendi gamely authored several of the artist texts, and we are grateful for her contributions, as well as for those of ICA LA senior curator Jamillah James and independent writer and curator Ana Briz. We thank editor Domenick Ammirati for his sensitive and critical work on every text in the book and proofreader Jane Bobko. The publication's exceptional design was created by Jessica Fleischmann, whose sensitivity to the subject made our collaboration both inspired and indispensable. We thank Mary DelMonico and D.A.P. for championing the book and managing its distribution.

Bringing together works from an international roster of artists and coordinating complex installations and projects requires a dedicated and talented team. At the Hammer, we thank registrar, exhibitions Linda Yun and director, registration and collections management Portland McCormick for coordinating all the shipping and loan arrangements. Manager, exhibition design and production Adam Peña planned the layout and worked diligently with each artist to facilitate their projects. Senior preparator Jason Pugh managed all details of a complex installation and worked closely with preparator Angelica Perez-Aguirre, assistant preparator Michael Terzano, our expert AV technicians museum and theater technical director Jim Fetterley and technical supervisor Tim Ferris, and the whole wonderful exhibitions team. At ICA LA, we thank registrar Bernie Sale and exhibitions manager Peter Gould, along with our team of preparators, for expertly managing all aspects of the registration and installation.

Public programs and performances are integral to the experience of *Witch Hunt*. Overseeing these important events are, at the Hammer, director of public programs Claudia Bestor; public programs manager Janani Subramanian; and at ICA LA, director of learning and engagement Asuka Hisa. We'd also like to thank associate director, academic programs Theresa Sotto and the academic programs staff.

For their heroic fundraising efforts and support, we thank the development team at the Hammer— Veridiana Pontes, Hannah Howe, Jessica Vrazilek, Sara Friedman, Kelly Connors—and Jimmy Freeman,

Adam Lee, Sonia Mak, Gisela Morales, and McKenna Warde at ICA LA. Expert marketing and promotion of the exhibition was spearheaded by the Hammer's Scott Tennent, chief communications officer, and Nancy Lee, public relations manager, working closely with Susan Edwards, associate director of digital content, Tara Morris, graphic designer, and Mitch Marr, associate director of communications and marketing.

For their collaboration we thank the following gallerists and other colleagues who work closely with the artists involved. They include Adams and Ollman, Portland; Air de Paris, France; Marcelle Alix, Paris; Anne Barlow, Tate St Ives; Tanya Bonakdar Gallery, New York and Los Angeles; Ellen de Brujine Projects, Paris; Capitain Petzel, Berlin; James Cohan, New York; Mor Charpentier, Paris; Pamela Echeverría, Labor, Mexico City; Galeria Foksal, Warsaw; Annet Gelink Gallery, Amsterdam; A Gentil Carioca, Rio de Janeiro; Goodman Gallery, Cape Town, Johannesburg, and London; Marian Goodman, New York, Paris, and London; Susan Inglett Gallery, New York; Kaufmann Repetto, New York and Milan; Anton Kern Gallery, New York; Peter Kilchmann, Zurich; KOW, Berlin and Madrid; kurimanzutto, Mexico City and New York; In Situ Fabienne Leclerc, Paris; Hector Martínez; Mendes Wood, São Paulo; Nasher Sculpture Center, Dallas; New Discretions, New York; Palais de Tokyo, Paris; Petzel Gallery, New York; Solomon R. Guggenheim Museum, New York; Sommer Contemporary Art, Tel Aviv; Galeria Luisa Strina, São Paulo; Studio Voltaire, London; Lumen Travo, Amsterdam; Shoshana Wayne Gallery, Los Angeles. We also thank the private lenders and other generous supporters of the exhibition, including Sam and Deborah Berkovitz, Nancy Berman, Armyan and Christine Bernstein, Kaleta A. Doolin, Betty Duker, Emily and Teddy Greenspan, Jill and Peter Kraus, Alice and Nahum Lainer, Kelsey Lee Offield, Eileen O'Kane Kornreich, Darren Star, and Wim van Dongen, each of whom contributed significant support to the project.

We feel it is worth noting that we began writing our curatorial texts in the fall of 2019, a year in advance of the 2020 presidential election, before the coronavirus pandemic that would change our world utterly, and prior to the movement for racial justice that was reignited in the spring of 2020. We could never have imagined what 2020 would hold as we wrote these words. But it is without question that our calls for real, meaningful, and genuine change—our expressions of rage and vulnerability—are only more imperative now.

Finally, our heartfelt thanks and deep admiration go to the artists in the exhibition. We are inspired by their work, awed by their rigor and their political and ethical commitment, and incredibly proud and grateful to have brought their work to Los Angeles, in many cases for the first time. In the words of feminist scholar Sarah Ahmed in her *Living a Feminist Life* (2017), "Where we find feminism matters; from whom we find feminism matters. Feminism as a collective movement is made out of how we are moved to become feminists in dialogue with others. A movement requires us to be moved." We are moved.

Connie Butler
Chief Curator,
Hammer Museum

Anne Ellegood
Good Works Executive Director,
Institute of Contemporary Art,
Los Angeles

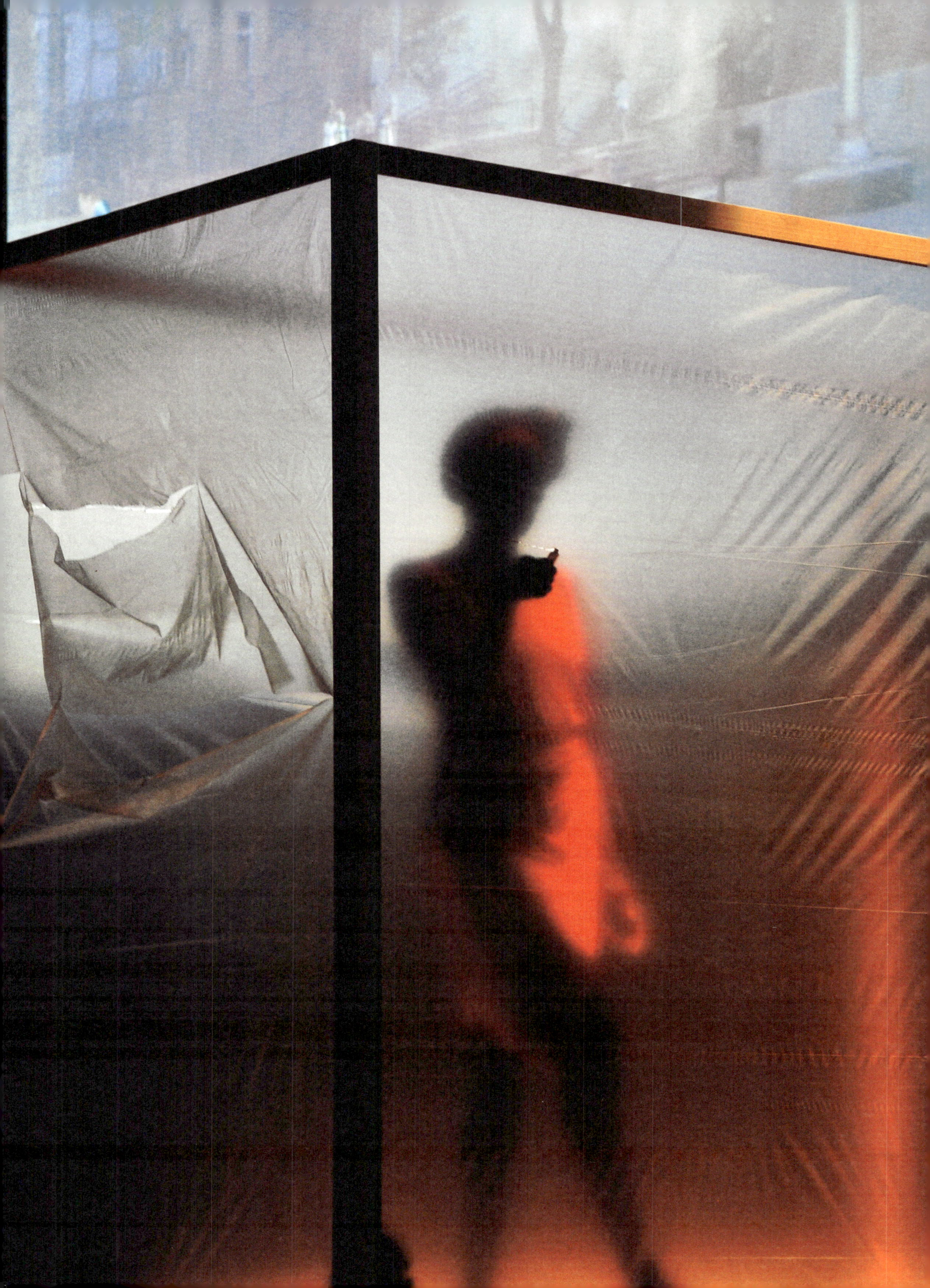

Days of Rage

Connie Butler

All my life I've had rage. Living as a woman in the United States under patriarchy breeds it. My memories are punctuated with moments that sharpened it, a slow, grinding anger. Marching in Washington, DC, for reproductive rights in 1992, seething at Operation Rescue and the phalanx of white men who would tell me what to do with my body—not to mention deprive me access to low-cost, confidential health care offered by doctors who we didn't yet call frontline workers. Delivering meals to homebound people with AIDS, whose lives were being foreclosed by a government that blocked their access to research and health care. For many women of my generation, watching the riveting testimony of Anita Hill on television in 1991 was a profound coming of age in terms of forming a personal, feminist politics. Her damning words continue to haunt our public discourse, echoing through recent Supreme Court confirmation hearings and the crescendo of #MeToo activism that's swept the culture like a tidal wave. The tenor of the moment is rage.

Art indelibly marked my experience of this history. Sometimes it was symbolic, affective. As a young dancer in 1984, I saw Pina Bausch's radical, frenzied reworking of *The Rite of Spring* (1975), a work of rage and promiscuous movement if ever there was one. The image and smell of naked bodies thrashing in the dark peat on stage was searing. In 1989, I had just arrived as a curator at Artists Space in New York when the controversy over *Witnesses: Against Our Vanishing* erupted, focused on David Wojnarowicz's scathing attack in the show's catalogue on myopic religious figures and politicians.[1] I shepherded this project forward while protests erupted outside the gallery even as Wojnarowicz spoke to me of his own suffering and rage; his was a formative voice in my ear that I will never forget. Two years later, in response to the reactionary political climate's threat to Roe v. Wade, I worked with artists Kathe Burkhart and Chrysanne Stathacos to realize *The Abortion Project*, an installation in which women who had had abortions signed the walls of Artists Space in red (Fig. 1). A reimagining of Simone de Beauvoir's 1971 "Manifesto of the 343," which published the names of signatories who had terminated pregnancies, the work gathered a community of women in protest and underscored the cyclical nature of these battles in the US.

Though the international group of artists in *Witch Hunt* represents a range of geographies and cultural positions, all came of age either during or in the wake of the events I describe. While their work can well be situated into a history of feminism, framing their endeavors through affect—through rage, a topic that traverses cultures and histories—seemed to me the most urgent way to address their extraordinary practices. While I have written about and curated second-wave feminist art from primarily a Euro-American context, such a focus is no longer

1 Wojnarowicz had excoriated New York's Cardinal O'Connor and Republican Senator Jesse Helms in the catalogue for the show, which was curated by Nan Goldin and addressed the dire impact of AIDS on the art community. The text caused the National Endowment for the Arts to cancel a grant for the exhibition.

Okwui Okpokwasili
Poor People's TV Room Solo, 2014

enough, when women in Africa, South and Central America, and within the United States itself face such varied economic, sociocultural, and political realities. In the words of Audre Lorde, "I am not free while any woman is unfree, even when her shackles are very different from my own."[2] What do we do with our rage? Lorde asks. Through methodologies involving deep and radical empathy, and an intimacy born of rage, the artists in *Witch Hunt* align themselves with political and social ruptures not only historical but also enduring and endured.

■

Writing in *Gore Capitalism* (2018) about Mexico and the so-called third world, Tijuana-based transfeminist activist Sayak Valencia compellingly argues that, in the twenty-first century, reality is synonymous with violence and death is the most profitable business in capitalist society.[3] What Valencia vividly calls "gore practices" stem from a condition she posits in Mexican culture in which "gender constructions are intimately tied to the construction of the state."[4] That state's decline disturbs those identities, the deep entrenchment of macho culture within the country, and the national idea of manliness. Among the effects this scenario produces is increased

violence against women. Though a massive surge in female homicide has been noted in Mexico since the early 1990s, 2020 saw an unprecedented rise in gender-based violence, with grisly and inexplicable murders occurring with increasing brazenness, leading women to protest openly across the country.[5] Valencia's text demands a transfeminism, a "daily insurrection" of resignification—a call to arms seeking nothing less than a theoretical and practical rethinking of the mechanisms of heteronormative, masculinist power.[6]

How can an artist respond to such a disturbing state of affairs? What does an ethical practice in this context even look like, and how can it make us look at the horror of social injustice and really see it, rather than turn away? In the early 1990s, Teresa Margolles began sketching the outlines of such an approach in Mexico City's morgue, where she worked, in a sense, embedded as an artist. As part of the SEMEFO art collective (a group active from 1990 to 1999 that took its name from the acronym for Mexico City's medical examiner's office),[7] she created ephemeral works that gained their power from the combination of her firsthand experience as an employee at the institution, and from the physical evidence of trauma and erasure that she gleaned and repurposed—at times literally. The tactic recalls the early work of the British artist Cosey

2 Audre Lorde, "The Uses of Anger: Women Responding to Racism," keynote at the National Women's Studies Association Conference, Storrs, Connecticut, June 1981. See the presentation's full text at https://www. blackpast.org/african-american-history/speeches-african-american-history/1981-audre-lorde-uses-anger-women-responding-racism/.

3 Sayak Valencia, "The Breakdown of the State as a Political Formation," in *Gore Capitalism* (Pasadena, CA: Semiotext(e), 2018), 35–36. I want to thank Nika Chilewitch for first bringing this text to my attention and for all of the energy and intelligence she brought to our project.

4 Ibid., 55.

5 See Robbie Whelan, "Pressure Builds on Mexican President over Rising Violence against Women," *Wall Street Journal*, February 19, 2020, https://www.wsj.com/articles/pressure-builds-on-mexican-president-over-rising-violence-against-women-11582120125.

6 Valencia, "Warning," in *Gore Capitalism*, 13.

7 The collective SEMEFO comprised Margolles, Arturo Ángulo Gallardo, Juan Luis García Zavaleta, and Carlos López Orozco, among others.

Fig. 1
Kathe Burkhart and Chrysanne Stathacos, *The Abortion Project*, 1991. Marker, signatures, silkscreen, painted floor. Installation view, Artist's Space, New York, 1991

Fanni Tutti, who worked as a model in porn photo shoots (showing the results in the infamous COUM Transmissions show *Prostitution* at London's Institute of Contemporary Art in 1976). Fanni Tutti inhabited the misogynist culture of pornography to increase the understanding of her own subject position and voice, in search of empowerment for herself and other sex workers. In a similarly complex and activist set of reversals, Margolles's early work often recuperated the physical remains of the anonymous victims of violence that stemmed from gangs and drug cartels, individuals whose identities had essentially been erased. After SEMEFO, in visceral installations made from the nearly invisible residue of human life and death, Margolles found form in a sculptural vocabulary that is hard boiled, minimal, and often abstract yet extremely affecting. She is masterful at subtly shifting the conditions of the viewing experience in such a way that her searing content operates only for those most closely attending to her material and conceptual choices. Few works linger in sense memory as much as her 2009 Venice Biennale installation, *¿De qué otra cosa podríamos hablar?* (What else could we talk about?), in which the floors of the fifteenth-century palazzo that houses the Mexican Pavilion were washed with mud-impregnated fabric that had been used to swab killing sites in Mexico (Fig. 2). The presence of the deceased was visceral as the bloody fabric was dampened and rubbed against the ground, a sort of inverted cleansing or ablution. Playing on the metaphor of silence and silencing, the quiet encounter of the viewer with the ongoing labor of the scrubbing was stark, mining what Jennifer Doyle has called the "affective density of the interaction between the artist and the audience."[8] The transfer of anonymous and unknowable horror, and the distillation of the numbness left in its wake, was profoundly unsettling and absolutely unforgettable.

Margolles's work attempts to make intimate the global and spectacular experience of violence, both symbolic and actual. She frequently collaborates with local communities, in a way going undercover in situations whose inhumane dimensions she empathizes with and is compelled to expose. Most recently, she has focused on contested borders. For a current project, Margolles has spent time living around the Simón Bolívar International Bridge which spans a river between Venezuela and Colombia and connects the two countries. Since 2019, the area has been flooded with people trying to escape the poverty and hunger inflicted by the Venezuelan dictatorship. In such margins between nation-states, the politics of food, health care, and shelter are exacted on human bodies as families flee and are forced to invent new modes of survival. Margolles

8 Jennifer Doyle, *Hold It Against Me: Difficulty and Emotion in Contemporary Art* (Durham, NC: Duke University Press, 2013), 3. Doyle theorizes that emotion, both as a material of the artist and a response in the viewer, creates an affective space around the object and reception of art.

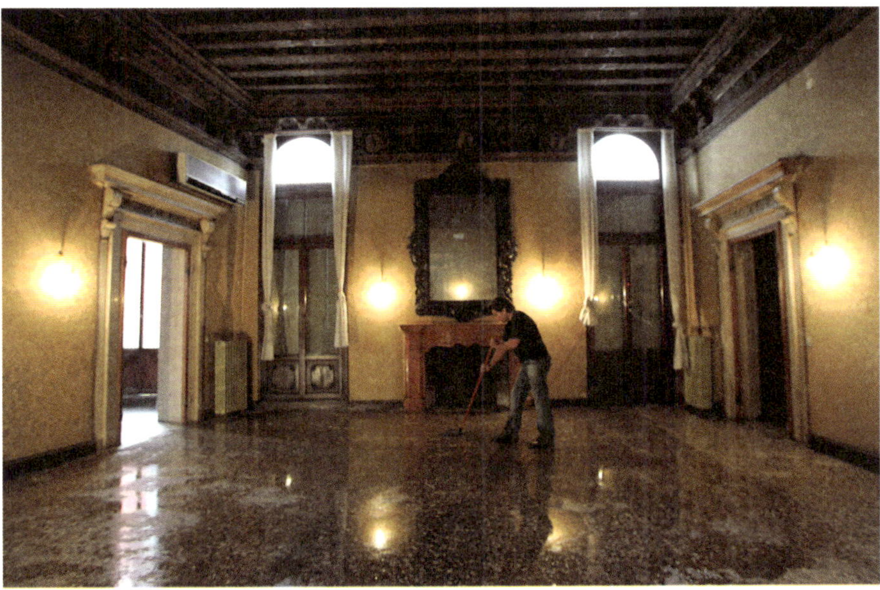

Fig. 2
Teresa Margolles, *¿De qué otra cosa podríamos hablar? Limpieza* (What else could we talk about? Cleaning), 2009. Installation view, Mexican Pavilion, Venice Biennale, 2009. Courtesy of the artist; Galerie Peter Kilchmann, Zurich; and James Cohan, New York

turns these economies of violence inside out, returning them to the viewer condensed into spare and disturbing objects and actions. Her experience at the Venezuelan border has informed her thinking for *Witch Hunt*, for which the artist turns her attention to the border between Mexico and the United States and the impact of border policies on immigration and gentrification issues in Los Angeles, where she has close family ties.

The feminist postcolonial theorist Sarah Ahmed has written, "To share a memory is to put a body into words."[9] An early dance-theater performance by Okwui Okpokwasili, *Pent Up: A Revenge Dance* (2010), explores just this nexus of memory, narrative, and the somatic. The work begins with images of Nigerian girls dancing and playing, projected onto the artist's bare back, making her torso a vessel for both personal and collective memory. After a few moments, Okpokwasili begins to writhe, her athletic body quaking in electrifying waves. She grunts and breathes heavily, pantomiming the labor and release of self-pleasure while also harnessing the disappeared histories of sexual violence, genital mutilation, and other ruptures carried in the bodies of women. After the opening solo, Okpokwasili lies down on the ground near her partner onstage, a younger woman, who begins to recite a tale of a little girl who obsessively touches her "swollen, desperate, wretched clit,"

with Okpokwasili taking the role of the mother figure. The tale possesses a dark subtext, given that, in Nigeria, girls are condemned for displays of sexuality: Nigeria has the highest rate of genital mutilation of any country, accounting for roughly a quarter of the world's cases.[10] The legacies of ongoing sexualized violence against women set the stage for the horrifying kidnapping of 276 young girls by the terrorist group Boko Haram in northern Nigeria in 2014.

Though Okpokwasili was born and grew up in the Bronx, her Igbo-Nigerian parents immigrated to the United States in the late 1960s to escape the Nigerian Civil War. The artist's conjuring of her family's village in southeastern Nigeria in *Pent Up* acts as a signifier for contemporary conditions in Africa for women and girls. The imagining that the piece elicits, of the contradiction between the girls' sweet innocence and the backdrop of violence and injustice that imperils them, recalls Adrian Piper's video *Please, God* (1990), in which the joyful dance of little girls on the streets of New York is set to the soundtrack of Billie Holiday singing "God Bless the Child" and "Strange Fruit" (Fig. 3). The text that scrolls over images of their ebullient happiness pleads for their protection and voices apprehension about their fragile lives.

Okpokwasili's multimedia works also resonate with the vernacular form of the dance play, a ritual

9 Sarah Ahmed, *Living a Feminist Life* (Durham, NC: Duke University Press, 2017), 23.

10 T. C. Okeke, U. S. B. Anyaehie, and C. C. K. Ezenyeaku, "An Overview of Female Genital Mutilation in Nigeria," *Annals of Medical and Health Sciences Research* 2, no. 1 (January–June 2012): 70–73, available at https://www.ncbi.nlm.nih.gov/pmc/articles/PMC3507121/.

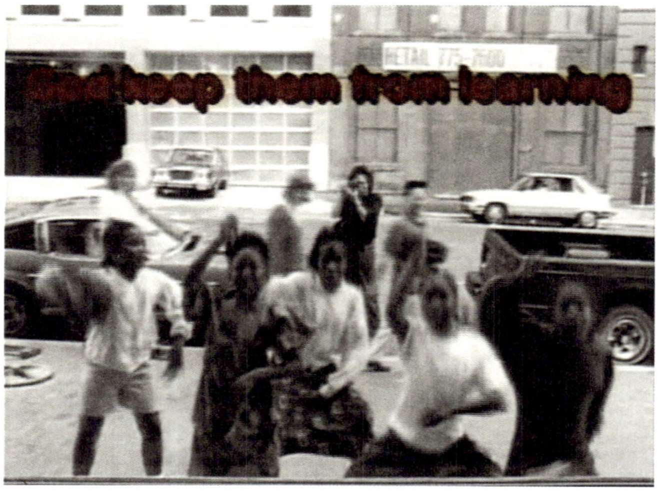

Fig. 3
Adrian Piper, *Please, God*, 1990.
Video, color, sound; 61 min.
Adrian Piper Research Archive
(APRA) Foundation Berlin.
© APRA Foundation Berlin

of song and dance practiced by Nigerian women to commemorate not only the milestones of life—death, marriage, birth—but also to mark the daily occasions of the market, the harvest, and religious celebration.[11] *Poor People's TV Room Solo* (2014), a performance that has become one of the artist's signatures, harnesses the central role of dance and song in the 1929 Women's War, a socioeconomic protest movement organized by women across six ethnic groups in southeastern Nigeria (Fig. 4).[12] Okpokwasili channels this history via her own mixture of song, dance, storytelling, and video. She performs on a small elevated platform shrouded in a milky, semi-opaque plastic that partially abstracts her body, with a projected backdrop of video images of dancing girls from the Ebo village where her family is from. The artist chants and sings while moving with increasing urgency to break free of the structure that confines her. Okpokwasili steadily shifts from a still, embryonic state to full frenzy, finally rupturing the walls of the encasement and becoming vividly, monumentally present, elevated above the audience. Crouching and swaying as though preparing to give birth, she is a cipher, a medium channeling the voices and spirits of Igbo women and girls and moving in and out of the audience's clear perception. The lyrics she sings offer oblique answers to the question of why the

women revolted in 1929, lifting phrases from the transcripts of the British colonial hearings around the incident. Okpokwasili performs actions that are both sexual and laborious—washing, scrubbing, beating, purging something from her body. *Poor People's TV Room Solo* can be performed live or experienced as an installation (as it will be shown in *Witch Hunt* after an initial performance). In both versions, her vocals linger. "Can't swear on no Bible, can't read your Bible," she sings as if to the authorities. "Look at this body, boy. . . . Have I swallowed enough, have I swallowed too much?"

■

Comedy does not exist independent of rage.
—José Esteban Muñoz[13]

As an emotional and psychological state, rage is less represented than inhabited, intimate in its proximity to the body and the histories it carries. In the case of Vaginal Davis, performance is something larger than what can be framed by a proscenium or stage. Davis's work involves the telling of tales scandalous to mainstream sensibilities through numerous invented personae that channel the roiling sentiments of a body

11 See Judith Lynne Hanna, "Dance and the 'Women's War,'" *Dance Research Journal* 14, nos. 1–2 (1981–82): 25. Okpokwasili did not knowingly draw on this tradition when she created *Poor People's TV Room Solo.*

12 See "Riot or Rebellion? The Women's Market Rebellion of 1929," American Historical Association website, https://www.historians.org/teaching-and-learning/teaching-resources-for-historians/ teaching-and-learning-in-the-digital-age/through-the-lens-of-history-biafra-nigeria-the-west-and-the-world/the-colonial-and -pre-colonial-eras-in-nigeria/ the-womens-market-rebellion-of-1929.

13 I return often to the writing of José Esteban Muñoz. See his "Jack's Plunger," preface to *Disidentification: Queers of Color and the Performance of Politics* (Minneapolis: University of Minnesota Press, 1999), xi.

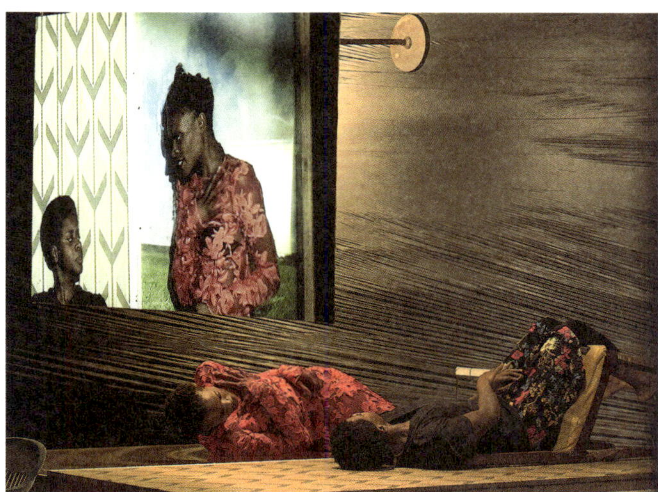

Fig. 4
Okwui Okpokwasili, *Poor People's TV Room*, 2016. Performance view, New York Live Arts, 2016. Courtesy of the artist. Photo: Paul B. Goode

beyond restriction and restraint. While Davis's recent art production includes charming, roughly drawn images of figures rendered on cardboard or paper out of makeup—the raw material of both performance onstage and the daily performance of femininity—Davis came of age as an artist in the Los Angeles punk rock scene of the late 1970s, performing with the band Afro Sisters and subsequent music acts. Creating zines such as *Fertile La Toyah Jackson* (early 1980s) and DIY videos such as *Dot* (1994), based on the life and acerbic writing of Dorothy Parker, Davis has crafted what the late queer theorist José Esteban Muñoz brilliantly called "terrorist drag."[14] Muñoz describes a mode of performance that he defines as disidentification, "a performative mode of tactical recognition that various minoritarian subjects employ in an effort to resist the oppressive and normalizing discourse of dominant ideology."[15] Davis takes her moniker and drag identity from Angela Davis, channeling the writer and activist's militant, far-left politics and invoking the era and ethos of Black Power, including her foremother's early life as a member of the Los Angeles chapter of the Black Panthers.

Davis bases her new audio work and installation for *Witch Hunt*, *Mary Mary* (2020), on her real-life mother, Mary Magdalene Duplantier, whose own mixture of fact and fabulation the artist renders with occasional larger-than-life detail. Duplantier was a Native/African American activist who moved to Los Angeles from Louisiana during the Great Migration. Her brief relationship with the artist's Mexican father resulted in the artist's conception. (Davis has explored the Chicana part of her heritage in various personae as well as the musical group ¡Cholita!, whose drag inspiration was the boy band Menudo.[16]) Duplantier hosted meetings at her home of a lesbian separatist group, and *Mary Mary* draws on a trove of her letters and ephemera—a lost history of lesbian activism found under her mother's bed that takes part in Davis's highly personalized invention of reality and biography. In the artist's words, "Mary Magdalene was a witch, born of an ancient coven. . . . She became radicalized in the 1960s through liberation theology and ties to a lesbian coven."[17] Mary also had ties to the Symbionese Liberation Army, which had a headquarters in the Pico Union district of Los Angeles where she and Davis lived. *Mary Mary* takes the form of a kind of audio portrait of the artist's mother, with Davis performing a soundtrack enhanced by relics and other objects, including an Eva Gabor–style wig, a branch of a healing plant from a yard in Los Angeles, a Creole amulet, Jean Naté perfume, and a Michelob, her mother's beer of choice. The performance, of

14 José Esteban Muñoz, "'The White to Be Angry': Vaginal Davis's Terrorist Drag," in "Queer Transexions of Race, Nation, and Gender," special issue, *Social Text*, nos. 52–53 (Autumn–Winter 1997): 80–103.

15 Ibid., 106.

16 Ibid., 105.

17 From a video trailer for *Mary Mary,* the audio work in progress for *Witch Hunt,* sent by the artist in April 2020.

which the audience only hears the audio recording, is funny, raunchy, honorific, and raw.

Davis's array of identities, the way she moves between ages, character types, and various relationships to passing, are all framed not only by the history of drag but by the history of Black stand-up comedy.[18] Sampling freely, Davis draws on this lineage which includes such predecessors as comedy pioneer Jackie "Moms" Mabley and Flip Wilson's drag character Geraldine Jones. Like Davis, these larger-than-life female personae used their exaggerated physicality to disarm audiences whose unconscious bias might mediate their experience of race or gender. The reconfiguration of gender identity via a comedic turn, moving from rage to the outrageous, has a long history within feminist practice as well: the play *Cock and Cunt* written by Judy Chicago and performed by Faith Wilding and others at Womanhouse in 1970, the current punk activist strategies of Pussy Riot, Kalup Linzy's soap-opera drag in the ongoing series *As Da Art World Might Turn* (2013–), and Mark Bradford's trans superhero character in his performance video *Superman* (2015). With no imagery other than analog-looking subtitles, the work is experienced in a gallery lit only by a spotlight and fogged by a smoke machine. Bradford's unhinged monologue in the persona of a trans woman takes down the

homophobic bent of Black comedians such as Eddie Murphy and Richard Pryor.[19]

Los Angeles–based artist Lara Schnitger also harnesses humor in her work, to temper and make more accessible the feminist agitprop of the textile-based sculptures that she has been making for more than two decades (Fig. 5). After moving from the Netherlands to Los Angeles in the early 1990s, Schnitger's initial works involved creating props, costumes, and scripts with the performance ensemble My Barbarian, whose members are Malik Gaines, Jade Gordon, and Alex Segade. "Schnitger's [work] is a sculptural enactment of the masquerade, a fluctuating position described by visual excess, detached from a biological determinant," Segade has written. "Schnitger makes costumes for a play with no actors but great parts."[20]

One of the most jarring and pleasurable aspects of Schnitger's art is her wrangling of appropriated text, presented with a bluntness that is humorous even as it packs a visual and conceptual punch. Her use of English is shaped by being a Dutch transplant to the United States, and in particular to the sunny sprawl of Los Angeles, where billboards shout corporate advertising across the city. Literally cutting and pasting, sewing and applying direct-address text to her "slut sticks" and banners, Schnitger uses slogans that are pithy

18 See Megan Sutherland, "Entertaining Identities, or the Politics of Variety Performance," in *The Flip Wilson Show* (Detroit: Wayne State University Press, 2008), 73.

19 In some ways, I was moved to write about rage in context of *Witch Hunt* after having reflected on Mark Bradford's exhibition *Scorched Earth*, which I curated at the Hammer Museum in 2015. Along with a number of paintings, the show included *Superman*.

20 Lara Schnitger, *Dance Witches Dance: Lara Schnitger and My Barbarian in Collaboration* (Sittard, Netherlands, Museum Het Domein, 2012).

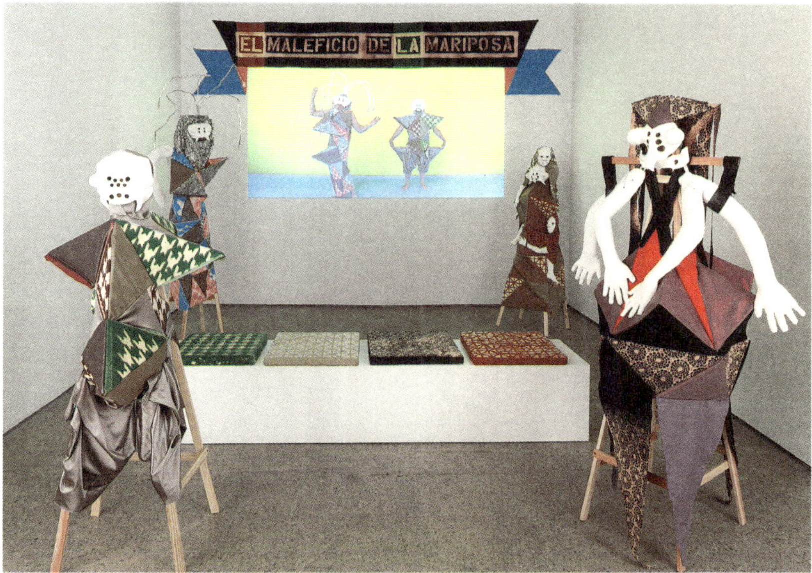

Fig. 5
Lara Schnitger, *The Butterfly's Evil Spell,* 2012. Installation view, Anton Kern Gallery, New York, 2012. Courtesy of the artist and Anton Kern Gallery, New York

and personal. Phrases like "Do Not Let the Boys Win," "No=No," "Proud Slut," "We Are Sexy," "Your Mom Is Nice Lady," and "Ride Your Bedroom," to sample a few, have a multigenerational resonance. Communicating a feminism that is both angry and broadly accessible, Schnitger's text is political but personal and user friendly. Inspired by the women's voting-rights movements of the early twentieth century, Schnitger's *Suffragette City* is a processional in which she and volunteers including children, students, and artist friends of all genders protest while carrying some of her declarative creations. First performed in Basel in 2015 in the effervescent context of an art fair, the performance was restaged at the Hammer Museum immediately following the 2016 election, and since then variously during the course of rolling #MeToo revelations. *Suffragette City* engages directly with politics while maintaining a comedic tone and a historical feminist inspiration.

Droll humor can also erupt into something like celebration, as in the work of Pauline Boudry / Renate Lorenz. In their video *Telepathic Improvisation* (2017), four people in uniformlike, red and white costumes engage with a tableau of moving sculptures and other items accompanied by a score based on an eponymous movement from Pauline Oliveros's 1974 *Sonic Meditations* (Fig. 6). Wall text at the entrance of

the viewing space entreats the viewer to telepathically communicate with those on-screen in an "experiment in inter-stellar telepathic transmissions," an instruction underscored in the video itself by performer MPA, who acts as a kind of interpretive emcee. This direct address activates Oliveros's intention that her score engage the viewer at a deep physiological level through deep listening and embodiment of sound. The absurdity of the scenario lightly mimics Oliveros's original composition, setting the stage for the actors' deadpan homage and the funny kinetic elements, which hum across the floor or rotate on their own like sentient beings.[21] Humans, nonhumans, movements, speeches, gestures, and music all consort on equal terms. A bright, flashing platform, each floor tile programmed and illuminated at intervals, suggests a dance floor and invites the audience to be titillated by its exuberant disco presence. The most animate object is a disc that glides occasionally around the space, bumping into walls and objects. This funny, minimalist puck haunts the video as it moves among the human participants with stealth and persistence. When installed in a gallery space, the video is sometimes accompanied by *HE EAR R* (2016), a rotating, spotlit platform with microphones that suggests the authority of the broadcast voice but that remains impotent, unactivated.

21 See the description of *Telepathic Improvisation* on the Boudry/Lorenz website, https://www. boudry-lorenz.de/telepathic-improvisation, and the text in the exhibition brochure *Pauline Boudry / Renate Lorenz: Ongoing Experiments with Strangeness*, Julia Stoschek Collection, Berlin, Germany, 2019, n.p.

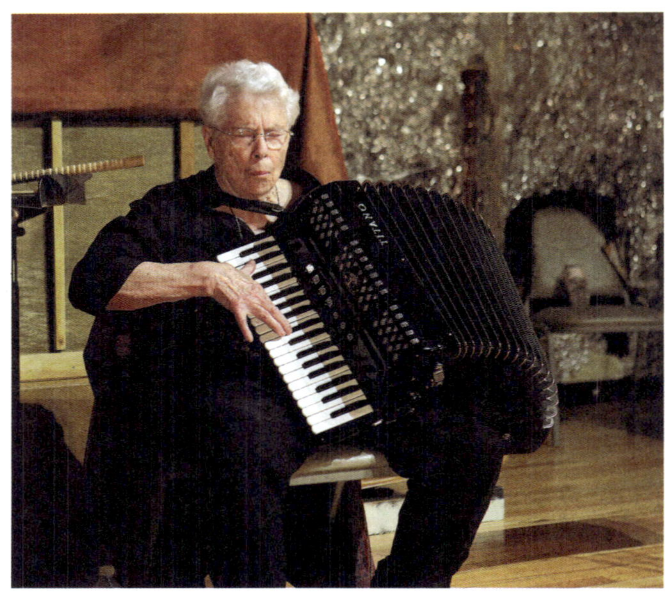

Fig. 6
Pauline Oliveros plays the accordion at Jack, New York, 1991. Courtesy Redux Pictures LLC. Photo: Hiroko Masuike/The New York Times/Redux

The performers in *Telepathic Improvisation*, Marwa Arsanios, MPA, Ginger Brooks Takahashi, and Werner Hirsch, display a range of affects and personal styles. Each is deployed in a way that highlights their body and personality. Hirsch, for example, a performer by training, is the most theatrical person onstage and the largest. A boxy white oxford and white shorts exaggerate the paleness of his skin as well as his ambiguous age and androgynous presentation. MPA, also a performance artist in her own practice, makes a riveting impression. *Telepathic Improvisation* is intended, according to the artists, to refer to current social conditions and their violent aspects; underscoring that theme, MPA recites excerpts from Ulrike Meinhof's 1968 essay "From Protest to Resistance," which opens with a paraphrase from Black Panther Fred Hampton: "Protest is when I say I don't like this. Resistance is when I see to it that the things that I don't like no longer occur."

■

Life in this society being, at best, an utter bore and no aspect of society being at all relevant to women, there remains to civic-minded, responsible, thrill-seeking females only to overthrow the government, eliminate the money system, institute complete automation and destroy the male sex.
—Valerie Solanas[22]

There is something elegiac in the way Boudry / Lorenz bring Oliveros's work into the contemporary moment, using Elizabeth Freeman's notion of "temporal drag" to "challenge notions of linear time by proposing queer, trans-chronic practices."[23] One example is the artists' relationship with the composer herself. Oliveros is something of an icon within queer and feminist art practice for her notions of making community through sound and deep listening, as well as for the all-woman performing group ♀ Ensemble she assembled around 1970. Oliveros inspired Boudry / Lorenz's *Telepathic Improvisation* and would have performed the score for it had she not died in 2016. The work expanded their exploration of Oliveros's output, which had begun a few years earlier when the duo took her

22 Valerie Solanas, *SCUM Manifesto* (London: Verso, 2004), 35.

23 *Ongoing Experiments with Strangeness*, n.p. See Elizabeth Freeman, *Time Binds: Queer Temporalities, Queer Histories*, (Durham, NC: Duke University Press, 2010).

composition *To Valerie Solanas and Marilyn Monroe in Recognition of Their Desperation* (1970) and rendered it as an installation and 16mm film of the same title. Solanas was the radical feminist author of the *SCUM Manifesto*, written in the same year, 1968, that she tried to assassinate Andy Warhol. The text is one of the late twentieth century's great rants, thrilling, poignant, and full of rage. Boudry / Lorenz's engagement with Solanas via Oliveros is yet another example of a networked history, the temporal drag sprung from a seed of rage against the repressions enacted by received narratives. Writing in 1979 about her *Telepathic Improvisation*, Oliveros said:

> In my mind the piece is directed to these women whose commonality was the desire to be heard and understood in terms of their inner needs as artists. The piece was not for their actions of desperation, suicide and attempted murder, but "in recognition of their desperation" in a society which was not listening to them, but forcefully imposing conceptions, which prevented their self-expression, finally leading to their anti-social acts.[24]

The desire to recuperate queer history martials resistance to the invisibility imposed by mainstream mechanisms of canonization; it also speaks to the power of history in forging community. The queering of time but also space practiced by Boudry / Lorenz is an approach they share with the many artists with whom they have collaborated, including Arsanios, Sharon Hayes, and Every Ocean Hughes. The *Witch Hunt* exhibition in fact sprang in part from an interest in how a generation of queer artists who came of age artistically in the early 2000s reinvested in the legacies of 1970s feminist practices, reinhabiting them to locate the lasting resistance and rage within them. The reactivation of such histories produces a community of the living, the dead, and those to come.

Bouchra Khalili and Leonor Antunes both focus on female artists and artisans whose stories have been deemphasized or lost over time. In her films, Khalili typically assumes the position of documentarian and witness, working to foreground the narratives of silenced voices and political minorities. Her focus in *Witch Hunt* is the Swiss documentary filmmaker and activist Carole Roussopoulos, one of the first women to own a video camera, who documented the Women's Liberation Movement in France (and who, as it happens, made a film about Solanas's *SCUM Manifesto* with her collaborator, the French

24 Pauline Oliveros, letter to Donal Henehan, December 12, 1979. Pauline Oliveros Collection. Excerpted in *WACK! Art and the Feminist Revolution*, ed. Lisa Gabrielle Mark (Cambridge, MA: MIT Press; Los Angeles: Museum of Contemporary Art, 2006), 275.

actress Delphine Seyrig, in 1976). Turning her position of relative privilege to one of activism, Roussopoulos used the new medium as a means of self-organizing and developing transnational alliances in order to give women and minorities, including migrant women, a voice. Khalili's interest in Roussopolos emerged from her work on Jean Genet, who suggested to the documentarian that she purchase her first Portapak video camera. This tool enabled her to make the film for which she is best known, *Genet parle d'Angela Davis* (1970). In 1975, Roussopolos formed an all-female video collective Les Insoumuses (Defiant Muses) with Seyrig and continued to use the lightweight, portable device to document the feminist political movement in France. Khalili is interested in the early history of video as a tool of activism and emancipatory women's politics.[25]

In sculptural installations and accumulations of reference-laden material, Antunes also mines the history of forgetting. The backbone of her practice is an archive of memory, a subjective and emotional relationship to artists, designers, and architects, often iconoclastic, secondary figures who lived in the shadows during their own lifetimes, even if as years have passed, they have been more recognized— women such as the artist Anni Albers, who helped found the Bauhaus; the radical Brazilian architect Lina Bo Bardi; and her contemporary Lygia Clark.

Borrowing vernacular traditions from her native Portugal as well as Mexico and South America, Antunes uses materials that reference the histories and practices of these artists and replicates or reanimates the crafts and processes they used. For *Witch Hunt*, she addresses the Pacific Rim diaspora by examining how spending the years 1940–46 in Japan impacted the work of Charlotte Perriand, the influential designer and architect. Perriand sought to integrate design and art objects into everyday life, particularly in ways that enhanced the lives of women and facilitated the kinds of labor they perform. Always interested in the parallel histories of women makers whose lives may or may not have intersected in real time, Antunes draws together Perriand's history with that of the little-known Japanese designer Michiko Yamawaki, who spent time at the Bauhaus while her husband, the photographer and architect Iwao Yamawaki, studied there. After returning to Japan, the couple taught at the New Architecture and Design College in Tokyo, disseminating the European modernism that evolved into a specifically Japanese version in the midcentury period. While little is known about Yamawaki's production, she did incorporate aspects of Bauhaus design into spaces and objects for the Japanese tea ceremony, a subject that Perriand took up in a design for a tea-ceremony space in 1939. Antunes

25 For more on Delphine Seyrig and her circle, see the exhibition *Defiant Muses: Delphine Seyrig and the Feminist Video Collectives in France in the 1970s and 1980s*, Museo Nacional Centro de Arte Reina Sofía, Madrid, 2019–20. The catalogue is available online at https://www.museoreinasofia.es/sites/default/files/publicaciones/catalogosPDF/musas_ingles-catalogo.pdf.

takes the titles for this group of works from a text Perriand wrote in 1936 titled "The Homemaker and Her Domain," which appeared in a weekly newspaper as an interview with a secretary about the pros and cons of modern furnishings and room arrangements, acknowledging both women's roles in defining traditional and popular taste and the realities of working-class budgets.[26]

The Brazilian artist Laura Lima also reflects on the gendered nature of specific kinds of labor and so-called women's work in her installation for *Witch Hunt*, titled *Tailor's Shop*. First realized at the Bonnefantenmuseum in the Netherlands in 2014, and subsequently at the Pinacoteca de São Paulo in 2018, the installation comprises a fully functioning tailoring workshop including all the necessary textiles, trimmings, equipment, and human labor. As realized in Los Angeles, the project specifically references the role of immigrant labor and the garment industry, an important part of the city's economy. Hired to work throughout the exhibition, the tailors produce a collection of garments that will function as portraits of subjects and subjectivities that Lima suggests and the tailors interpret. The results are then stretched on frames and mounted in the gallery, accumulating as the exhibition progresses. The activation of the space by the garment workers raises the complex issue of the relationship of their

labor to the viewers in the museum, what it means to stage such labor in the museum context, and what parallels might exist between the work of the tailors and the work of artists in art making.

In all of her work, Lima makes visible the nature and ethics of individual versus collective behavior; working in Rio de Janiero for many years, she operates in the historical context of Brazilian Neo-Concrete art and the radical social proposals of artists such as Lygia Clark. Lima is also the cofounder (along with Ernesto Neto and Márcio Botner) of A Gentil Carioca, an artist-run gallery and center for experimental art in Rio. In her trajectory, the artist's practice explicitly expands on an avant-garde in which some of the most radical artists were women whose own projects enlarged the possibilities for making art.

Beverly Semmes's Feminist Responsibility Project (FRP), which the artist began in 2003, takes a self-reflexive and retrospective look at feminism's complicated relationship to pornography. Extending the legacy of Martha Rosler's powerful protest collage series such as House Beautiful: Bringing the War Home (ca. 1967–72, Fig. 7), Semmes mines vintage *Penthouse* magazines, a collection of '90s porn she was given in 2002, and recuperates the recumbent, disempowered bodies and individuals that appear there. She draws and paints on centerfolds with

26 From an email correspondence with the artist, January 26, 2021.

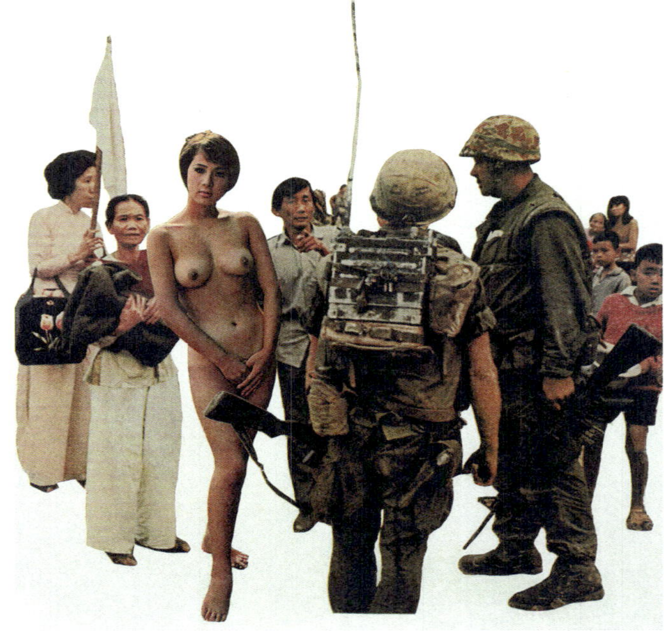

Fig. 7
Martha Rosler, *Playboy (On View)*, from the series House Beautiful: Bringing the War Home, ca. 1967–72. Photomontage. 19 11/16 × 19 7/8 in. (50 × 50.5 cm). © Martha Rosler. Courtesy of the artist and Mitchell-Innes & Nash, New York

broad gestures that add up to a kind of blanketing, leaving just enough of the body visible to both orient the viewer and upset the question of who has agency in these pictures. The result is a new menagerie of bodily fragments, colorful and ambivalently erotic. The altered magazine pages exist as works in their own right, but Semmes has also digitally enlarged the small works and used them as the basis for painted canvases. The artist, who has also made numerous oversize textile-based installations and sculptures (and has an ongoing fashion collaboration called CarWash Collective with designer Jennifer Minniti), is interested in the various ways these abstracted bodies can find new agency as monumentally scaled hybrids whose recombinant bodies seem to stare back at the viewer with resolute frontality, even as their actual gaze is often obscured. At a time when sexual display and body positivity is a sign of empowerment, particularly for younger women, Semmes mocks her own older-white-lady-feminist persona by embracing the prudish implications of her project of covering-up. Semmes is well aware of the ambiguities inherent in the impetus to "rescue" women involved in pornography, even as an array of pornographic images of women's bodies occupy a numbing amount of visual space in our public sphere. The artist attends to their vulnerability and also to the specificity of their identities. Like Rosler's Vietnam-era collages, the FRP includes women of color in ways that underscore the complexities of her subject and introduces class as part of an underlying critique of labor. Semmes harnesses her own empathic response to these women and their presumed powerlessness in an industry that exploits them through a posthuman reinvention for visual culture now.

The ceremonious absurdity of Semmes's project, the "fixing" of porn, possesses an element of camp and pseudo-grandiosity. Curator Ingrid Schaffner has written of the FRP, "It disrupts the normal flow of pornography by strategically amplifying the awkward and obvious construction of the pose, the gaze, the exploitation, and the bodies that make it work. And it calls to order Feminism, along with social issues and political responsibilities that, in so-called post-Feminist culture, we may not care to embrace."[27] The work becomes yet more freighted in the #MeToo era, when the revealing of personal stories, narratives of vulnerability and violence, takes on enormous potency and demands an almost impossible navigation. Semmes's puritanical gesture of covering becomes almost more prurient, even as bodies in the FRP are superseded by the erotics of touch and paint.

27 Ingrid Schaffner, "FRP: An Induction," *The Feminist Responsibility Project*, exh. cat. (Glassboro, NJ: Rowan University Art Gallery, 2011), 5, available at https://sites.rowan.edu/ artgallery/_docs/beverly-semmes _web-catalog_rowan-university. pdf. Elsewhere in this print-on-demand catalogue, Catherine Liu discusses the Super Puritan, the authorial character whom Semmes posits as behind the FRP. See her "Beverly Semmes: The Feminist Responsibility Project," 11.

■

The problem, simply stated, is that one must believe in the existence of the person in order to recognize the authenticity of her suffering. Neither men nor women believe in the existence of women as significant beings.
—Andrea Dworkin[28]

Yael Bartana's work *What if Women Ruled the World?* (2017) began with aspirational thinking. The artist's own description of the initial performance at the Volksbühne in Berlin, which now exists in video versions of its three live stagings, begins with a quote from the Bulletin of the Atomic Scientists: "It is two and a half minutes to midnight, the clock is ticking, global danger looms. Wise public officials should act immediately, guiding humanity away from the brink. If they do not, wise citizens must step forward and lead the way."[29] Bartana's work often reanimates historical memory; here she delves into masculinist tropes such as the war room and the negotiating table, and the gendered drive towards endless war. Staging an experimental politics by replicating the physical trappings of the governmental nerve center depicted in Stanley Kubrick's *Dr. Strangelove or: How I Learned to Stop Worrying and Love the Bomb* (1964), she populates the space with both actors

and an international group of experts, politicians, scientists, scholars, and peace activists, all women, who grapple with nuclear disarmament but inevitably veer into other issues of today including climate change and racial and economic inequity. Bartana replaces Kubrick's satiric irony with something much more affecting. As the women converse, soliloquize, and respond with genuine proposals to stop the doomsday clock, an unfamiliar combination of earnestness, deep wisdom, and hope emerges. Through the simple device of replacing white men with female protag-onists, Bartana suggests a completely different mode for governance.

With climate change now occupying the status of the most urgent issue of our time and our sense that time is running out, perhaps the most startling thing about *What if Women Ruled the World?* is the future it imagines. Only ten percent of United Nations member countries are led by women; the United States has never had a female leader. In the performance, Bartana creates a situation that is seldom if ever seen: women from diverse backgrounds sitting together in a room exchanging ideas and inventing solutions for war and the destruction of the planet. It less argues for a separatist utopia than suggests a better future that relies on inclusive models of power and governance. There are also moments of great humor and self-awareness in *What If Women*

28 Andrea Dworkin, "Right Wing Women" (1983), in *Last Days at Hot Slit: The Radical Feminism of Andrea Dworkin*, ed. Johanna Fateman and Amy Scholder (South Pasadena, CA: Semiotext(e), 2019), 179.

29 Quoted in *"What if Women Ruled the World?, 2017,"* Yael Bartana's website, http://yaelbartana.com/project/what-if-women-ruled-the-world-2017#info.

Ruled the World? When a shirtless male waiter enters the war room, for example, he is treated with the same dismissal that might have greeted a female attendant in the conventional all-male boardroom. His appearance leads to a rousing discussion and is a reminder that one must not simply reinscribe existing forms of oppressive power relations. Such moments underscore Bartana's argument in favor of new models of authority: "it's a kind of outcry . . . about how we have to find an alternative to a world dominated by men."[30]

Similarly conjuring an alternate reality as a theoretical and political call to arms, the artist Every Ocean Hughes (formerly Emily Roysdon) began in 2009 to articulate something she called Ecstatic Resistance. In many ways, my thinking for *Witch Hunt* began with this concept, which I encountered via EOH's manifesto on the subject and the experience of the artworks it generated when I saw her solo exhibition at New York's Art in General in 2011. In a text titled "From 'Social Movement' to 'Ecstatic Resistance,'" EOH spells out the terms of the approach, which she derived from examining her own work and that of her peers. "The ecstatic is: taking a leap, doing something beyond logic and reason, form that exceeds itself, becoming an other to yourself," she writes. Working toward Ecstatic Resistance encompasses a few goals:

The first is to develop a position of the impossible and to think about all that is unthinkable/unspeakable. The realm of the impossible is political, never naïve, and always shifting. Asking what is "impossible" about the boundaries of humanness, intelligibility and power. . . . Second, I want to explore the possibility of creating, of a new imaginary, through projects that deconstruct historical categories and history itself, through projects that build new systems, structures, perspectives from the ruins. . . . Last, I want to think about the sets of strategies that create ecstatic resistance— excessive, humorous, loving, confrontation, sublime, grotesque, obsessive.[31]

EOH's ideas emerged out of queer and feminist political and aesthetic engagement with what is literally unthinkable and unspeakable within the current white masculinist order. She and her peers, notably those with whom she formed the feminist, genderqueer collective LTTR (along with artists K8 Hardy and Ginger Brooks Takahashi), are important members of the generation who reimagined second-wave feminism through strategies that were both inclusive and separatist.

30 Elodie Evers, "Interview with Yael Bartana on 'What if Women Ruled the World?'" Volksbühne Berlin, 2017, https://www. volksbuehne.berlin/en/news/ 4319/interview-with-yael- bartana-on-what-if-women- ruled-the-world.

31 Every Ocean Hughes [as Emily Roysdon], "From 'Social Movement' to 'Ecstatic Resistance,'" *Public*, no. 39 (2009), 111.

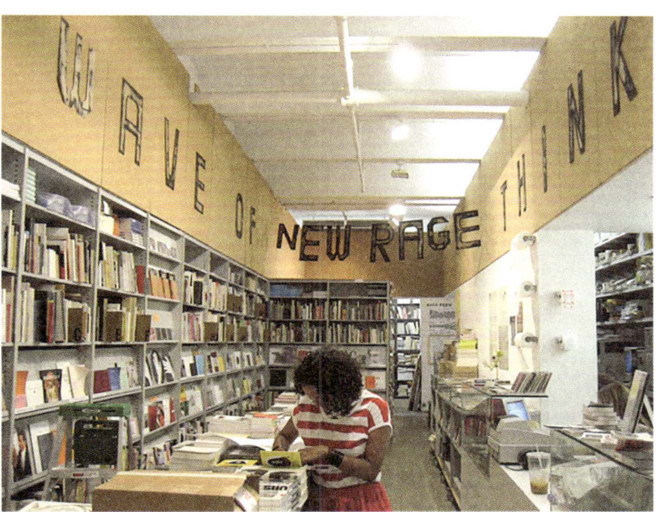

Fig. 8
LTTR, Radical Read In: A Wave of New Rage Thinking, 2005. Residency at Printed Matter, New York. Photo: Every Ocean Hughes

In 2005, LTTR staged an event titled Radical Read In: A Wave of New Rage Thinking at Printed Matter in New York (Fig. 8).[32] Based on the tradition of activist teach-ins, workshop participants gathered to promote reading as a radical act. Participants bookmarked significant passages in the volumes on the shelves at Printed Matter as a way of inspiring conversations both during the program and afterward. Participants were also invited to bring a text that had changed their lives and to share it. This way of generating conversation, of reading together in public, was also a way to preserve and activate histories—of artists, identities, and underknown artistic practices—that were under threat of disappearance. Thinking through rage, and conceptualizing it as a positive, constructive force, is an ethos that only a generation emerging in the aftermath of 1990s multiculturalism and the undoing of canonical thinking could generate. Riffing on forms such as the consciousness-raising groups of second-wave feminism, LTTR was an organized but open community of women-identified, queer, explicitly feminist artists inspired by the past but imagining something else: a new way of thinking about aesthetic production, a new configuration of the body beyond language, a new way of being.

When Nigerian-born artist Otobong Nkanga speaks about finding new ways of being human, she proposes a choir of positives. In her work is the making of a movement setting its sights on nothing less than addressing the planet itself. She expresses a clear and unapologetic sense of an essential connection to nature, and of reconnecting the land to notions of the feminine. Nkanga's non-Western feminism addresses the colonialist and hegemonic violence that inflicts itself on the land, literally pillaging the deserts and mountains of Africa, her home continent. She responds with a vision of a future where respect for the earth is paramount and nonnegotiable. She conducts her business of healing through visually engaging, sensual objects including minerals, weavings, carpets populated with sensuous, crystalline objects, and drawings that elaborate the quasi-narrative iconography of her ongoing investigations. Her performances are emotional and often funny, usually featuring Nkanga as the solo or lead voice. In a performance and video titled *Remains of the Green Hill* (2015), she stands barefoot at the edge of a mining sinkhole in Tsumeb, Namibia, arms outstretched and balancing on one leg with rocks balanced on her head. Singing and speaking to the land, she meets the land, as she says, searching for the provenance of her materials.[33] Moved by the violence done to the environment by industries such as the rampant mining in Nigeria and throughout Africa,

32 The archive of LTTR's activities is maintained online, and Hughes has coordinated several archival exhibitions of the group's history. For the Radical Read In, see https://www.lttr.org/events/radical-read-in-a-wave-of-new-rage-thinking-residency-at-printed-matter.

33 See "Otobong Nkanga in conversation with Clare Molloy at Kadist Paris," 2015, https://vimeo.com/144554605.

Nkanga responds with immediate action and direct address. Her works in *Witch Hunt* come from a number of key recent projects on the politics of the landscape proposing, in her words, "multiple ways of understanding how we can be here together."[34]

The Afrofuturist vision of science fiction writer Octavia Butler conjures the arid landscape of California's desert interior in novels like *Parable of the Sower* (1993). Strong female characters time travel or possess superpowers, such as an excess of empathy, that enable them to navigate a world altered by climate change and income inequality. What Butler imagines is nothing less than survival on a new planet, engineered and powered by the diasporic recolonization of women-centered narratives. Nkanga's Afrofuturist worlds, the multipart installations in which she creates an emotional and political space with objects and images activated by her very powerful presence, are rooted in a notion of deep empathy with the land. The human head, the artist believes, carries too much information; hence the absence of heads on figures in her drawings and sumptuous tapestries. Instead, it is through the body that we enter the constellations of minerals and residue of the earth as well as the geological conditions that her work represents in archival photographs and video. Nkanga takes up the urgent, manmade disasters that are shaping the planet,

such as mining, which forms the subject of her tapestry *Infinite Yield* (2015). She questions the acceleration of this mutilation in places that have been colonized, calling out how it deranges the fundamental structure of a place. In another body of work, titled *In Pursuit of Bling* (2014), Nkanga directly cites different landscapes in crisis, admonishing humanity for its dependency and addiction to catastrophic habits. Histories of the earth can only be transformed if, she says, we become a group singing with different voices.[35]

This voice, a voice of rage and joy, urges us to connect to the land and attend to the consequences of human action. The artist is a time traveler, a contemporary goddess sent to reconnect with a radical embodied empathy.

34 Tate, "Artist Otobong Nkanga—'Imagining the Scars of a Landscape, Tate,'" video for *From Where I Stand* exhibition, Tate St Ives, United Kingdom, 2019–20, https://www.youtube.com/watch?v=qZZruEToDCl.

35 Conversation with the author, January 2020.

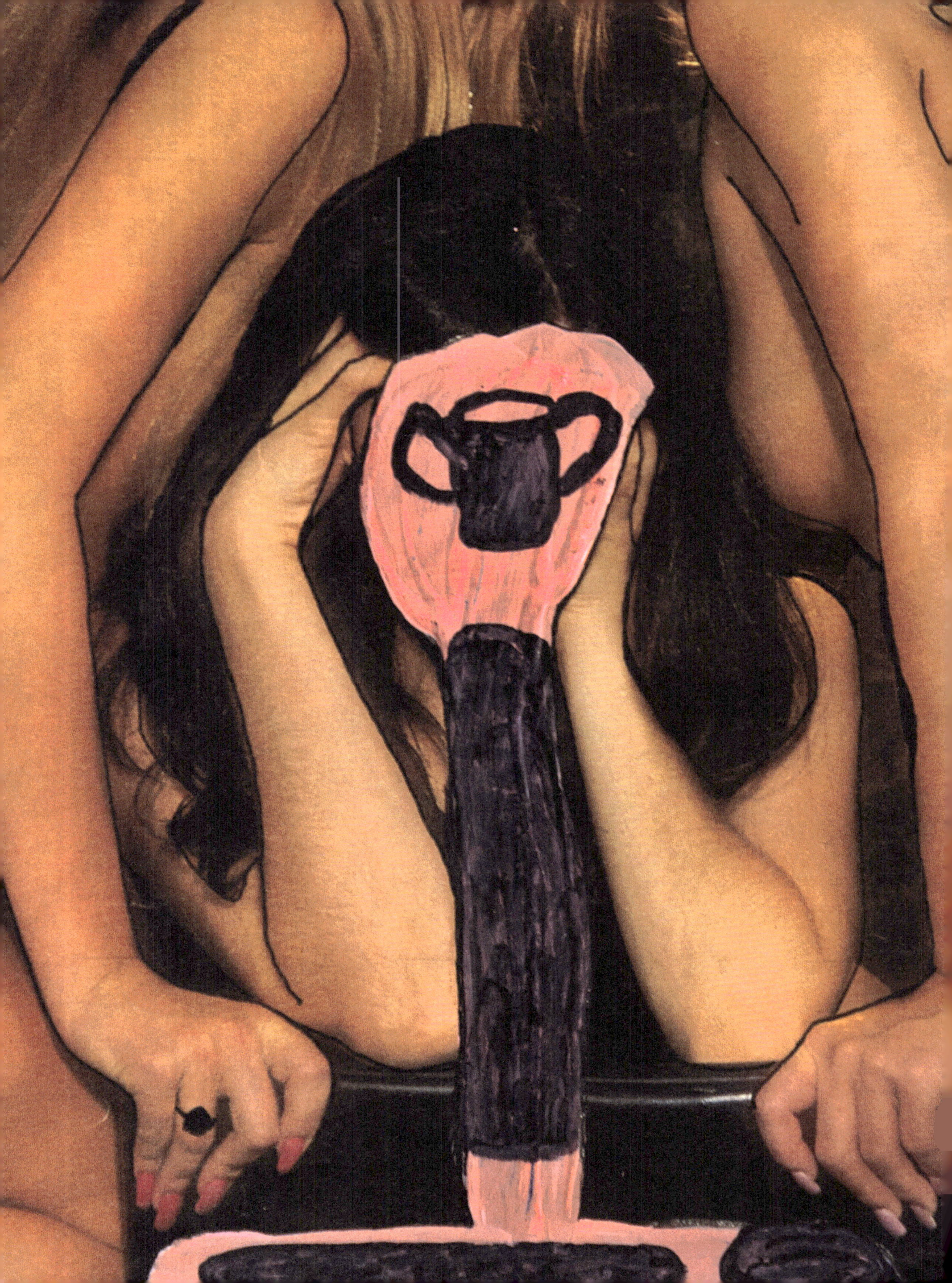

Visibility and Vulnerability

Anne Ellegood

> Sexism wears a lab coat; misogyny goes on witch hunts. . . .
> Sexism has a theory; misogyny wields a cudgel.
> —Kate Manne, *Down Girl: The Logic of Misogyny*

> We are working in a context of oppression and threat, the cause
> of which is . . . virulent hatred leveled against all women, people
> of Color, lesbians and gay men, poor people—against all of us
> who are seeking to examine the particulars of our lives as we
> resist oppressions, moving toward coalition and effective action.
> —Audre Lorde, *The Uses of Anger: Women Responding to Racism*

Since Donald Trump was elected president in 2016, he has tweeted the phrase "witch hunt" more than three hundred fifty times.[1] While his apparent lack of awareness of the facts of real, historical witch hunts—in which women, mostly, are accused of bringing harm to their communities and cast out or even killed—is in and of itself offensive, his incessant allegations that he is the one being wronged are even more so. It doesn't take a seasoned political strategist to understand that his behavior is a cynical effort to reverse the gender dynamics of these histories and position himself as a victim (Fig. 1). Trump's steady stream of claims that he is being unfairly persecuted relies on a contemporary vernacular use of "witch hunt," which generalizes any perceived injustice or slight as a concerted attack on an unwitting innocent. The irony is likely beyond Trump's comprehension: he invokes egregious incidents of "unhinged"

(one of his favorite terms) mob-mentality misogyny to attach a meme-ready tagline to his personal grievance at having to answer for his unethical, if not illegal, actions in a democratic system that relies on checks and balances to curtail abuses of office. Trump cries "Witch hunt!" not just as a means to sway public opinion but, more frighteningly, as a justification for his own obstruction of justice, to encourage others to also delay or reject conventional protocols of congressional processes, and as a tactic to attempt to derail any and all investigations into his administration.

While Trump started tweeting about witch hunts when concerns over Russian interference into the United States 2016 elections surfaced, the official announcement of an impeachment inquiry by the House of Representatives on October 31, 2019, provoked him to declare that effort "The Greatest Witch Hunt in American History" on Twitter.[2] Trump

1 As of March 8, 2020. See the Trump Twitter Archive, http://www.trumptwitterarchive.com/archive/Witch%20Hunt. This essay was written in late 2019 and 2020 when Trump was still in office.

2 For further discussion of Trump's use of the term, see Alice Markham-Cantor, "What Trump Really Means When He Cries 'Witch Hunt,'" *The Nation*, October 28, 2019, https://www.thenation.com/article/archive/trump-witch-hunt/.

Beverly Semmes
Handle, 2015 (detail)

is not the first politician or public figure to resort to this rhetoric. The headline of an article by Bob Woodward and Carl Bernstein on July 22, 1973, in the *Washington Post* read, "Nixon Sees 'Witch-Hunt,' Insiders Say," more than a year before Richard Nixon resigned from office during the Watergate investigations when an impeachment hearing was imminent (Fig. 2). But Trump might be the most vociferous user of such language. And the paradox that he relies on claims of a witch hunt to call his base to action when his behavior is under scrutiny is not lost on feminists around the world, who continue to hope that one day he may face repercussions for his bald-faced sexism, transgressions against women, and race baiting. As the writer Alice Markham-Cantor has summarized, "When Trump cries witch hunt, it is a rallying cry. It is not designed to prove his innocence but to whip his listeners into a frenzy, to turn their ire upon those who were so bold as to think they could hold him accountable. Donald Trump, like witch hunters throughout history, has proved skillful at flipping the narrative, writing himself as the victim even when he is the aggressor. When Trump cries witch hunt, it is to summon the hunters."[3]

Most Americans are aware of the witchcraft trials in colonial Salem, Massachusetts, in which more than two hundred people were accused of being witches during the Puritan religious reform movement of the late seventeenth century. Nineteen were found guilty and hanged while another five died in jail, making it the deadliest such outbreak in the country's history. While the Salem episode may seem like a historical anomaly driven by the hysteria and irrationality of a bygone era, witch hunts continue today. Women accused of being "sperm bandits"—of allegedly kidnapping and raping men in order to take their semen to sell on the black market for ritual purposes—are being sent to jail in Zimbabwe and South Africa. Feminist scholar and historian Silvia Federici has argued that the rise of witch hunts correlates with disruptions to capitalism's reliance on free domestic labor provided by women in societies with rigid gender roles. The women accused of being witches in early modern Europe, Federici notes, often had a role in keeping reproductive choices in the hands of women: midwives, abortion providers, and herbalists who could provide contraception.[4] Federici claims a parallel process is happening in contemporary Africa as capitalism expands, compounded by the rise of fundamentalist Christianity, which results in more women being accosted, and even murdered, for being witches.[5]

From all these various accounts and diverse circumstances, it is clear that misogyny rears its ugly head when women—including, importantly, trans

---

3 Ibid.

4 See Silvia Federici, *Caliban and the Witch: Women, the Body and Primitive Accumulation* (Brooklyn: Autonomedia, 2004).

5 See Sady Doyle, "How Capitalism Turned Women Into Witches," *In These Times*, January 31, 2019, https://inthesetimes.com/article/21592/capitalism-witches-women-witch-hunting-sylvia-federici-caliban.

6 Thomas Erdbrink, "Iran's Shaming of Young Dancer Draws Backlash," *New York Times*, July 9, 2018, https://www.nytimes.com/2018/07/09/world/middleeast/irans-instagram-dancer-teen.html

7 Paul B. Preciado, "Dissident Interfaces: Shu Lea Cheang's 3×3×6 and the Digital Avant-Garde," in 3×3×6, exh. cat., Taiwan Pavilion, Venice Biennale 2019 (Taipei: Taipei Fine Arts Museum, 2019), 83.

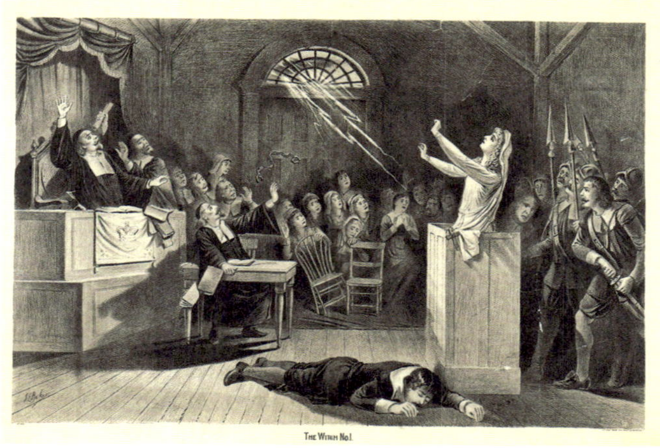

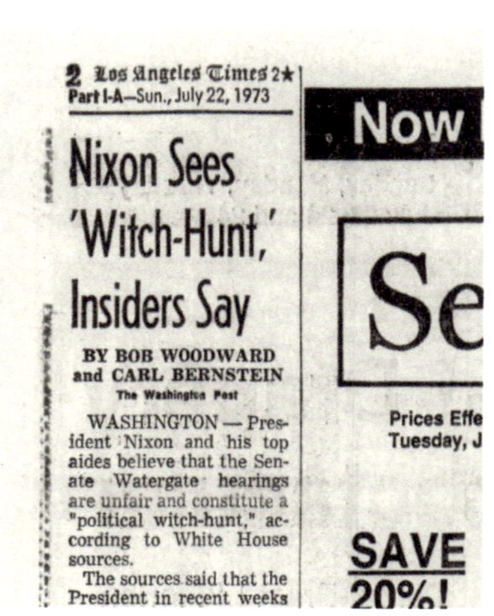

2 Los Angeles Times 2★
Part I-A—Sun., July 22, 1973

Nixon Sees 'Witch-Hunt,' Insiders Say

BY BOB WOODWARD
and CARL BERNSTEIN
The Washington Post

WASHINGTON — President Nixon and his top aides believe that the Senate Watergate hearings are unfair and constitute a "political witch-hunt," according to White House sources.

The sources said that the President in recent weeks

Now
Se
Prices Effe
Tuesday, J
SAVE
20%!

Fig. 1
Joseph E. Baker, *The Witch no. 1,* ca. 1892. Lithograph. 28 ⅛ × 41 ½ in. (71.4 × 105.4 cm)

Fig. 2
Bob Woodward and Carl Bernstein, "Nixon Sees 'Witch-Hunt,' Insiders Say," *Los Angeles Times*, July 22, 1973

women and anyone who presents as feminine—step outside the boundaries of their socially prescribed roles. Women are seen as threats especially when they reject limitations based on gender and attempt to expand into arenas conventionally considered men's domains, prompting fears that women are infringing on the special access to power and privileges men have for so long enjoyed. Witch hunts are just one form that such targeted attacks have taken under centuries of patriarchy, with manifestations ranging from the pernicious and subtle to the brazenly violent. In our technologized age, persecutions of course extend to life online. Writing about Shu Lea Cheang's video installation 3×3×6 (2019, Fig. 3), curator Paul Preciado discusses the witch hunts occurring today in which women's use of social media is monitored and deployed as evidence against them. An eighteen-year-old woman in Iran, Maedeh Hojabri, for example, was arrested for "indecent" dancing after she recorded herself moving to pop music in her bedroom without a hijab and posted it to Instagram.[6] Describing digital platforms as the new frontier of witch hunts, Preciado writes:

> This hunt is happening mostly, and above all, within the digital space of the Internet and on apps such as Instagram, Twitter,

and Facebook, where images and discourses are created and new forms of value produced. Against the image of the Internet as a free, genderless space, such accusations against women define the emergence of a new form of techno-patriarchy regulated by a digital authoritarianism, where women's bodies and actions are harshly surveilled.[7]

The National Center for Education Statistics reported an increase in cyberbullying in 2019, with three times as many girls as boys reporting being bullied.[8] Women and people of color experience acute online harassment, especially when they speak out against sexism, racism, or injustice of any kind.[9] Although officially banned on Reddit and Twitter and now outlawed in several states, the nonconsensual posting of intimate photographs, often called "revenge porn," remains a problem with real-life impacts. In October 2019, Democratic Congresswoman Katie Hill resigned after a conservative media outlet, Red State, reported that she had had a (consensual) sexual relationship with a campaign staffer. To accompany the story, the website published nude photos of her, likely provided by her estranged husband whom she was in the process of divorcing. In her final speech to Congress, Hill took

---

8 Associated Press, "Cyberbullying Is on the Rise, and Girls Report Three Times More Harassment than Boys," *USA Today*, July 26, 2019, https://www.usatoday.com/story/tech/2019/07/26/harassment-social-media-cyberbullying-reports-rise-among-girls/1835431001/.

9 To cite only a couple of prominent examples, actor Leslie Jones temporarily left Twitter after an onslaught of racist, sexist slurs were hurled at her following the 2016 release of an all-female version of the film *Ghostbusters*; as part of the Gamergate episode in 2014 attacking women in the gaming industry, media critic Anita Sarkeesian was inundated daily with violent threats—called a bitch and a whore, threated with rape and even murder. Sarkeesian described it as a "sustained intimidation campaign" that highlighted the acute sexism she had called out in the industry. See Sarkeesian, "One Week of Harrassment on Twitter," Tumblr, January 20, 2015, https://femfreq.tumblr.com/post/109319269825/one-week-of-harassment-on-twitter.

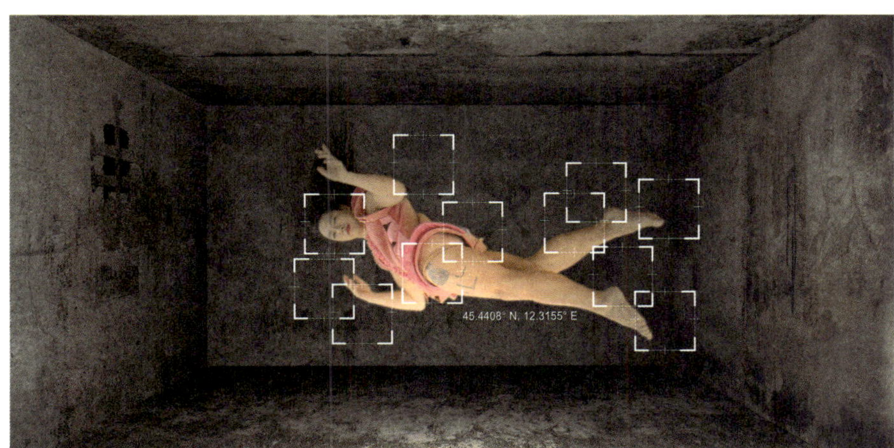

Fig. 3
Shu Lea Cheang, *CASANOVA X*, 2019. 4K video, color, sound; 10 min. From 3×3×6, 2019. Courtesy of the artist

aim at the double standards women are forced to endure: "I am leaving because of a misogynistic culture that gleefully consumed my naked pictures, capitalized on my sexuality and enabled my abusive ex to continue that abuse, this time with the entire country watching."[10] As Jessica Bennett pointed out in the *New York Times*, while Hill resigned from her position ten days into the controversy, Trump remains president despite dozens of credible allegations of sexual misconduct against him.[11]

It is no coincidence that the rise of Trump—memorably described as our "misogynist in chief" by Congresswoman Kim Schrier[12]—has occasioned numerous media stories attempting to define just exactly what misogyny is. The results are mixed, at times within the same piece. In the *New York Times*, Nina Renata Aron pegged an article on the topic with the statement "Misogyny is having a moment," the tone of which, like the rest of her introduction, seemed to dismiss the current public discourse about misogyny as somehow trendy—even as the essay acknowledges that, indeed, misogyny has been woven into the fabric of patriarchal societies for centuries.[13] Despite example upon example of the ways in which misogyny serves as a socially sanctioned tool for keeping women in their place, a major misconception about it persists: that it resides simply in the minds of particular men.

Rather than acknowledging misogyny as a *systemic* problem rooted in patriarchy, it is most commonly discussed and evaluated as a state of mind, located in the psychology of specific individuals. Men who perpetuate misogynistic acts—sexual harassers and assaulters like Harvey Weinstein and Matt Lauer, or mass murderers like Elliot Rodger, who posted a video raging against "spoiled, stuck-up blonde slut" sorority women before his rampage[14]—are often described as having never learned to respect women or as having an irrational vendetta against a particular woman or type of women. Misogyny quickly becomes about the misogyn*ist*, making it a defect of one man here and another there rather than a social problem. In a maneuver that recalls the argument propagated by gun lobbyists that the mass shootings that now take place almost weekly in the United States are the perverse and hateful acts of the mentally ill, situating misogyny solely within the individual has become a convenient way to sidestep real action toward ameliorating gender inequities throughout society.

Of course, the argument that the hatred of women at the heart of misogyny is structural has been made by feminists for decades, from Andrea Dworkin and Audre Lorde to more recent writers such as Roxane Gay and Rebecca Traister. Yet we are still inundated with excuses for a host of maladies:

10 Sarah D. Wire, "Katie Hill: 'I Am Leaving Because of a Misogynistic Culture That Gleefully Consumed My Naked Pictures,'" *Los Angeles Times*, October 31, 2019, https://www.latimes.com/politics/story/2019-10-31/katie-hills-gives-her-final-floor-speech.

11 Jessica Bennett, "The Complicated Case of Katie Hill," *New York Times*, November 1, 2019, https://www.nytimes.com/2019/11/01/us/katie-hill-photos-relationship.html.

12 Dr. Kim Schrier (@DrKimSchrier), "Inspiring and exciting to see women stepping up and WINNING all across the country. It turns out that when you elect a misogynist in chief who grabs women's bodies, women will grab right back!," Twitter, May 28, 2018, 2:39 pm, https://twitter.com/DrKimSchrier/status/1001171140482555904.

13 Nina Renata Aron, "What Does Misogyny Look Like?" *New York Times*, March 8, 2018, https://www.nytimes.com/2019/03/08/style/misogyny-women-history-photographs.html.

incessant violence against women and transgender people; perpetually unequal pay based on gender; the inability of women to ascend to the highest positions of power in our society (as I write this, all the female candidates for the Democratic nomination to the 2020 presidential ticket are out, and two white, heterosexual, cisgender, elderly men remain in the primary race); and contempt for any woman or gender-nonconforming person who tries to realize their full potential. We are consistently encouraged to believe that endemic, corrosive behaviors are merely the acts of individual perpetrators—an angry husband, a bad boss, an immature frat boy, or a power-drunk politician; ignorant chauvinists who maintain "old-fashioned" ideas about the natural differences between the sexes; "boys will be boys" innocents shaped by their environment; or, in the worst cases, pathological predators.

As philosopher Kate Manne argues, this enduring explication—what she refers to as a "naïve definition"—not only misdefines misogyny but empowers it to remain intact by distracting from the actual issues at hand. "Misogyny, though often personal in tone, is most productively understood as a political phenomenon," she writes. "Misogyny ought to be understood as the system that operates within a patriarchal social order to police and enforce women's subordination and to uphold male dominance."[15] The alleged current popularity of the term *misogyny* makes it "less harsh to hear," according to Aron, the argument being that its common use somehow dissipates the strength of its claim. Yet Aron recognizes the urgency of leveling it as an accusation, too: "It captures the cognitive dissonance of our moment, in which women are seemingly reviled and revered, running for president and still fighting for paid maternity leave."[16] Thus, the fact that the rhetoric relating to individual stories of bad behavior has, to some extent, distracted from more substantive debates and calls to action does not by any means imply that perpetrators of loathsome acts against women should *not* be called out. The #MeToo movement has brought a wellspring of attention to the widespread sexual harassment (and much worse) intrinsic to many workplaces, from the United States Senate to Hollywood, and is responsible for many men losing their positions and status. This necessary culling of in some cases very high-powered sexists who had been sheltered from retribution has not only served to rid these work environments of these predators, it has also opened up space for women to be promoted and given more power and oversight.[17] Admittedly, much work remains to be done, but these are at least some small victories.

14 "Transcription: Video Details Plan for 'Retribution,'" NBC 4 Los Angeles website, May 24, 2014, https://www.nbclosangeles.com/news/california-news/isla-vista-uc-santa-barbara-shooting-rampage-gunman-video-elliot-rodger-transcription/70292/.

15 Kate Manne, *Down Girl: The Logic of Misogyny* (Oxford: Oxford University Press, 2018), 33.

16 Aron, "What Does Misogyny Look Like?"

17 Audrey Carlsen et al., "#MeToo Brought Down 201 Powerful Men. Nearly Half of Their Replacements Are Women." *New York Times*, October 29, 2018, https://www.nytimes.com/interactive/2018/10/23/us/metoo-replacements.html.

Just as Kate Manne argues that we must stop focusing on the acts of individual men when articulating the contours of the immense societal hatred toward women, the artists in *Witch Hunt* choose to represent the experiences of those who are disempowered and suppressed by structural misogyny. Misogyny is, as Manne notes, a political phenomenon, and its political reality serves as the foundation for their work, no matter the subject, medium, or methodology. The female, trans, and genderqueer artists in *Witch Hunt* address systemic, institutional forms of misogyny to reflect on the nuanced ways in which it functions as a tool of the patriarchal order, extending a genealogy that includes such trailblazers as Lorraine O'Grady (Fig. 4), Mary Kelly, Adrian Piper, and Martha Rosler. Together, the work of the artists in *Witch Hunt* might be considered a collective action to bring greater visibility to the damage misogyny inflicts on women and transgender people from the perspective of its victims rather than its culprits.

Visibility, then, is critically important in a great deal of feminist art making. This emphasis is not new, however. The politics of representation were a driving force behind feminist practices that first emerged in the 1970s, just as they were in the works of artists of color and others who had historically been marginalized within both mainstream culture and the art world. In the decades since, artists have worked to remedy the misrepresentations and stereotypes that continue to dominate so many cultural outlets, or their own invisibility within them, working to address what Rosler called the "impoverishment of representational strategies" (Fig. 5).[18] As critic Craig Owens articulated in the 1980s, investigations into who has been allowed to be represented are undertaken "in order to expose that system of power that authorizes certain representations while blocking, prohibiting or invalidating others."[19] Even as much feminist work insists on visibility for the marginalized and oppressed, acknowledging the dignity of each human being, it also encounters a paradox. Providing platforms for those who have been othered and encouraging debate about corrupt and damaging social systems may increase visibility, but those steps also often highlight the vulnerabilities of the subjects presented, reducing them to victims in ways that can minimize the fullness of their identities.

The portraits that make up Teresa Margolles's series Pistas de baile (Dance floors, 2016) are poignant reminders of how art can shed light on structural violence while also capturing the transformational sense of autonomy that can attend the act of

<hr>

18 Martha Rosler, "In, Around, and Afterthoughts (On Documentary Photography)," in *Decoys and Disruptions: Selected Writings, 1975–2001* (Cambridge, MA: MIT Press; New York: International Center of Photography, 2004), 191. In this section of her lengthy analysis of documentary photography, Rosler discusses her influential work *The Bowery in two inadequate descriptive systems* (1974–75).

19 Craig Owens, "The Discourse of Others: Feminists and Postmodernism," in *Beyond Recognition: Representation, Power, Culture* (Berkeley: University of California Press, 1994), 168.

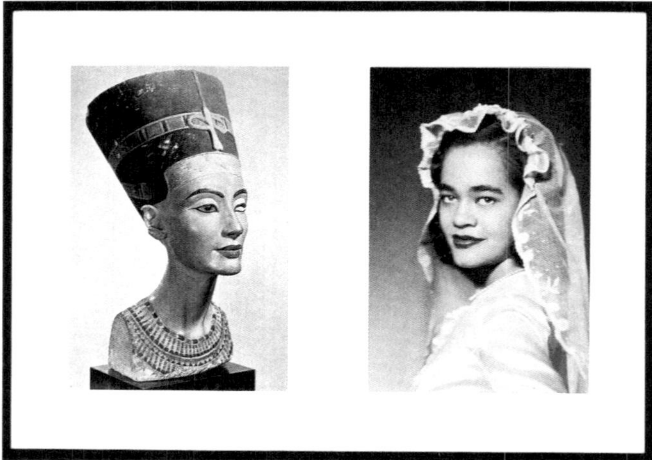

Fig. 4
Lorraine O'Grady, *Miscegenated Family Album (Sisters I), L: Nefernefruaten Nefertiti; R: Devonia Evangeline O'Grady*, 1980/1994. Cibachrome print. 26 × 37 in. (66 × 94 cm). Courtesy of the artist and Alexander Gray Associates, New York. © Lorraine O'Grady/Artists Rights Society (ARS), New York

being a willing subject in front of the camera (Fig. 6). Margolles's photographs feature transgender sex workers in Ciudad Juárez—a city on the border between Mexico and the United States where the disappearances and murders of women and transgender people are pervasive—posing alone on the dance floors of the demolished nightclubs where they formerly worked. They stand tall and proud, many with their hands defiantly on their hips, among the ruins of city blocks razed by officials intent on gentrifying the city center and removing not just buildings but also human beings whom they considered blights on the urban landscape. Margolles provides an opportunity for her subjects to present themselves however they like, and in so doing, there is much beauty in the images. Nonetheless, the works also bring to the viewer's attention the pronounced vulnerability these trans sex workers face, a kind of double-edged sword of discrimination, as trans women in a misogynistic society where violence against women is a real danger and as sex workers who are socially devalued and uprooted from their ability to make a living. As in much of Margolles's practice, the artist embedded herself in the work's context, moving to Juárez from Mexico City to work closely with her subjects in order to understand their daily experiences and build relationships with them. The

revelations that accompany increased visibility, such as the daily hardships faced by these sex workers, can be both emotionally devastating and empowering to subject, artist, and observer, revealing truths so hard-hitting it seems implausible they could have ever been kept underground.

Visibility can also exceed documentarian-style verisimilitude and move into the realm of fantasy, role playing, and futuristic imaginings. Cheang's *3×3×6*, which premiered at the 2019 Venice Biennale, was described by the artist as a work of "trans punk fiction, queer, and anti-colonial imaginations hacking the operating system of the history of sexual subjection." The multichannel video installation presents historical and contemporary figures victimized by prejudices surrounding gender and sexuality, showing facets of their experiences of imprisonment and repression alongside scenes of ecstatic realization in which they are allowed to be their true selves. *3×3×6* recalls sexual persecution throughout history, starting with Giacomo Casanova, who was imprisoned in Venice for disrespecting common decency and religious doctrines in the eighteenth century, to a 2018 case in which a Muslim woman was held in solitary confinement in a French prison for ten months after being accused of sexual assault and rape. Using three rooms of the Palazzo delle Prigioni, which was Venice's central

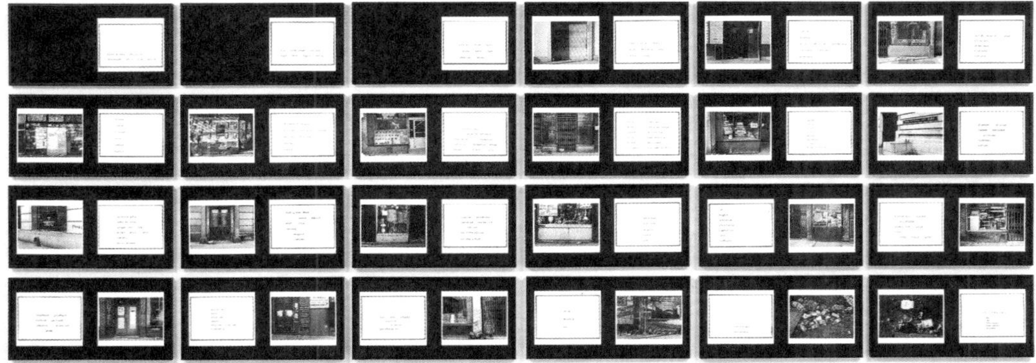

Fig. 5
Martha Rosler, *The Bowery in two inadequate descriptive systems*, 1974–75. 45 gelatin silver prints. Each framed board: 10 × 22 in. (25.4 × 55.9 cm). © Martha Rosler. Courtesy of the artist and Mitchell-Innes & Nash, New York

prison from the sixteenth century until 1922, Cheang transformed the eerie space into a high-tech site of surveillance and image projection, with the title referring to the typical size of cells within the increasingly standardized prison-industrial complex. One room featured ten monitors situated on the floor, each telling the story of a different individual, including the aforementioned Casanova and Hojabri as well as Michel Foucault, the Marquis de Sade, and figures drawn from other contemporary cases. Cheang pays homage to revolutionaries who paved the way for the gender noncomformity more openly expressed today and who continue to battle on the frontlines in spheres where aggressive tactics are used to stifle anything outside accepted norms.

Candice Breitz's video installation *TLDR* (2017) is a collaborative project made with sex workers from Cape Town affiliated with SWEAT (Sex Workers Education and Advocacy Taskforce) (Fig. 7). Its centerpiece is a remarkably entertaining musical drama done in the DIY style of community theater, with handmade props and a minimal stage set, featuring sex workers fighting for basic human rights. Originally from South Africa and now splitting her time between Berlin and Cape Town, Breitz became acquainted with SWEAT while active in local protests to protect sex workers from violence. The work grew out of years of research, including in-depth interviews with sex-work activists and a workshop with the collaborators to determine the video's structure and approach.

TLDR (the social-media acronym for "Too Long, Didn't Read") tells the true story of the conflict between activists fighting to decriminalize sex work and a well-meaning but naïve group called the Coalition Against Trafficking in Women (CATW), who understood their position against sex work as staunchly feminist. CATW argued for abolishing all prostitution, which would by default further criminalize the very sex workers about whom they are ostensibly concerned and who are engaged in their own struggles for legal recognition. The activists were endorsed by Amnesty International, while CATW enlisted the support of numerous privileged white women Hollywood celebrities. *TLDR* unwinds the tangled tale of the clash between two distinct, culturally specific forms of feminism—one initiated and enacted by sex workers themselves, the other by a group with no direct experience of the issues at hand. Nonetheless, CATW felt entitled to determine the best course of action—to "rescue" the sex workers from themselves—buoyed by celebrities who likely hadn't bothered to become genuinely informed on the subject. Breitz's video is narrated by a precocious twelve-year-old named Xanny Stevens, the child of a sex-work activist.

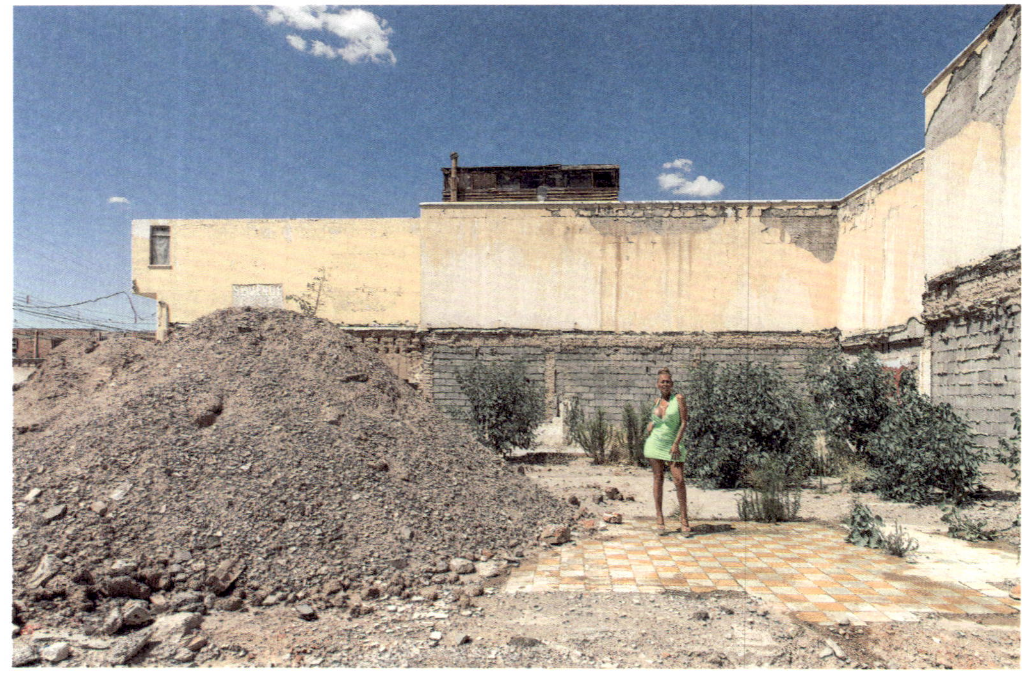

Fig. 6
Teresa Margolles, *Nancy, Pista de baile del club "Arthur's"* (Nancy, dance floor from the club Arthur's), 2016. Pigmented inkjet print. Framed: 17 13⁄16 × 25 3⁄8 in. (45 × 64.5 cm). Courtesy of the artist; Galerie Peter Kilchmann, Zurich; and James Cohan, New York

A Greek chorus of eleven members of SWEAT flanks the narrator, animating the story through song and movement. Occasionally, they hold up signs featuring a variety of protest slogans drawn from their own ongoing activism; familiar emoji expressions of feelings and states of mind; the pithy acronyms of social media; and the last names of well-known sexual predators, including Trump, Weinstein, Tyson, Ailes, Polanski, Zuma, and Mthethwa.

TLDR reflects the multiplicity of feminisms and how feminist ideologies necessarily intersect with a range of other social categories used to discriminate, including race, class, age, ability, and religion. It also reveals how opinions and modes of activism among feminist movements can widely diverge, conjuring up past tensions in the women's movement when those who were socially empowered were called out for ignoring the experiences of certain other groups of women—women of color, lesbian and queer women, poor women. As a white, middle-class South African, Breitz is sensitive to her position of privilege. In an interview about the work, she said:

> There was no way to make this piece without including a layer of reflection on the violence that is inherent to white privilege. . . . It needs to be constantly addressed and deconstructed. You can try to use it

against itself by extending some of the visibility that attaches to whiteness to issues and communities that are generally denied broader visibility. To a large extent *TLDR* is about how attention tends to land in the wrong places for the wrong reasons. One of the big challenges of the piece is to try to ensure that attention lands in some of the right places for a change.[20]

In *TLDR*, the narrator speaks directly to the audience, invoking the personal pronouns *I* and *you* throughout the work. This direct address implicates the viewer in their own position of privilege, causing each of us to evaluate our personal roles in perpetuating social systems of discrimination and what we are doing to change it. This tactic has been adopted by many feminist artists over the years, such as Piper and Jenny Holzer, as a strategy to break down the perceived barrier between the work (or the speaker/author) and the viewer to create a sense of at-times-uncomfortable intimacy. With reference to Barbara Kruger's use of the same operation, Craig Owens breaks down its effects via gender: "Kruger uses a term with no fixed content, the linguistic shifter ('I/you'), in order to demonstrate that masculine and feminine themselves are not

20 Josie Thaddeus-Johns, "Candice Breitz: Too Long, Didn't Read," *Elephant*, May 24, 2019, https://elephant.art/candice-breitz-long-didnt-read/.

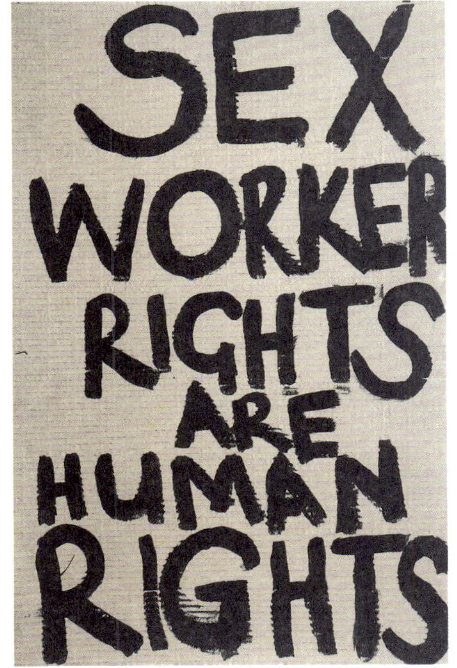

Fig. 7
Candice Breitz, *TLDR*, 2017 (detail). Thirteen-channel video installation, color, sound. Room A: 60 min. loop; room B: approx. 12 hour loop. Courtesy of the artist; Goodman Gallery, Johannesburg and London; Kaufmann Repetto, Milan and New York; and KOW, Berlin

stable identities, but subject to exchange" (Fig. 8).[21] As Breitz has articulated about her decision to take action in relationship to complex social issues: "Those of us who can afford to speak out—and we should never forget that being able to speak out is a privilege—are no longer willing to be complacent or remain silent."[22] The moments of internal reckoning that may result, small and large, can function as encouragement to act in the world.

The works by Margolles, Cheang, and Breitz all explicitly work through the matrix of the body, particularly its reproductive and sexual functions. This focus should be no surprise. As Federici writes, "The body has been for women in capitalist society what the factory has been for male waged workers, the primary ground of their exploitation and resistance."[23] The work of Minerva Cuevas examines the influence of colonial histories on the construction of identity and the impact of global capitalism on the body as a site of labor and production. Using a range of mediums, often juxtaposing the visual languages of corporate branding and museological displays, she makes visible the complex social, political, and economic systems that enact pronounced dynamics of power and hierarchy on daily existence. In her 2015 installation *Feast and Famine*, Cuevas uses an evaluation of chocolate as a global commodity to present fraught histories

of human suffering inflicted by the economics of colonialism and the ways in which the marketing of certain foods have participated in racial and gendered stereotyping. The project began with Cuevas's research into the coin collection at the museum of ethnography in Frankfurt, which revealed the prominence of cacao in pre-Hispanic cultures including its use as currency, as well as how its mass cultivation today is implicated in exploitative labor practices. The piece includes numerous images and objects that borrow from popular chocolate brands—Hershey's, Toblerone—to comment on the drive toward continuous consumption and how these brands perpetuate notions of value. Contrasting ideas of abundance, pleasure, and satiation with lack of food and resources, one centerpiece of the installation is the work *Famine 3.6* (2015), which consists of a machine that drips melted chocolate from the ceiling every six seconds, the rate at which people die of starvation around the world. Over time, the deliciously seductive chocolate forms an oozing mound of waste on the floor, more like a bodily fluid, excrement, or science experiment than a food considered a luxury by some. Works like *Feast, Nest*, and *Nigger Heads* (all 2015) point to how globalized industries leverage biases and fabricated distinctions among people— with the help of disciplines like anthropology—

21 Owens, "The Discourse of Others," 184.

22 Kimberly Bradley, "The Machinery of Identity," *Flash Art*, September/ October 2019. https://flash---art. com/article/the-machinery-of- identity-candice-breitz/

23 Federici, *Caliban and the Witch*, 16.

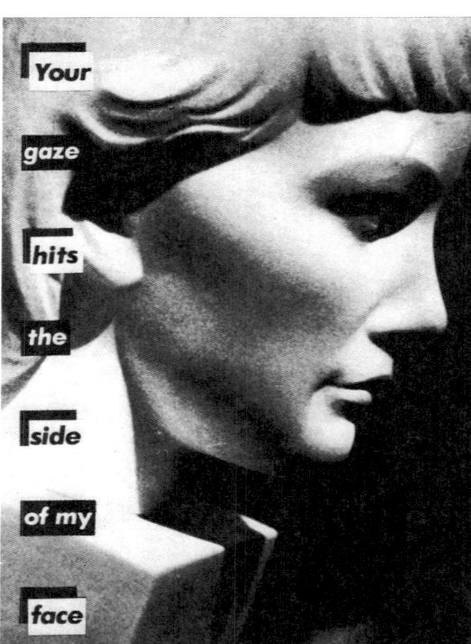

Fig. 8
Barbara Kruger, *Untitled (Your gaze hits the side of my face)*, 1981. Photograph and type on paperboard. 18 ⅞ × 15 ⅜ × 1 ¾ in. (47.9 × 39.1 × 4.4 cm)

to justify centuries of oppression and violence. Cuevas's commitment to exposing these histories of exploitation becomes a reminder of the need for active resistance and the power of collection action.

Beverly Semmes's Feminist Responsibility Project (FRP) (2003–) takes up issues surrounding the body, visibility, and its relationship to vulnerability from a different perspective (Fig. 9). For the past several years, the artist has been painting on pages torn from vintage pornographic magazines to obscure or highlight details of their imagery. In some images, the female figure has been almost completely obliterated, rendered an amorphous blob out of what can feel like an urgent need to convert these sexualized portrayals into abstract shapes and washes of color, even while the women's bodies resist eradication under the swaths of pigment. In some works, the provocative poses, while disguised, are still largely legible, with women's genitalia foregrounded or their augmented breasts kept intact. And in some pieces, Semmes emphasizes rather than conceals the titillating details, fragmenting the body to acknowledge how the objectification of the female anatomy has had very real social consequences in the lives of women while playfully participating in this absurd and fetishistic obsession. Semmes's figures teeter between the monstrous, with faces obfuscated

or eyes peering out from inside a morass of repetitive line work, and the slightly ridiculous, as if depicting cartoon characters.

At first glance, Semmes's overlays appear to be acts of censorship or masking. Indeed, the artist herself initially felt her gestures to be "protective to the viewer, protective to the subject," and even "nurturing."[24] But Semmes's attitude, and the works themselves, have become more layered and complex as the project has gone on. Recent works from the Feminist Responsibility Project abandon physical magazine pages in favor of greatly enlarged appropriated images of women in familiar pornographic poses, as well as of fashion models striding down the runway, printed on canvas and adorned with vibrant color and line rendered in paint and ink. At this larger scale, the embellishment seems more celebratory, adding energy and dynamism to the remarkably banal original images of print pornography, which often traffic in suggestion and quotation more than depict actual sex. The shapes she applies, mimicking the contours of the original imagery, also recall Semmes's sculptural work, in particular the unwieldy yet alluring ceramic vessels she has been making for many years. The necessity of pleasure emanates from both these bodies of work, a pleasure that vacillates between the tactile and the mediated.

24 "Interviews: Beverly Semmes," as told to Lauren O'Neill-Butler, *Artforum*, February 5, 2014, https://www.artforum.com/ interviews/beverly-semmes-talks-about-her-current-solo-exhibitions-45150.

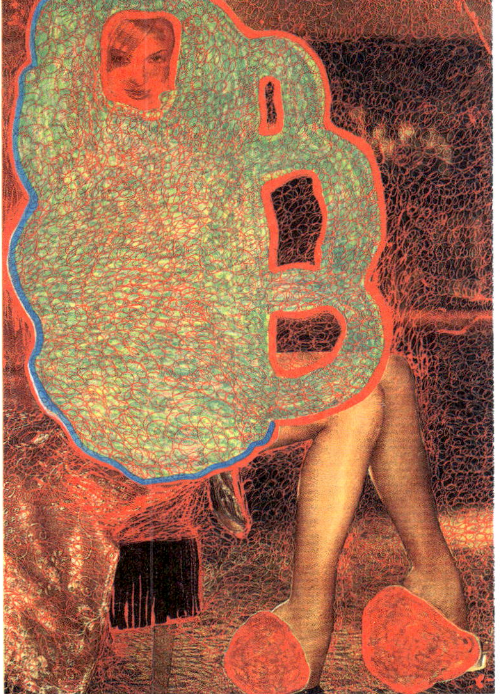

Fig. 9
Beverly Semmes, *Slip*, 2019. Ink and acrylic on photograph printed on canvas. 72 ½ × 50 in. (184.15 × 127 cm). Courtesy of the artist and Susan Inglett Gallery, New York. Photo: Jason Mandella, New York

Semmes explores the humorous ungainliness of physicality, the ridiculous artificiality of representation, and the rich terrain that exists when they are brought together.

The hyperexposure considered in works like Semmes's yields also to the opposite problem for women and genderqueer people: the sense of being absent from the cultural landscape. In some cases, this concern is addressed in direct representations of these other bodies and consciousnesses. But it may also be suggested through more subtle means. In their performance-based video projects, Pauline Boudry / Renate Lorenz are intent on focusing on the violence of visibility strategies that have marked certain bodies, in their words, "as 'other,' freaky, perverse, racialised or socially outcast."[25] The duo resists the demeaning, demoralizing modes of representation to which their queer subjects have often been exposed by creating safe, isolated, theatrical settings where private collaborative performances are captured on video. Responsive to historical examples of struggles for survival and protests against patriarchy—with references ranging from the German militant Ulrike Meinhof to the iconic writer Oscar Wilde, female Kurdish guerilla fighters, and the experimental composer Pauline Oliveros—the artists' works articulate the power that can issue from intentional forms

of community and resistance. The tone can range from emphatic and serious to optimistic and joyous. *Telepathic Improvisation* (2017), described by writer and curator André Lepecki as "telepathically transmitting queer-feminist-militant-resistant toxicity-cure,"[26] takes the form of a video installation that includes objects specifically related to theatricality and speech—stage lights, a smoke machine, an elevated stage with panels that light up on a preprogrammed sequence, and a suite of microphones (Fig. 10). Created in response to the current anxious political and social climate, the work looks to historical instances of resistance or pleasure, such as actions by the Black Panther Party or the safe spaces incarnated by queer clubs, and uses them as jumping-off points to imagine alternative communities and better futures. Four performers move in and out of a dark stage setting, creating moments of interaction and independence, continuously negotiating the space and their relationships to one another. They are all dressed in red and white, indicating their deliberate alliance with one another, their commitment to creating a new form of community. The queer body takes center stage. One performer, the artist MPA, stares directly into the camera and becomes a conduit to voice what Meinhof once said, herself echoing the words of Black Panther Party member Fred

25 "Stages: A Conversation Between Andrea Thal, Pauline Boudry, and Renate Lorenz," Berlin, September 2010, http://www.boudry-lorenz.de/texts/. Cited in Gregg Bordowitz, "Repetition and Change: The Film Installations of Pauline Boudry and Renate Lorenz," *Afterall* 31 (Autumn/Winter 2012), https://www.afterall.org/journal/issue.31/repetition-and-change-the-film-installations-of-pauline-boudry-and-renate-lorenz.

26 André Lepecki, "The Telepathic Drive: The Event Horizon: The Protest: The Resistant Movement," 6, in Lepecki et al., *Telepathic Improvisation* (Houston: Contemporary Arts Museum, 2018), available at https://www.boudry-lorenz.de/media/AndréLepecki_VTM1rOF.pdf.

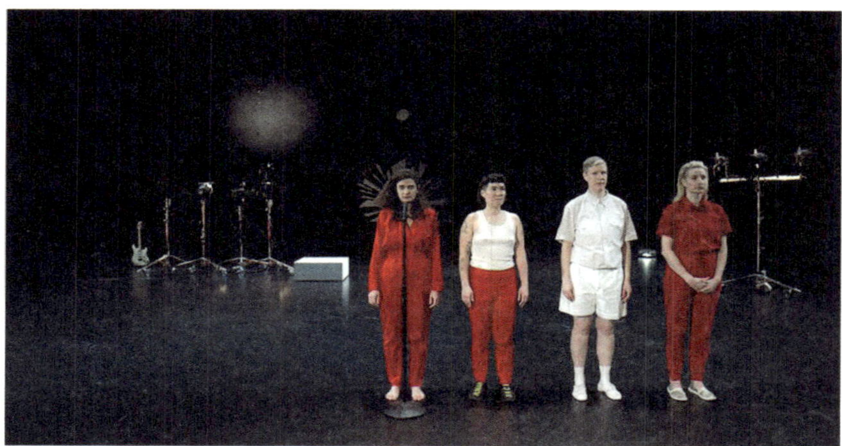

Fig. 10
Pauline Boudry / Renate Lorenz, *Telepathic Improvisation*, 2017. HD video, color, sound with mixed-media installation. Video: 20 min., installation dimensions variable. Courtesy of the artists; Ellen de Bruijne Projects, Amsterdam; and Marcelle Alix, Paris

Hampton: "Protest is when I say I don't like this. Resistance is when I put an end to what I don't like." As Gregg Bordowitz said of the role of posing in this work, "Posing for the camera . . . is a form of self-defence in the age of surveillance. It's an act of self-authorship."[27]

The tensions between historical fact and contemporary interpretation, between self-assertion and playacting that reside at the core of Boudry/Lorenz's works return to the problematics of visibility. While a political necessity, visibility can also bring increased vulnerability. As feminist writer Jia Tolentino has written about the fast-moving solidarity and pronounced spotlight that has accompanied movements such as #MeToo and #YesAllWomen, "These hashtags have at least partially reified the things they're trying to eradicate: the way that womanhood can feel like a story of loss of control. They have made feminist solidarity and shared vulnerability seem inextricable, as if we were incapable of building solidarity around anything else."[28] In a conversation with artist Juliana Huxtable about the ways in which a higher public profile can lead to backlash against perceived acceptance and political power, the writer Che Gossett describes how certain forms of visibility can also become distractions of a sort—"visibility as a deadlock." Gossett warns, "It's representation but not really. Scattering of people without any real redistribution of power."[29]

Gossett's statement is a call for the need to create spaces for truly transgressive forms of representation that strive to dismantle the racist patriarchal order. The works in *Witch Hunt* provide models for ways this may occur: revelations of the labored body, the empowerment of those on the margins, the reincarnation of histories deemed unworthy of articulation, the creation of intoxicating spaces of desire, pleasure, and community. When feminist artists tell stories, the structural reality of misogyny is made evident, and their capacity to offer counternarratives provides a path forward.

27 Bordowitz, "Repetition and Change."

28 Jia Tolentino, "The I in the Internet," in *Trick Mirror: Reflections on Self Delusion* (New York: Random House, 2019), 28.

29 "Existing in the World: Blackness at the Edge of Trans Visibility, Che Gossett and Juliana Huxtable in Conversation," in *Trap Door: Trans Cultural Production and the Politics of Visibility*, ed. Reina Gossett, Eric A. Stanley, and Johanna Burton (Cambridge, MA: MIT Press, 2017), 45.

This checklist reflects the works included in *Witch Hunt* as of April 2021.

Leonor Antunes
Hammer Museum
The homemaker and her domain, 2021
Various works
Dimensions variable
Courtesy of the artist;
kurimanzutto, Mexico City and New York; Marian Goodman Gallery, London; Galeria Luisa Strina, São Paulo; and Taka Ishi Gallery, Tokyo and Hong Kong

Yael Bartana
Hammer Museum
Patriarchy Is History, 2020
Neon
78 × 73 in. (198.4 × 185.3 cm)
Courtesy of the artist; Annet Gelink Gallery, Amsterdam; Sommer Contemporary, Tel Aviv; Galeria Raffaella Cortese, Milan; Petzel Gallery, New York; and Capitain Petzel, Berlin

Two Minutes to Midnight, 2021
Digital video, color, sound
Approx. 47 min.
Courtesy of the artist; Annet Gelink Gallery, Amsterdam; Sommer Contemporary, Tel Aviv; Galeria Raffaella Cortese, Milan; Petzel Gallery, New York; and Capitain Petzel, Berlin

Pauline Boudry / Renate Lorenz
Hammer Museum
HE EAR R, 2016
Microphones, microphone stands, spotlights, C-stands, wood, paint, mechanical turntable
Dimensions variable
Courtesy of the artists; Ellen de Bruijne Projects, Amsterdam; and Marcelle Alix, Paris

Telepathic Improvisation, 2017
HD video, color, sound, with mixed-media installation
Video: 20 min., installation dimensions variable
Courtesy of the artists; Ellen de Bruijne Projects, Amsterdam; and Marcelle Alix, Paris

Stage Piece (Untimely Collaboration), 2018
Stage, light
Dimensions variable
Courtesy of the artists; Ellen de Bruijne Projects, Amsterdam; and Marcelle Alix, Paris

Candice Breitz
ICA LA
TLDR, 2017
Thirteen-channel video installation, color, sound
Room A: three-channel projection, 60 min. (loop); room B: ten-channel video installation, approx. 12 hours (loop)
Featuring interviews with Zoe Black, Connie, Duduzile Dlamini, Emmah, Gabbi, Regina High, Jenny, Jowi, Tenderlove, and Nosipho "Provocative" Vidima. Narrator: Xanny "The Future" Stevens. Grim Reaper: Buhle Nobuzana.

Conceived in dialogue with SWEAT (Sex Workers Education and Advocacy Taskforce), Cape Town. In memory of Nokuphila Kumalo
Commissioned by the B3 Biennial of the Moving Image, Frankfurt am Main
Courtesy of the artist; Goodman Gallery, Johannesburg and London; Kaufmann Repetto, Milan and New York; and KOW, Berlin

Shu Lea Cheang
Hammer Museum
UKI Virus Rising, 2018
Three-channel digital video, color, sound
10 min.
Courtesy of the artist

Minerva Cuevas
ICA LA
Feast and Famine, 2015
Selected works from mixed-media installation
Dimensions variable
Courtesy of the artist and kurimanzutto, Mexico City and New York

As-yet-untitled site-specific outdoor mural, 2021
Commissioned by the Institute of Contemporary Art, Los Angeles

Vaginal Davis
ICA LA
Mary Mary, 2020
Audio and mixed-media installation
Dimensions variable
Courtesy of the artist; Adams and Ollman, Portland; Galerie Isabella Bortolozzi, Berlin; and New Discretions, New York

Women on the Verge (50 plus years of influence), 2021
Selection of paintings on paper
Mixed media including eye shadow, eyeliner, rouge, foundation, coconut oil, nail polish, perfume, hair conditioner, hair spray, watercolor pencil, hydrogen peroxide, and glycerin on paper
Dimensions variable
Courtesy of the artist; Adams and Ollman, Portland; Galerie Isabella Bortolozzi, Berlin; and New Discretions, New York

Every Ocean Hughes
ICA LA
Help the Dead, 2019
Performance
60 min.
Performers: Colin Self and Geo Wyeth
Courtesy of the artist

One Big Bag, 2021
HD video, color, sound
Approx. 40 min.
Courtesy of the artist

Bouchra Khalili
Hammer Museum
The Magic Lantern Project, 2021
Mixed-media installation with video projection
Dimensions variable
Courtesy of the artist and Mor Charpentier, Paris

Laura Lima
Hammer Museum
Alfaiataria (Tailor shop), 2014–
Mixed-media installation
Dimensions variable
Courtesy of the artist; Tanya Bonakdar Gallery, Los Angeles and New York; A Gentil Carioca, Rio de Janeiro; and Galeria Luisa Strina, São Paulo

Teresa Margolles
Hammer Museum
As-yet-untitled mixed-media installation, 2021
Dimensions variable
Courtesy of the artist and James Cohan, New York

Otobong Nkanga
Hammer Museum
The Collection: Biotologicalymica I, 2013–14
C-print
24 ⅝ × 16 ¹¹⁄₁₆ in. (62.5 × 42.5 cm)
Courtesy of the artist; In Situ Fabienne Leclerc, Paris; and Lumen Travo, Amsterdam

The Collection: Fragments of Tsumeb, MfN Berlin, 2013–14
C-print
24 ⅝ × 16 ¹¹⁄₁₆ in. (62.5 × 42.5 cm)
Courtesy of the artist; In Situ Fabienne Leclerc, Paris; and Lumen Travo, Amsterdam

The Collection: Models, Musée de minéralogie Strasbourg, 2013–14
C-print
24 ⅝ × 16 ¹¹⁄₁₆ in. (62.5 × 42.5 cm)
Courtesy of the artist; In Situ Fabienne Leclerc, Paris; and Lumen Travo, Amsterdam

The Collection: Muscovitalogicalymica I, 2013–14
C-print
24 ⅝ × 16 ¹¹⁄₁₆ in. (62.5 × 42.5 cm)
Courtesy of the artist; In Situ Fabienne Leclerc, Paris; and Lumen Travo, Amsterdam

In Pursuit of Bling—Coalition, 2014
C-print
24 ⅝ × 16 ¹¹⁄₁₆ in. (62.5 × 42.5 cm)
Courtesy of the artist; In Situ Fabienne Leclerc, Paris; and Lumen Travo, Amsterdam

In Pursuit of Bling—Desire, 2014
C-print
24 ⅝ × 16 ¹¹⁄₁₆ in. (62.5 × 42.5 cm)
Courtesy of the artist; In Situ Fabienne Leclerc, Paris; and Lumen Travo, Amsterdam

The Apparatus, 2015
Acrylic and acrylic modeling paste on paper
70 ½ × 49 ⅝ in. (179 × 126 cm)
Collection of Wim van Dongen

Solid Maneuvers, 2015
Make-up, vermiculite, metals, PVC foamboard, acrylic, tar
55 ½ × 57 ⅞ × 81 ⅛ in. (141 × 147 × 206 cm)
Courtesy of the artist; In Situ Fabienne Leclerc, Paris; and Lumen Travo, Amsterdam

Tsumeb Fragments, 2015
Powder-coated steel; cement with malachite, azurite, and mica; electromagnet; copper; photographic prints on Galala limestone and acrylic; lightbox; high-definition monitor with headphones
Dimensions variable
Courtesy of the artist; In Situ Fabienne Leclerc, Paris; and Lumen Travo, Amsterdam

Infinite Yield, 2015
Woven textile, mohair, organic cotton, polyester, viscose bast
113 ⅜ × 68 ⅞ in. (288 × 175 cm)
Courtesy of the artist; In Situ Fabienne Leclerc, Paris; and Lumen Travo, Amsterdam

Steel to Rust—Meltdown, 2016
Tapestry
87 ⅜ × 120 ½ in. (222 × 306 cm)
Courtesy of the artist; In Situ Fabienne Leclerc, Paris; and Lumen Travo, Amsterdam

The Leftovers, 2017
Tapestry
65 × 102 ⅜ in. (165 × 260 cm)
Courtesy of the artist; In Situ
Fabienne Leclerc, Paris; and
Lumen Travo, Amsterdam

Double Plot, 2018
Woven textile with five inkjet
prints on PVC foamboard
104 ⁵⁄₁₆ × 303 ³⁄₁₆ in. (265 × 770 cm)
Courtesy of the artist; In Situ
Fabienne Leclerc, Paris; and
Lumen Travo, Amsterdam

Okwui Okpokwasili
Hammer Museum
Poor People's TV Room Solo,
2014/2021
Video and mixed-media installation
Dimensions variable
Purchased jointly by the Hammer
Museum, Los Angeles, with funds
from the Board of Advisors,
and the Whitney Museum of
American Art, New York

Lara Schnitger
ICA LA
Warts and All, 2021
Mixed-media installation,
including wood, fabric, fake fur,
nylon, elastic, ribbons, lingerie,
quilts, pins, hardware
Dimensions variable
Courtesy of the artist and
Anton Kern Gallery, New York

Beverly Semmes
Hammer Museum
Cake, 2012
Ceramic, epoxy, paint
45 × 24 × 24 in. (114.3 × 61 × 61 cm)
Nasher Sculpture Center, Dallas,
Acquired through the Kaleta A.
Doolin Acquisitions Fund for
Women Artists

Fish, 2012
Ceramic, epoxy, paint
56 × 27 × 27 in. (142.2 × 68.6 ×
68.6 cm)
Courtesy of the artist and
Susan Inglett Gallery, New York

Glove, 2012
Ceramic, epoxy, paint
49 × 22 × 22 in. (124.5 × 55.9 × 55.9 cm)
Courtesy of the artist and
Susan Inglett Gallery, New York

Plant, 2012
Ceramic, epoxy, paint
41 ½ × 15 × 10 in. (105.4 × 38.1
× 25.4 cm)
Courtesy of the artist and
Susan Inglett Gallery, New York

Rooster, 2012
Ceramic, epoxy, paint
52 × 18 × 18 in. (132.1 × 45.7 × 45.7 cm)
Courtesy of the artist and
Susan Inglett Gallery, New York

Smoke, 2012
Ceramic, epoxy, paint
53 × 16 × 16 in. (134.6 × 40.6 ×
40.6 cm)
Courtesy of the artist and
Susan Inglett Gallery, New York

Suitcase, 2012
Ceramic, epoxy, paint
56 × 16 × 16 in. (142.2 × 40.6 ×
40.6 cm)
Courtesy of the artist and
Susan Inglett Gallery, New York

Helmet, 2018
Ink and acrylic on printed canvas
70 ½ × 50 in. (179.1 × 127 cm)
Courtesy of the artist and
Susan Inglett Gallery, New York

Legs, 2018
Ink and acrylic on printed canvas
78 ¹³⁄₁₆ × 50 in. (200.2 × 127 cm)
Private collection

Silver Hat, 2018
Ink and acrylic on printed canvas
82 ⁷⁄₁₀ × 50 in. (210.1 × 127 cm)
Collection of Sam and
Deborah Berkovitz

Antenna, 2019
Ink and acrylic on printed canvas
82 ½ × 50 in. (209.1 × 127 cm)
Collection of Jill and Peter Kraus

Poodle, 2019
Ink and acrylic on printed canvas
81 ¾ × 50 in. (207.6 × 127 cm)
Courtesy of the artist and
Susan Inglett Gallery, New York

Silver Heart, 2019
Ink and acrylic on printed canvas
81 ⅛ × 50 in. (206.1 × 127 cm)
Courtesy of the artist and
Susan Inglett Gallery, New York

Blue Moon, 2020
Ink and acrylic on printed canvas
65 ¾ × 40 in. (167 × 101.6 cm)
Collection of Eileen O'Kane
Kornreich

Contributors

Vanessa Arizmendi is a curatorial assistant at the Hammer Museum, where she has supported exhibitions including *Made in L.A. 2018*, *Adrian Piper: Concepts and Intuitions, 1965–2016* (2018), *Lari Pittman: Declaration of Independence* (2019), *Hammer Projects: Ja'Tovia Gary* (2020), *No Humans Involved* (2021), and *Hammer Projects: noé olivas* (2021). Her 2019 group exhibition, *Nowhere Better than This Place*, featured work by Felix Gonzalez-Torres, Rebecca Morales, Gala Porras-Kim, and Analia Saban. She has also organized numerous performances and public programs at the Hammer by artists including EJ Hill, Mónica Mayer, Regina Silveira, and Cecilia Vicuña.

Ana Briz is an independent researcher, writer, and curator. Born in Guayaquil, Ecuador, and raised in Miami, Florida, she lives and works in Los Angeles. Her research is situated in the field of performance and performativity and is primarily focused on contemporary performance art with an emphasis on queer, feminist, and antiracist work by BIPOC in California. Her most recent exhibitions include *CARE NOT CAGES: Processing a Pandemic (*2020), cocurated with Alexandre Dorriz online in collaboration with the Crenshaw Dairy Mart and GALLERYPLATFORM. LA; *This Body Can't Be All There Is* (2020), cocurated with Johnny Forever at the USC Roski Graduate Gallery; and *By the rivers, I stood and stared into the Sun* (2019), cocurated with Star Montana at the USC Roski MFA Gallery. Briz is currently a PhD student in American studies and ethnicity at the University of Southern California and holds an MA in curatorial practices and the public sphere from the University of Southern California and a BA in art history from Florida International University.

Connie Butler is chief curator at the Hammer Museum, where since 2013 she has organized numerous exhibitions including *Lari Pittman: Declaration of Independence* (2019), *Made in L.A. 2014*, *Mark Bradford: Scorched Earth* (2015), and *Marisa Merz: The Sky Is a Great Space* (2017). She cocurated *Adrian Piper: A Synthesis of Intuitions, 1965–2016* (2018), which opened at the Museum of Modern Art (MoMA), New York, and traveled to the Hammer Museum, and also oversaw the curatorial team for *Radical Women: Latin American Art, 1960–1985* (2017). From 2006 to 2013, she was Robert Lehman Foundation Chief Curator of Drawings at MoMA, where she cocurated *Lygia Clark: The Abandonment of Art, 1948–1988* (2014) and *On Line: Drawing through the Twentieth Century* (2010). Butler also organized the groundbreaking survey *WACK! Art and the Feminist Revolution* (2007) at the Museum of Contemporary Art, Los Angeles, where she was curator from 1996 to 2006. In 2020, Butler received the Bard College Audrey Irmas Award for Curatorial Excellence.

Nika Chilewich is a curatorial assistant at the Hammer Museum. She is a founding member of the subcritical studies collective Los Yacuzis, whose most recent show was *Melquiades Herrera. Reportaje plástico de un teorema cultural* (2019) at the Museo Universitario de Arte Contemporáneo in Mexico City. She holds a BA in Latin American literature from Bard College in New York and an MA in art history and curatorial studies from the National Autonomous University of Mexico (UNAM). Her curatorial work includes *B L I S S* (2019), *Trapos sucios* (2018), *Sabroso veneno* by Radamés "Juni" Figueroa (2017), and *Juan Acha: Por una nueva problemática artística* with Los Yacuzis at the Modern Art Museum of Mexico (2016–17). In 2018, she founded LAR, a nonprofit dedicated to supporting female identifying artists. She also coedits *Erizo, A Journal of the Arts*, a bilingual journal of poetry and art from the Americas.

Anne Ellegood has been the Good Works Executive Director of the Institute of Contemporary Art, Los Angeles (ICA LA) since September 2019. She was senior curator at the Hammer Museum from 2009 to 2019, where in addition to organizing exhibitions and building the collection, she oversaw the Hammer Projects series and the Public Engagement program. She cocurated *Made in L.A. 2018* and *Take It or Leave It: Institution, Image, Ideology* (2014). Ellegood organized the first North American retrospective of the work of Jimmie Durham, which opened at the Hammer in January 2017 and traveled to the Walker Art Center in Minneapolis, the Whitney Museum of American Art in New York, and the Remai Modern in Saskatoon, as well as numerous other solo exhibitions, including those with Diana Al-Hadid, Kevin Beasley, Shannon Ebner, Latifa Echakhch, Charles Gaines, Yunhee Min, Tschabalala Self, Frances Upritchard, and Lily van der Stokker.

Jamillah James is curator at the Institute of Contemporary Art, Los Angeles. James is cocurating the 2021 edition of the New Museum Triennial with Margot Norton. Recent exhibitions include *No Wrong Holes*, the most comprehensive exhibition to date of artist, educator, and curator Nayland Blake; *This Has No Name*, the first US survey of B. Wurtz; and solo presentations of Harold Mendez, Lucas Blalock, Maryam Jafri, rafa esparza, Abigail DeVille, and Sarah Cain. Prior to joining ICA LA in 2016, James was assistant curator at the Hammer Museum where she organized exhibitions of Simone Leigh, Alex Da Corte, and Njideka Akunyili Crosby, among others, for the museum and the nonprofit Art + Practice. She has held curatorial positions at the Studio Museum in Harlem, New York, and the Queens Museum, Flushing, New York, and independently organized exhibitions, performances, screenings, and public programs at alternative and artist-run spaces throughout the United States and Canada since 2004.

Illustrations

Every reasonable effort has been made to identify, contact, and acknowledge rights holders. If there are errors or omissions, please contact the Hammer so they can be addressed in subsequent editions.

All works are © the artist(s); all images appear courtesy of the artist(s) and the lenders or owners of the materials depicted. The following illustration list is organized according to page number.

1. Okwui Okpokwasili, *Poor People's TV Room Solo*, 2014. Performance view, David Rubenstein Atrium, Lincoln Center, New York, 2014. Photo: Caitlin McCarthy

2. Vaginal Davis, *Joanne Woodward Seven*, 2012. Britney Spears eye shadow, Wet n Wild Nail Polish, Afro Sheen Hair Conditioner, Aqua Net Extra Super Hold Hair Spray, watercolor pencil, and glycerin on cornflakes box. 10 ¼ × 7 ¼ in. (26 × 18.4 cm). Courtesy of the artist; Adams and Ollman, Portland; Galerie Isabella Bortolozzi, Berlin; and New Discretions, New York

3. Lara Schnitger, *Day Is Done*, 2019. Stretched velvet. 28 × 22 in. (71.1 × 55.9 cm). Courtesy of the artist; Grice Bench, Los Angeles; and Anton Kern Gallery, New York. Photo: Joshua White

4. Minerva Cuevas, *Be always disposed to do something desperate*, 2018. Acrylic on newspaper. 17 × 11 in. (43.1 × 27.9 cm). Courtesy of the artist and kurimanzutto, Mexico City and New York

5. Duduzile Dlamini on the set of Candice Breitz, *TLDR*, 2017. Thirteen-channel video installation, color, sound. Room A: 60 min. loop; room B: approx. 12 hour loop. Featuring interviews with Zoe Black, Connie, Duduzile Dlamini, Emmah, Gabbi, Regina High, Jenny, Jowi, Tenderlove, and Nosipho "Provocative" Vidima. Narrator: Xanny "The Future" Stevens. Grim Reaper: Buhle Nobuzana. Conceived in dialogue with SWEAT (Sex Workers Education and Advocacy Taskforce), Cape Town. In memory of Nokuphila Kumalo. Commissioned by the B3 Biennial of the Moving Image, Frankfurt am Main. Courtesy of the artist; Goodman Gallery, Johannesburg and London; Kaufmann Repetto, Milan and New York; and KOW, Berlin. Photo: Sydelle Willow Smith

6. Beverly Semmes and Jennifer Minniti with Dean Sidaway, *Carwash Performance*, 2018 (detail). Performance view, Susan Inglett Gallery, New York, 2018. Performance: Grace Choi. Courtesy of the artist and Susan Inglett Gallery, New York. Photo: Nate Bozeman

Leonor Antunes

9. Leonor Antunes, *Lygia #1, #2, #3, #4*, 2019 (details). Stainless steel. Installation view, *joints, voids and gaps*, Casa de Vidro, São Paulo, 2019. Courtesy of the artist and Galeria Luisa Strina, São Paulo. Photo: Nick Ash

10–11. Leonor Antunes, installation view, *joints, voids and gaps*, Museu de Arte de São Paulo, 2019. Courtesy of the artist and Galeria Luisa Strina, São Paulo. Photo: Nick Ash

12. Leonor Antunes, *Oaxacan textile I + II*, 2018 (detail). Brass. Dimensions variable. Installation view, *discrepancias con C. P.*, Museo Tamayo, Mexico City, 2018. Courtesy of the artist and kurimanzutto, Mexico City and New York

13. Leonor Antunes, installation view, *discrepancias con C. P.*, Museo Tamayo, Mexico City, 2018. Courtesy of the artist and kurimanzutto, Mexico City and New York

14. Leonor Antunes, installation view, *the frisson of the togetherness*, Whitechapel Gallery, London, 2017–18. Courtesy of the artist and kurimanzutto, Mexico City and New York; Marian Goodman Gallery, London; and Galeria Luisa Strina, São Paulo

15. Leonor Antunes, installation view, *the last days in Galliate*, Pirelli Hangar Bicocca, Milan, 2018–19. Courtesy of the artist and kurimanzutto, Mexico City and New York; Marian Goodman Gallery, London; and Galeria Luisa Strina, São Paulo

16–17. Leonor Antunes, installation view, *Resonating Spaces*, Fondation Beyeler, Riehen/Basel, 2019–20. Courtesy of the artist and kurimanzutto, Mexico City and New York; Marian Goodman Gallery, London; and Galeria Luisa Strina, São Paulo

Yael Bartana

19–21 top. Yael Bartana, *What if Women Ruled the World?*, 2017. Performance views, Filmby Aarhus, European Capital of Culture Aarhus 2017, Denmark. Courtesy of the artist. Photo: Birgit Kaulfuss

21 bottom. Yael Bartana, *What if Women Ruled the World?*, 2017. Performance view, Volksbühne, Berlin, 2018. Courtesy of the artist. Photo: Birgit Kaulfuss

22. Yael Bartana, *What if Women Ruled the World?*, 2017. Performance view, Filmby Aarhus, European Capital of Culture Aarhus 2017, Denmark. Courtesy of the artist. Photo: Birgit Kaulfuss

23. Yael Bartana, *What if Women Ruled the World?*, 2016. Neon. 94 × 43 in. (250 × 97.5 cm). Courtesy of the artist; Annet Gelink Gallery, Amsterdam; Sommer Contemporary, Tel Aviv; Galleria Raffaella Cortese, Milan; and Petzel Gallery, New York. Photo: Hans-Georg Gaul

24–25. Yael Bartana, *Bury Our Weapons, Not Our Bodies!*, 2018. Performance views, Philadelphia Museum of Art, 2018. Courtesy of the artist. Photo: Constance Mensch

26. Yael Bartana, *Wild Seeds*, 2005. Two-channel digital video projection, color, sound; 6:40 min. Courtesy of the artist; Annet Gelink Gallery, Amsterdam; and Sommer Contemporary Art, Tel Aviv

27 top left. Yael Bartana, *Mary Koszmary* (Nightmares), 2008. Video, color, sound; 11 min. Courtesy of the artist; Annet Gelink Gallery, Amsterdam; and Foksal Gallery Foundation, Warsaw

27 middle and bottom left. Yael Bartana, *Zamach* (Assassination), 2011. Video, color, sound; 35 min. Courtesy of the artist; Annet Gelink Gallery, Amsterdam; and Sommer Contemporary Art, Tel Aviv

27 right. Yael Bartana, *Mur i wieża* (Wall and tower), 2009. Video, color, sound; 15 min. Courtesy of the artist; Annet Gelink Gallery, Amsterdam; and Sommer Contemporary Art, Tel Aviv

Pauline Boudry / Renate Lorenz

29–31. Pauline Boudry / Renate Lorenz, *Telepathic Improvisation*, 2017. HD video, color, sound, with mixed-media installation. Video: 20 min., installation dimensions variable. Performance: Marwa Arsanios, MPA, Ginger Brooks Takahashi, and Werner Hirsch. Courtesy of the artists; Ellen de Bruijne Projects, Amsterdam; and Marcelle Alix, Paris

32 top. Pauline Boudry / Renate Lorenz, *HE EAR R*, 2016. Microphones, microphone stands, spotlights, C-stands, wood, paint, mechanical turntable. Installation view, Julia Stoschek Collection, Berlin, 2019. Courtesy of the artists; Ellen de Bruijne Projects, Amsterdam; and Marcelle Alix, Paris. Photo: Alwin Lay

32 bottom. Pauline Boudry / Renate Lorenz, *Stage Piece (Untimely Collaboration)*, 2018. Stages, lights. Installation view, Julia Stoschek Collection, Berlin, 2019. Courtesy of the artists; Ellen de Bruijne Projects, Amsterdam; and Marcelle Alix, Paris. Photo: Alwin Lay

33. Pauline Boudry / Renate Lorenz, *I Want*, 2015. Two-channel digital video installation, color, sound; 16 min. Performance: Sharon Hayes. Courtesy of the artists; Ellen de Bruijne Projects, Amsterdam; and Marcelle Alix, Paris. Photo: Andrea Thal

34. Pauline Boudry / Renate Lorenz, *Silent*, 2016. HD video, color, sound; 7 min. Performance: Aérea Negrot. Courtesy of the artists; Ellen de Bruijne Projects, Amsterdam; and Marcelle Alix, Paris. Photo: Martin Argyroglo

35. Pauline Boudry / Renate Lorenz, *Silent*, 2016. HD video, color, sound; 7 min. Performance: Aérea Negrot. Installation view, Nuit Blanche, Paris, 2017. Courtesy of the artists; Ellen de Bruijne Projects, Amsterdam; and Marcelle Alix, Paris. Photo: Martin Argyroglo

36. Pauline Boudry / Renate Lorenz, *Moving Backwards*, 2019. HD video installation, color, sound; 23 min. Performance: Julie Cunningham, Werner Hirsch, Latifa Laâbissi, Marbles Jumbo Radio, and Nach. Courtesy of the artists; Ellen de Bruijne Projects, Amsterdam; and Marcelle Alix, Paris

37. Pauline Boudry / Renate Lorenz, *Moving Backwards*, 2019. HD video installation, color, sound; 23 min. Installation view, Swiss Pavilion, Venice Biennale, 2019. Performance: Julie Cunningham, Werner Hirsch, Latifa Laâbissi, Marbles Jumbo Radio, and Nach. Courtesy of the artists; Ellen de Bruijne Projects, Amsterdam; and Marcelle Alix, Paris. Photo: Anick Wetter

Candice Breitz

39. Candice Breitz, *Love Story*, 2016. Seven-channel video installation, color, sound; 73:42 min. Performance: Alec Baldwin and Julianne Moore. Based on and including interviews with José Maria João, Mamy Maloba Langa, Sarah Ezzat Mardini, Farah Abdi Mohamed, Luis Ernesto Nava Molero, and Shabeena Francis Saveri. Commissioned by the National Gallery of Victoria, Outset Germany, and Medienboard Berlin-Brandenburg. Courtesy of the artist; Goodman Gallery, Johannesburg and London; Kaufmann Repetto, Milan and New York; and KOW, Berlin

40. Candice Breitz, *Her*, 1978–2008. Seven-channel video installation, color, sound; 23:56 min. Installation view, Kunstmuseum Bonn, 2020. Commissioned by Outset Contemporary Art Fund, London. Courtesy of the artist; Goodman Gallery, Johannesburg and London; Kaufmann Repetto, Milan and New York; and KOW, Berlin. Photo: David Ertl

41 top. Candice Breitz, *King (A Portrait of Michael Jackson)*, 2005. Sixteen-channel video installation, color, sound; 42:20 min. Installation view, Grand Palais, Paris, 2018. Courtesy of the artist; Goodman Gallery, Johannesburg and London; Kaufmann Repetto, Milan and New York; and KOW, Berlin. Photo: Alex Fahl

41 bottom. Candice Breitz, *Queen (A Portrait of Madonna)*, 2005. Thirty-channel HD video installation, color, sound; 73:30 min. Installation view, White Cube, London, 2005. Courtesy of the artist; Goodman Gallery, Johannesburg and London; Kaufmann Repetto, Milan and New York; and KOW, Berlin. Photo: Stephen White

42–43. Candice Breitz, *Love Story*, 2016. Seven-channel video installation, color, sound; 73:42 min. Installation view, South African Pavilion, Venice Biennale, 2017. Performance: Alec Baldwin and Julianne Moore. Based on and including interviews with José Maria João, Mamy Maloba Langa, Sarah Ezzat Mardini, Farah Abdi Mohamed, Luis Ernesto Nava Molero, and Shabeena Francis Saveri. Commissioned by the National Gallery of Victoria, Outset Germany, and Medienboard Berlin-Brandenburg. Courtesy of the artist; Goodman Gallery, Johannesburg and London; Kaufmann Repetto, Milan and New York; and KOW, Berlin. Photo: Andrea Rossetti

44–45. Candice Breitz, *TLDR,* 2017. Thirteen-channel video installation, color, sound. Room A: 60 min. loop; room B: approx. 12 hour loop. Featuring interviews with Zoe Black, Connie, Duduzile Dlamini, Emmah, Gabbi, Regina High, Jenny, Jowi, Tenderlove, and Nosipho "Provocative" Vidima. Narrator: Xanny "The Future" Stevens. Grim Reaper: Buhle Nobuzana. Conceived in dialogue with SWEAT (Sex Workers Education and Advocacy Taskforce), Cape Town. In memory of Nokuphila Kumalo. Commissioned by the B3 Biennial of the Moving Image, Frankfurt am Main. Courtesy of the artist; Goodman Gallery, Johannesburg and London; Kaufmann Repetto, Milan and New York; and KOW, Berlin

46–47. Candice Breitz, *TLDR,* 2017. Thirteen-channel video installation, color, sound. Room A: 60 min. loop; room B: approx. 12 hour loop. Installation view, Kunstmuseum St. Gallen, Switzerland, 2018. Featuring interviews with Zoe Black, Connie, Duduzile Dlamini, Emmah, Gabbi, Regina High, Jenny, Jowi, Tenderlove, and Nosipho "Provocative" Vidima. Narrator: Xanny "The Future" Stevens. Grim Reaper: Buhle Nobuzana. Conceived in dialogue with SWEAT (Sex Workers Education and Advocacy Taskforce), Cape Town. In memory of Nokuphila Kumalo. Commissioned by the B3 Biennial of the Moving Image, Frankfurt am Main. Courtesy of the artist; Goodman Gallery, Johannesburg and London; Kaufmann Repetto, Milan and New York; and KOW, Berlin

Shu Lea Cheang

49. Shu Lea Cheang, *Brandon: A One-Year Narrative Project in Installments,* 1998–99. Web and mixed-media installation. Installation view, Waag Society, Amsterdam, 1998–99. Solomon R. Guggenheim Museum, New York. Courtesy of the artist

50–51. Shu Lea Cheang, *UKI Virus Rising,* 2018. Three-channel digital video, color, sound; 10 min. Installation views, Gwangju Biennale, South Korea, 2018. Courtesy of the artist

52–53. Shu Lea Cheang, *3×3×6,* 2019. Ten-channel 4K video installation. Installation views, Taiwan in Venice, Venice Biennale, 2019. Courtesy of the artist. Photos: Guan-ming Lin

54 top. Shu Lea Cheang, *FAUCAULT X,* 2019. 4K video, color, sound; 10 min. From *3×3×6,* 2019. Courtesy of the artist

54 bottom. Shu Lea Cheang, *OOX,* 2019. 4K video, color, sound; 10 min. From *3×3×6,* 2019. Courtesy of the artist

55. Shu Lea Cheang, *Baby Love,* 2005. Mixed-media installation. Installation view, Palais de Tokyo, Paris, 2005. Courtesy of the artist. Photo: Florian Kleinefenn

56–57. Shu Lea Cheang, *3×3×6,* 2019. Ten-channel 4K video installation. Videos: 10 min each., dimensions variable. Installation view, Taiwan in Venice, Venice Biennale, 2019. Courtesy of the artist

Minerva Cuevas

59. Minerva Cuevas, *De la serie Caníbal,* 2015. Chocolate screen prints on cotton paper. Dimensions variable. Installation view, kurimanzutto, Mexico City, 2015. Courtesy of the artist and kurimanzutto, Mexico City and New York. Photo: Omar Luis Olguín

60 top. Minerva Cuevas, *Melate,* 2000. Acrylic on wall. Dimensions variable. Public artwork in Mexico City as part of *Mejor Vida Corp.,* 1997–. Courtesy of the artist and kurimanzutto, Mexico City and New York

60 bottom. Minerva Cuevas, *Awake Is Aware,* 2000. Poster. Public artwork in New York as part of *Mejor Vida Corp.,* 1997–. Courtesy of the artist and kurimanzutto, Mexico City and New York

61. Minerva Cuevas, *Mejor Vida Corp.,* 1998–. Mixed media. Various dimensions. Installation view, Museo de la Ciudad de México, Mexico City, 2012. Courtesy of the artist. Photo: Estudio Michel Zabé

62. Minerva Cuevas, *Égalité,* 2004. Five thousand water bottles with altered labels. Dimensions variable. Installation view, Le Grand Café, Centre d'Art Contemporain, Saint-Nazaire, France, 2007. Courtesy of the artist. Photo: Marc Domage

63. Minerva Cuevas, *Del Montte: Bananeras,* 2003. Acrylic on wall, one hundred relabeled tomato cans. Dimensions variable. Installation view, Museo de la Ciudad de México, 2012. Courtesy of the artist. Photo: Estudio Michel Zabé.

64. Minerva Cuevas, installation view, *Feast and Famine,* kurimanzutto, Mexico City, 2015. Courtesy of the artist and kurimanzutto, Mexico City and New York. Photo: Omar Luis Olguín

65 top. Minerva Cuevas, *Feast,* 2015 (detail). Metal table, plastic bones, mixed media. Approximately 43 5/16 × 94 1/2 × 57 1/16 in. (110 × 240 × 145 cm). Installation view, kurimanzutto, Mexico City, 2015. Courtesy of the artist and kurimanzutto, Mexico City and New York. Photo: Omar Luis Olguín

65 bottom. Minerva Cuevas, *Like a Tzompantli,* 2015. Chocolate ears in vitrine. 37 × 36 × 24 7/16 in. (94 × 91.5 × 62 cm). Installation view, kurimanzutto, Mexico City, 2015. Courtesy of the artist and kurimanzutto, Mexico City and New York. Photo: Omar Luis Olguín

66. Minerva Cuevas, *Feast and Famine,* 2015. Installation view, kurimanzutto, Mexico City, 2015. Courtesy of the artist and kurimanzutto, Mexico City and New York. Photo: Omar Luis Olguín

67. Minerva Cuevas, *Famine 3.6,* 2015 (details). Stainless steel, chocolate. Dimensions variable. Installation view, kurimanzutto, Mexico City, 2015. Courtesy of the artist and kurimanzutto, Mexico City and New York. Photo: Omar Luis Olguín

Vaginal Davis

69. Vaginal Davis, *Book of Salma and Suvad*, 2017. Watercolor pencil, nail varnish, lip stain, eye shadow, glycerin, hydrogen peroxide, witch hazel, coconut oil, cocoa butter, perfume, hair spray, Anacin Fast Pain Relief Tablets, Excedrin Migraine and Headache Tablets, and Lydia E. Pinkham Women's Compound and Health Tonic on found paper. 2 × 1 ⅝ in. (5.1 × 3.8 cm). Courtesy of the artist; Adams and Ollman, Portland; Galerie Isabella Bortolozzi, Berlin; and New Discretions, New York

70. Vaginal Davis, *Book of Sawab and Suvur*, 2018. Watercolor pencil, nail varnish, lip stain, eye shadow, glycerin, hydrogen peroxide, witch hazel, coconut oil, cocoa butter, perfume, hair spray, Anacin Fast Pain Relief Tablets, Excedrin Migraine and Headache Tablets, and Lydia E. Pinkham Women's Compound and Health Tonic on found paper. 8 ⅛ × 5 ¹¹⁄₁₆ in. (20.6 × 14.5 cm). Courtesy of the artist; Adams and Ollman, Portland; Galerie Isabella Bortolozzi, Berlin; and New Discretions, New York

71. Vaginal Davis, *Heart and Sparks*, 2018. Watercolor pencil, nail varnish, lip stain, eye shadow, glycerin, hydrogen peroxide, witch hazel, coconut oil, cocoa butter, perfume, hair spray, Anacin Fast Pain Relief Tablets, Excedrin Migraine and Headache Tablets, and Lydia E. Pinkham Women's Compound and Health Tonic on found paper. 11 ¹¹⁄₁₆ × 8 ¹¹⁄₁₆ in. (29.7 × 22.1 cm). Courtesy of the artist; Adams and Ollman, Portland; Galerie Isabella Bortolozzi, Berlin; and New Discretions, New York

72 top. Vaginal Davis, trailer for *Mary Mary*, 2020. Digital video, color, sound; 2:43 min. Courtesy of the artist; Adams and Ollman, Portland; Galerie Isabella Bortolozzi, Berlin; and New Discretions, New York

72 bottom left. Vaginal Davis, *Le Spectre Vert*, 2018. Watercolor pencil, nail varnish, lip stain, eye shadow, glycerin, hydrogen peroxide, witch hazel, coconut oil, cocoa butter, perfume, hair spray, Anacin Fast Pain Relief Tablets, Excedrin Migraine and Headache Tablets, and Lydia E. Pinkham Women's Compound and Health Tonic on found paper. 7 ⅜ × 5 ½ in. (19.3 × 13 cm). Courtesy of the artist; Adams and Ollman, Portland; Galerie Isabella Bortolozzi, Berlin; and New Discretions, New York

72 bottom right. Vaginal Davis, *This for Zahed*, 2018. Watercolor pencil, nail varnish, lip stain, eye shadow, glycerin, hydrogen peroxide, witch hazel, coconut oil, cocoa butter, perfume, hair spray, Anacin Fast Pain Relief Tablets, Excedrin Migraine and Headache Tablets, and Lydia E. Pinkham Women's Compound and Health Tonic on found paper. 8 ³⁄₁₆ × 5 ¹³⁄₁₆ in. (20.8 × 14.7 cm). Courtesy of the artist; Adams and Ollman, Portland; Galerie Isabella Bortolozzi, Berlin; and New Discretions, New York

73. Vaginal Davis, *Proper Butch Goddess Freya*, 2015. Clay, stucco fragments, Wet n Wild Brickhouse Nail Varnish, neon nail lacquer, Rival de Loop nylon nail enamel, hydrogen peroxide, glycerin, witch hazel, Pam, Aqua Net Extra Super HoldHair Spray, Jean Naté perfume. 6 × 6 × 4 ¾ in. (15.2 × 15.2 × 12.1 cm). Courtesy of the artist; Adams and Ollman, Portland; Galerie Isabella Bortolozzi, Berlin; and New Discretions, New York

74 top. Vaginal Davis as the Whoracle at Delphi in Zackary Drucker and Rhys Ernst, *She Gone Rogue*, 2012. HD video, color, sound; 23 min. Courtesy of the artists and Luis de Jesus, Los Angeles

74 bottom. Vaginal Davis as Graciela Grejalya in a promotional still for ¡Cholita!, the Female Menudo, 1990. Styling: I Love Ricky/Cloutier. Courtesy of the artist; Adams and Ollman, Portland; Galerie Isabella Bortolozzi, Berlin; and New Discretions, New York. Photo: Beulah Love (aka Rick Castro)

75 top. Vaginal Davis, trailer for *Mary Mary*, 2020. Digital video, color, sound; 2:43 min. Courtesy of the artist; Adams and Ollman, Portland; Galerie Isabella Bortolozzi, Berlin; and New Discretions, New York

75 bottom. Vaginal Davis, *That Fertile Feeling*, 1982. Video, color, sound; 8:28 min. Directed by Vaginal Davis, John "Quasi" O'Shea, and Gomorrah Wednesday (aka Keith Holland). Courtesy of the artist; Adams and Ollman, Portland; Galerie Isabella Bortolozzi, Berlin; and New Discretions, New York

76. Vaginal Davis and the Afro Sisters in *Interview* magazine, 1986. Styling: Beulah Love (aka Rick Castro) and I Love Ricky/Cloutier. Courtesy of the artist; Adams and Ollman, Portland; Galerie Isabella Bortolozzi, Berlin; and New Discretions, New York. Photo: Alberto Sánchez

77 top. Vaginal Davis in Pedro, Muriel, and Esther (PME)'s *Advanced Capitalism Reunion: Reparations and Retardations*, 2009. Performance view, Santos Party House, New York, 2009. Courtesy of the artist; Adams and Ollman, Portland; Galerie Isabella Bortolozzi, Berlin; and New Discretions, New York. Photo: Mark Tusk

77 bottom. Vaginal Davis as Heike in *Overture Machine Shop*. Performance view, *The Magic Flute: An Opera in Six Steps*, 80WSE Gallery, New York University, 2015. Directed by Susanne Sachsse, written by Vaginal Davis, and produced by Jonathan Berger, with music by Xiu Xiu. Photo: Hector Martínez, 2015

Every Ocean Hughes

79–80. Every Ocean Hughes, *Help the Dead*, 2019. Performance views, KW Institute for Contemporary Art, Berlin, 2019. Performance: Colin Self and Geo Wyeth. Courtesy of the artist. Photos: Frank Sperling

81. Every Ocean Hughes, *Uncounted (performance 9)*, 2017. Performance view, Tate Modern, London, 2017. Performance: Every Ocean Hughes and Ain Bailey. Courtesy of the artist. Photo: Brotherton-Lock

82. Every Ocean Hughes, *Reading the Shade of a Pink Triangle*, 2013. Metal and acrylic on concrete wall. 120 × 180 in. (304.8 × 457.2 cm). Installation view, Portland Institute for Contemporary Art, Oregon, 2013. Courtesy of the artist

83. Every Ocean Hughes, *Comedy of Margin Theatre*, 2015. Acrylic, handmade clocks, costumes. Dimensions variable. Installation view, Secession, Vienna, 2015. Courtesy of the artist and Secession, Vienna. Photo: Iris Ranzinger

84. Every Ocean Hughes, *Sense and Sense*, 2010. Two-channel video, color, silent, and digital chromogenic prints. Video: 15:25 min.; prints: 19 × 17 in. (48.3 × 43.2 cm) each. Performance view: Konsthall C, Stockholm, 2010. In collaboration with MPA. Courtesy of the artist

85. Every Ocean Hughes, *A Gay Bar Called Everywhere (With Costumes and No Practice)*, 2011. Performance view, The Kitchen, New York, 2011. Performance: Becca Albee, Vanessa Anspaugh, Aretha Aoki, Nao Bustamante, Jibz Cameron, Elaine Cardberry, Yve Laris Cohen, Dean Daderko, Celeste Dupuy-Spencer, N-Pop Eisenman, Barbara Hammer, K8 Hardy, Tami Hart, Thomas J. Lax, Charles Ryan Long, Tara Mateik, Neal Medlyn, MPA, Jeanine Oleson, Will Rawls, JD Samson, A. L. Steiner, and Sacha Yanow. Courtesy of the artist

86. Every Ocean Hughes, poster for *Uncounted*, 2015. 24 × 19 in. (61 × 48.3 cm). Designed with Carl Williamson. Courtesy of the artist

87. LTTR event flyer, 2006. 3 × 5 in. (7.6 × 12.7 cm). Courtesy of the artist

Essay Opening Images

98. Okwui Okpokwasili, *Poor People's TV Room Solo*, 2014. Performance view, David Rubenstein Atrium, Lincoln Center, New York, 2014. Courtesy of the artist. Photo: Caitlin McCarthy

114. Beverly Semmes, *Handle*, 2015. Ink on magazine page. 7¾ × 7 in. (19.7 × 17.8 cm). Courtesy of the artist and Susan Inglett Gallery, New York

Bouchra Khalili

147–48 top. Bouchra Khalili, *The Tempest Society*, 2017. 2K video, color, sound; 60 min. Courtesy of the artist and Mor Charpentier Gallery, Paris

148 bottom. Bouchra Khalili, *The Tempest Society*, 2017. 2K video, color, sound; 60 min. Installation view, documenta 14, Athens, 2017. Courtesy of the artist and Mor Charpentier Gallery, Paris. Photo: Stathis Mamalakis

149–50. Bouchra Khalili, *Foreign Office*, 2015 (video stills). Fifteen photographs, silkscreen print, and HD video, color, sound; 22 min. Dimensions variable. Commissioned for the Sam Art Prize, 2015. Courtesy of the artist and Mor Charpentier Gallery, Paris

151. Bouchra Khalili, *The Mapping Journey Project*, 2008–11 (detail). One channel of eight-channel video, color, sound; duration variable. Courtesy of the artist and Mor Charpentier Gallery, Paris

152 top. Bouchra Khalili, *The Mapping Journey Project*, 2008–11. Eight-channel video, color, sound; duration variable. Installation view, Museum of Modern Art, New York, 2016. Courtesy of the artist and Mor Charpentier Gallery, Paris. Photo: Jonathan Muzikaro. © The Museum of Modern Art/Licensed by SCALA/Art Resource, New York

152 bottom. Bouchra Khalili, *The Mapping Journey Project*, 2008–11 (detail). One channel of eight-channel video, color, sound; duration variable. Courtesy of the artist and Mor Charpentier Gallery, Paris

153. Bouchra Khalili, *Twenty-Two Hours*, 2018. 4K video, color, sound; 45 min. Courtesy of the artist and Mor Charpentier Gallery, Paris

154–55. Bouchra Khalili, *Twenty-Two Hours*, 2018. 4K video, color, sound; 45 min. Installation view, Museum Folkwang, Essen, Germany, 2018. Courtesy of the artist and Mor Charpentier Gallery, Paris

155. Bouchra Khalili, *Twenty-Two Hours*, 2018. 4K video, color, sound; 45 min. Courtesy of the artist and Mor Charpentier Gallery, Paris

Laura Lima

157–58. Laura Lima, *Alfaiataria* (Tailor shop), 2014–. Installation views, Pinacoteca Octágono, São Paulo, 2018. Courtesy of the artist; Tanya Bonakdar Gallery, Los Angeles and New York; A Gentil Carioca, Rio de Janeiro; and Galeria Luisa Strina, São Paulo. Photo: Isabelle Matheus

159. Laura Lima, sketches for *Alfaiataria* (Tailor shop) 2014–. Courtesy of the artist; Tanya Bonakdar Gallery, Los Angeles and New York; A Gentil Carioca, Rio de Janeiro; and Galeria Luisa Strina, São Paulo. Photo: Isabelle Matheus

160–61. Laura Lima, *Alfaiataria* (Tailor shop), 2014–. Installation view, Tanya Bonakdar Gallery, New York, 2019. Courtesy of the artist; Tanya Bonakdar Gallery, Los Angeles and New York; A Gentil Carioca, Rio de Janeiro; and Galeria Luisa Strina, São Paulo. Photo: Isabelle Matheus

162. Laura Lima, *Gelatina (H=c/M–c)* (Jelly [M=f/W=f]), 1996. Performer, gelatin, wood, cord. Installation view, *Antártica artes com a folha*, Galeria Casa Triângulo, São Paulo, 1999. Courtesy of the artist; Tanya Bonakdar Gallery, Los Angeles and New York; A Gentil Carioca, Rio de Janeiro; and Galeria Luisa Strina, São Paulo

163 top. Laura Lima, *Marra (M=f/W=f)*, 1996/2002/ 2011. Performers, fabric. Installation view, Bonniers Konsthall, Stockholm, 2011. Courtesy of the artist; Tanya Bonakdar Gallery, Los Angeles and New York; A Gentil Carioca, Rio de Janeiro; and Galeria Luisa Strina, São Paulo. Photo: Olle Kirchmeir

163 bottom. Laura Lima, *Doped (M=f/W=f)*, 1997/ 2002/2006/2014. Performer, crochet tube. Installation view, Instituto Inhotim, Minas Gerais, Brazil, 1997. Courtesy of the artist; Tanya Bonakdar Gallery, Los Angeles and New York; A Gentil Carioca, Rio de Janeiro; and Galeria Luisa Strina, São Paulo. Photo: Eduardo Eckenfels

164. Laura Lima, *Pheasants with Food*, 2005–06. Wood, fishing net, golden ink, faience porcelain, birds, food, water, soil, fruits, vegetables, bread. Dimensions variable. Installation view, Museo de Arte Contemporáneo de Santiago, 2006. Courtesy of the artist; Tanya Bonakdar Gallery, Los Angeles and New York; A Gentil Carioca, Rio de Janeiro; and Galeria Luisa Strina, São Paulo. Photo: Laura Lima, Ana Torres, Paulo Innocêncio

165. Laura Lima, notes on *Man=flesh/Woman=flesh*, 1995–98. Ink on paper and fabric. Courtesy of the artist; Tanya Bonakdar Gallery, Los Angeles and New York; A Gentil Carioca, Rio de Janeiro; and Galeria Luisa Strina, São Paulo

Teresa Margolles

167. Teresa Margolles, *Aproximación al lugar de los hechos* (Proximity to the scene), 2020. Steel, twenty hot plates, dripping system, water extracted from sites where women were murdered in Sydney and its surrounding suburbs, red industrial curtains. Plates, 23 ⅝ × 23 ⅝ in. (60 × 60 cm) each, 196 ⅞ × 669 ¼ × 236 ¼ in. (500 × 1700 × 600 cm) overall. Installation view, National Art School, Biennale of Sydney 2020. Commissioned by the Biennale of Sydney. Courtesy of the artist; Galerie Peter Kilchmann, Zurich; and James Cohan, New York. Photo: Zan Wimberley

To create this installation, Margolles and a group of students from the National Art School in Sydney executed a series of performative actions in which they poured water onto the ground where homicides and the disappearances of women had taken place, absorbing the material traces of each violent act. Encircled in red industrial curtains, the resulting artwork comprised twenty steaming iron plates onto which drops of water fall from above, laced with the material residue of violence.

168 top. Teresa Margolles, *Autorretratos (No 2)* (Self-portraits [No. 2]), 1998. Color photographic print. 40 ½ × 48 ⅜ in. (103 × 123 cm). Courtesy of the artist; Galerie Peter Kilchmann, Zurich; and James Cohan, New York

168 bottom. Teresa Margolles, *¿De qué otra cosa podríamos hablar? Limpieza* (What else could we talk about? Cleaning), 2009. Performance carried out by one to three people mopping the floors of the exhibition space with a liquid containing water obtained from wetting fabrics that previously absorbed fluids and material residue of crime scenes from several cities in northern Mexico. Installation view, Mexican Pavilion, Venice Biennale, 2009. Courtesy of the artist; Galerie Peter Kilchmann, Zurich; and James Cohan, New York

169 top. Teresa Margolles, *¿De qué otra cosa podríamos hablar? Narcomensajes* (What else could we talk about? Narcomessages), 2009. Fabrics impregnated with blood gathered in places where murders took place in Ciudad Juárez, Mexico, and progressively embroidered throughout the course of the exhibition. Installation view, Mexican Pavilion, Venice Biennale, 2009. Courtesy of the artist; Galerie Peter Kilchmann, Zurich; and James Cohan, New York

169 bottom. Teresa Margolles, *En el aire Ciudad Juárez* (In the air Ciudad Juárez), 2011. Bubbles produced with water infused with the material residue of violent acts that took place on the outskirts of Ciudad Juárez. Installation view, Musée d'Art Contemporain de Montréal, Canada, 2017. Courtesy of the artist; Galerie Peter Kilchmann, Zurich; and James Cohan, New York. Photo: Richard-Max Tremblay

170–71. *Karla, Hilario Reyes Gallegos*, 2016 (detail). Black-and-white photographic print, facsimile of death certificate, sound piece, found object from the crime site. Dimensions variable. Courtesy of the artist; Galerie Peter Kilchmann, Zurich; and James Cohan, New York

Karla was a transsexual sex worker beaten to death at the age of sixty-four on December 22, 2015, in Ciudad Juárez.

172. Teresa Margolles, *La promesa* (The promise), 2012–17. Twenty-two tons of rubble from the remains of a demolished house in Ciudad Juárez. Installation view, Musée d'Art Contemporain de Montréal, Canada, 2017. Courtesy of the artist; Galerie Peter Kilchmann, Zurich; and James Cohan, New York

173. Teresa Margolles, *La sombra* (The shade), 2016. Concrete structure. 19 ft. 8 in. × 19 ft. 8 in. × 45 ft. 11 in. (6 × 6 × 14 m). Courtesy of the artist; Galerie Peter Kilchmann, Zurich; and James Cohan, New York

Over the course of eighteen months, Margolles and a crew of helpers visited roughly one hundred sites around Los Angeles where individuals had been killed in violent crimes. Water was poured onto these locations and then absorbed into fabric pieces used to transfer the organic material from the ground into bottles of water, each labeled with the name of the person who had been killed and the date and site of their death. This infused water was subsequently used to mix concrete poured to create the sculpture *La sombra*, placed at Echo Park Lake as a part of the biennal Current: LA Water.

174–75. Teresa Margolles, *Carretilleras sobre el Puente Internacional Simón Bolívar* (Porters on the Simón Bolívar International Bridge), 2018. Color photographic print. 42 ⅛ × 81 ½ in. (107 × 202 cm). Courtesy of the artist; Galerie Peter Kilchmann, Zurich; and James Cohan, New York

Venezuelan economic collapse has resulted in women taking on the traditionally male labor of carrying goods across the Colombia-Venezuela border. The photograph depicts women forming a line in an area called La Parada near the Simón Bolívar International Bridge at the artist's request.

Otobong Nkanga

177. Otobong Nkanga, *In Pursuit of Bling*, 2014. HD video, color, sound; 11:59 min. Courtesy of the artist

178–79. Otobong Nkanga, *Constellation to Appease*, 2019. Found objects and materials, stainless steel, rubber-coated rope, string. Dimensions variable. Performance view, Tate St Ives, United Kingdom, 2019. Courtesy of the artist. Photo: © Tate (Oliver Cowling)

180. Otobong Nkanga, *Contained Measures of a Kolanut*, 2012 (detail). Kola nut extract dripping from a decanter onto handmade cotton paper. Installation view, Bétonsalon—Centre d'Art et de Recherche, Paris, 2012. Courtesy of the artist

181. Otobong Nkanga, *Contained Measures of a Kolanut*, 2012. Tables, handmade cotton paper, inkjet photographs on PVC, wood, kola nuts, kola nut extract, glass plates, knife, gloves, cushions, decanter, stand. Performance and installation view, Szalon at the Logan Center Gallery, Chicago, 2014. Courtesy of the artist. Photo: Marco G. Ferrari

182. Otobong Nkanga, *In Pursuit of Bling*, 2014. Inkjet prints, light box, metal structure, minerals, objects, texts, HD videos (color, sound), woven textiles. Installation view, Berlin Biennale for Contemporary Art, KW Institute for Contemporary Art, 2014. Courtesy of the artist. Photo: Anders Sune Berg

183. Otobong Nkanga, *In Pursuit of Bling: Reflections of the Raw Green Crown*, 2014. HD video, color, sound; 2:52 min. Commissioned and coproduced by the Berlin Biennale for Contemporary Art with the support of DAAD. Courtesy of the artist

184. Otobong Nkanga, *The Weight of Scars*, 2015. Woven textile with viscose bast, mohair, polyester, cotton, linen, acrylic yarns, ten inkjet photographs on PVC. Four panels, 99 ⁹⁄₁₆ × 60 ⅛ in. (253 × 153 cm) each. Installation view, Museum of Contemporary Art Chicago, 2018. Courtesy of the artist. Photo: © MCA Chicago

185. Otobong Nkanga, *From Where I Stand*, 2015 (foreground, detail). Chromojet-printed carpet, various objects. 245 ⁵⁄₁₆ × 440 ⅛ in. (623 cm × 1118 cm). Installation view, Tate St Ives, United Kingdom, 2019–20. Courtesy of the artist. Photo: © Tate (Joe Humphrys and Oliver Cowling)

Okwui Okpokwasili

187. Okwui Okpokwasili, *Poor People's TV Room*, 2016. Performance view, New York Live Arts, 2016. Courtesy of the artist. Photo: Paul B. Goode

188. Okwui Okpokwasili, *Bronx Gothic*, 2014. Performance views, Danspace Project, New York, 2014. Courtesy of the artist. Photos: Ian Douglas

189. Okwui Okpokwasili, *Poor People's TV Room Solo*, 2014. Performance view, David Rubenstein Atrium, Lincoln Center, New York, 2014. Photo: Caitlin McCarthy

190–91. Okwui Okpokwasili, *Poor People's TV Room*, 2016. Performance view, Lincoln Center Atrium, New York, 2016. Courtesy of the artist. Photo: Paul B. Goode

191 right. Okwui Okpokwasili, *Poor People's TV Room*, 2016. Performance view, American Dance Institute, Rockville, Maryland, 2016. Courtesy of the artist. Photo: Mena Burnett

192–95. Okwui Okpokwasili, *Poor People's TV Room*, 2016. Performance views, New York Live Arts, 2016. Courtesy of the artist. Photos: Paul B. Goode

Lara Schnitger

197. Lara Schnitger, *Lick My Legs*, 2012. Quilted and bleached fabric. 75 ⅝ × 58 ¾ in. (192.1 × 149.2 cm). Courtesy of the artist and Anton Kern Gallery, New York. Photo: Joshua White

198. Lara Schnitger, installation view, *Helper's Little Mother,* Bonnefantenmuseum, Maastricht, Netherlands, 2014. Collection of the Bonnefantenmuseum, Maastricht, Netherlands. Photo: Peter Cox

199 top left. Lara Schnitger, *High Heeled Honey*, 2005. Stencil on fabric, ribbon, eyelets, cord, wood, pins. 129 × 59 × 61 in. (328 × 150 × 155 cm). Collection of the Hall Art Foundation, Derneburg, Germany. Photo: Joshua White

199 top right. Lara Schnitger, *Rebel Rouser*, 2005. Handmade T-shirts, I Love NY T-shirts, fabric, buttons, cotton, wood, ribbon, pins. 116 × 67 × 87 in. (295 × 170 × 220 cm). Courtesy of the artist and Anton Kern Gallery, New York. Photo: Joshua White

199 bottom left. Lara Schnitger, *Dix-huit+*, 2005. Lycra, stencil on fabric, ribbon, wood, pins. 114 × 79 × 47 in. (290 × 200 × 120 cm). Collection of the Linda Pace Foundation, Ruby City, San Antonio. Photo: Joshua White

199 bottom right. Lara Schnitger, *Betty Ford*, 2005. Wood, fabric, fake fur, pins. 91 × 86 × 62 in. (231.1 × 218.4 × 157.5 cm). Fogg Museum, Harvard Art Museums, Cambridge, Massachusetts. Photo: Joshua White

200–201. Lara Schnitger, installation view, *Victory Garden*, Grice Bench, Los Angeles, 2019. Courtesy of the artist; Anton Kern Gallery, New York; and Grice Bench, Los Angeles. Photo: Joshua White

202 left. Lara Schnitger, *Suffragette City Dresden*, 2017. Performance view, Kunsthaus Dresden, Germany, 2017. Courtesy of the artist and Anton Kern Gallery, New York. Photo: Swen Rudolph

202 right. Lara Schnitger, *Suffragette City Los Angeles*, 2016. Performance view, Hammer Museum, Los Angeles, 2016. Courtesy of the artist and Anton Kern Gallery, New York. Photo: Joshua White

203 top. Lara Schnitger, installation view, *Too Nice Too Long*, Anton Kern Gallery, New York, 2017. Courtesy of the artist and Anton Kern Gallery, New York. Photo: Thomas Mueller

203 bottom. Lara Schnitger, installation view, *Suffragette City Reims*, FRAC Champagne-Ardenne, Reims, France, 2015. Courtesy of the artist and Anton Kern Gallery, New York. Photo: Martin Argyroglo

204. Lara Schnitger, *I Am Evil,* 2019. Fabric, wood, silkscreen, pins. 72 × 78 × 116 in. (180.3 × 198.1 × 294.6 cm). Courtesy of the artist; Anton Kern Gallery, New York; and Grice Bench, Los Angeles. Photo: Joshua White

205. Lara Schnitger, *Leto's Party*, 2017. Cotton, resin, nylon, feathers, button, wig, wood. 120 × 99 × 108 in. (304.8 × 251.5 × 274.3 cm). Museum of Contemporary Art, San Diego. Photo: Joshua White

Beverly Semmes

207. Beverly Semmes, *Pink Pot*, 2008. Ink on magazine page. 7 ½ × 10 ¹³⁄₁₆ in. (19.1 × 27.5 cm). Courtesy of the artist and Susan Inglett Gallery, New York. Photo: Peter McClennan

208. Beverly Semmes, *Red Dress*, 1992. Velvet, clothes hanger. Dimensions variable. Courtesy of the artist; Susan Inglett Gallery, New York; and Shoshana Wayne Gallery, Los Angeles

209. Beverly Semmes, installation view, *Red Pots, Crystal Chandeliers*, Weatherspoon Art Museum, Greensboro, North Carolina, 2015. Courtesy of the artist and Susan Inglett Gallery, New York

210. Beverly Semmes, *Silver Hat*, 2018. Ink and acrylic on printed canvas. 82 ¹¹⁄₁₆ × 50 in. (210.1 × 127 cm). Courtesy of the artist and Susan Inglett Gallery, New York

211. Beverly Semmes, *Helmet*, 2018. Ink and acrylic on printed canvas. 70 ½ × 50 in. (179.1 × 127 cm). Courtesy of the artist and Susan Inglett Gallery, New York

212. Beverly Semmes, *Legs*, 2018. Ink and acrylic on printed canvas. 78 ½ × 50 in. (200.2 × 127 cm). Courtesy of the artist and Susan Inglett Gallery, New York

213. Beverly Semmes, *Antenna*, 2019. Ink and acrylic on printed canvas. 82 ⁵⁄₁₆ × 50 in. (209.1 × 127 cm). Courtesy of the artist and Susan Inglett Gallery, New York

214. Beverly Semmes, *Silver Heart*, 2019. Ink and acrylic on printed canvas. 81 ⅛ × 50 in. (206 × 127 cm). Courtesy of the artist and Susan Inglett Gallery, New York

215. Beverly Semmes, *Blue Moon*, 2020. Ink and acrylic on printed canvas. 65 ¾ × 40 in. (167 × 101.6 cm). Courtesy of the artist and Susan Inglett Gallery, New York

216. Pauline Boudry / Renate Lorenz, *Moving Backwards*, 2019. HD video installation, color, sound; 23 min. Choreography/performance: Julie Cunningham, Werner Hirsch, Latifa Laâbissi, Marbles Jumbo Radio, and Nach. Courtesy of the artists; Ellen de Brujine Projects, Amsterdam; and Marcelle Alix, Paris

217. Yael Bartana, *Patriarchy Is History*, 2019. Neon. 78 ⅛ × 72 ¹⁵⁄₁₆ in. (198.4 × 185.3 cm). Courtesy of the artist; Annet Gelink Gallery, Amsterdam; Sommer Contemporary Art, Tel Aviv; and Galleria Raffaella Cortese, Milan; Petzel Gallery, New York; and Captain Petzel, Berlin. Photo: Tom Haartsen

218. Bouchra Khalili, *The Archipelago*, 2015. Silkscreen print. 29 ½ × 19 ⅝ in. (75 × 50 cm). From *Foreign Office*, 2015. Courtesy of the artist and Lisson Gallery, London

219. Laura Lima, *Bale literal* (Literal dance), 2019. Installation view, A Gentil Carioca, Rio de Janeiro, 2019. Courtesy of the artist; Tanya Bonakdar Gallery, Los Angeles and New York; A Gentil Carioca, Rio de Janeiro; and Galeria Luisa Strina, São Paulo. Photo: Pedro Agilson

220. Shu Lea Cheang, *UKI Virus Rising*, 2018. Three-channel digital video, color, sound; 10 min. Installation view, *Fluidités, Le humain qui vient, Le Fresnoy*, Studio National des Arts Contemporains, Tourcoing, France, 2020. Courtesy of the artist and DICRéAM, Le Centre National du Cinéma, France. Photo: Yves Boutry

221. Every Ocean Hughes, *Ecstatic Resistance (schema)*, 2009. Silkscreen ink and chine-collé on paper. 34 ½ × 25 in. (87.6 × 63.5 cm). Designed with Carl Williamson. Courtesy of the artist

222. Otobong Nkanga, *Borrowed Light*, 2019 (detail). Acrylic on plywood and steel coach screws. Dimensions variable. Courtesy of the artist. Photo: © Tate (Joe Humphrys and Oliver Cowling)

223. Leonor Antunes, installation view, *discrepancias con C. P.* (discrepancies with C. P.), Museo Tamayo, Mexico City, 2018. Courtesy of the artist and kurimanzutto, Mexico City and New York

224. Teresa Margolles, *Pesquisas* (Inquiries), 2016–19 (detail). Thirty-three color photographic print installation. 118 ½ × 277 ⅜ in. (301 × 704.5 cm). Courtesy of the artist; Galerie Peter Kilchmann, Zurich; and James Cohan, New York

Pesquisas (inquiries) are photocopied portraits of disappeared women that have been plastered throughout the streets of Ciudad Juárez from the late 1990s to the present. The posters consist of a photograph and information about the victims. Over time, the information on the posters fades as they become discolored and torn, part of the urban landscape. External agents such as weather and people play a role in their transformation, at times making the portraits unrecognizable. Though the local government has tried to prohibit people from posting these images, the *pesquisas* continue. They represent the demands of both the families and civil society in the face of tragedy. The International Human Rights Commission notes that in the past four years, more than fourteen thousand women have disappeared in Mexico.

Hammer Museum

This book was published on the occasion of the exhibition *Witch Hunt*, organized and presented by the Hammer Museum, Los Angeles, and the Institute of Contemporary Art, Los Angeles, October 10, 2021–January 9, 2022.

The exhibition is curated by Connie Butler, chief curator of the Hammer, and Anne Ellegood, Good Works Executive Director of ICA LA, with Nika Chilewich, Hammer curatorial assistant.

Witch Hunt is made possible by lead funding from the Kaleta A. Doolin Foundation. Major support is provided by Kelsey Lee Offield, with generous funding from Darren Star, Jill and Peter Kraus and from Hope Warschaw and John Law. The exhibition is also supported by Bill Hair, Emily and Teddy Greenspan, and by Étant donnés Contemporary Art, a program developed by FACE Foundation and the Cultural Services of the French Embassy in the United States, with lead funding from the French Ministry of Culture and Institut Français-Paris, the Florence Gould Foundation, the Ford Foundation, the Helen Frankenthaler Foundation, Chanel USA, the ADAGP, and the CPGA. Additional support is provided by Artis and Betty Duker.

At ICA LA, major support for the exhibition is provided by the Vera R. Campbell Foundation and the Younes and Soraya Nazarian Family Foundation. The exhibition is also generously funded by grants from the Pasadena Art Alliance, the Art Dealers Association of America Foundation, and the Henry Moore Foundation, as well as contributions from Christine Meleo Bernstein and Armyan Bernstein, Alice and Nahum Lainer, Marla and Jeffrey Michaels, and members of the Curator's Council.

Published in 2021 by the Armand Hammer Museum of Art and Cultural Center, Inc.

Hammer Museum
10899 Wilshire Boulevard
Los Angeles, CA 90024-4201
310.443.7000
www.hammer.ucla.edu

DelMonico Books available through
ARTBOOK | D.A.P.
75 Broad Street, Suite 630
New York, NY 10004

www.artbook.com
www.delmonicobooks.com

Designer: Jessica Fleischmann / Still Room
Editor: Domenick Ammirati
Proofreader: Jane Bobko
Director, exhibition and publication management: Melanie Crader
Project manager: Claire Dilworth
Color separations: Echelon, Santa Monica
Printer: Conti Tipocolor, S.p.A., Florence, Italy

The book is typeset in Lelo by Katharina Köhler
and printed on Gardamatt Ultra and Munken Print paper.

Front and back covers: Pauline Boudry / Renate Lorenz, *Telepathic Improvisation*, 2017. HD video, color, sound, with mixed-media installation. Performance: Marwa Arsanios, MPA, Ginger Brooks Takahashi, and Werner Hirsch. Courtesy of the artists; Ellen de Bruijne Projects, Amsterdam; and Marcelle Alix, Paris

Printed and bound in Florence, Italy

Library of Congress Control Number: 2021933430

ISBN: 978-1-942884-75-0

Bouchra Khalili

b. 1975, Morocco. Lives and works in Berlin, Germany.

Encompassing video, installation, photography, and printmaking, Bouchra Khalili's practice explores strategies and discourses of resistance, often from the perspective of those at the margins. Operating at the intersection of the grand sweep of received history and micronarratives that are typically overlooked, her work combines research and archival practices with documentary film to investigate questions of self-representation, agency, and forms of resistance employed by suppressed communities. Khalili's approach is deeply informed by the legacy of post-independence avant-gardes and the vernacular traditions of her native Morocco. It combines various strategies of performing narrative, reactivating "civil poetry" as defined by Italian poet and filmmaker Pier Paolo Pasolini as well as the Moroccan tradition of the *halqa*, an ancient form of public storytelling.

In the video installation *The Mapping Journey Project* (2008–11), Khalili focuses on the personal stories told by individuals from various backgrounds—immigrants, undocumented workers, stateless citizens—who describe their journeys across various borders from North Africa and neighboring Arab countries to Europe. "I hope that I can get papers and be able to live like everyone else, here in Europe. To work, that is all," declares one speaker. Meanwhile, we see his hand tracing a trajectory in permanent marker on a map, wending from northern Tunisia through Libya, across the Mediterranean Sea to Italy, and finally ending in Marseille. Each of the eight channels features a different story and a different map of the Mediterranean basin, with a marker's line traversing and overriding geographic borders. Despite the danger and instability inherent in migrating without documentation, the speakers recount their stories of trauma, loss, detention, and deportation calmly, as matters of fact. They often end their narratives by focusing on the practical, proclaiming a need for the stateless and the rightless to have the obstacles to their passage removed—and also to have a chance at happiness.

Khalili emphasizes the importance of marginalized voices being heard directly, not speaking on their behalf or rendering them figuratively; her process is to listen rather than ask questions. The speakers claim authorship of their own narratives, reinstating their agency and recasting migration due to political and economic circumstances as a mode of resistance. Those who appear in *The Mapping Journey Project* are one example. By refusing to be held under state control, they challenge preconceived notions of immigration and statehood. In Khalili's video trilogy *The Speeches Series* (2012–13), migrants recite translated passages from various political or literary texts, devise manifestos on notions of citizenship and belonging, and reflect on oppression. Their performances, which take up writings such as Aimé Césaire's 1950 "Discourse on Colonialism," focus on redefining citizenship as inclusive of those most vulnerable and typically deprived of their civic rights: migrants, exiles, and refugees. Khalili's collaborators engage the past in ways that echo the present under neocolonialism, creating an understanding of how history and experience remain ever evolving across time.

In her work, Khalili listens just as intently to figures from the past as she does to the living, parsing out what is left unsaid from historical accounts and records and emphasizing voices made marginal. For *Witch Hunt*, Khalili examines the life and internationalist work of radical feminist filmmaker Carole Roussopoulos, a reoccurring figure in Khalili's work. *The Magic Lantern Project* (2021) takes as its starting point lesser-known parts of Roussopoulos's output—her videos about Jordan, the Black Panther Party, and Algiers—and aims to revive the ghosts haunting these forgotten tapes. Roussopoulos's deployment of filmmaking as a revolutionary practice meets the most ancient form of projected imagery, the magic lantern, to create a collective experience of revolutionary history. *The Magic Lantern Project* includes a video that restages the phantasmagoria of the precinematic age, performative shows that used a magic lantern to make ghosts speak in public. With reference to that device, as well as to the Sony Portapak video camera, which Roussopoulos used in her early work, Khalili's contribution to *Witch Hunt* meditates on media as a nomadic and dissident form of witnessing. Through the project, the artist hopes to fill history's gaps with imagination, calling forth phantoms as viewers stand in solidarity.

—Ana Briz

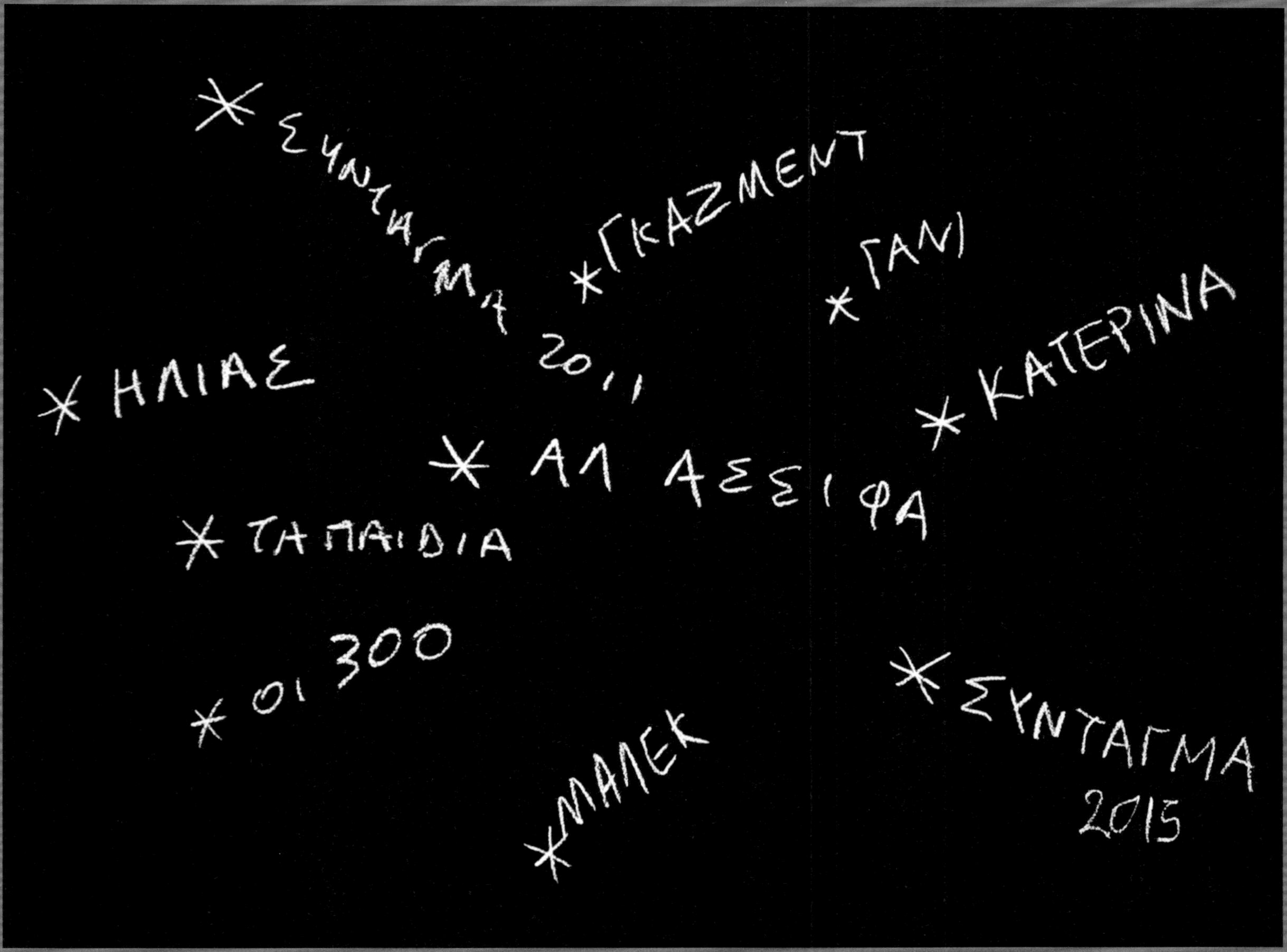

ΣΥΝΤΑΓΜΑ 2011
ΓΚΑΖΜΕΝΤ
ΓΑΝΙ
ΗΛΙΑΣ
ΚΑΤΕΡΙΝΑ
ΑΛ ΑΣΣΙΦΑ
ΤΑ ΠΑΙΔΙΑ
ΟΙ 300
ΜΑΛΕΚ
ΣΥΝΤΑΓΜΑ 2015

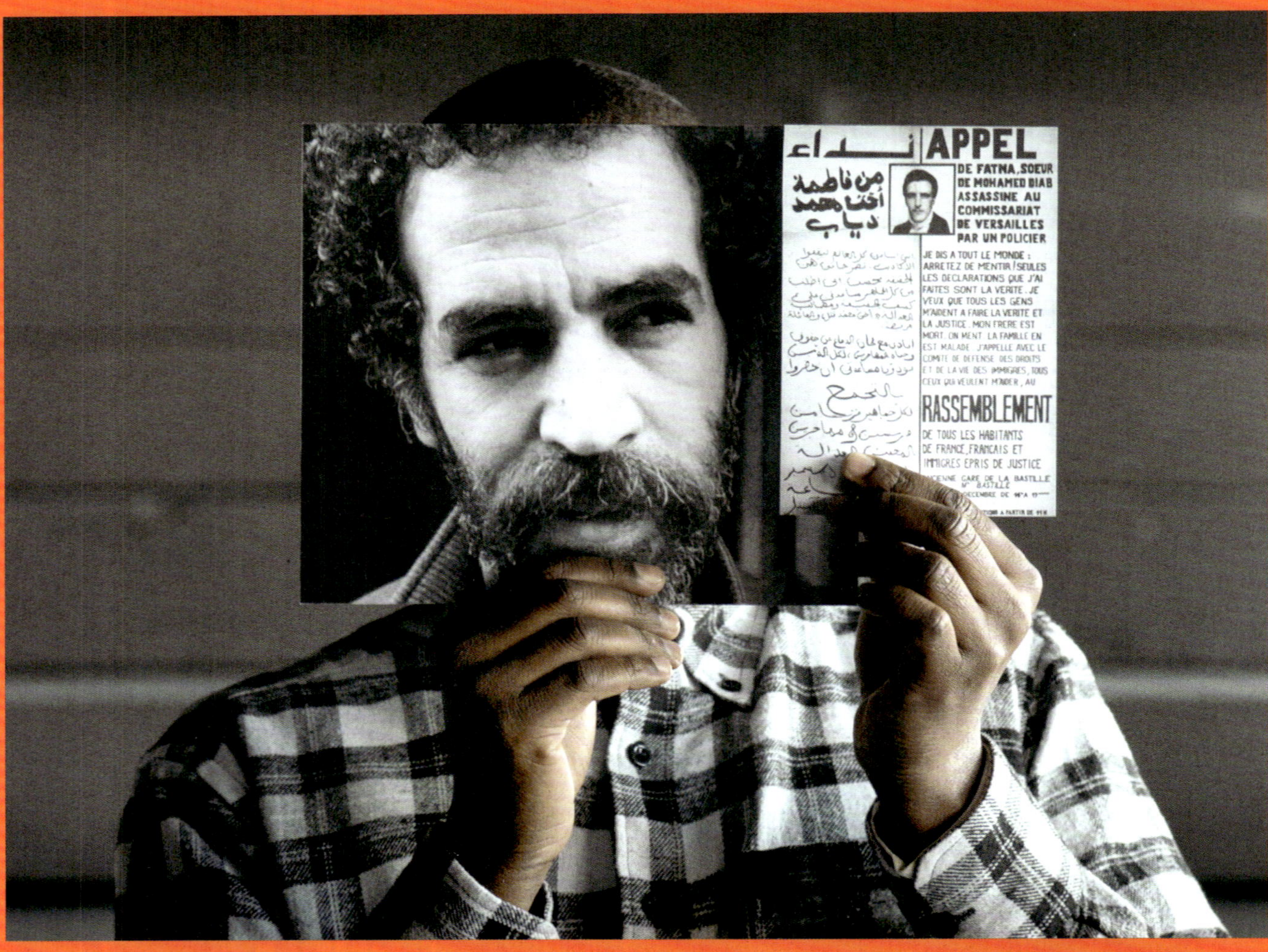

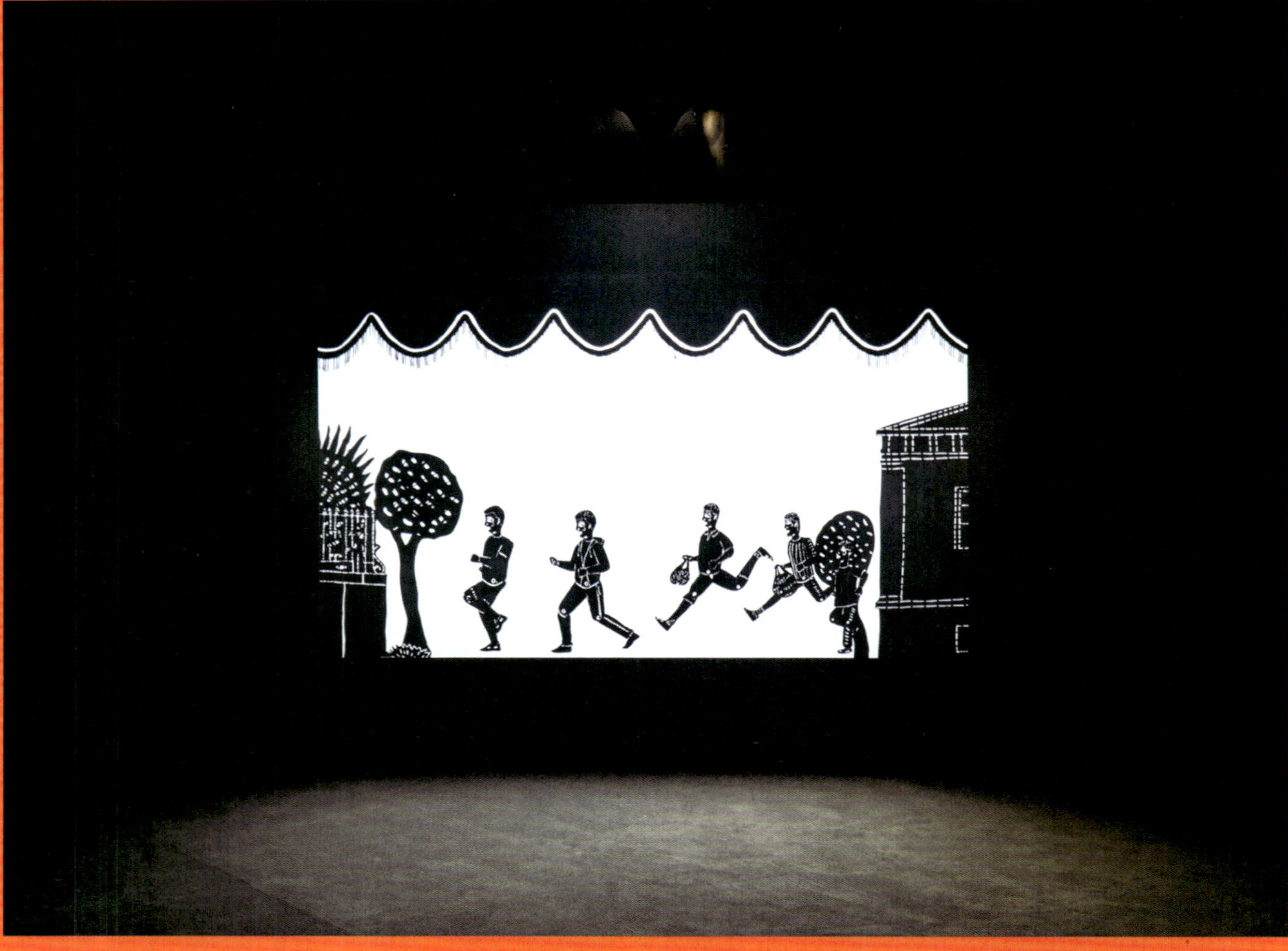

The Tempest Society, 2017

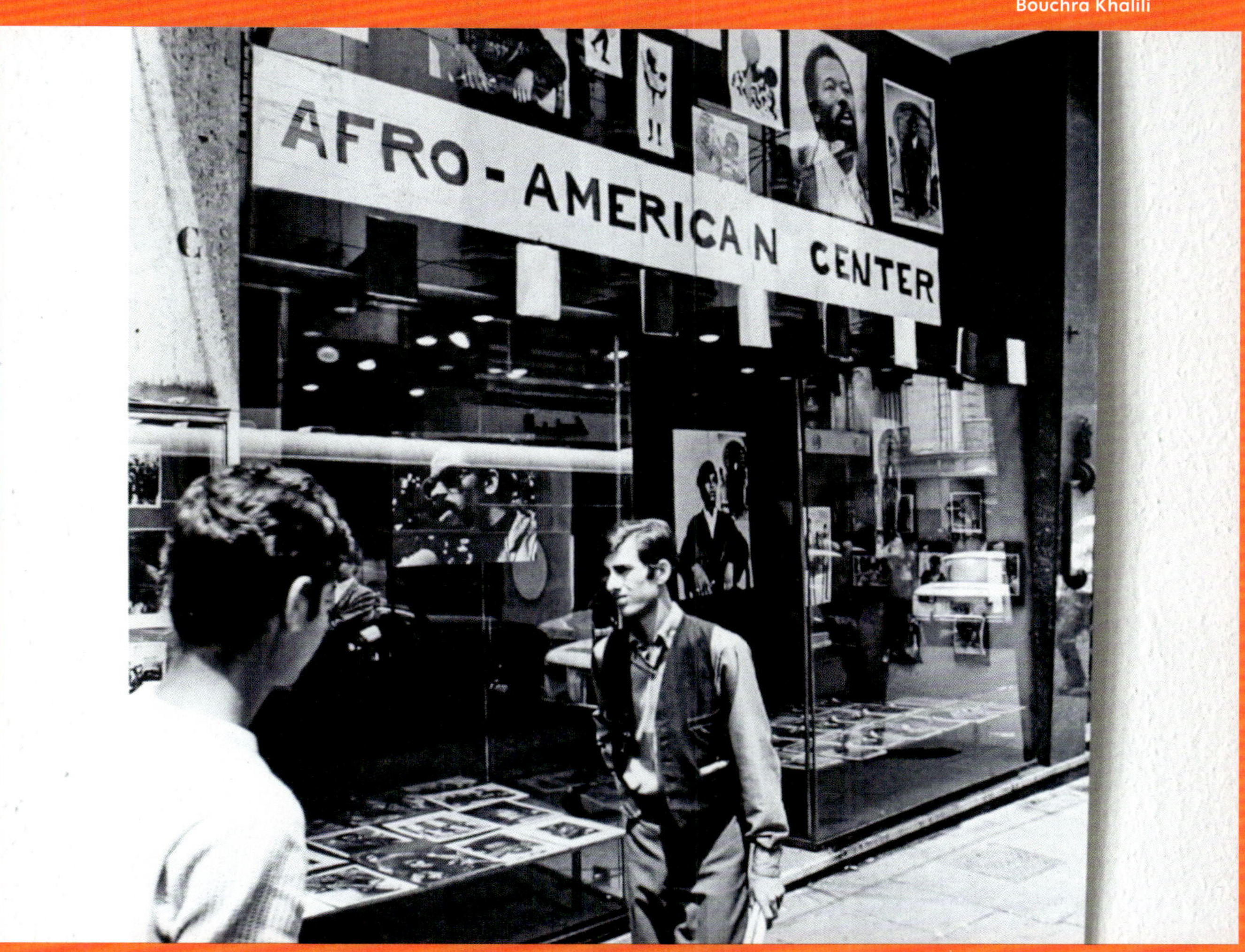

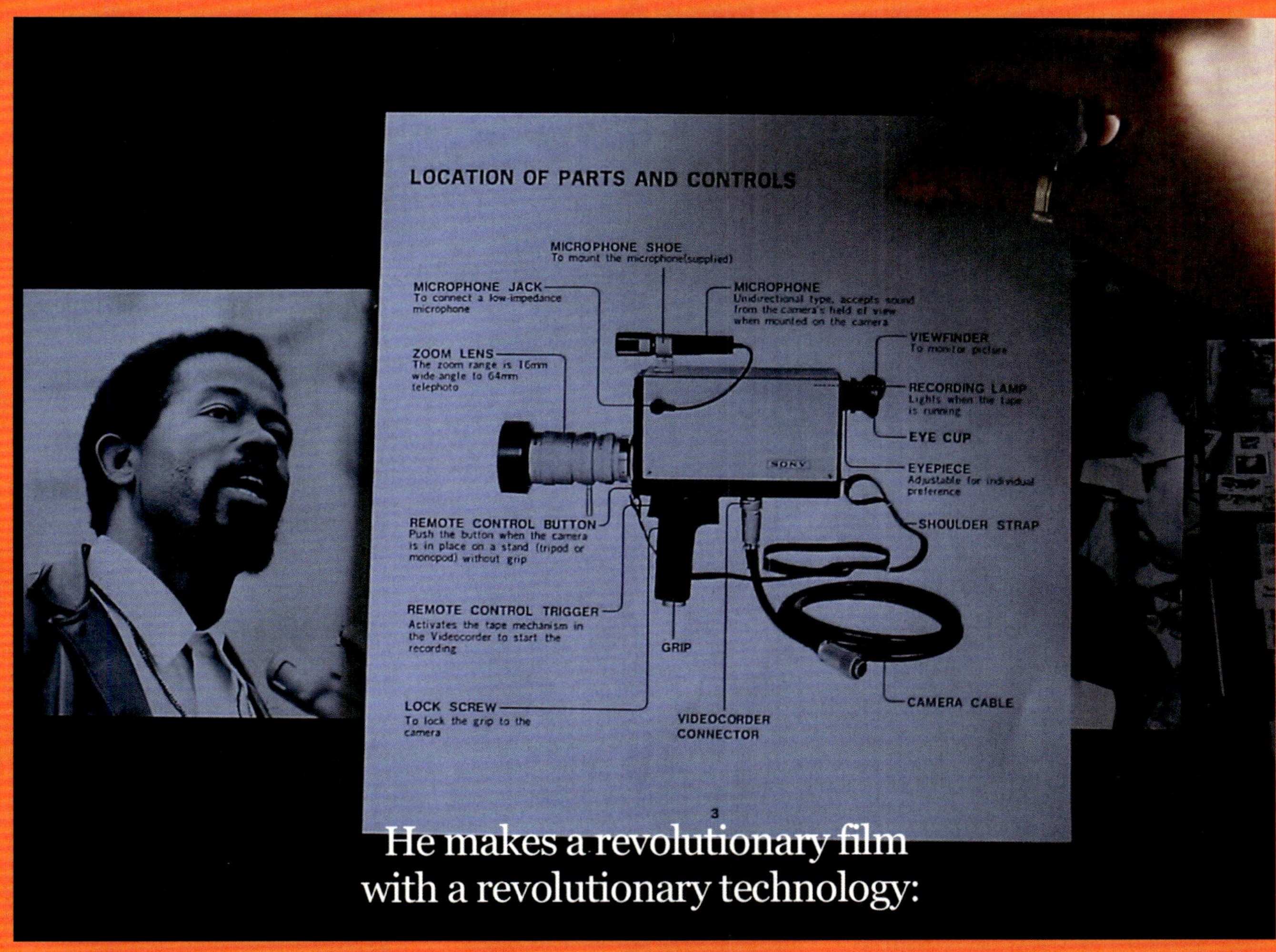

He makes a revolutionary film
with a revolutionary technology:

Foreign Office, 2015

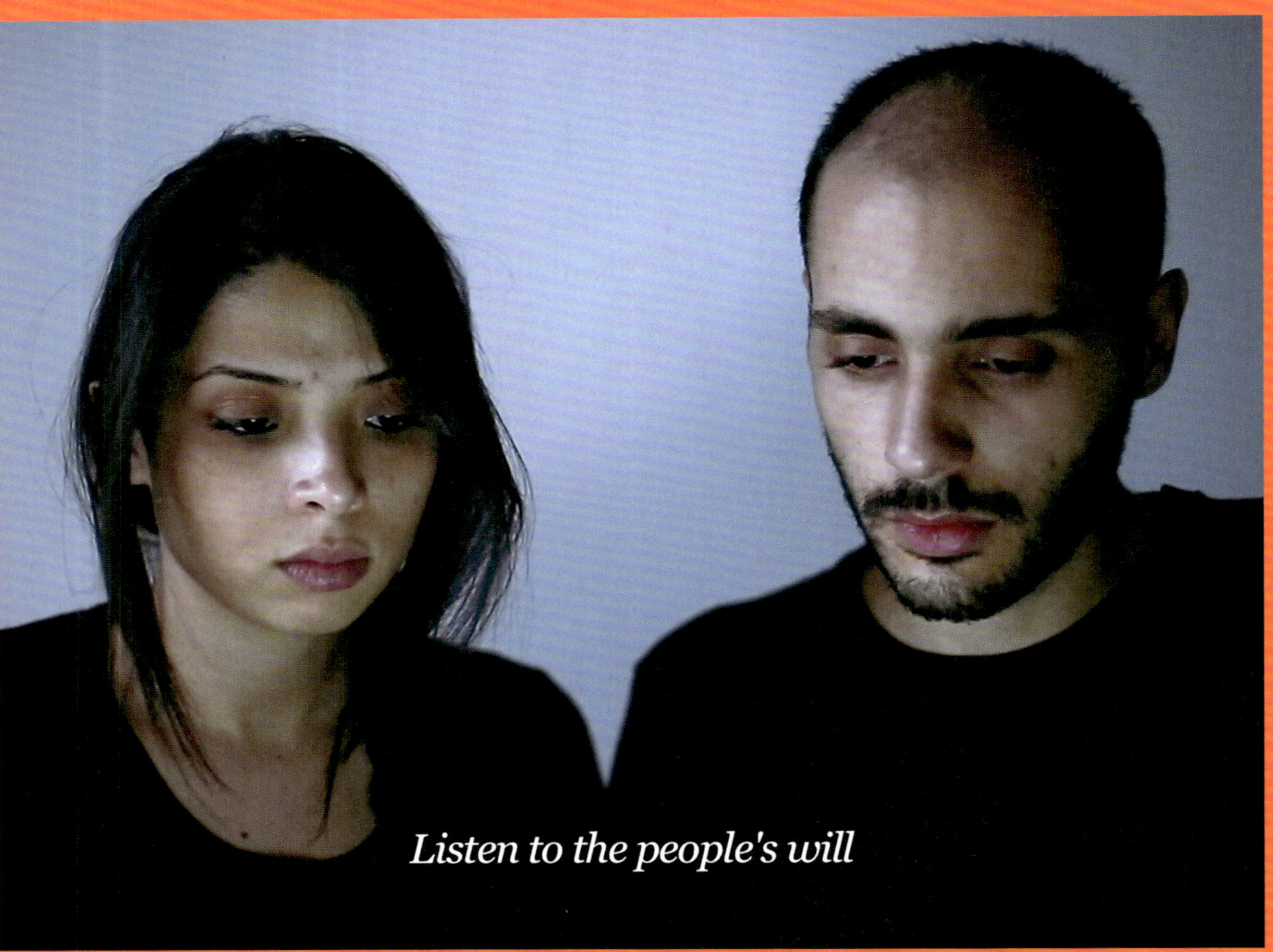

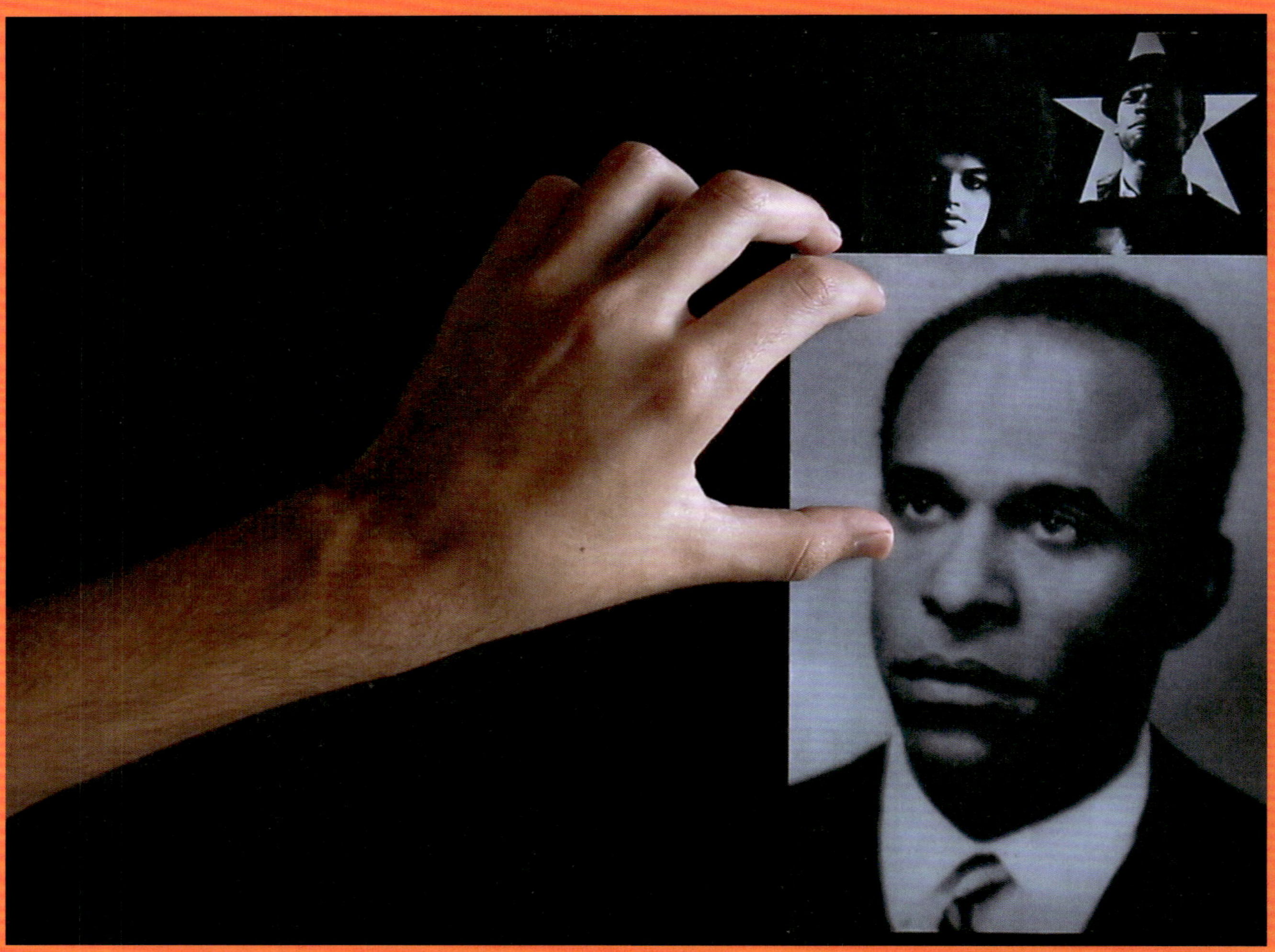

Foreign Office, 2015

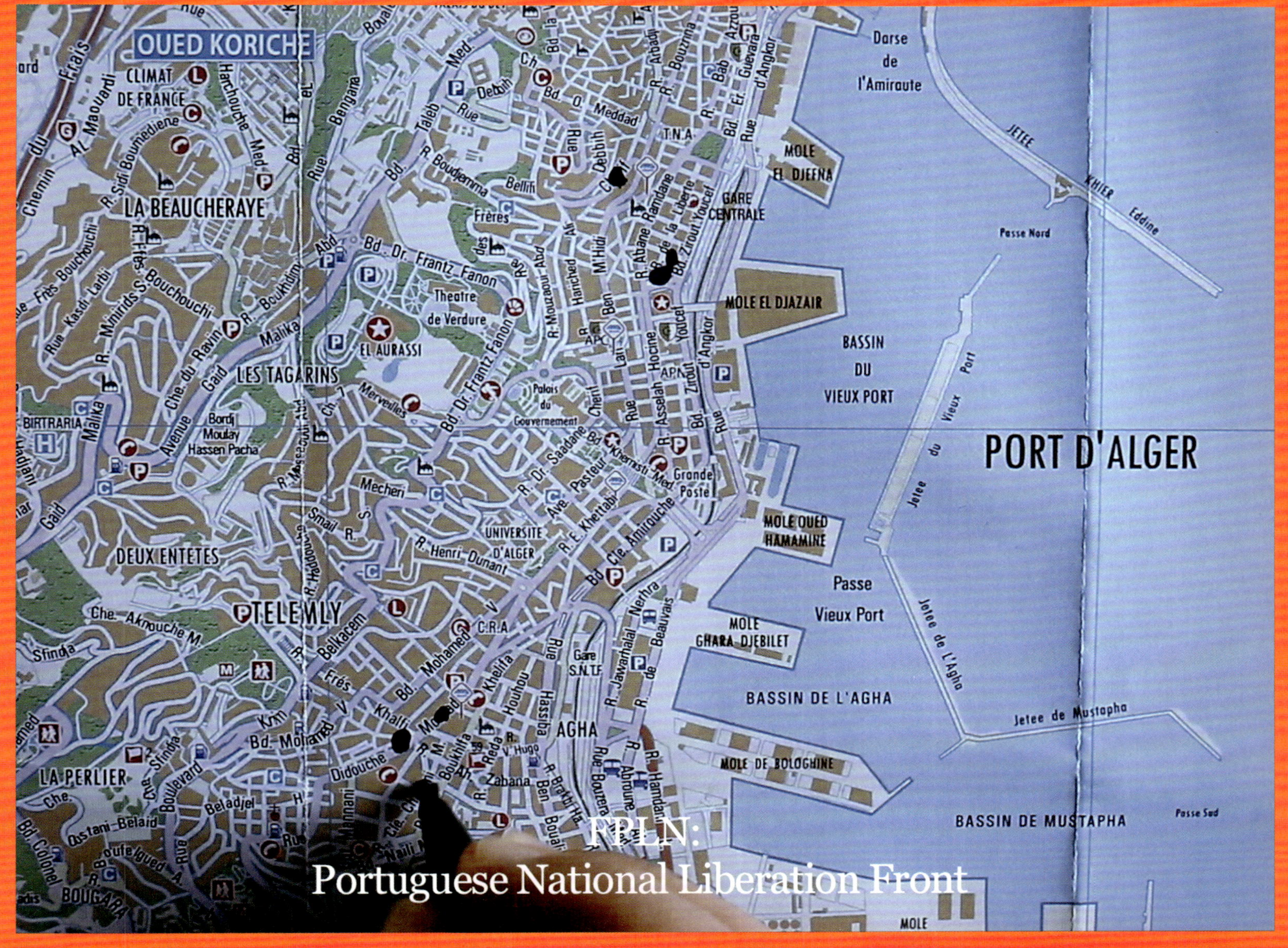
OUED KORICHE
LA BEAUCHERAYE
LES TAGARINS
EL AURASSI
DEUX ENTETES
PTELEMLY
LA PERLIER
AGHA
PORT D'ALGER
BASSIN
DU
VIEUX PORT
MOLE EL DJAZAIR
MOLE
EL DJEFNA
GARE
CENTRALE
MOLE OUED
HAMAMIRE
Passe
Vieux Port
MOLE
GHARA DJEBILET
BASSIN DE L'AGHA
MOLE DE BOLOGHINE
BASSIN DE MUSTAPHA
Jetee de Mustapha
Darse
de
l'Amiraute
Passe Nord
Passe Sud
FPLN:
Portuguese National Liberation Front

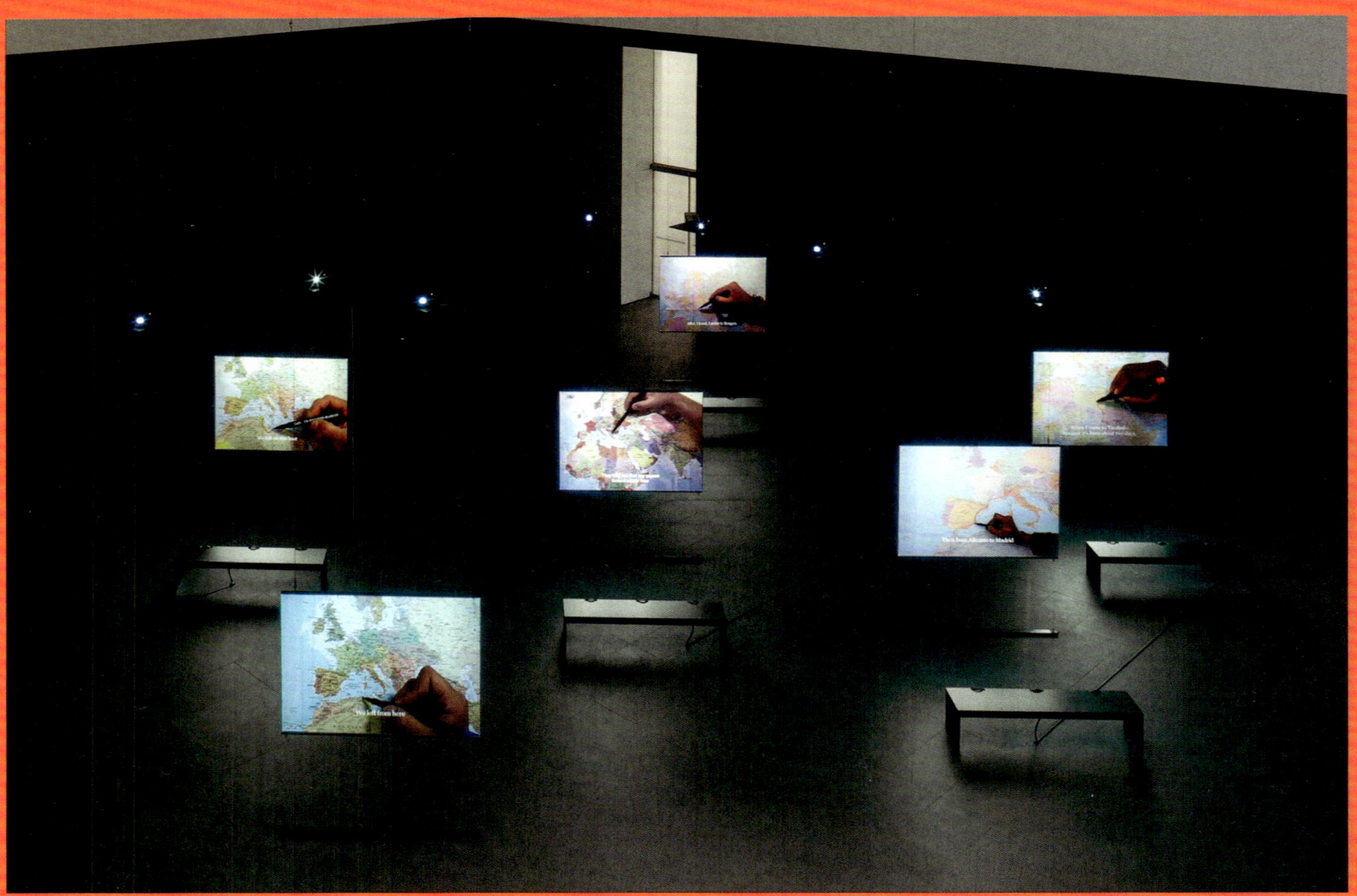

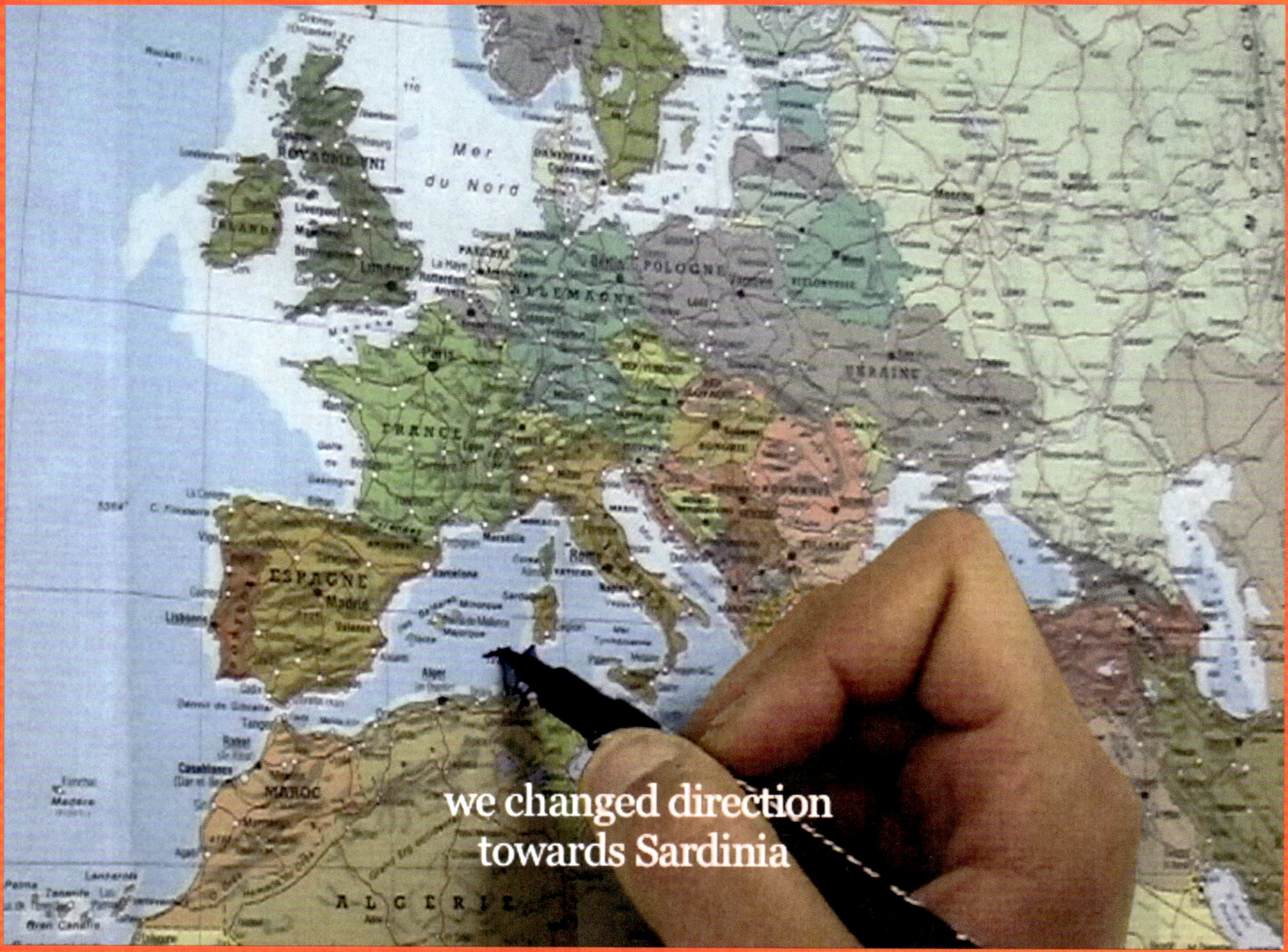

The Mapping Journey Project, 2008–11

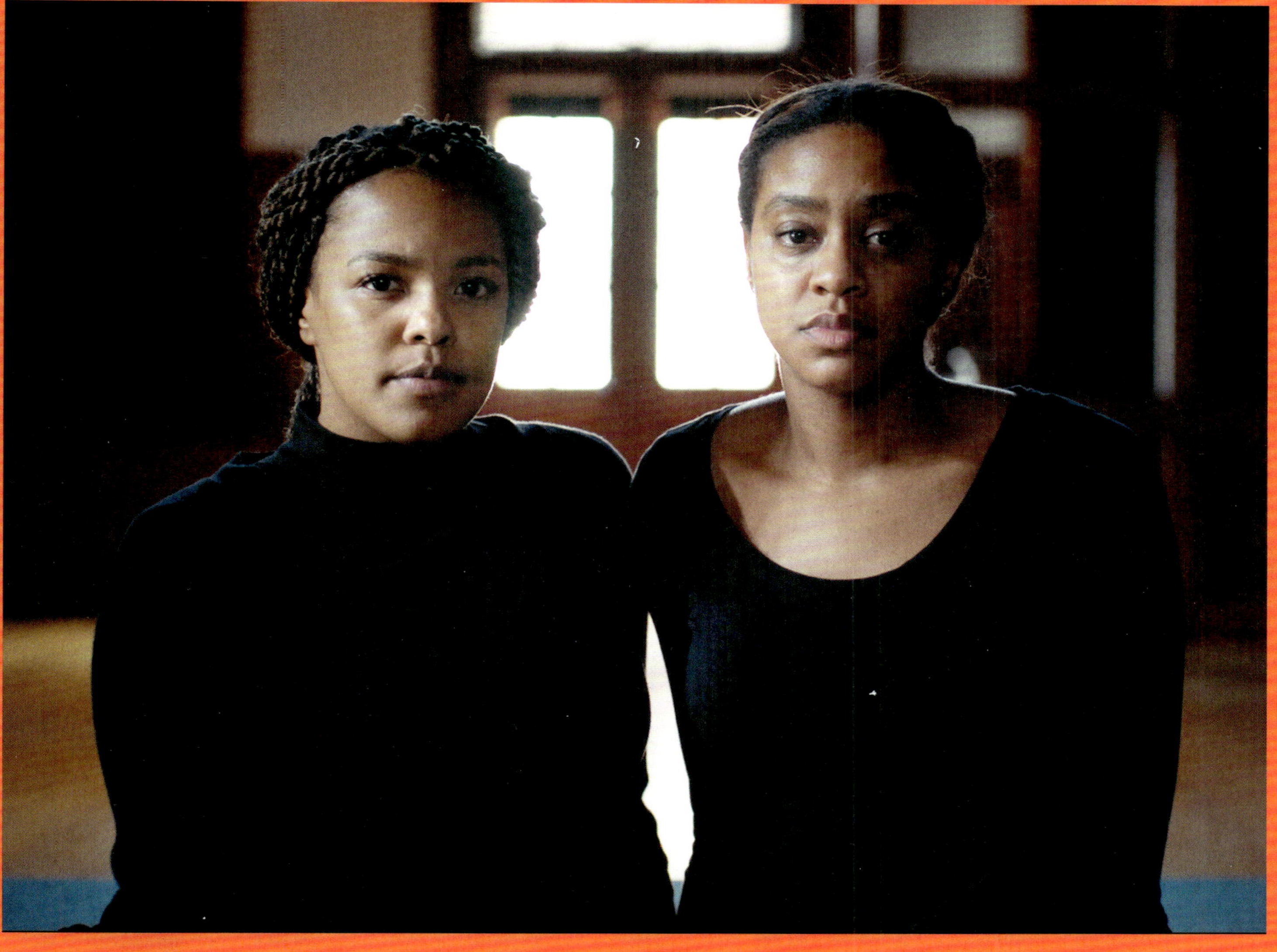

Twenty-Two Hours, 2018

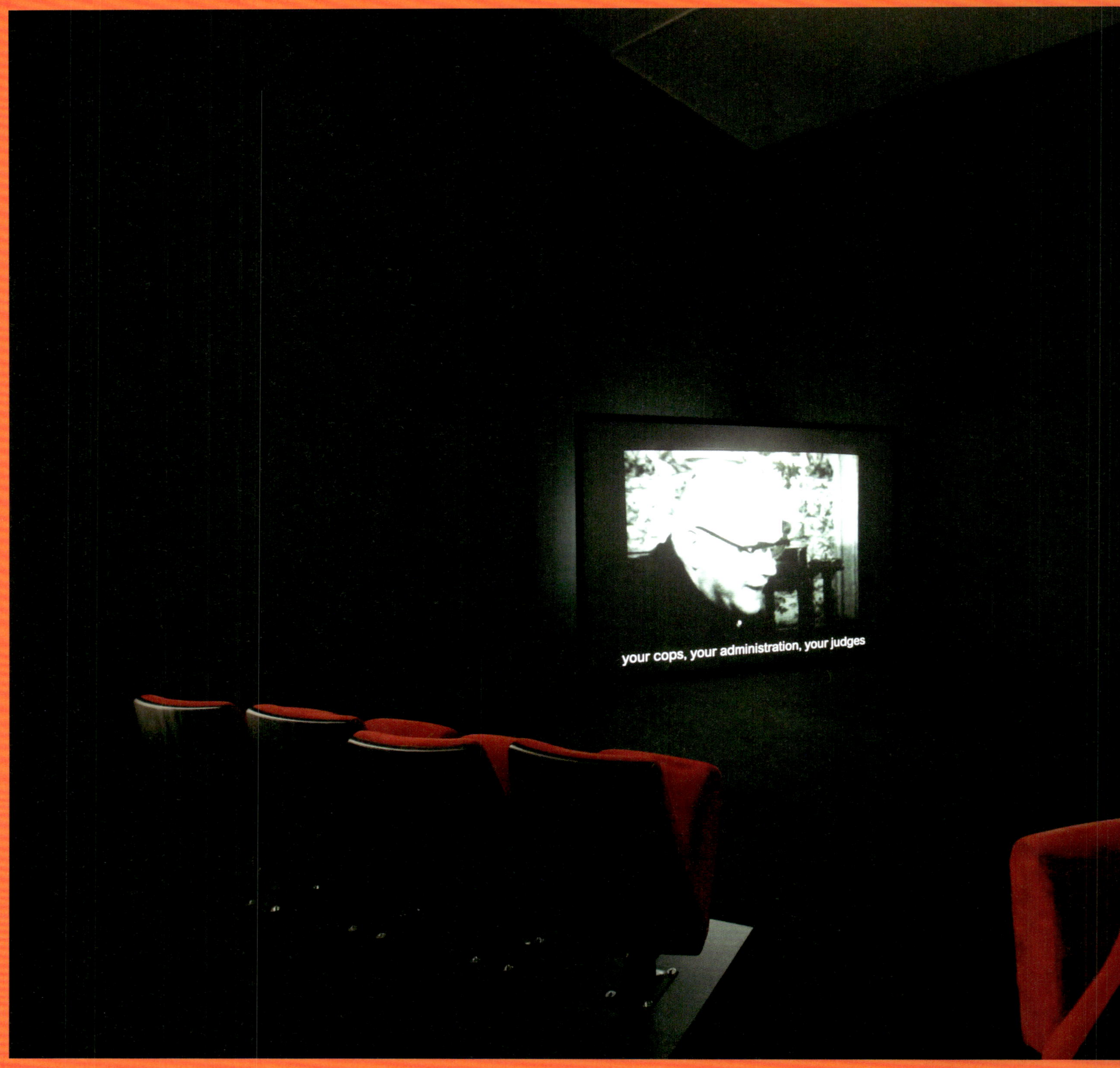

Twenty-Two Hours, 2018

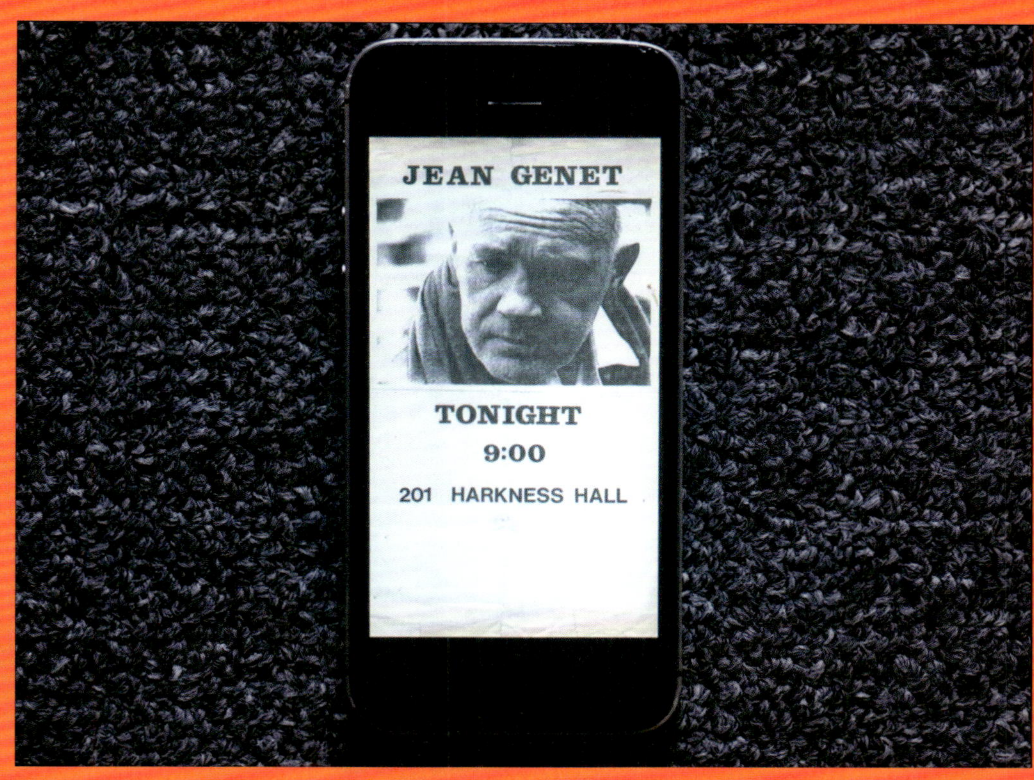

JEAN GENET
TONIGHT
9:00
201 HARKNESS HALL

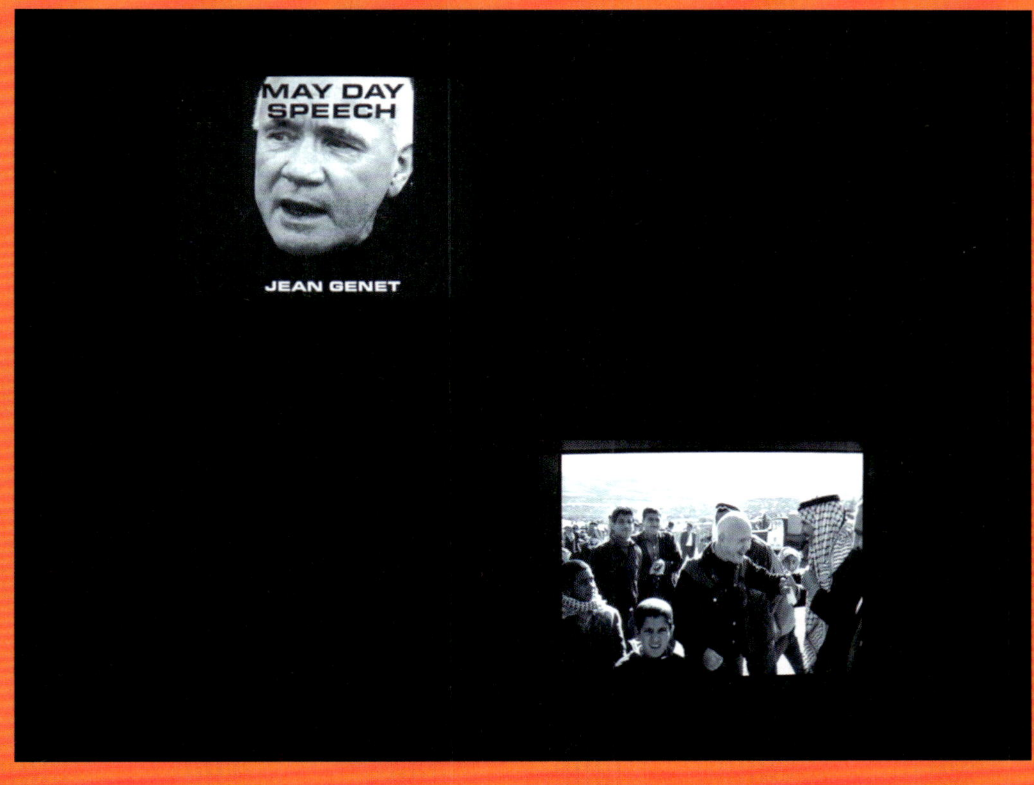

MAY DAY
SPEECH
JEAN GENET

Laura Lima

b. 1971, Brazil. Lives and works in Rio de Janeiro, Brazil.

In 1994, Laura Lima transplanted a single black cow from the Brazilian countryside to the sunny shores of Ipanema Beach. For one day, tourists and beachgoers in the storied Rio de Janeiro neighborhood frolicked in the waves while the cow freely pastured on the sand. This early work set the tone for Lima's practice ever since. Operating in the realm of the surreal, the dreamlike, and the mythical, Lima offers unexpected encounters in everyday contexts in order to disrupt viewers' common perceptions of reality.

While Lima's work blurs distinctions between performance, installation, and event, at the core of her methodology is the idea of the total image. In this way of conceiving how humans orient themselves in the world, beings and objects are identified as belonging or not belonging depending on the image created by their presence in a particular space. Thus, in works like *Cow (M=f/W=f)*, the absurdist "painting" (to use Lima's term) of a cow grazing on an urban beach becomes a critical engagement with ideas of existence, materiality, and truth. The notion of painting with living matter is key to the artist's body of work titled *Homen=carne/Mulher=carne* (Man=flesh/Woman=flesh, 1994–98). In the group of works, Lima reduces human bodies to pure flesh, which she considers equal to any other material she might use to realize a work. The *carne* gestures are never rehearsed or scripted but instead dictated by a brief set of instructions, a prop, an environmental context, and the untrained participants (animal or human) tasked with carrying out the action, which is usually quite simple—a naked man pulling on the columns of a building with a set of thick ropes to which he is attached in *Puxador paisagem (H=c/M=c)* (The landscape puller [M=f/W=f], 1998/1999/2000/2013/2015), for example, or a young girl in a white dress jumping rope in a pool of red gelatin in *Gelatina (H=c/M=c)* (Jelly [M=f/W=f], 1996). In the real-time context of a gallery or the street, however, the resultant image takes on a fantastical and disruptive quality, upending the viewer's understanding of what is real or possible. Lima's poetry lies in the teasing out of such surrealities. In *Bar restaurante* (Bar restaurant, 2010/2013), twenty-four abstract sculptures fill the tables of a restaurant installation while a bartender replenishes their beer glasses, which somehow regularly empty as if being consumed. The abstract figurations make a subtle nod to certain artistic legacies that Lima cites, namely, those of Lygia Clark, Hélio Oiticica, and Lygia Pape; in particular, Clark's Bichos (1960–66) are recalled by the shapes turned sentient bodies. But Lima's invitation to the viewer to accept the magical as real—she insists, for example, that the details of the beer-draining system remain a mystery—stands as more significant a strategy than art-historical references in her work. With a sleight of hand, ordinary spaces and objects become imbued with mystical power.

In Lima's universe, magic and the imaginary take on deeper meaning in the context of the museum. In *Nuvem* (Cloud, 2009), a gallery is filled with the scents of mint, smoke, and chocolate while human hands protrude from the walls, offering paintings, mirrors, jewelry, lamps, and delicately rolled cigars for the public to enjoy. In *Alfaiataria* (Tailor shop, 2014–)—a work premiered at the Bonnefanten Museum in the Netherlands that will be re-created for *Witch Hunt*—a team of local tailors translates Lima's portrait drawings into paintings of their own, which take the form of garments stretched over empty frames. During the exhibition, visitors witness the museum's transformation into a fully functioning workshop, with works of art executed right in front of them. By unveiling the processes of production and giving them shape through the actions of bodies in the museum, Lima asks the viewer to reconsider the magic and value of both commercial and artistic labor.

—Vanessa Arizmendi

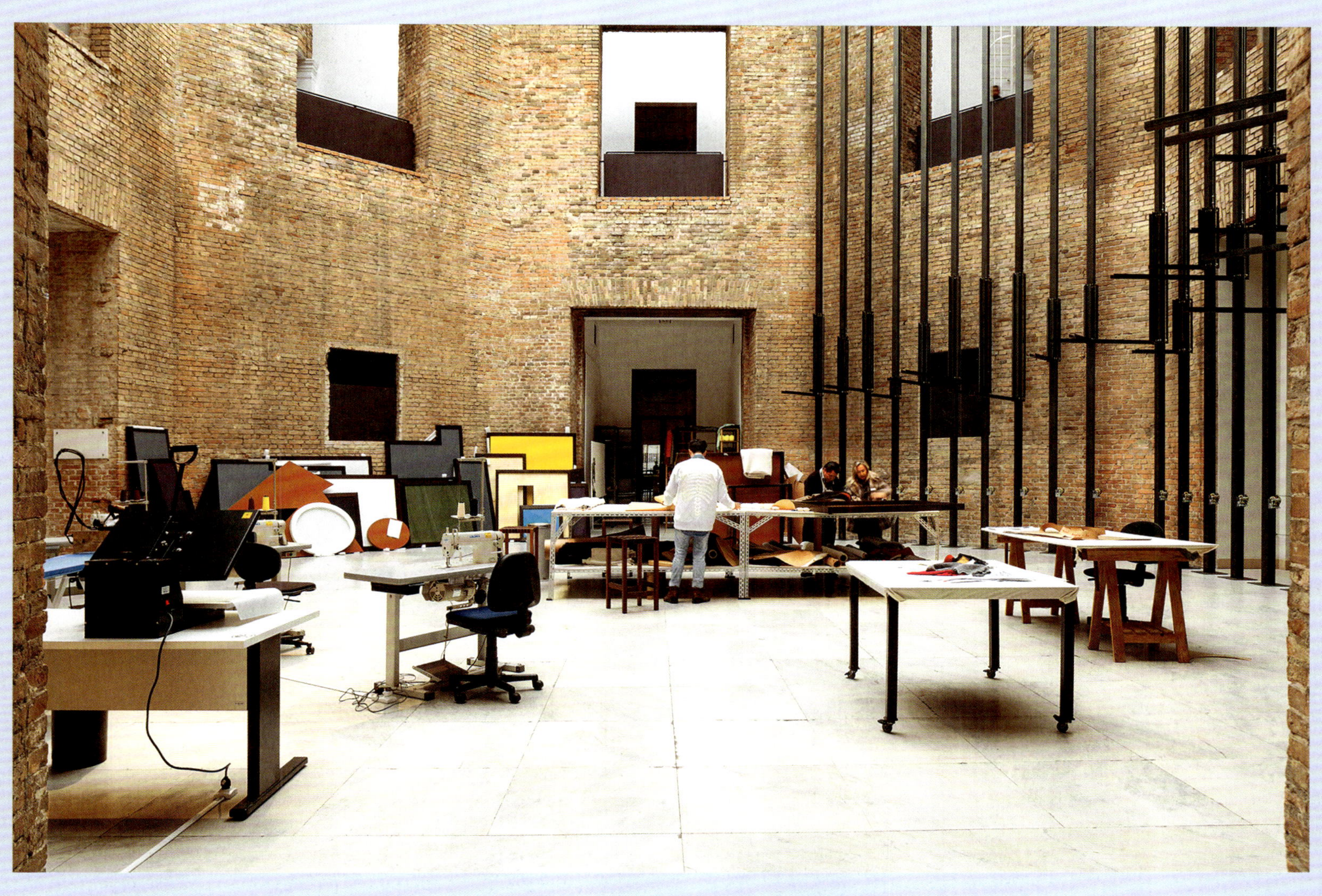

Alfaiataria (Tailor shop), 2014–

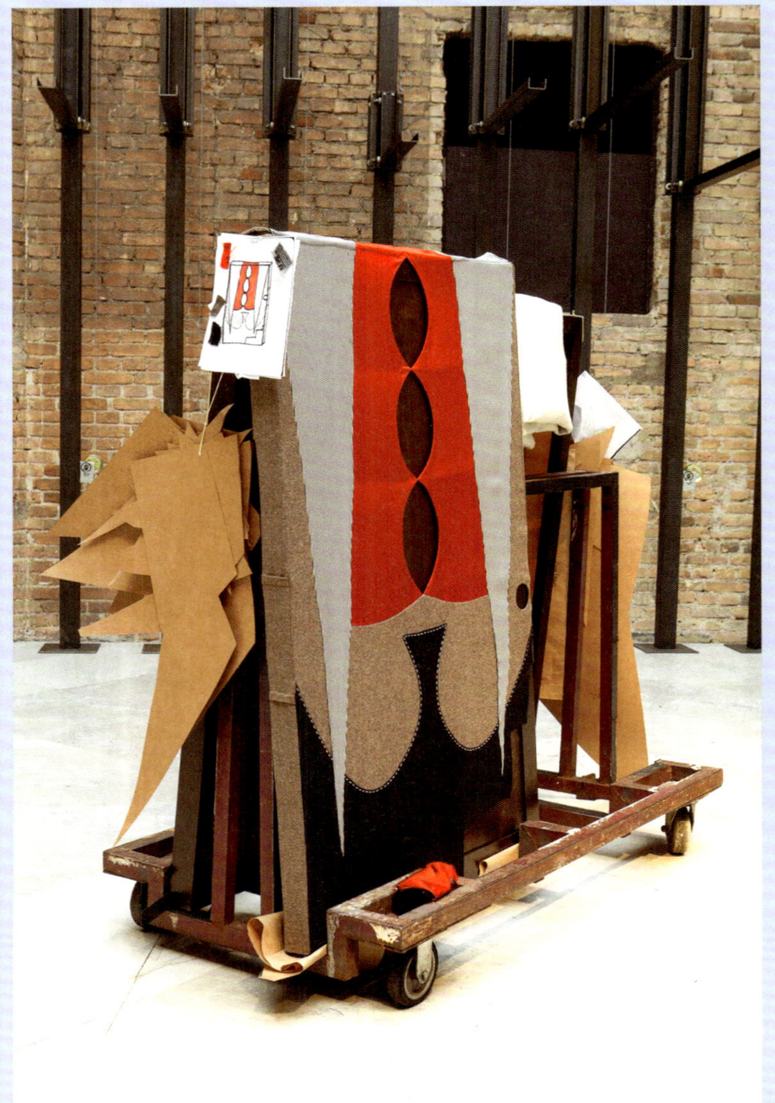

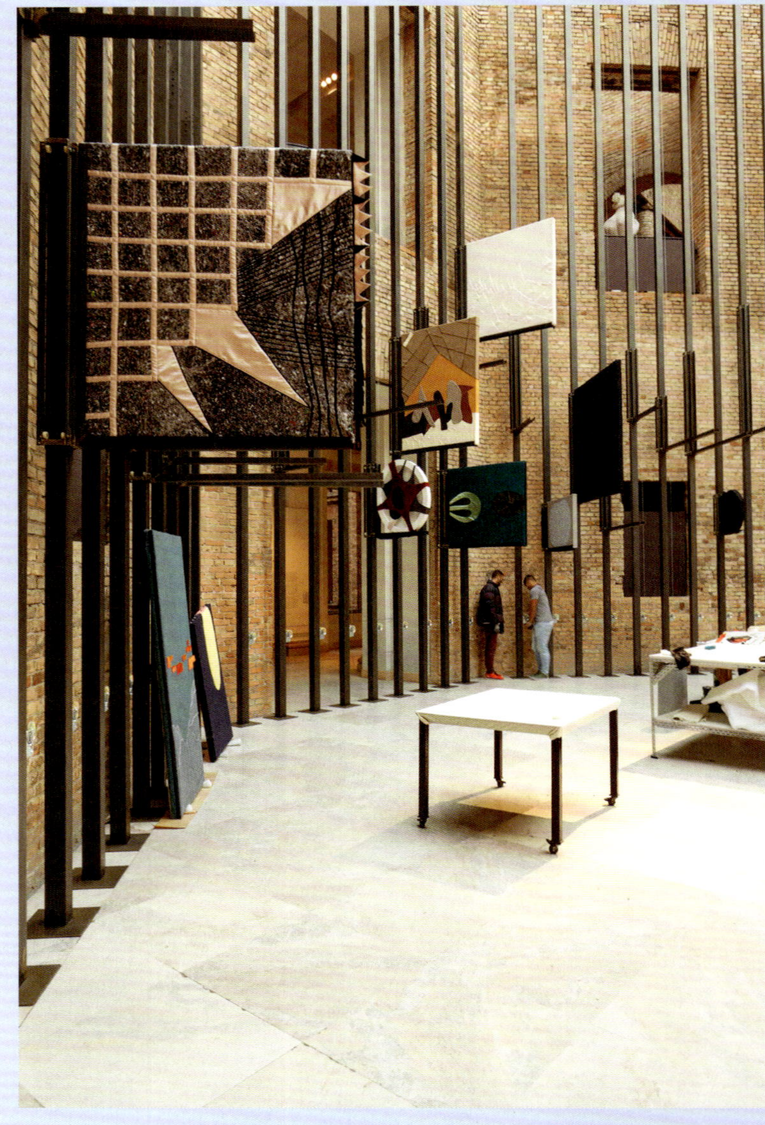

Alfaiataria (Tailor shop), 2014–

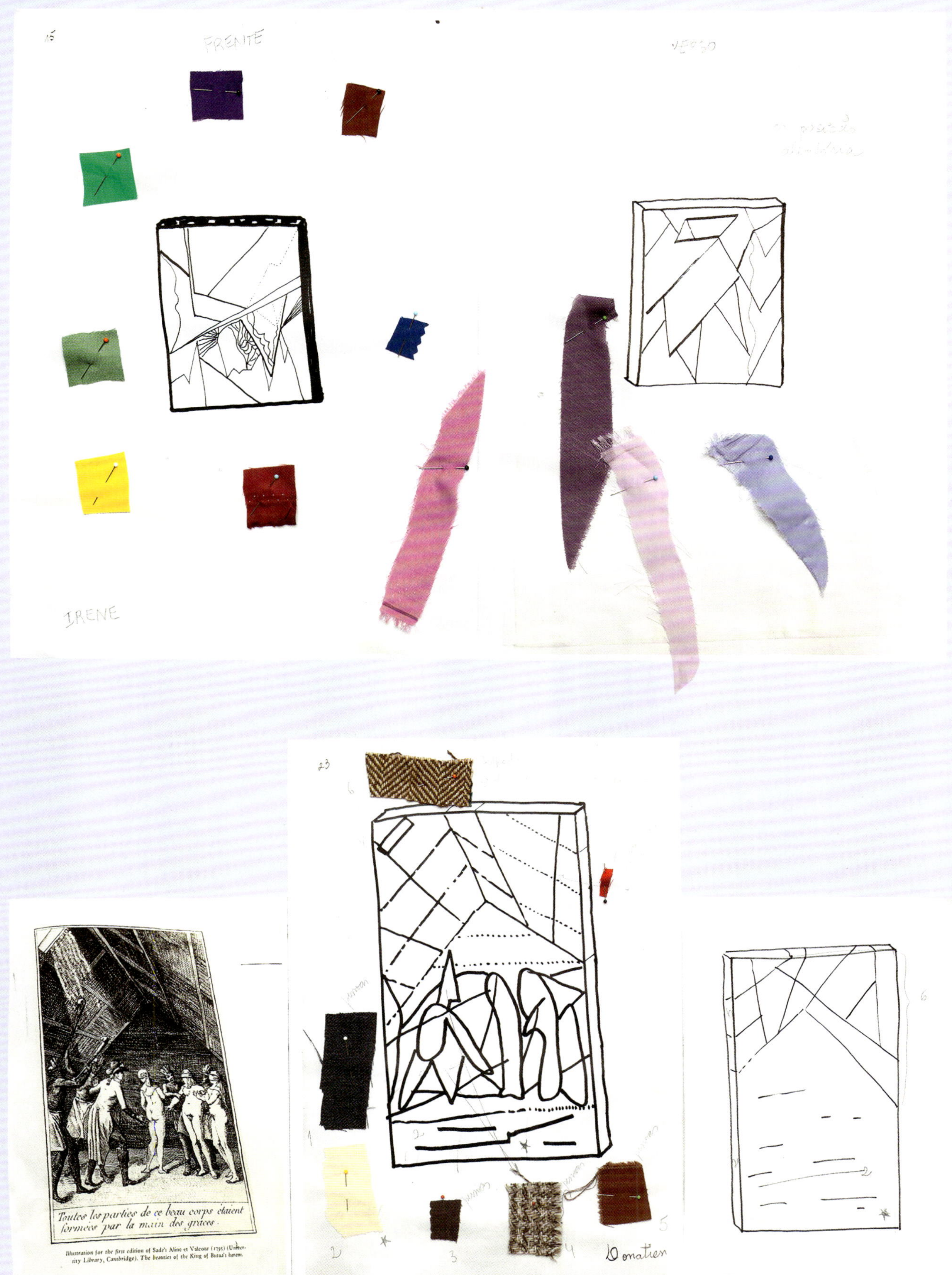

sketches for *Alfaiataria* (Tailor shop), 2014–

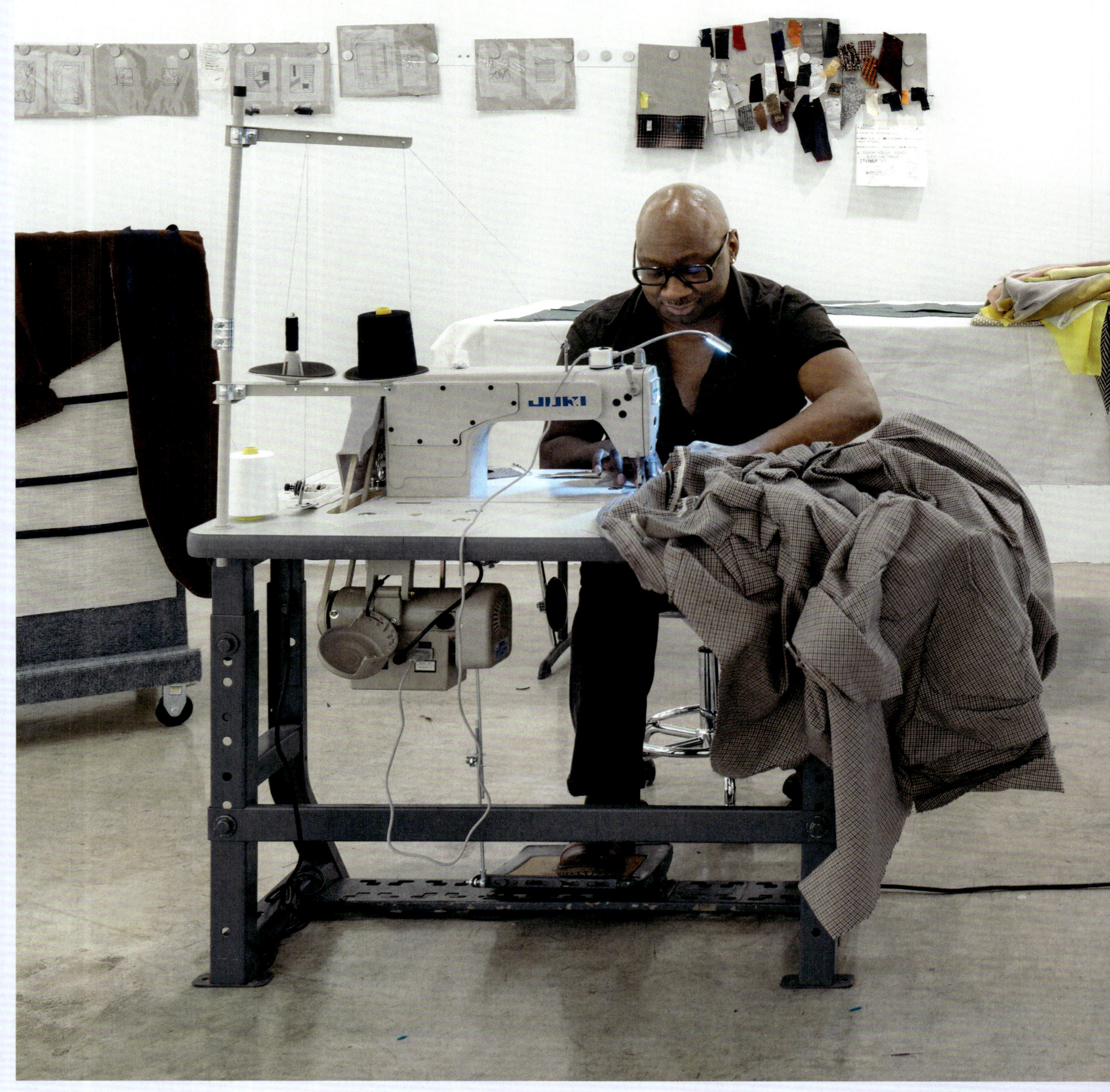

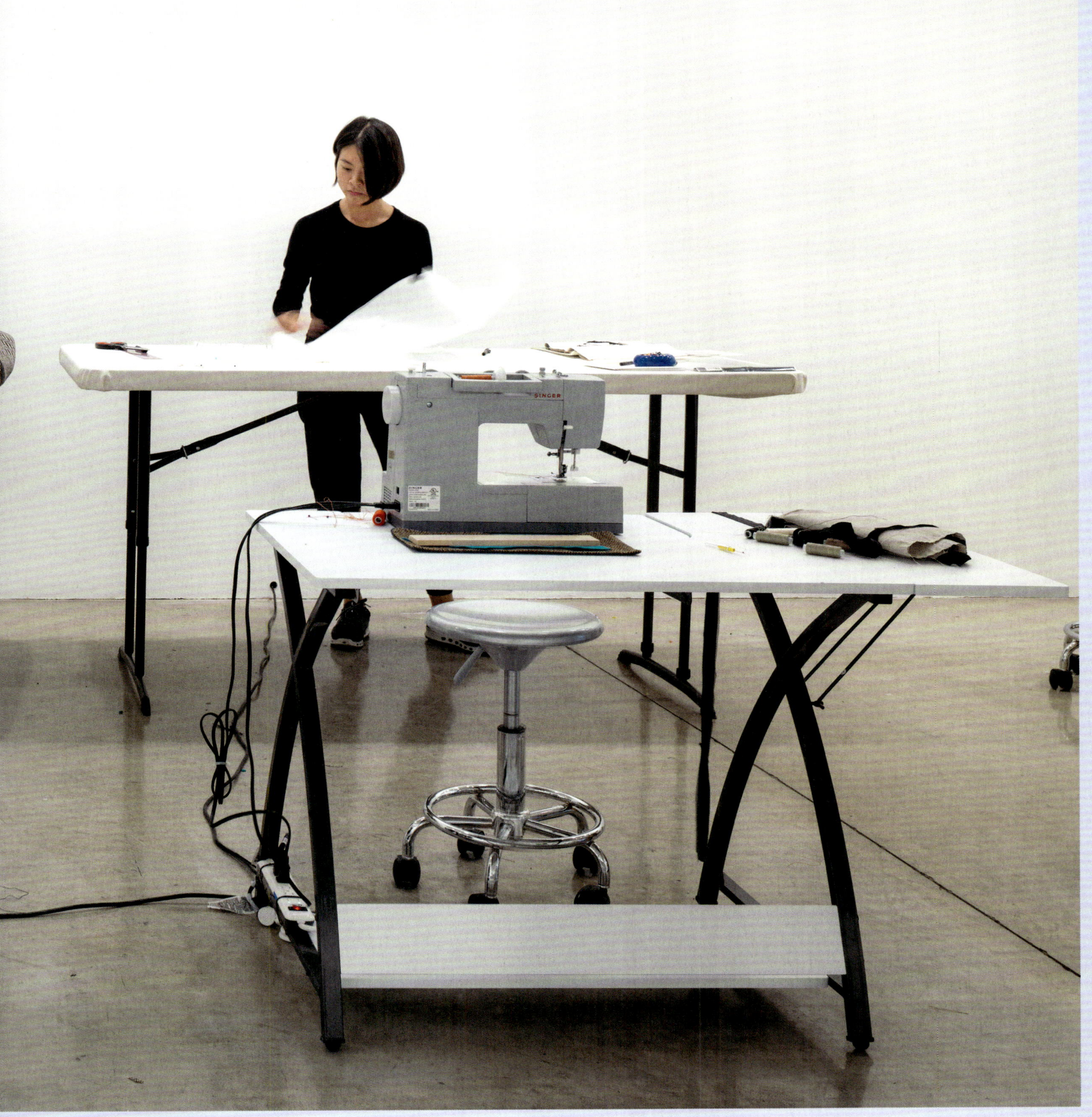

Alfaiataria (Tailor shop), 2014–

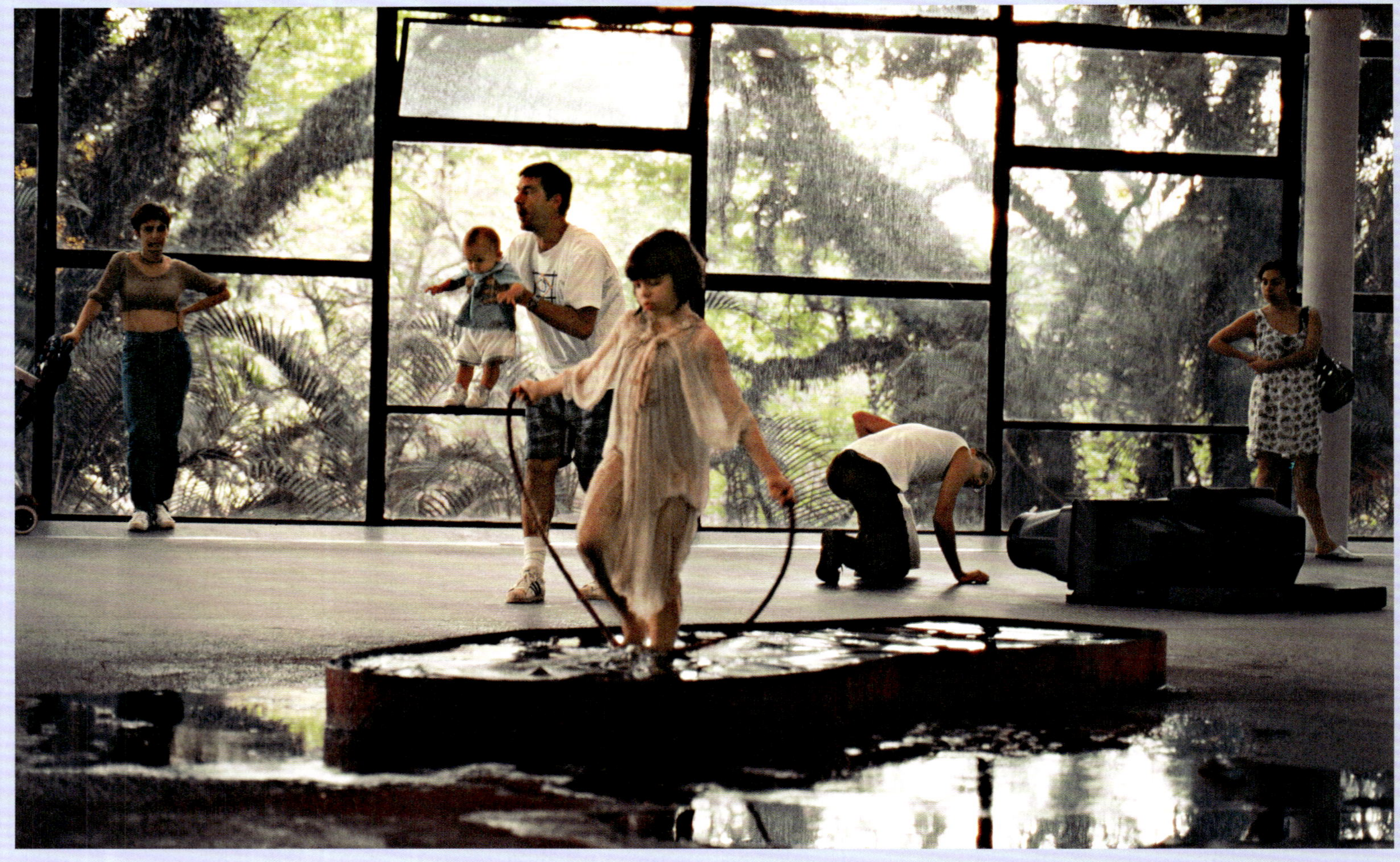

Gelatina (H=c/M=c) (Jelly [M=f/W=f]), 1996

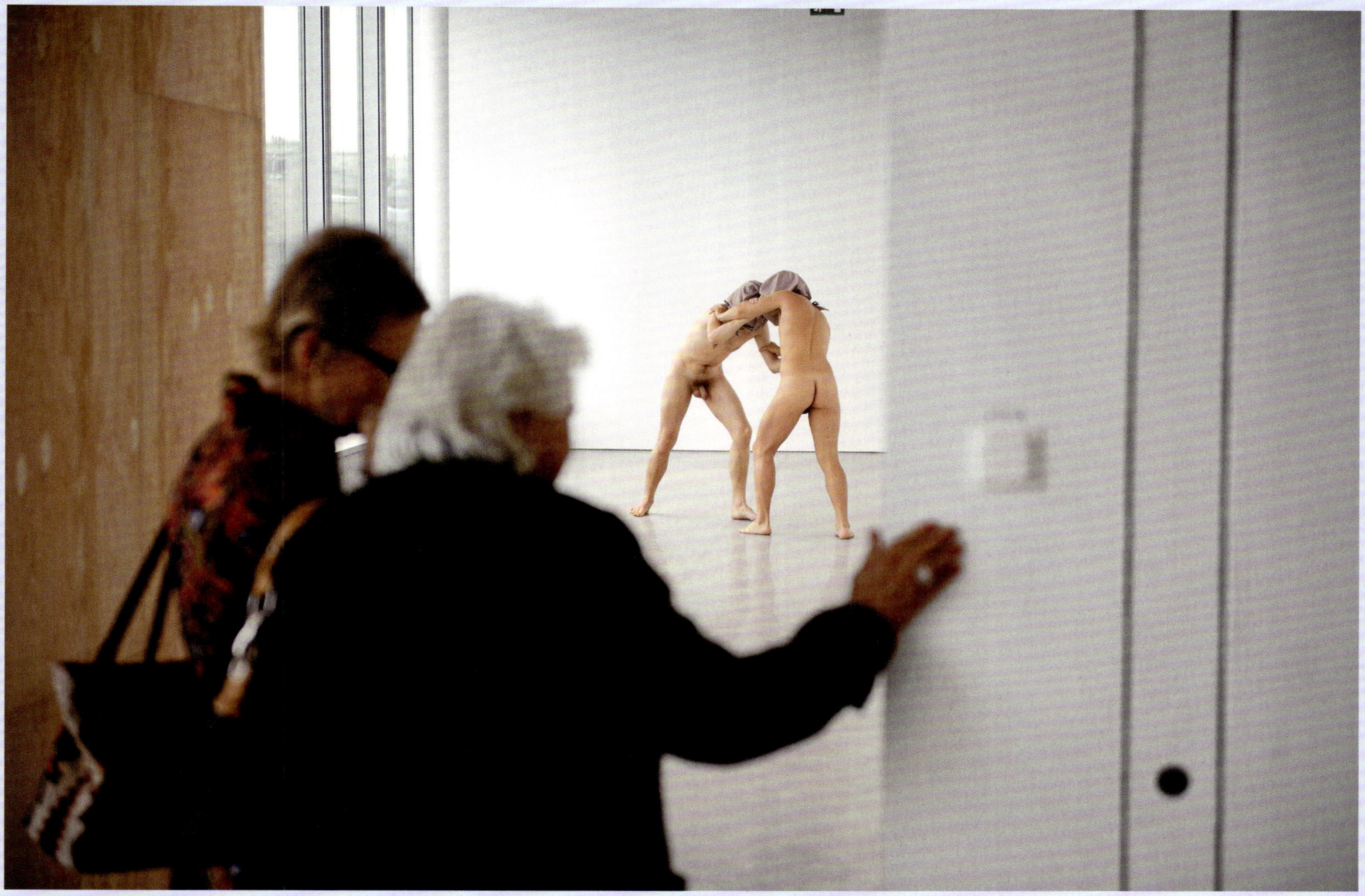

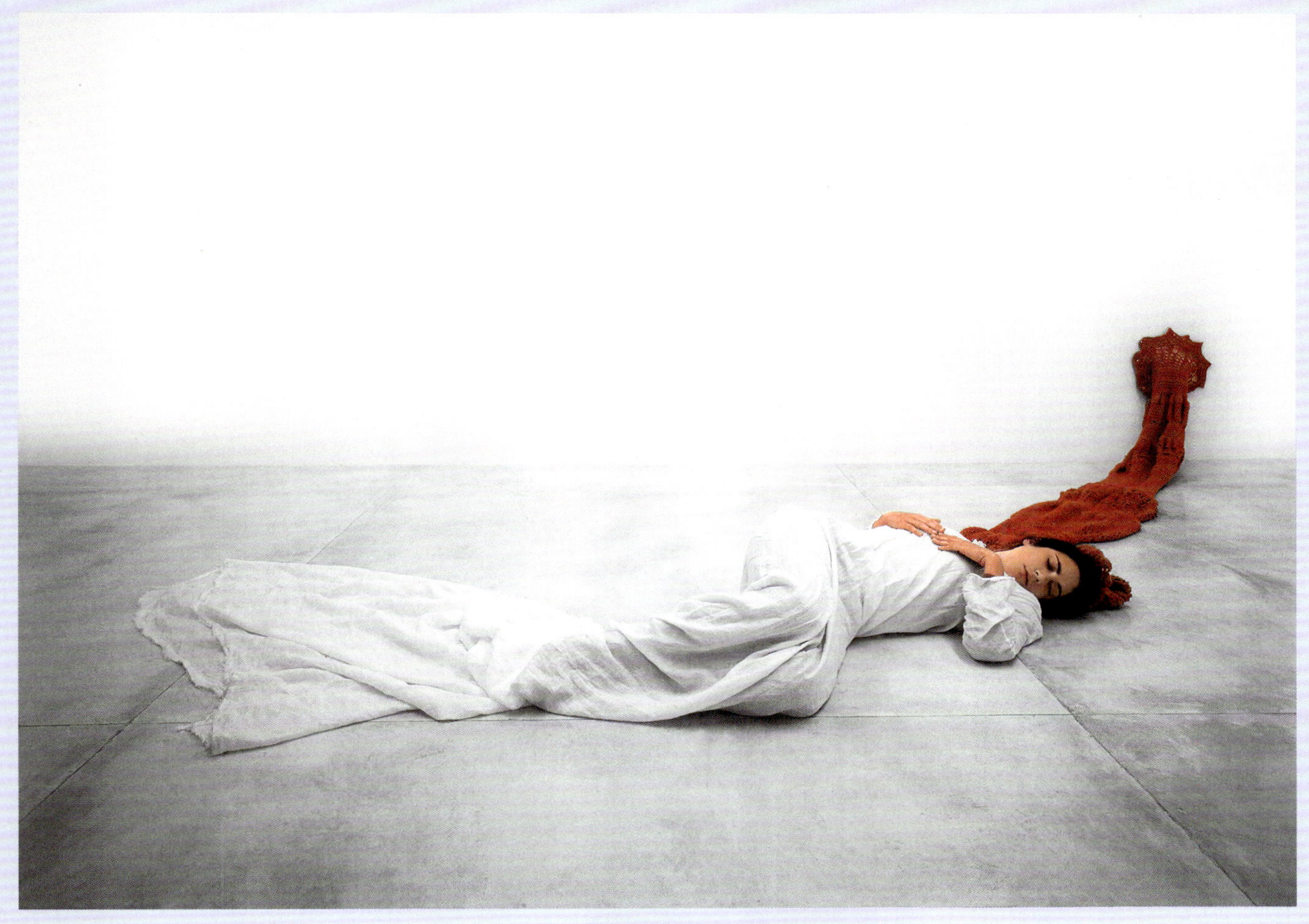

Marra (M=f/W=f), 1996/2002/2011
Doped (M=f/W=f), 1997/2002/2006/2014

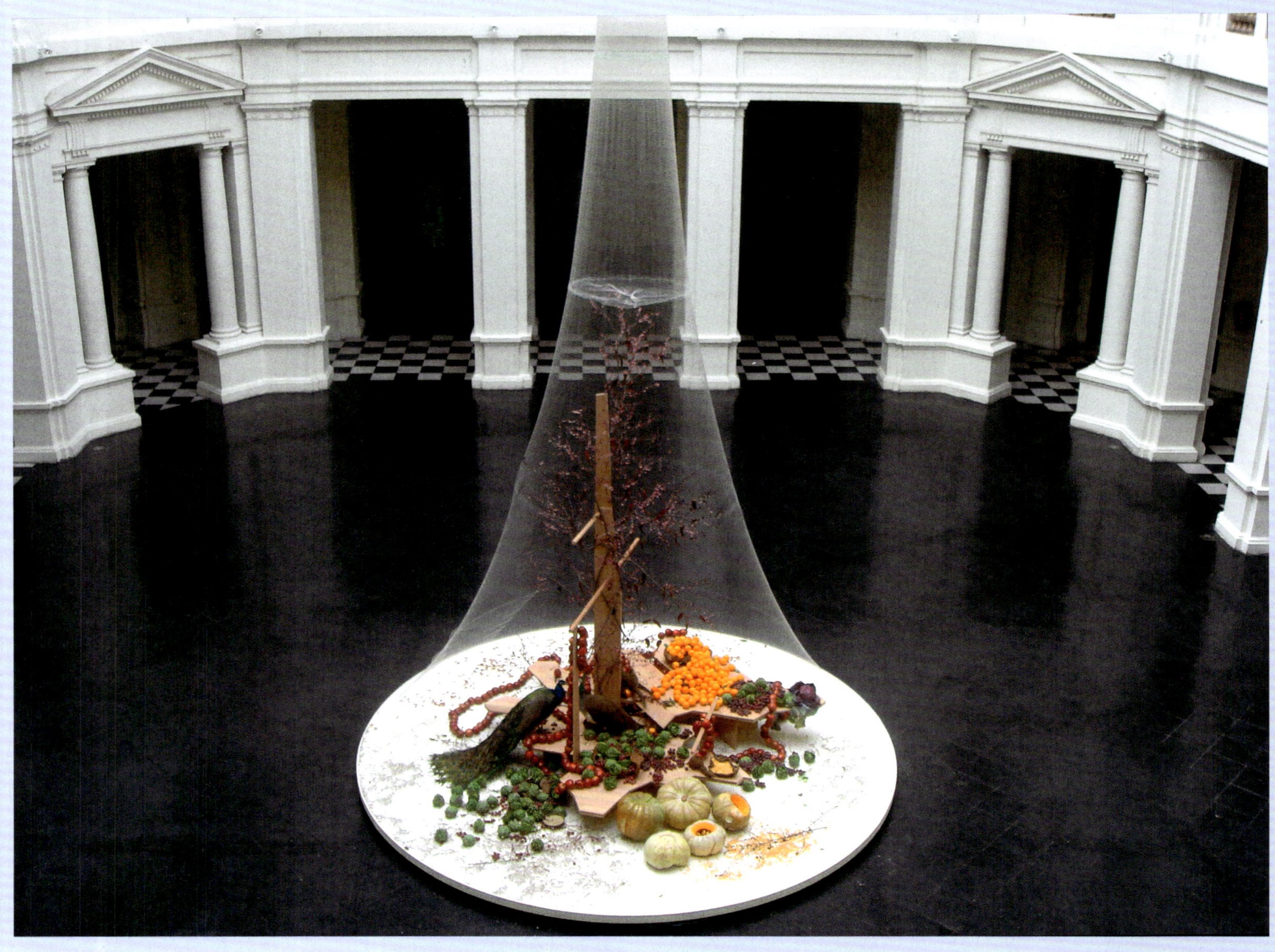

Pheasants with Food, 2005–2006

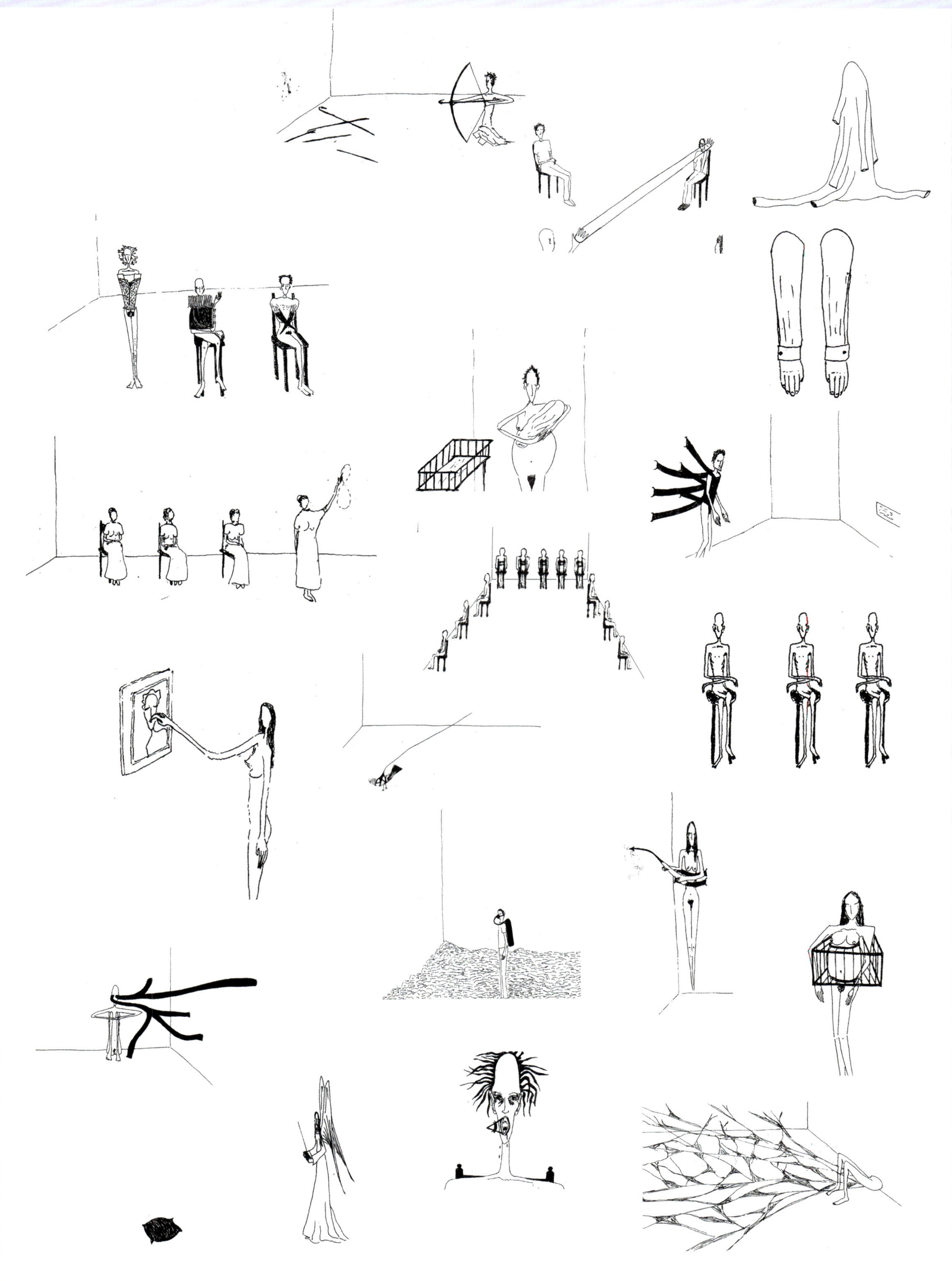

notes on *Man=flesh/Woman=flesh*, 1994–98

Teresa Margolles

b. 1963, Mexico. Lives and works in Madrid, Spain, and Ciudad Juárez, Mexico.

Teresa Margolles began her artistic career as a member of the Mexico City–based collective SEMEFO, which formed in the 1990s as an informal group of young artists interested in exploring questions of sociocultural violence. The collective's gatherings resulted in a series of confrontational exhibitions emblematic of their anarchist approach toward Mexico's brutal sociopolitical and economic landscape. Interventions involving human and animal remains, such as *Lavatio corporis* (The final washing of a corpse, 1994) and *Dermis* (1996), approached the painful, hypocritical, and violent state of Mexican life as a space of morbid tension. Margolles herself worked as a morgue technician for more than a decade, using Mexico's forensic medical system to source materials for SEMEFO's work and her own. For Margolles, the morgue functioned as a repository of life in the country. Her experience there would become the foundation for the artist's engagement with the materiality of institutional violence, and the effects that economic and political corruption have on the lives of a society's most vulnerable.

In her subsequent work, Margolles has used the morgue as a representational tool for exploring the state of life in Mexico. The series Autorretratos en la morgue (Self-portraits in the morgue, 1998) consists of simple self-portraits with bodies the artist encountered on the job; for *Lengua* (Tongue, 2000), the artist mounted the severed tongue of an adolescent boy who was murdered and whose family was unable to afford a funeral. Using a minimalist approach, Margolles's installations seduce the viewer into brutal and visceral encounters with state-sanctioned violence. In *Vaporización* (Vaporization, 2001), she created a vapor sculpture that enveloped the viewer in mist made from water used to clean corpses. In *En el aire* (In the air, 2003), she employs the same material to make bubbles that create a discordantly playful atmosphere. As relentless as they are gentle, these works take on a reverent quality, a conceptual and material distillation of life and death that creates a space to mourn the innumerable acts of unthinkable violence.

For the Mexican Pavilion at the 2009 Venice Biennale, Margolles moved beyond the walls of the morgue, creating objects from extended periods of field work along the Mexico–United States border. The result, *¿De qué otra cosa podríamos hablar?* (What else could we talk about?), comprised a series of interventions using large-scale fabrics stained with earth and blood that the artist used to absorb matter from sites where murders had occurred along the border. Some fabrics hung bare on the wall, while others floated atop the waters of the canals as part of a performative ritual or were collectively embroidered with narcomessages pulled from reporting on the brutal cartel violence. In a gesture of protest before the Biennale's opening, three were hung outside the windows and doors of the United States Pavilion as a reminder of the shared responsibility the country bears for the economic, social, and political violence in Mexico. These fabrics were soaked in buckets of water, activating the material residue of death each contained. The artist then invited family and friends of the deceased individuals to clean the floor of the Mexican Pavilion at distinct times each day.

Recently, Margolles has expanded her work to include a wider range of subjects across the Mexico-US border, shifting her focus to explore greater themes of loss, anger, and fear faced by transgender and cisgender women. *Pesquisas* (Inquiries, 2016–19) takes the form of a mural made from missing-person flyers found on the streets of Ciudad Juárez, where thousands of women are murdered every year. The series Pistas de baile (Dance floors, 2016) comprises portraits of trans sex workers— many of whom have themselves since been murdered—standing powerfully over the ruins of nightclubs where they have worked.

Over the past two years, Margolles has conducted extensive fieldwork along different borders throughout the Americas, where the artist has lived and worked with communities in Chile, Colombia, Venezuela, Mexico, and the United States. Her contribution to *Witch Hunt* represents the culmination of those efforts, with a project tackling issues related to the Mexico-US border and the unthinkable atrocities being enacted on migrants by the United States government. In this new work, Margolles once again employs her unique blend of research and ritual to create visibility and dignity for the experiences of communities otherwise ignored.

—Nika Chilewich

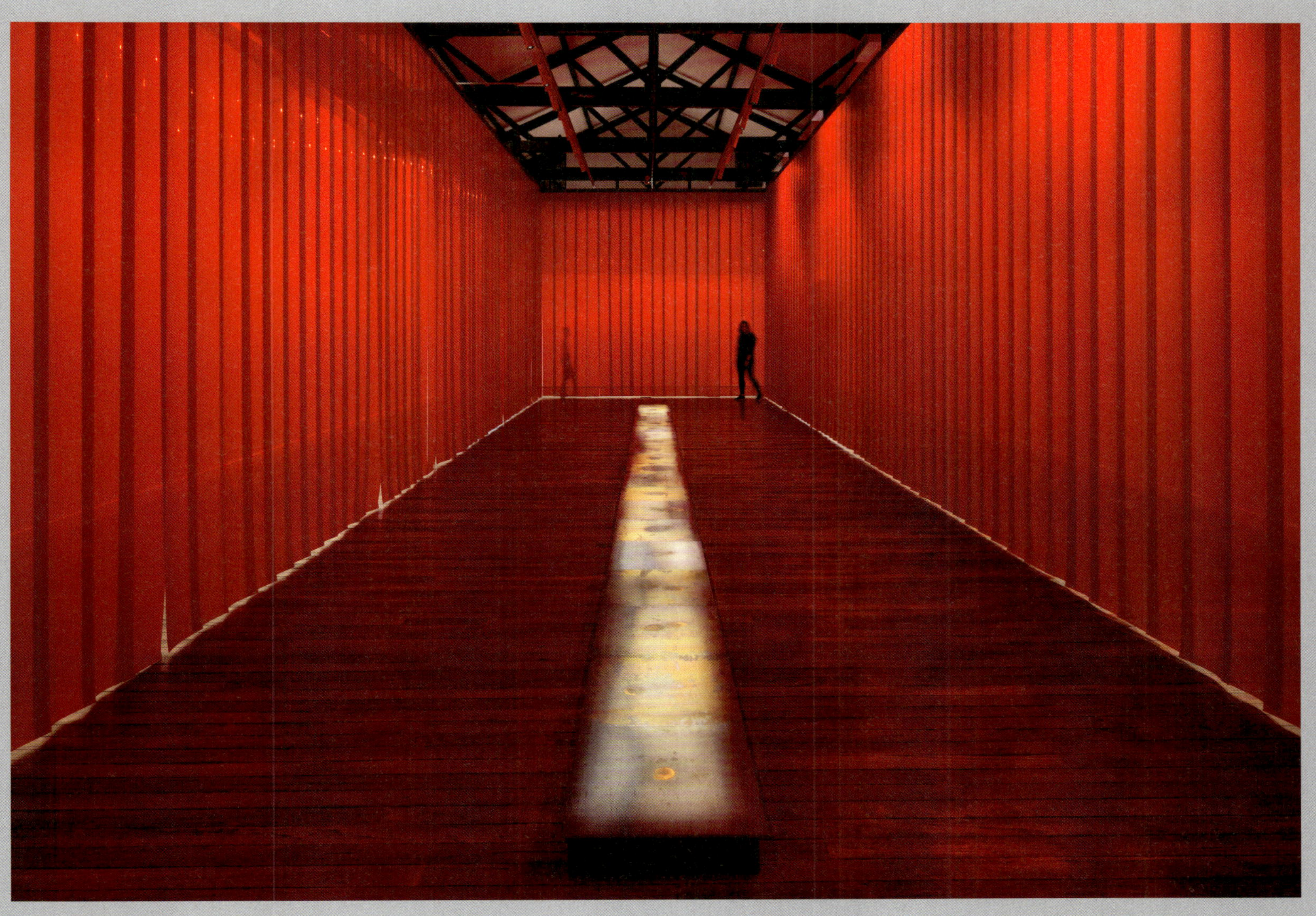

Aproximación al lugar de los hechos (Proximity to the scene), 2020

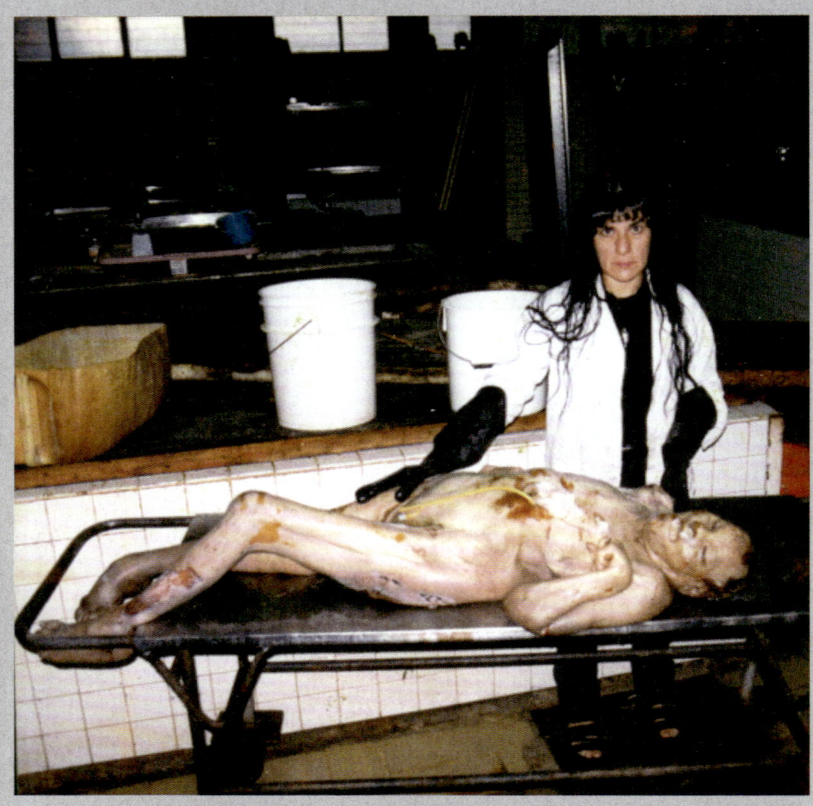

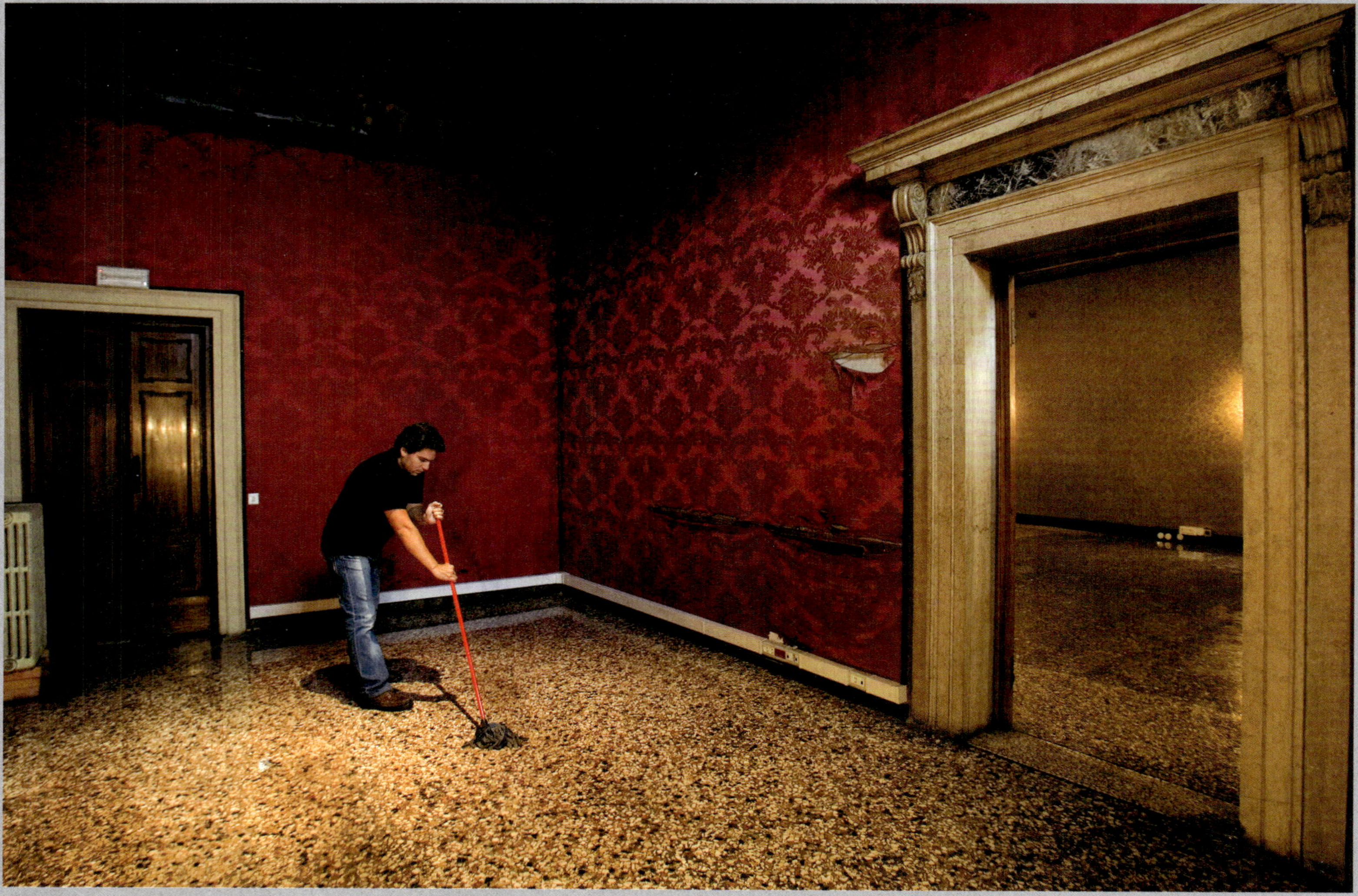

Autorretratos (No 2) (Self-portraits [No. 2]), 1998
¿De qué otra cosa podríamos hablar? Limpieza (What else could we talk about? Cleaning), 2009

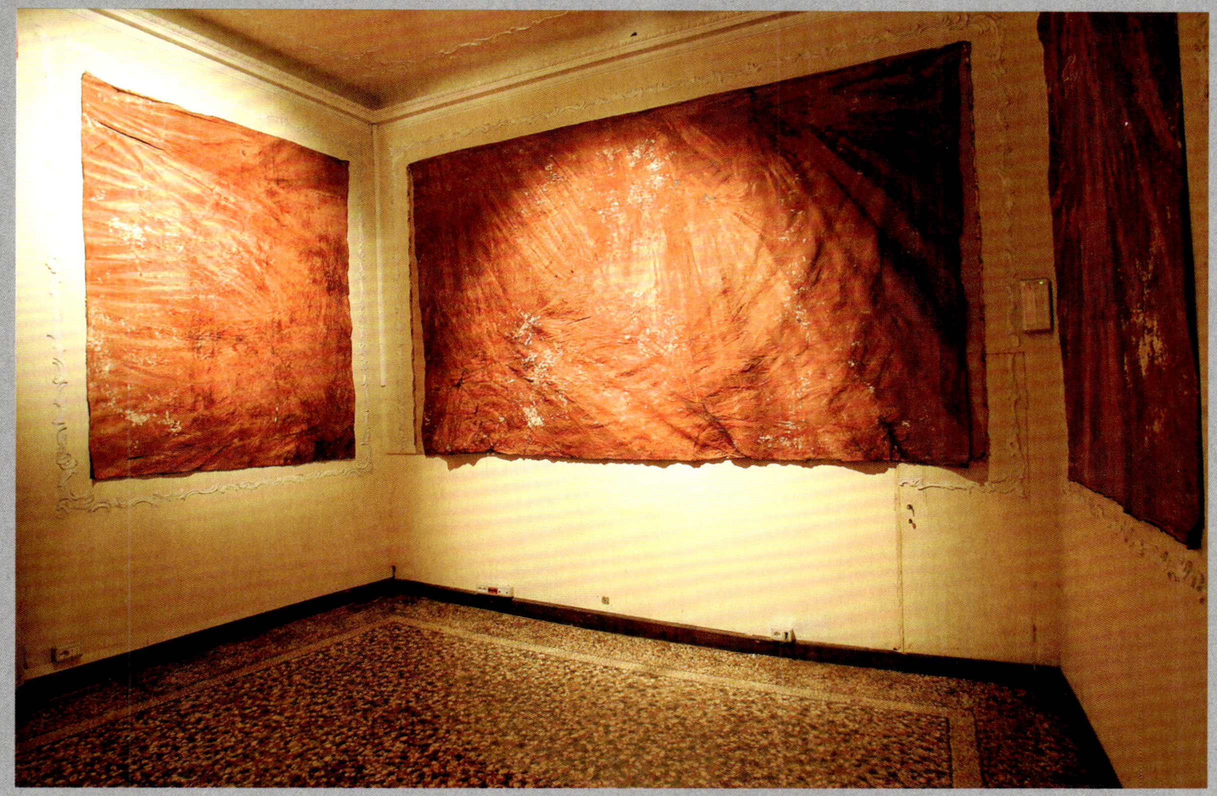

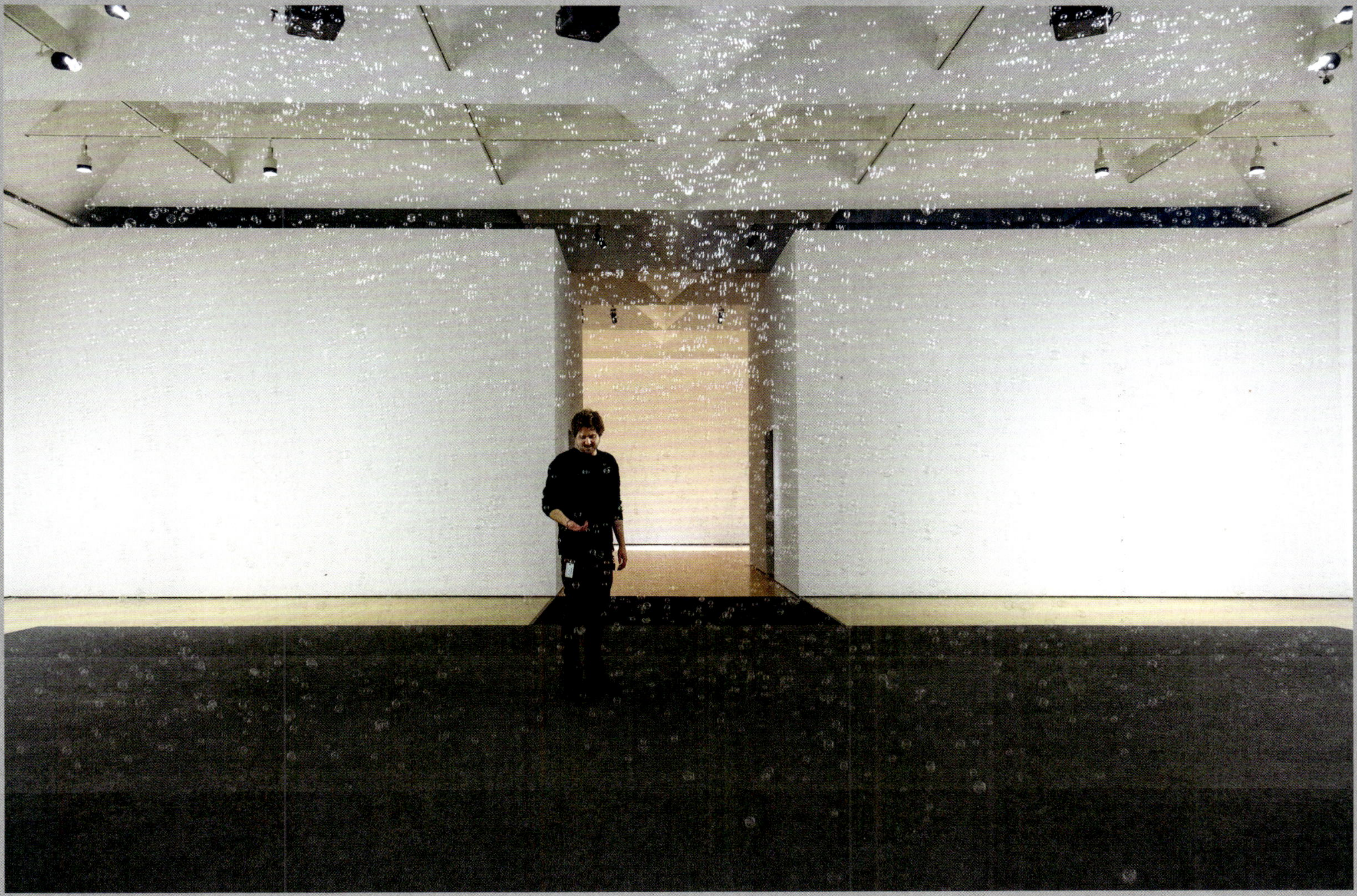

¿De qué otra cosa podríamos hablar? Narcomensajes (What else could we talk about? Narcomessages), 2009
En el aire Ciudad Juárez (In the air Ciudad Juárez), 2011

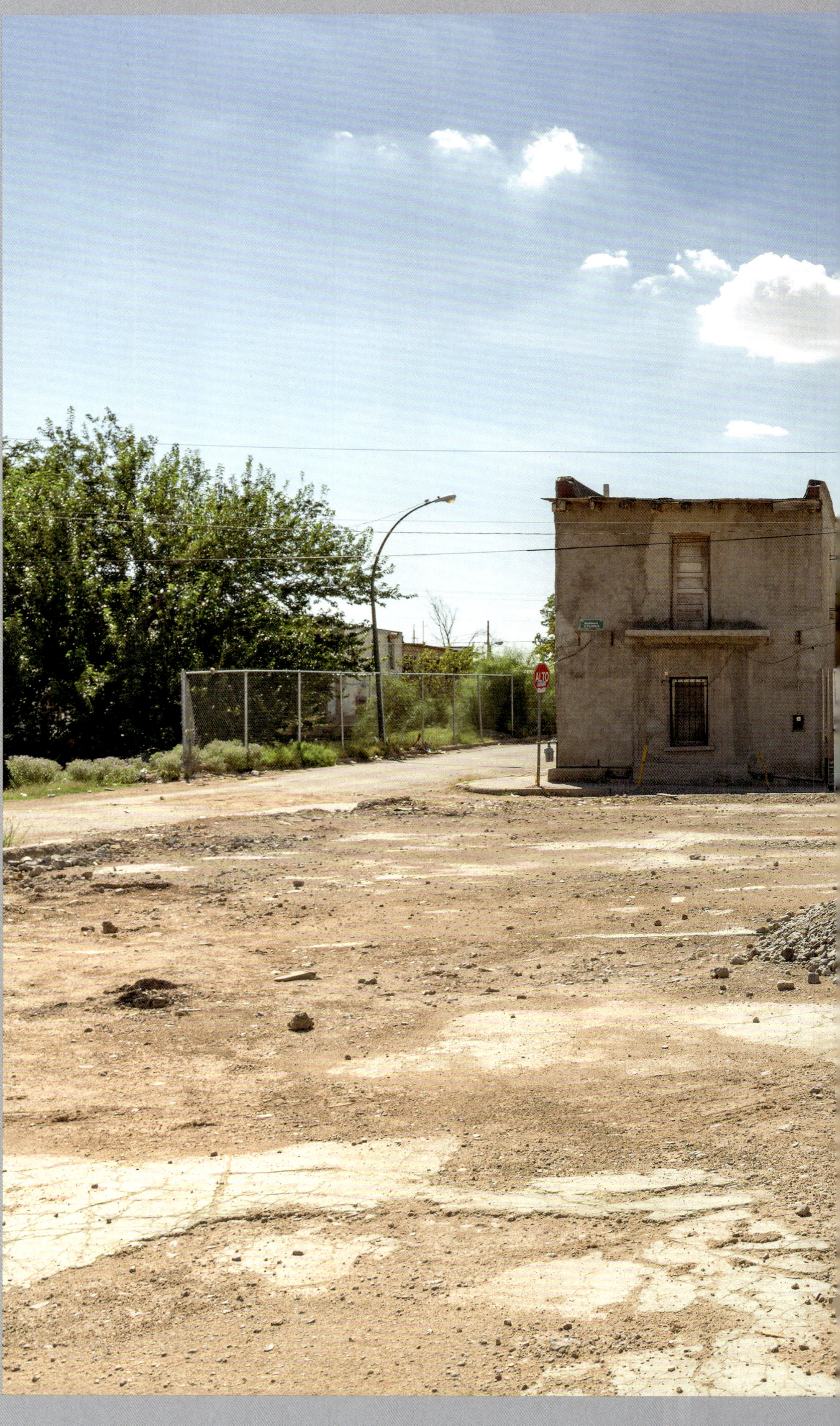

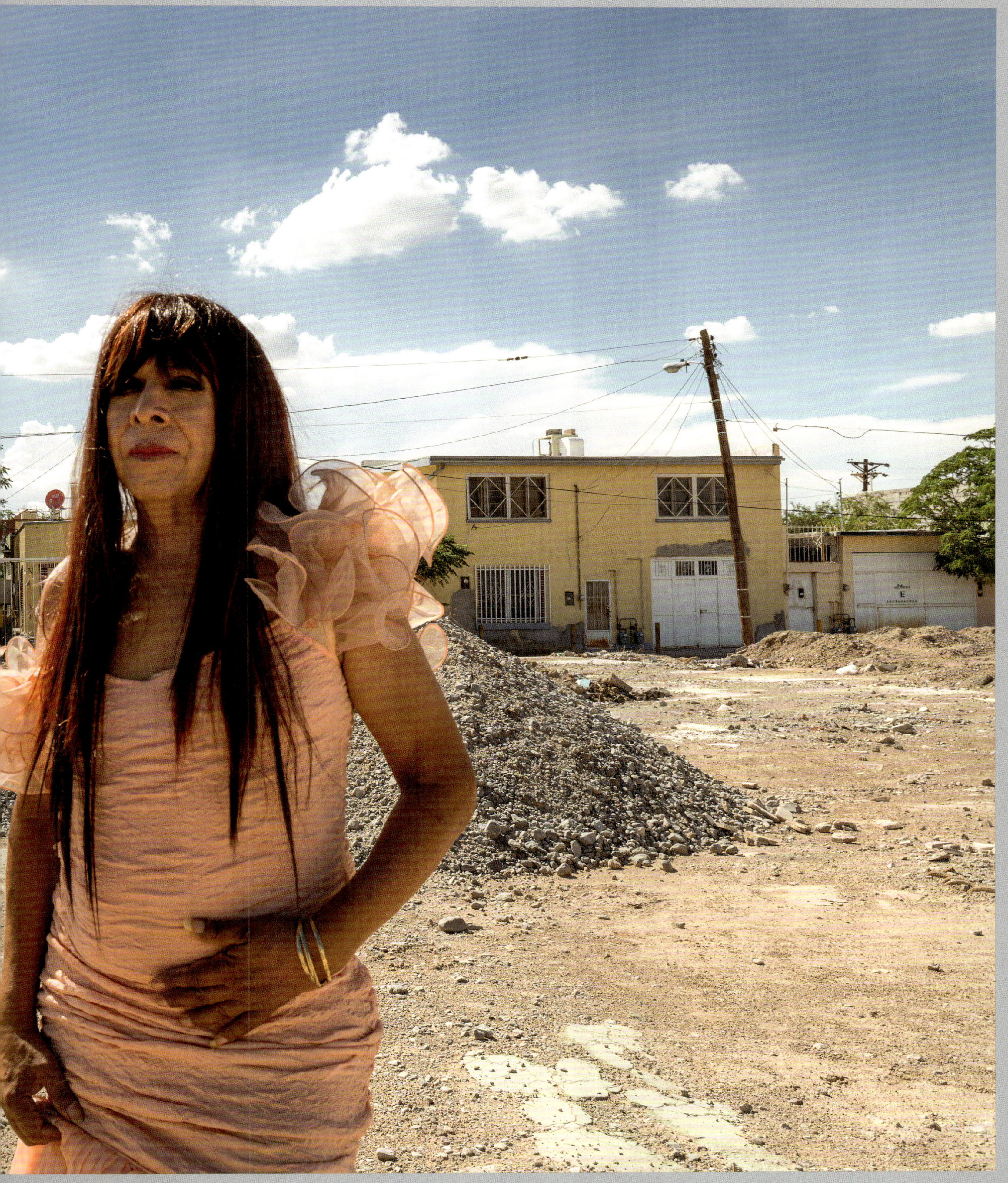

Karla, Hilario Reyes Gallegos, 2016

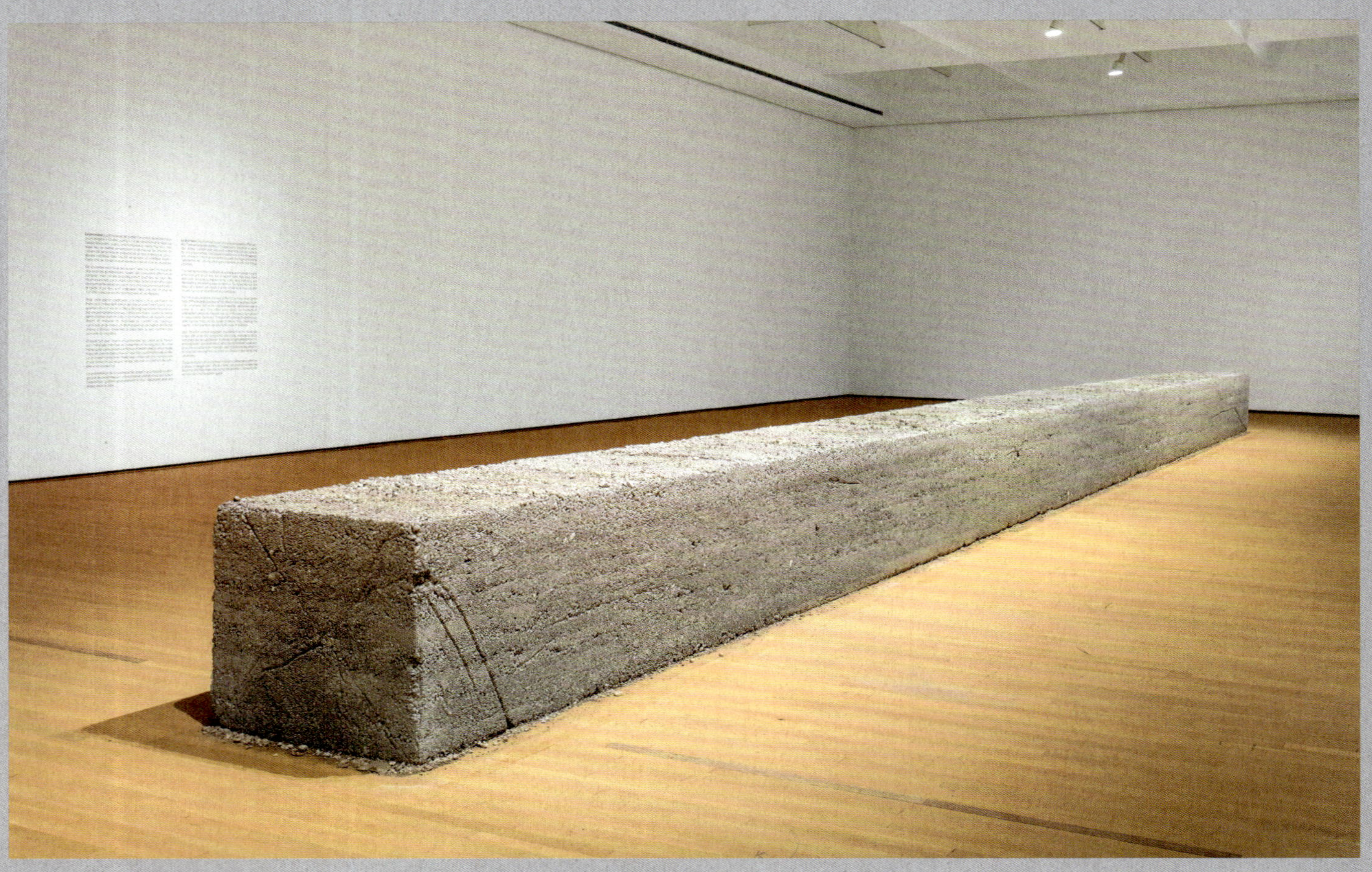

La promesa (The promise), 2012–17

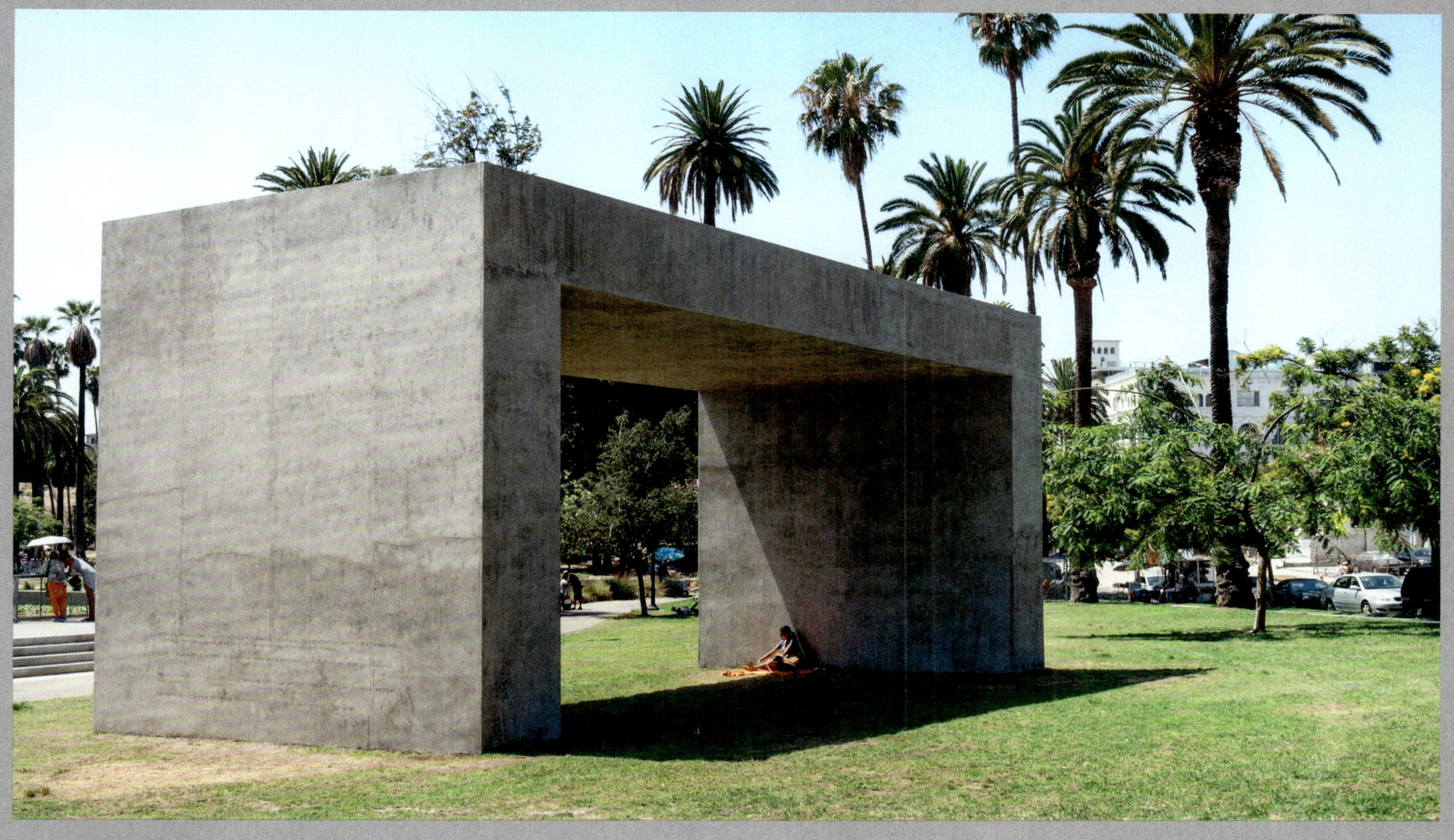

La sombra (The shade), 2016

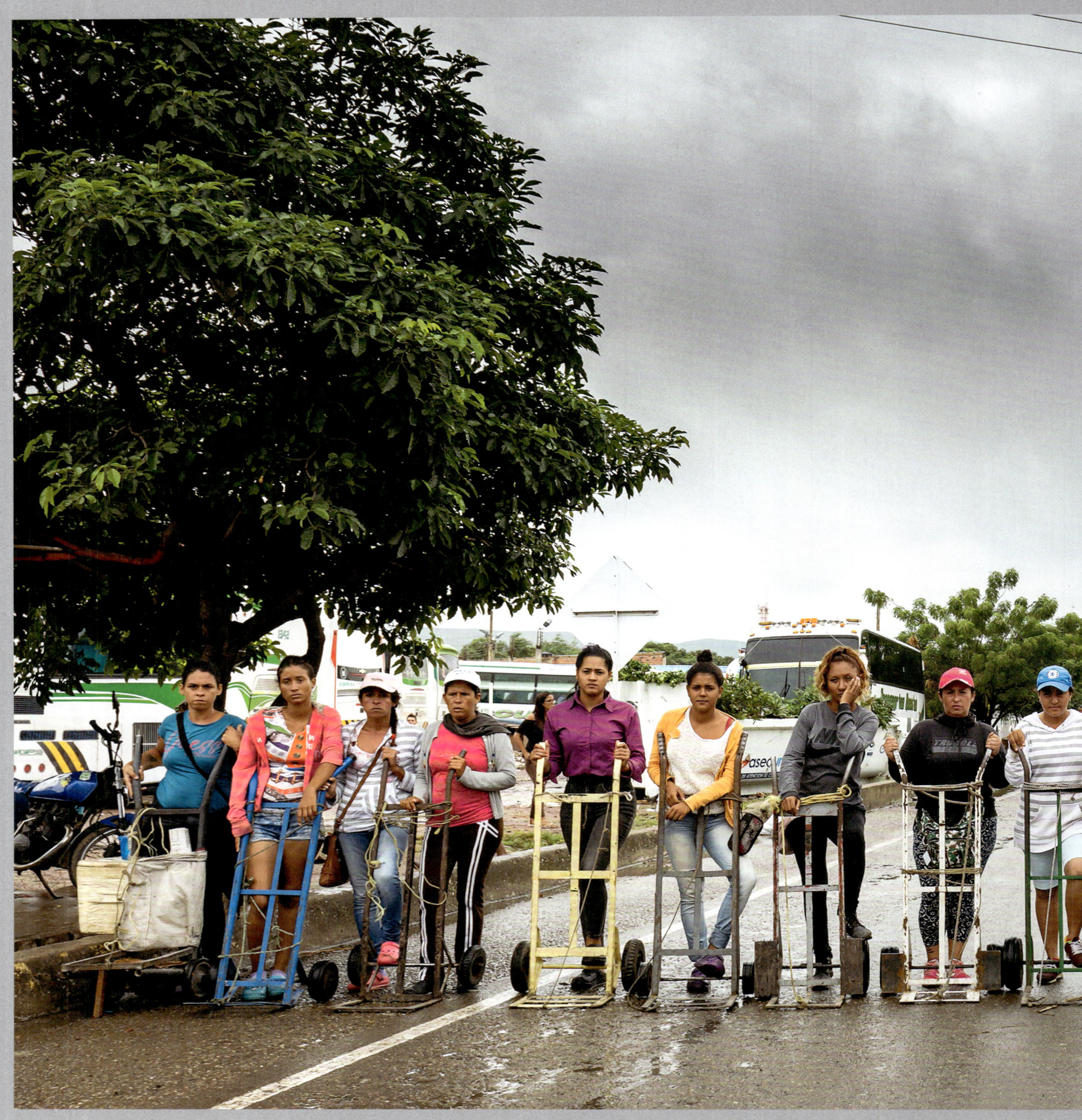

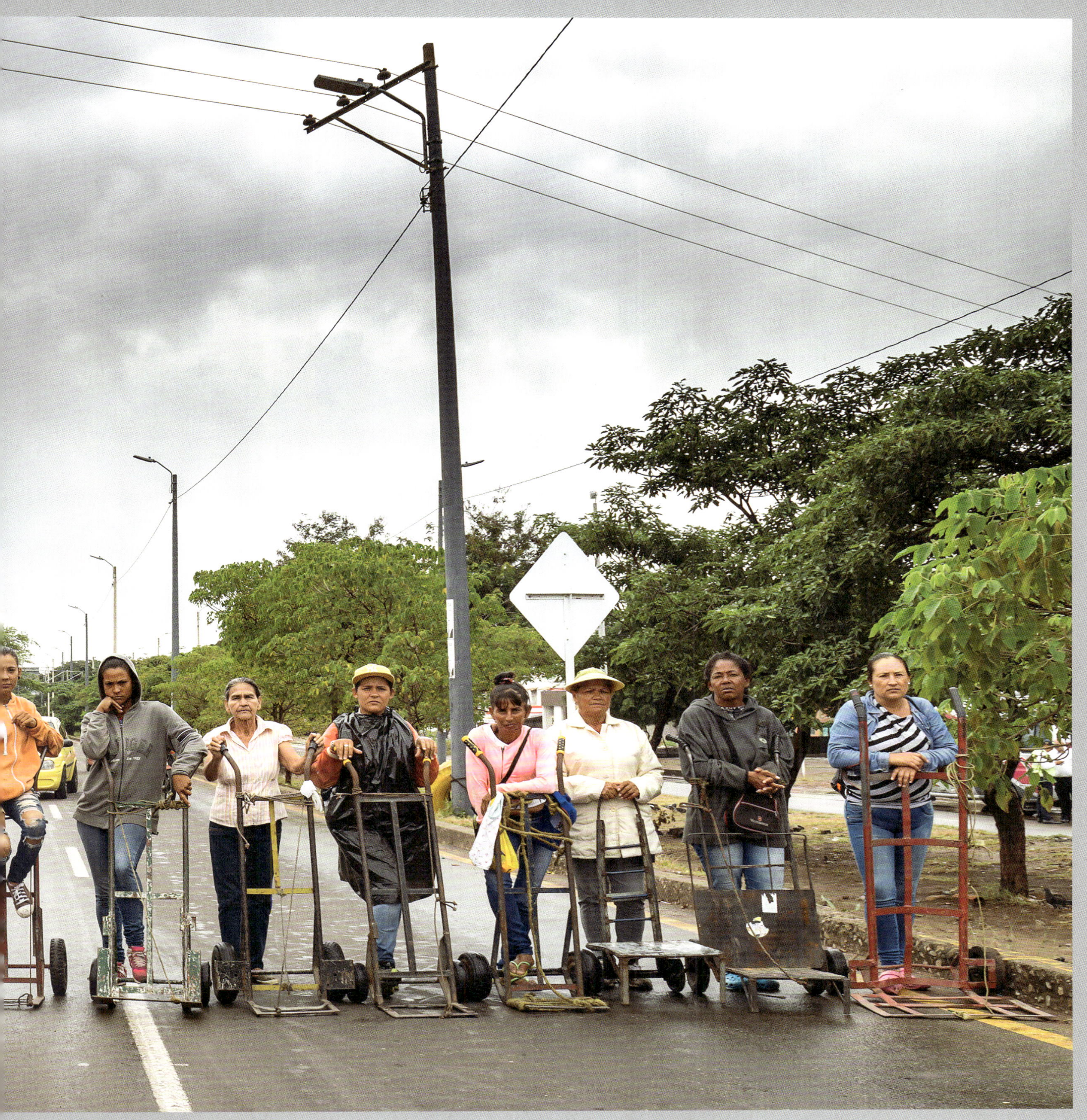

Carretilleras sobre el Puente Internacional Simón Bolívar (Porters on the Simón Bolívar International Bridge), 2017

Otobong Nkanga

b. 1974, Nigeria. Lives and works in Antwerp, Belgium.

Otobong Nkanga's work uses a combination of drawing, textiles, sculpture, video, and performance to explore the relationship between the body and the natural world. Often structured around the history of a particular mineral or site, the artist's installations reflect extensive research and travel throughout Africa and Europe, consultations with institutional archives, and engagement with local communities. Nkanga's expression of communal knowledge from throughout Africa and its diasporas posits ways of relating to the natural world outside the industrialized lust for materials that has been foundational to colonialism and our globalized economy.

Nkanga's installations are architectural and diagrammatic, made up of modular structures built for displaying and narrating often-contradictory histories that incorporate a performative element usually including the artist herself. In *Contained Measures of a Kolanut* (2012), Nkanga sits amid a simple, almost scientific display of documentation relating to the titular nut and the West African communities where it has a long history in rituals of hospitality, spirituality, community, and trade. A second chair allows one viewer at a time to sit and engage with the artist, who offers tastes of the nut's different varieties—a popular custom where Nkanga is from in Nigeria—as she explains its legacy within popular African tradition as well as its place within colonial histories. Archival documents, taken largely from the Historical Library of CIRAD (Centre for International Cooperation in Agronomic Research for Development) and from BREUIL Horticulture, both in France, appear juxtaposed with the raw material itself in different forms, including a glass funnel where liquid extracted from the kola nut drips onto homemade cotton paper.

The natural world takes on a multifaceted, animated place in Nkanga's work. A video titled *Reflections of the Raw Green Crown* (2014)—which, shown on a monitor embedded in a table, forms one component of the installation *In Pursuit of Bling* (2014)—documents a performance in which the key prop is a sculptural crown of malachite (also included in the installation) that the artist wears. Adorned with the mineral source of copper ore, Nkanga speaks to the copper-domed churches of

Berlin. She performs *as* the voice of copper, addressing the sorrow of the material's violent history in Africa. By imbuing the element with consciousness, Nkanga communicates the scars felt by the land as well as by the communities forced to mine the mineral to crown Christian religious institutions in Europe.

Across mediums, Nkanga employs a consistent visual language. In her tapestries and drawings, which often serve as anchors for her installations, simplified forms using flat blocks of color depict fragmented landscapes and body parts to create allegories of destruction of nature, displacement, and labor. The approach references non-Western pictographic and hieroglyphic visual languages. In the drawing series Social Consequences IV (2013), Nkanga demonstrates her narrative approach to iconicity by connecting fragmented figures to images of natural destruction and urban development with lines that suggest a diagrammatic connecting of the dots— or, at times, impalement. Titles of works in the series like *The Takeover* (2013) and *The Search* (2013) root the imagery within histories of colonialism and greed while also in their bareness lending the works a mythical tone. In the expansive textile *The Weight of Scars* (2015), Nkanga creates a fractured landscape scarred by extractive histories that was inspired by her research into the abandoned mines of northwestern Namibia, the colors and images of the materials once extracted there, the faceless masses forced to work in them, and the cracked earth that remains.

Nkanga's work can be seen as a mode of expression rather than a form of representation in the Western sense, a search for lost methods of understanding our relationship to the natural world. In *Witch Hunt,* the artist has reimagined a constellation of works from her retrospective solo project *From Where I Stand* at the Tate St Ives in 2019, which includes drawings, installations, and tapestries. Together, the works tell a story of shared wounds and collective memory that posits an alternative to Western feminism as a tool for healing our current addiction to natural resources.

—Nika Chilewich

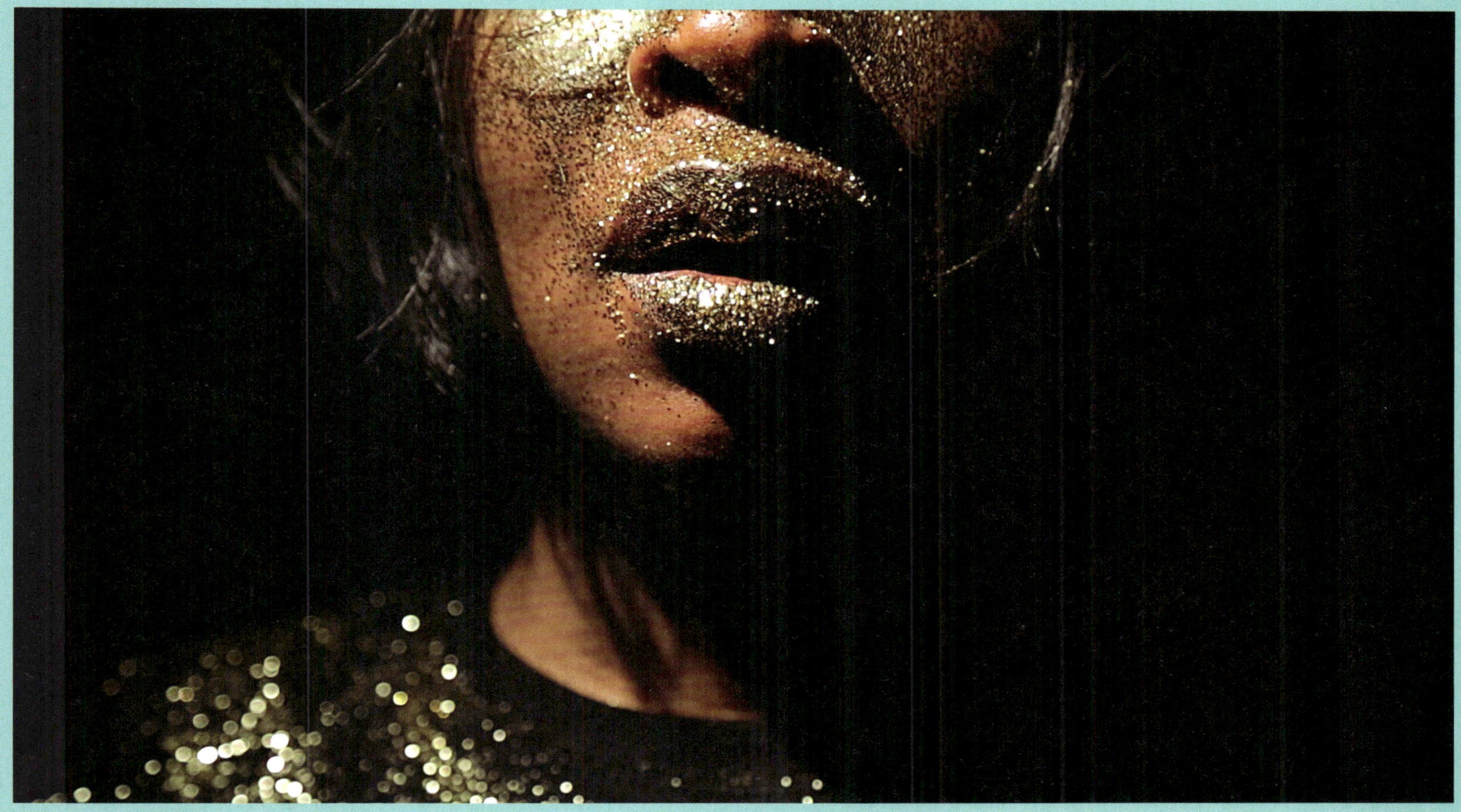

In Pursuit of Bling, 2014

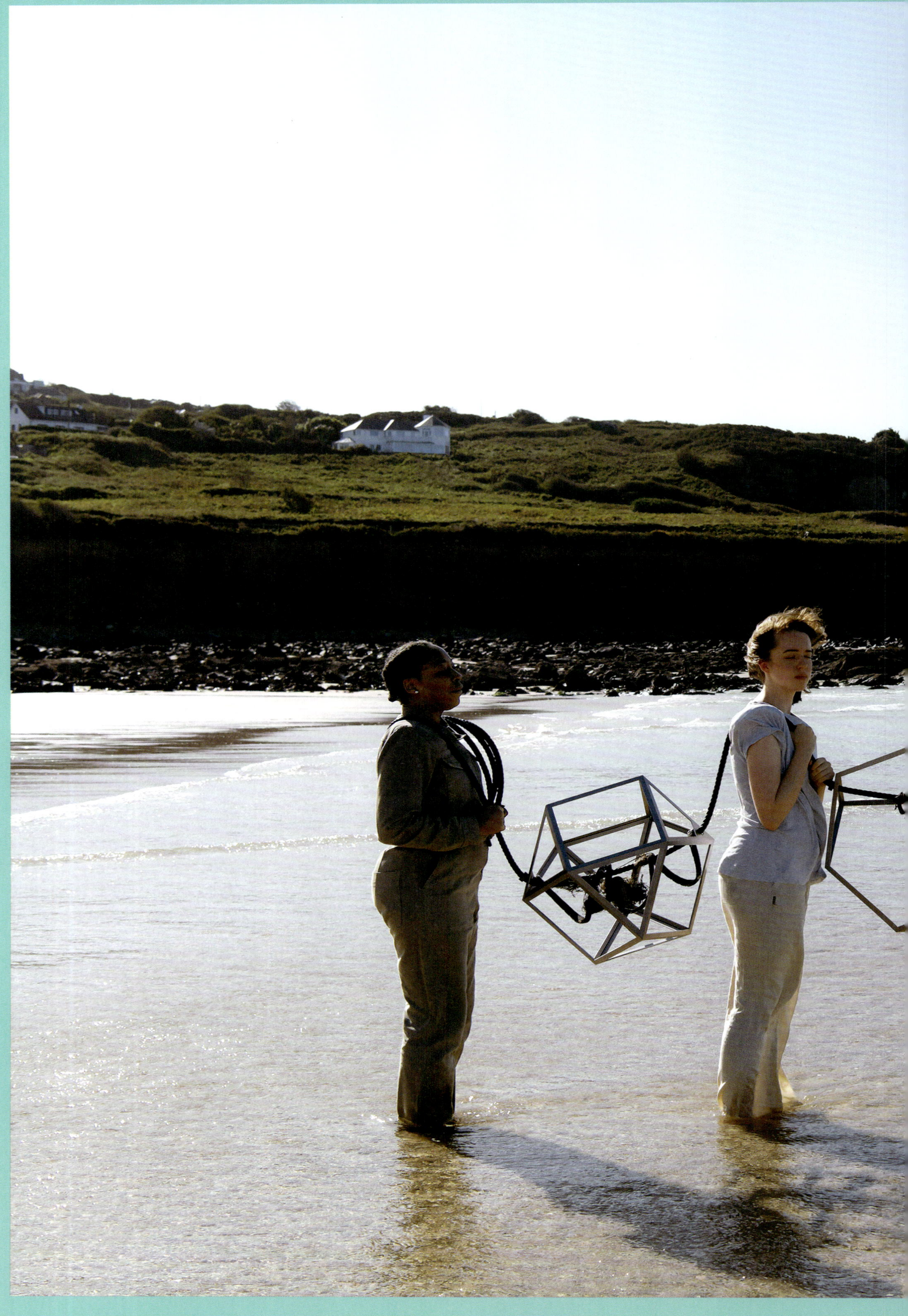

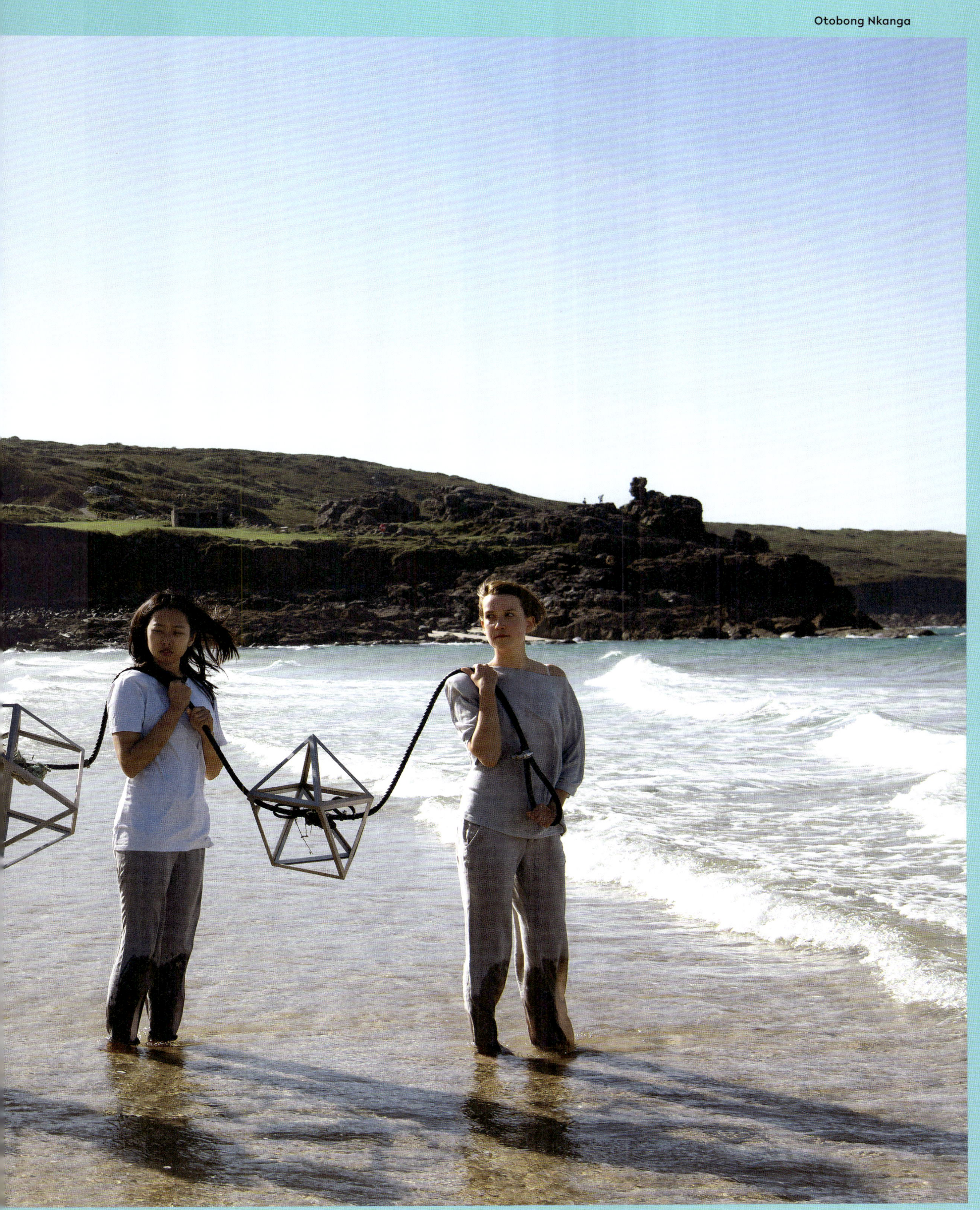

Constellation to Appease, 2019

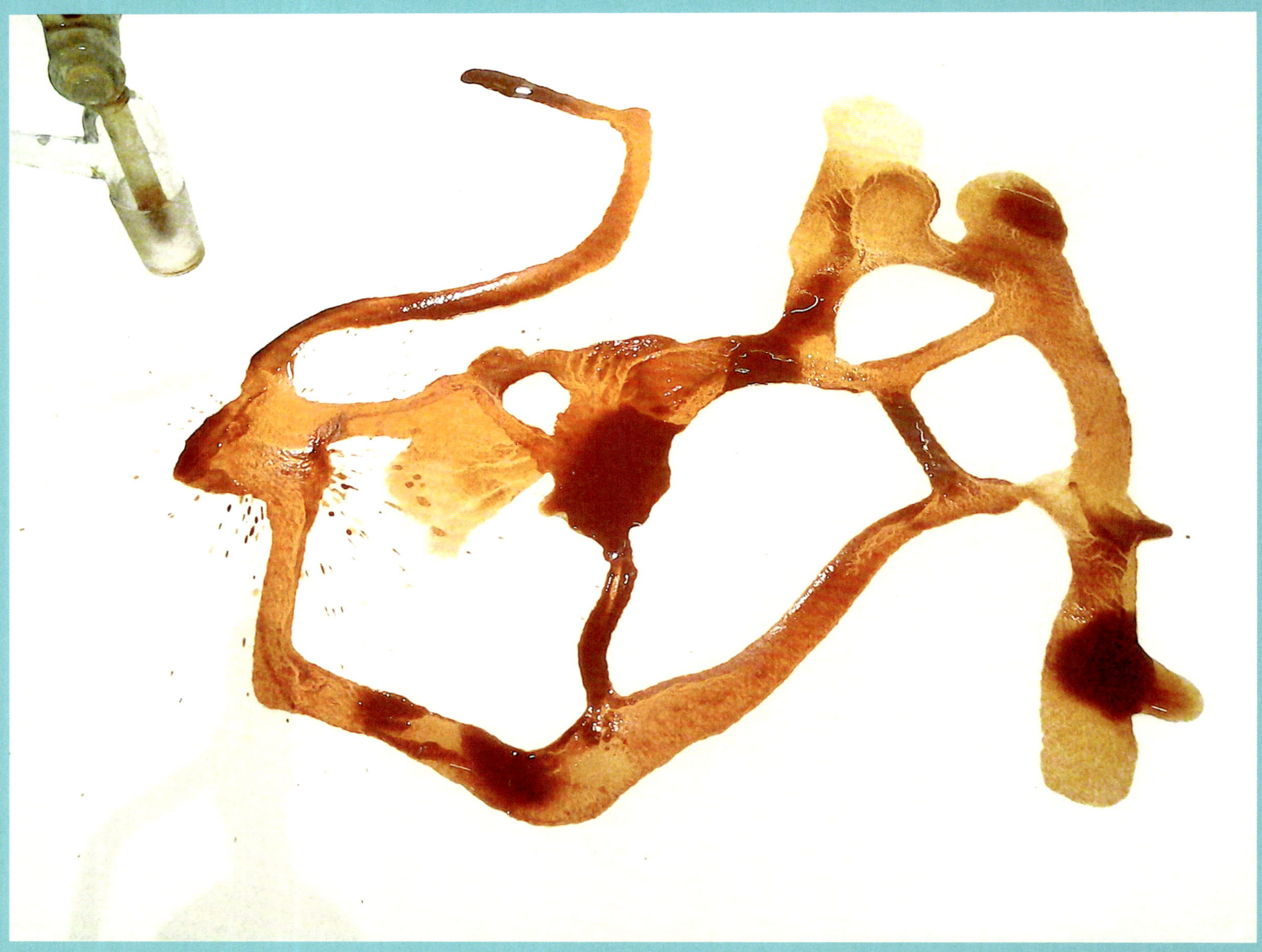

Contained Measures of a Kolanut, 2012

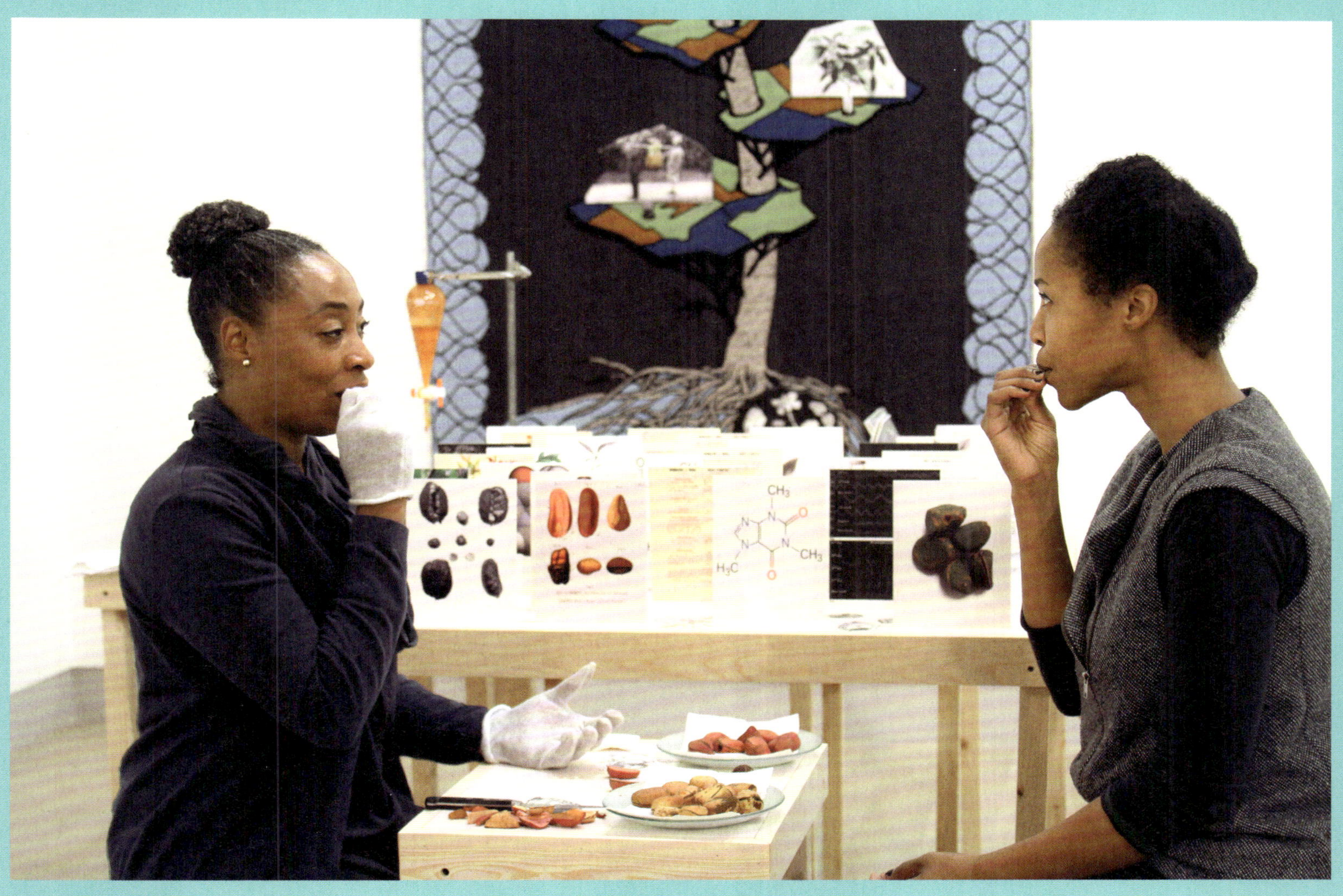

Contained Measures of a Kolanut, 2012

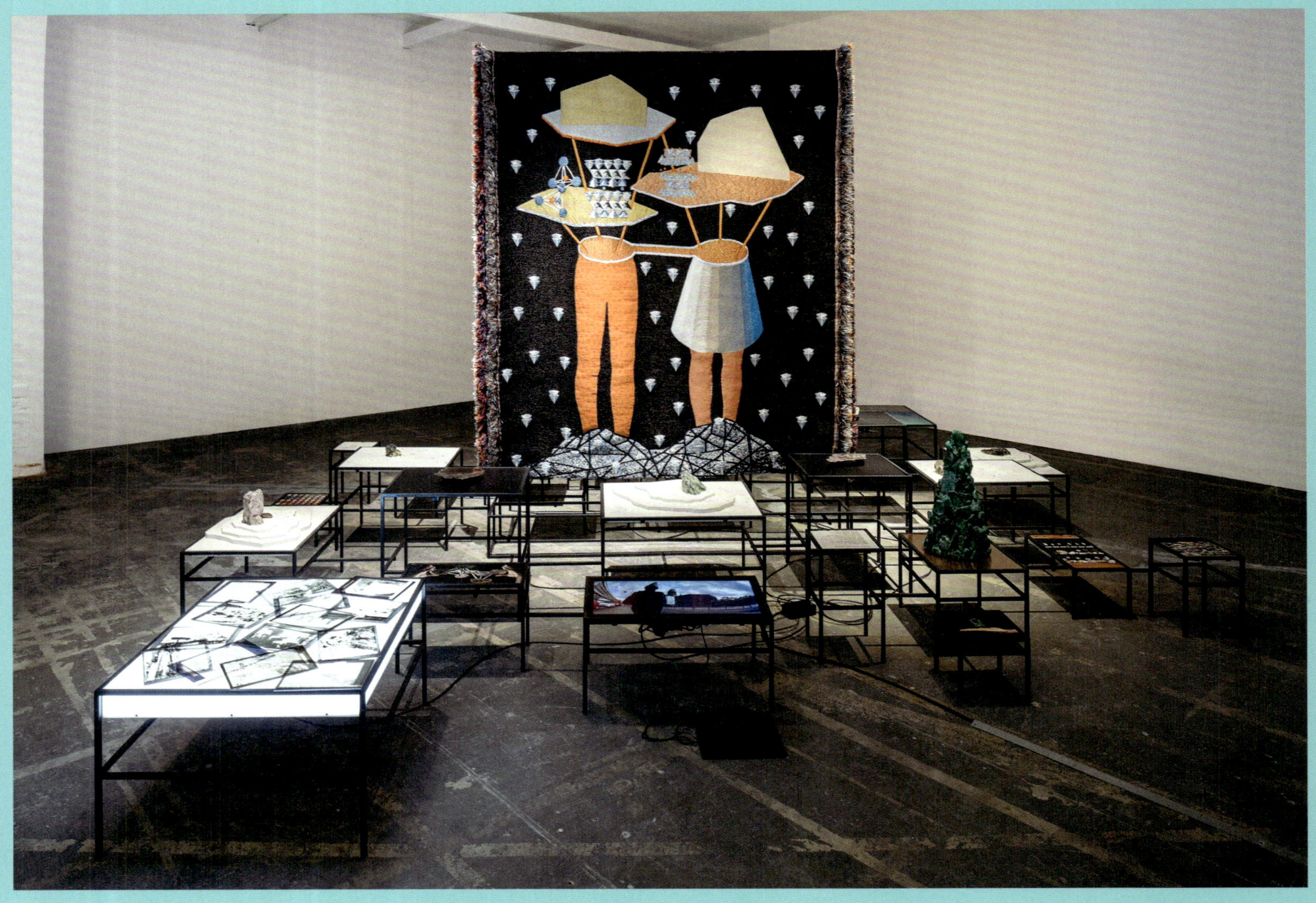

In Pursuit of Bling, 2014

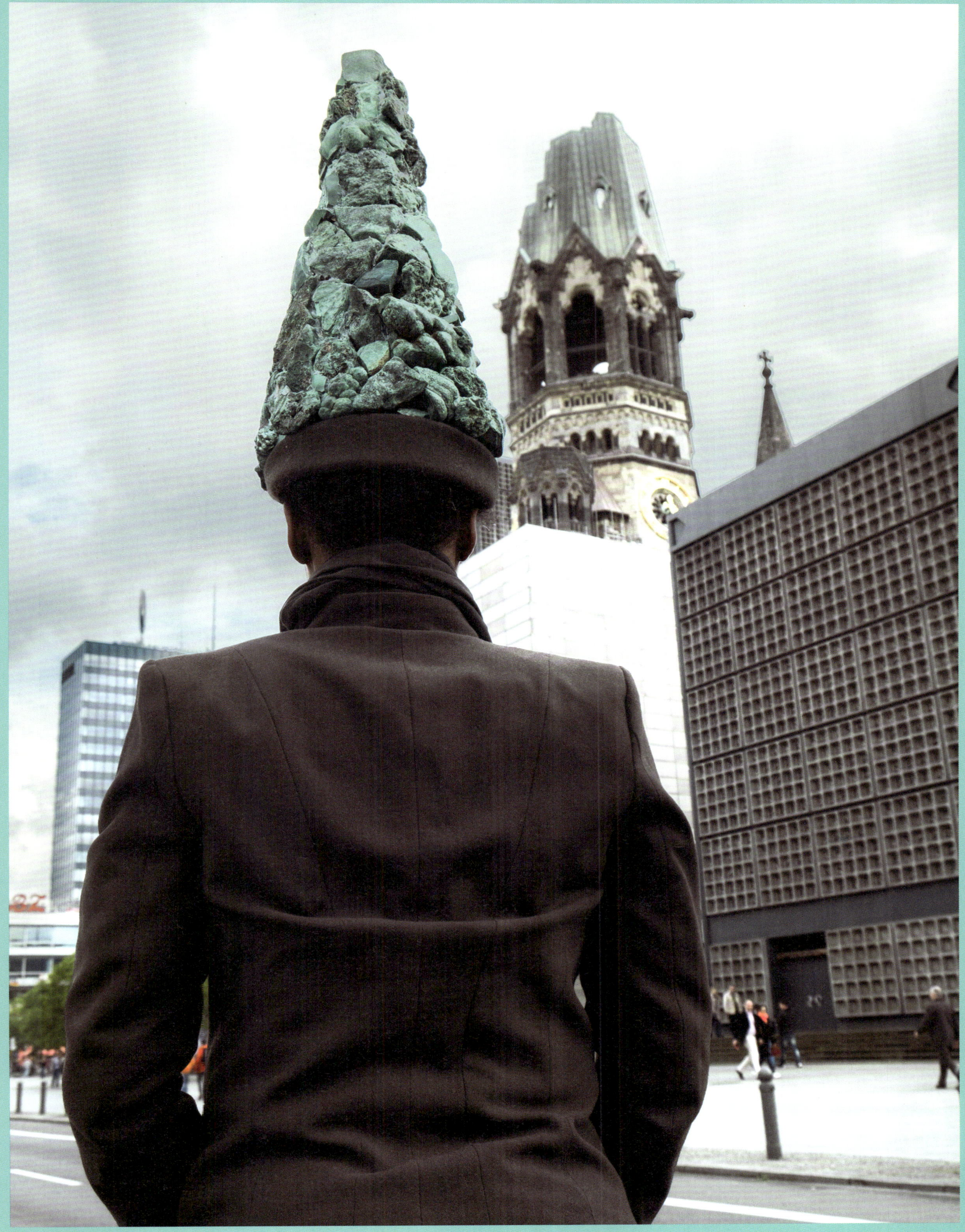

In Pursuit of Bling: Reflections of the Raw Green Crown, 2014

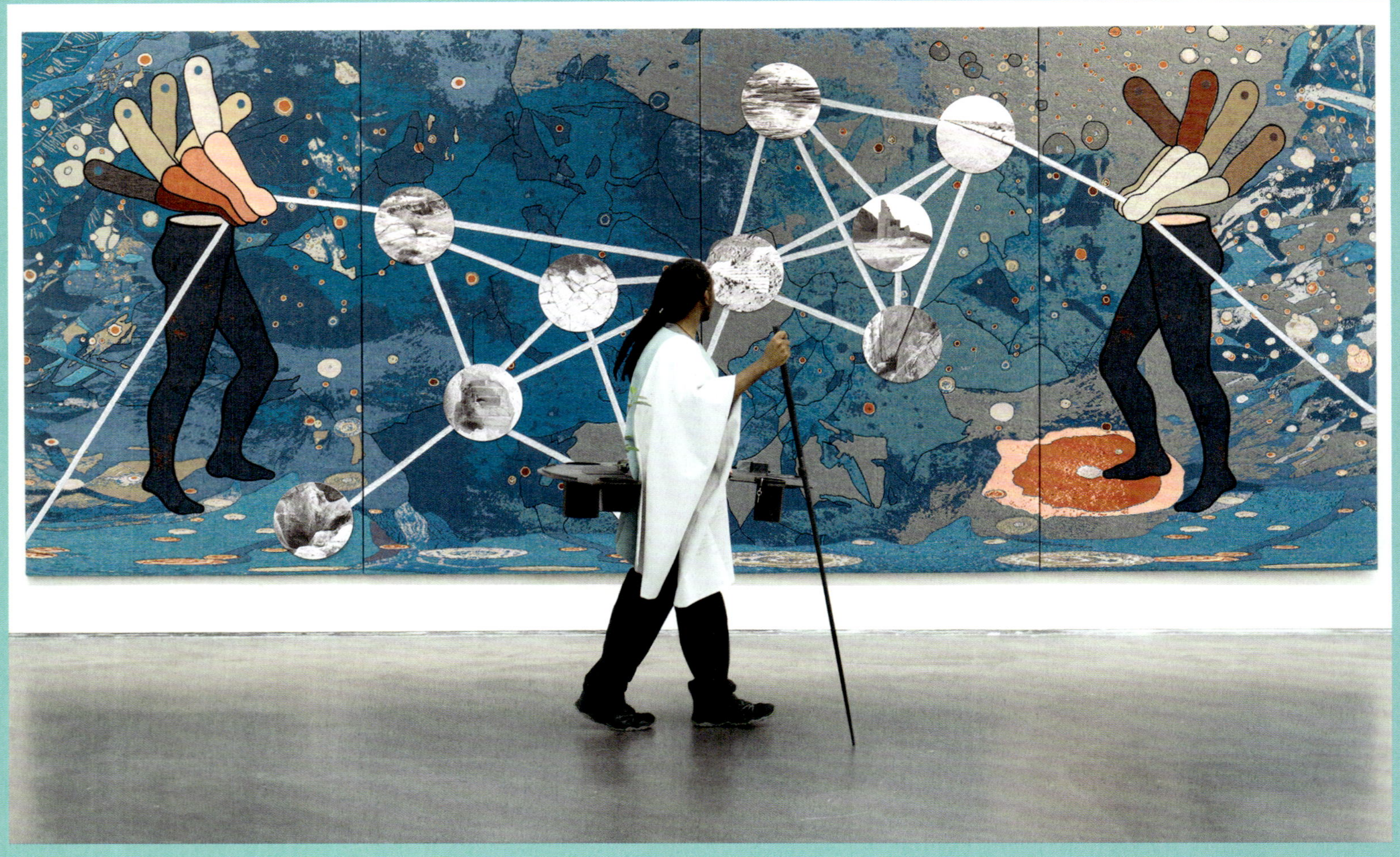

The Weight of Scars, 2015

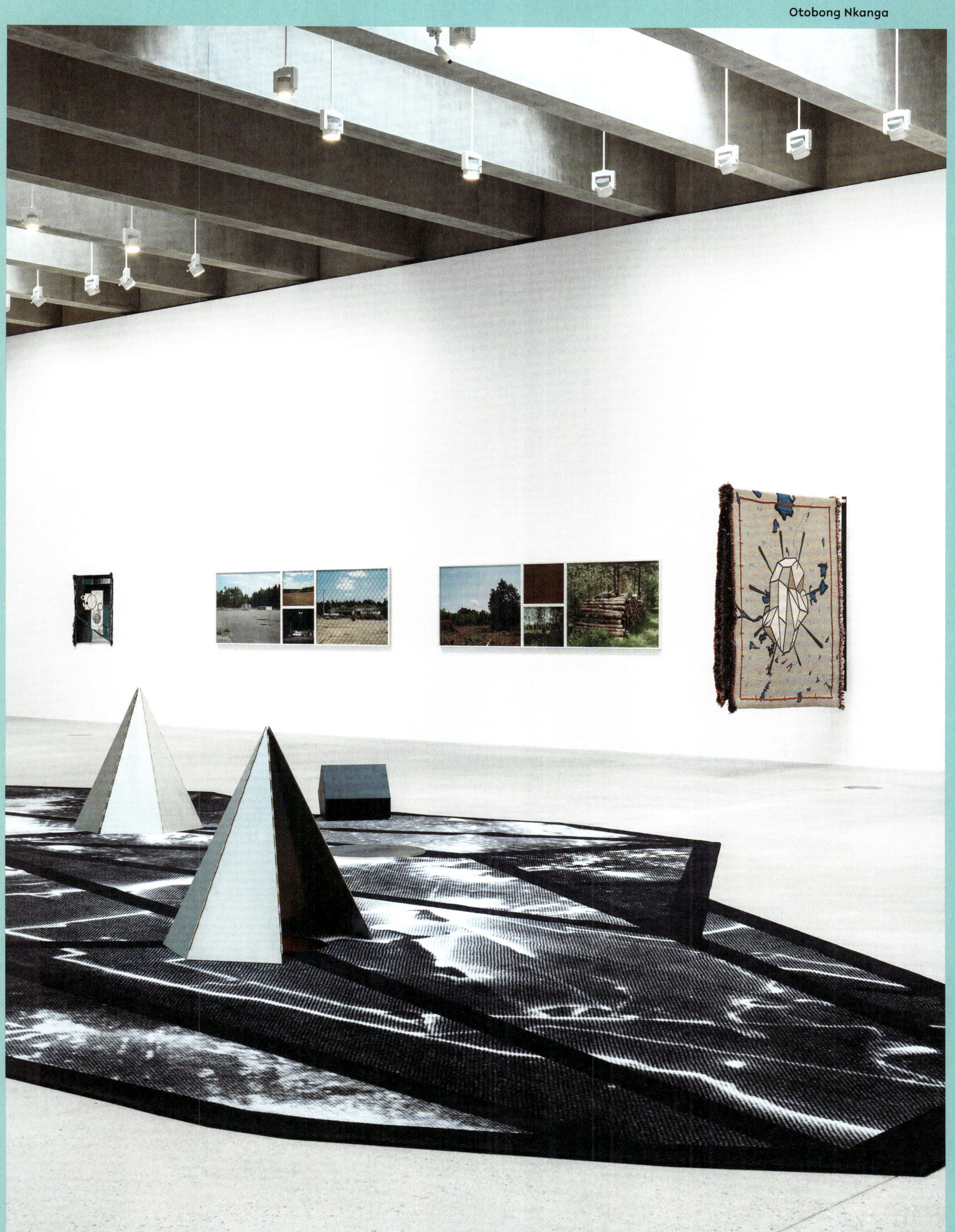

From Where I Stand, 2015

Okwui Okpokwasili

b. 1972, United States. Lives and works in New York, New York.

Combining elements of theater and dance, Okwui Okpokwasili's performances foreground the experiences of Black women, focusing on how history is embodied and transmitted and on how acts of resistance prevail amid the pervasive racist and sexist bias they experience—misogynoir, as the feminist scholar Moya Bailey has put it. The communion of bodies and voices is a central strategy throughout Okpokwasili's work. In the solo piece *Bronx Gothic* (2014), for example, she performs in the voices of two girls, presenting diaristic accounts of their burgeoning womanhood and sexuality. Even before she begins to speak, Okpokwasili is seen shaking in one corner of the stage with her back to the audience, the shadows of her convulsions cast against the curtained backdrop. Through her movement, she is summoning voices. "Maybe that's what I'm also trying to facilitate—the potential for a body to be possessed," the artist told an interviewer for the Walker Art Center in 2017. "What have we transferred through skin? Through genetics? What kind of pain? What kind of confusion? The body has these tunnels, these secrets, these pathways that can be opened up."

The first major performance by Okpokwasili, a Nigerian American raised in the Bronx, was *Pent Up: A Revenge Dance* (2009), in which the performer explores the tumultuous relationship between a mother and daughter. Elsewhere, her work engages more explicitly with politics. Performances such as *Poor People's TV Room* (2016), and the related works *When I return, who will receive me?* (2016) and *Sitting on a Man's Head* (2018), connect resistance movements spearheaded by African and African American women in response to violence or other abuses committed by the state. *Poor People's TV Room* began in part as a response to the kidnapping of 276 Chibok schoolgirls by the Nigerian terrorist group Boko Haram, and to the deaths of Trayvon Martin, Michael Brown, and Eric Garner, which catalyzed the Black Lives Matter movement. Okpokwasili focused on a historical forerunner of such movements, the 1929 Women's War in Nigeria, when women of several tribes organized an effective pressure campaign against local warrant chiefs and British colonizers. In response to their increased marginalization in politics, the economy, and tribal operations, the women waged an idiosyncratic form of protest called "sitting on a man's head"—gathering outside the homes of men who are guilty of a misdeed, wearing headdresses made of ferns (symbolizing war), wielding sticks wrapped in palms to invoke the power of their female ancestors, and singing songs that mock the targets of their ire.

In one version of *Poor People's TV Room*, Okpokwasili and three intergenerational collaborators sing in unison and perform movements that physicalize acts of solidarity, literally supporting one another and moving together, collapsing time and geography in the service of redressing shared conflict. The echoing, hypnotic incantations of the performers are a hybrid of protest chants and choral singing. Phrases like "mighty overtaking" and "I will swear on a sword, I can read your sword" suggest a power dynamic between speaker and listener that builds and changes with each verse. Moving behind a translucent plastic scrim for the duration of the piece, their individual bodies are not always visible, creating a mass of shadows in degrees of relief that inflect how the audience witnesses the work and is enveloped by its sounds and sights.

Staged as a solo performance for *Witch Hunt*, *Poor People's TV Room* finds the artist performing inside a booth constructed of plywood and plastic sheeting, singing short, poetic fragments. The shadows that Okpokwasili casts, along with footage projected behind her of Nigerian women congregating in various sites, suggest a critical mass of bodies, the legacy of their struggle contained within her frame, their power amplifying with every gesture and word.

—Jamillah James

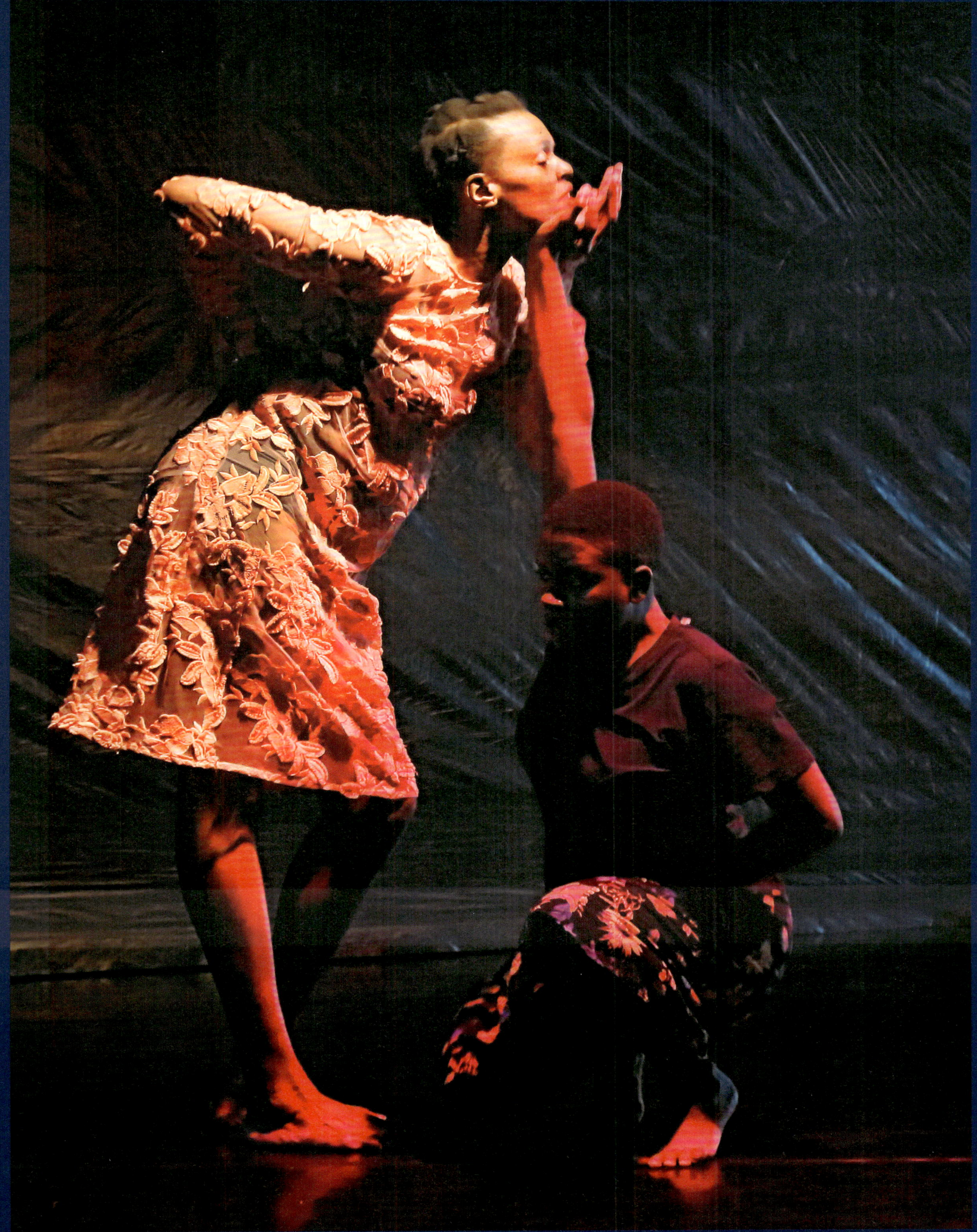

Poor People's TV Room, 2106

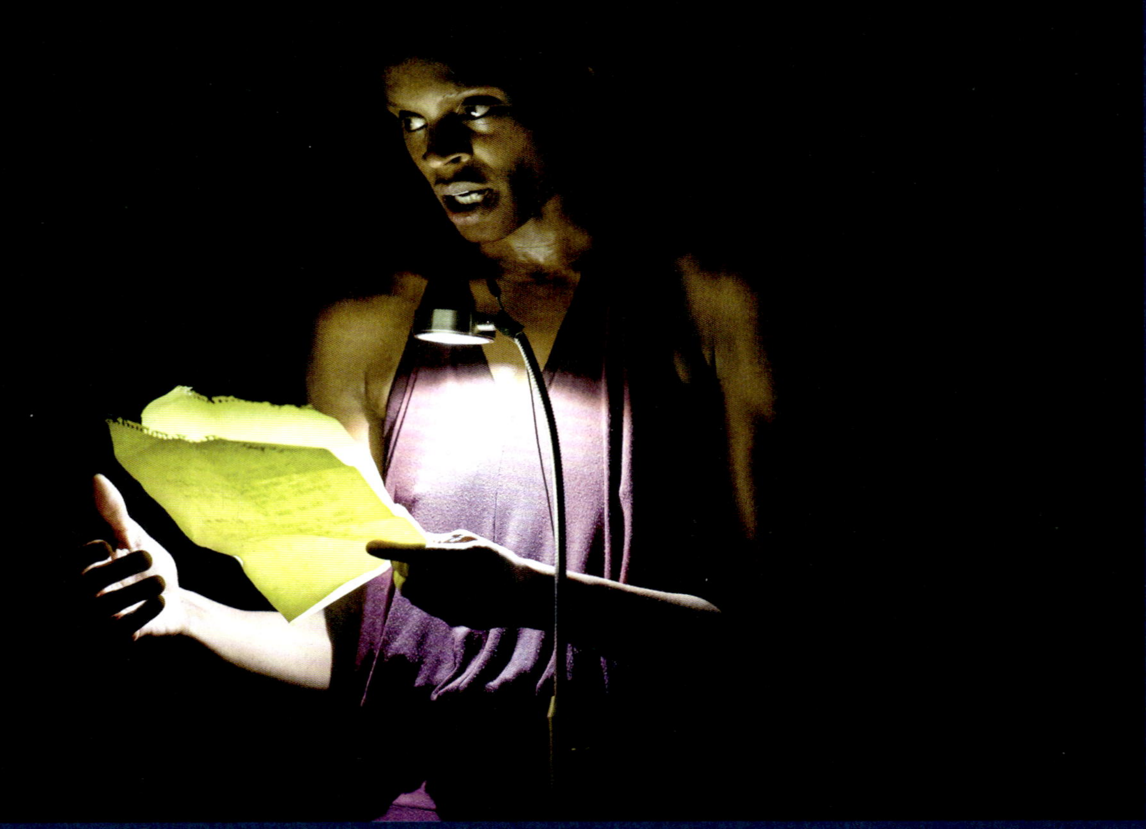

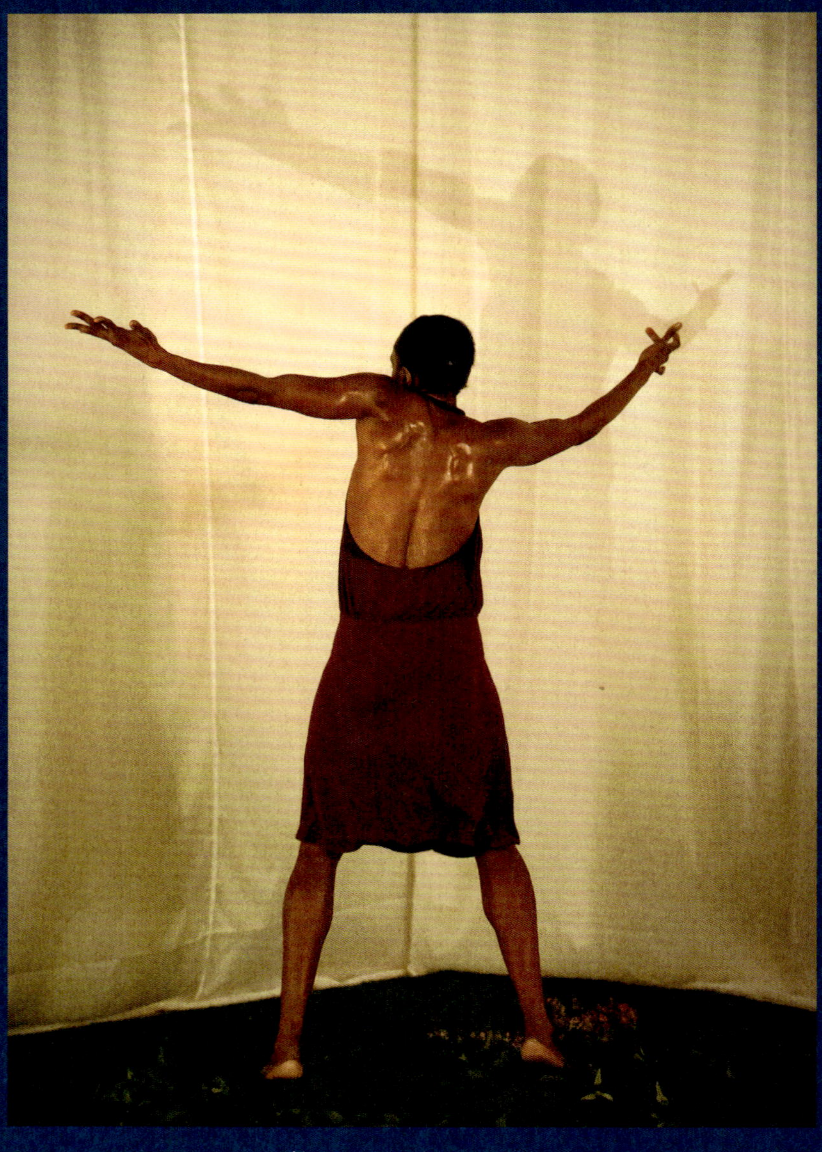

Bronx Gothic, 2014

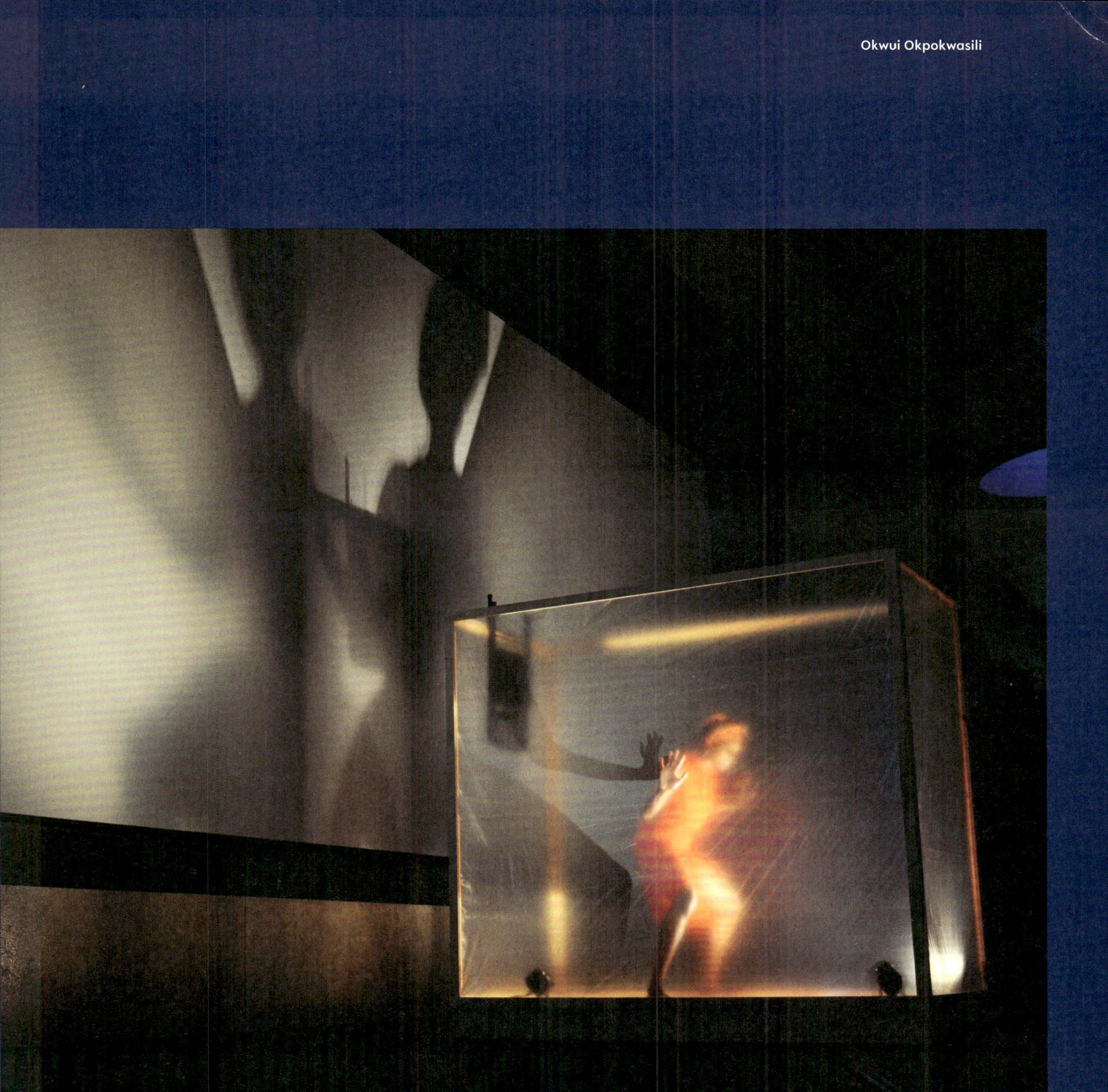
Okwui Okpokwasili

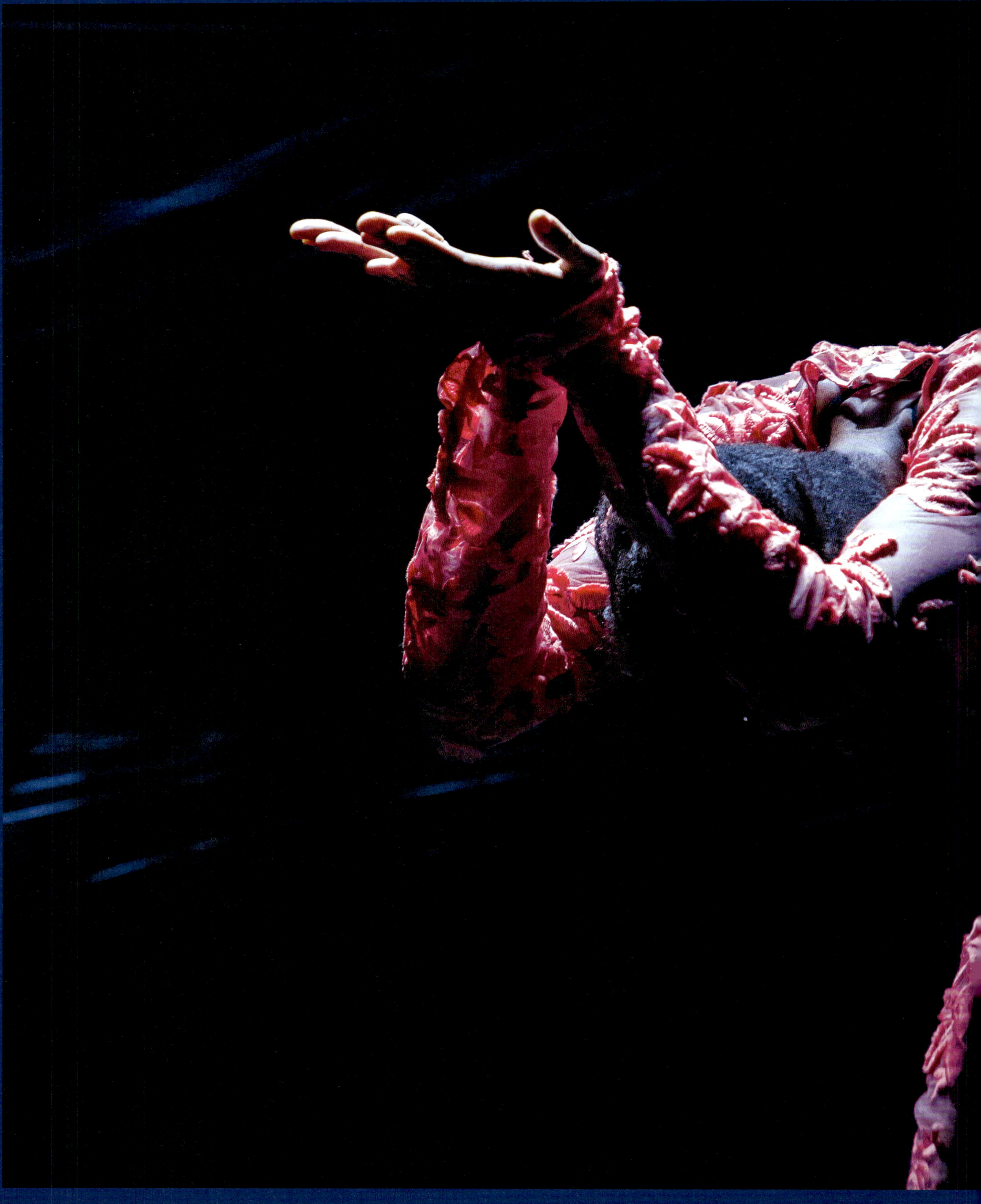

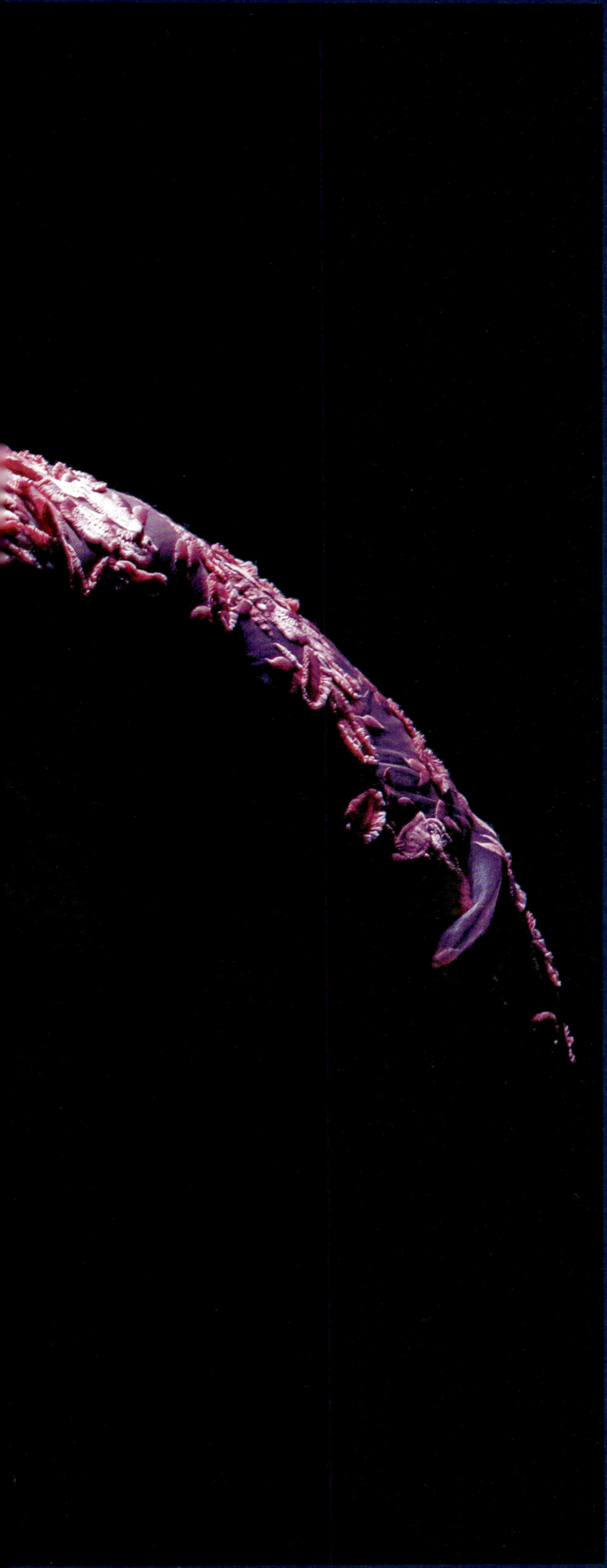

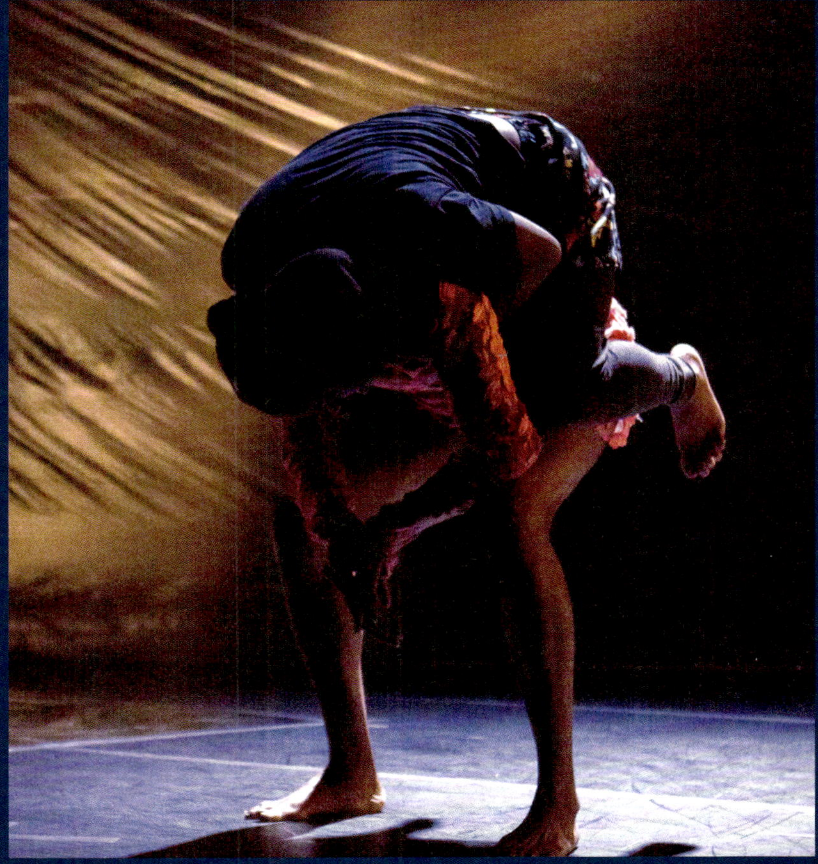

Poor People's TV Room, 2016

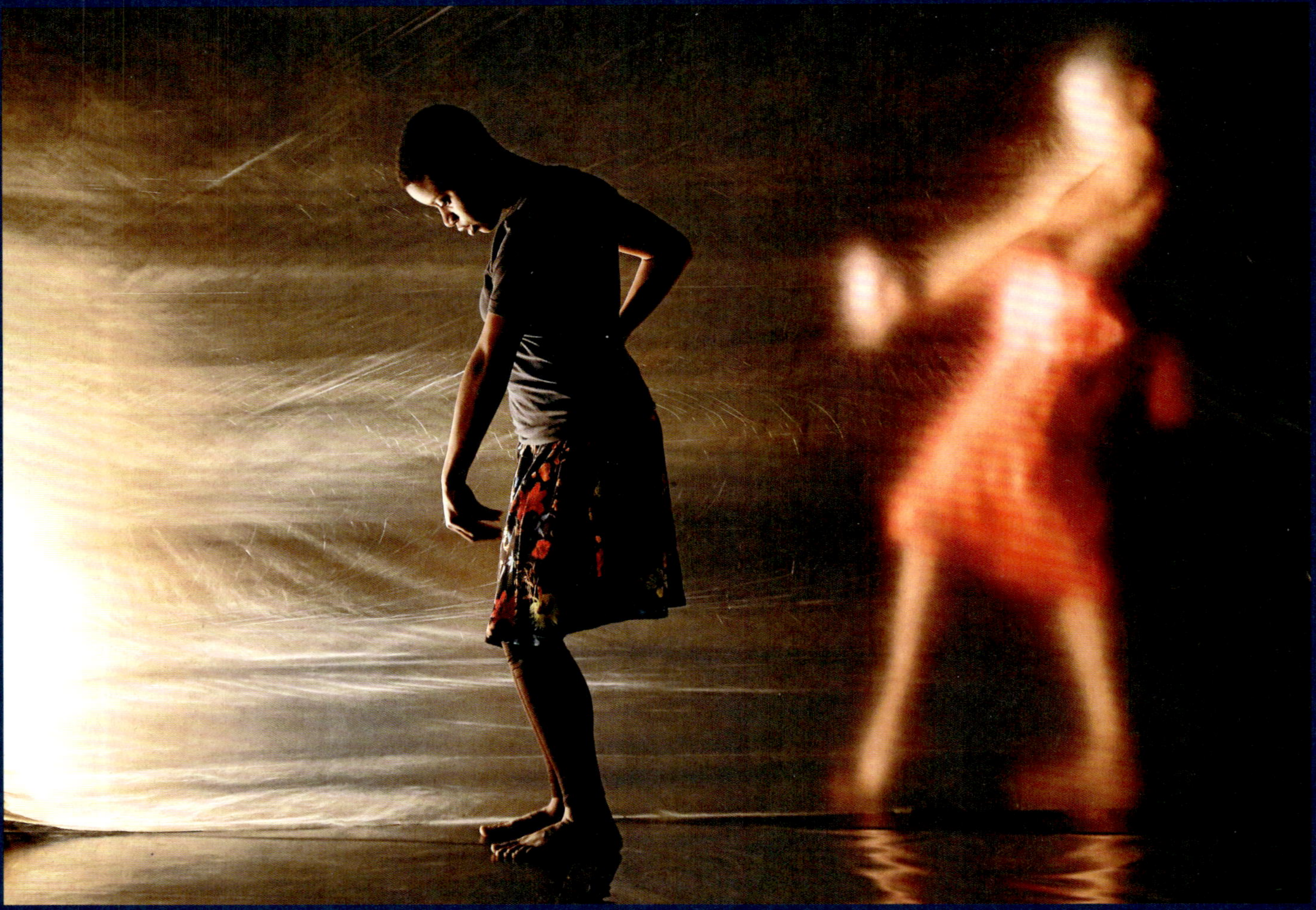

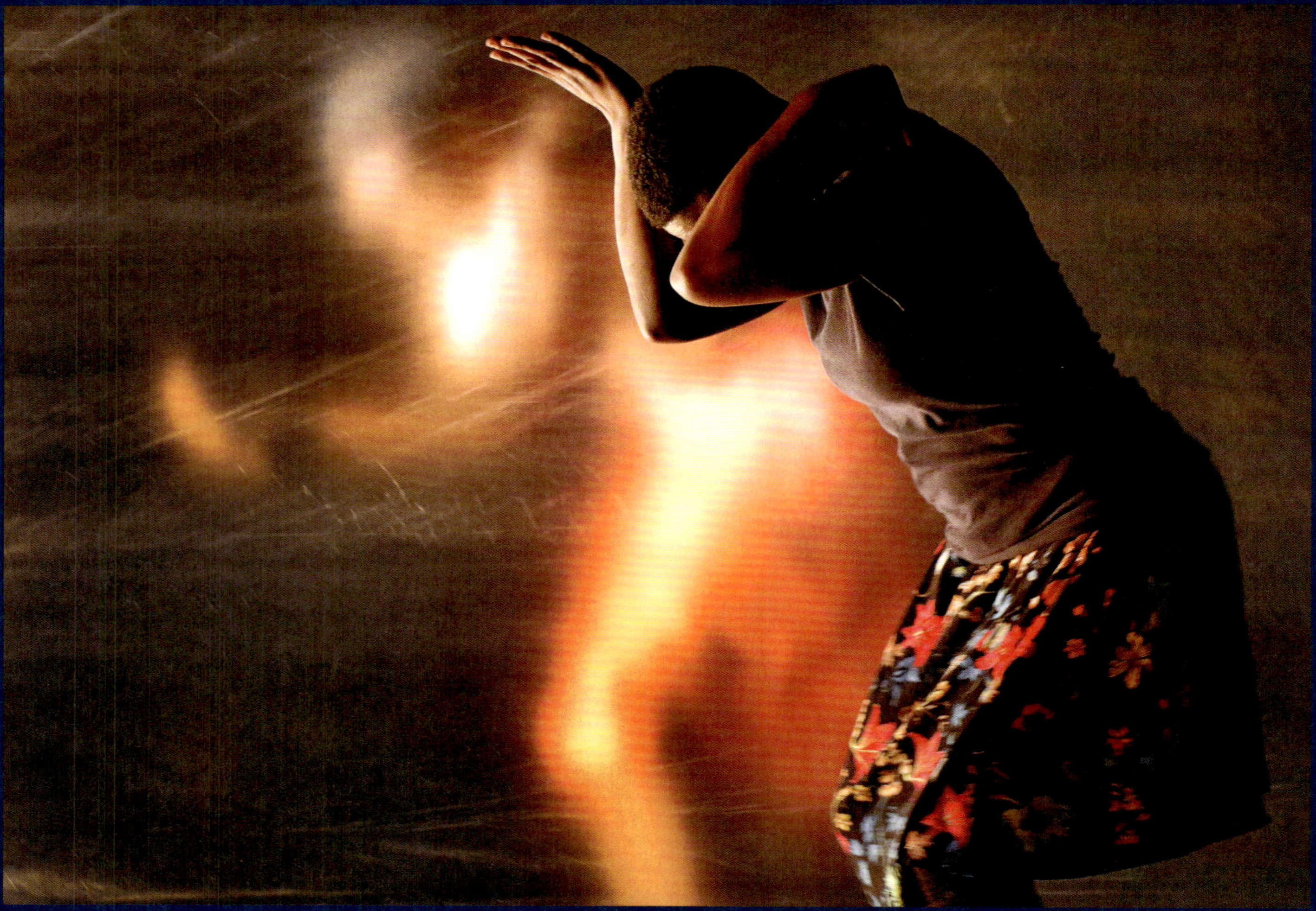

Poor People's TV Room, 2016

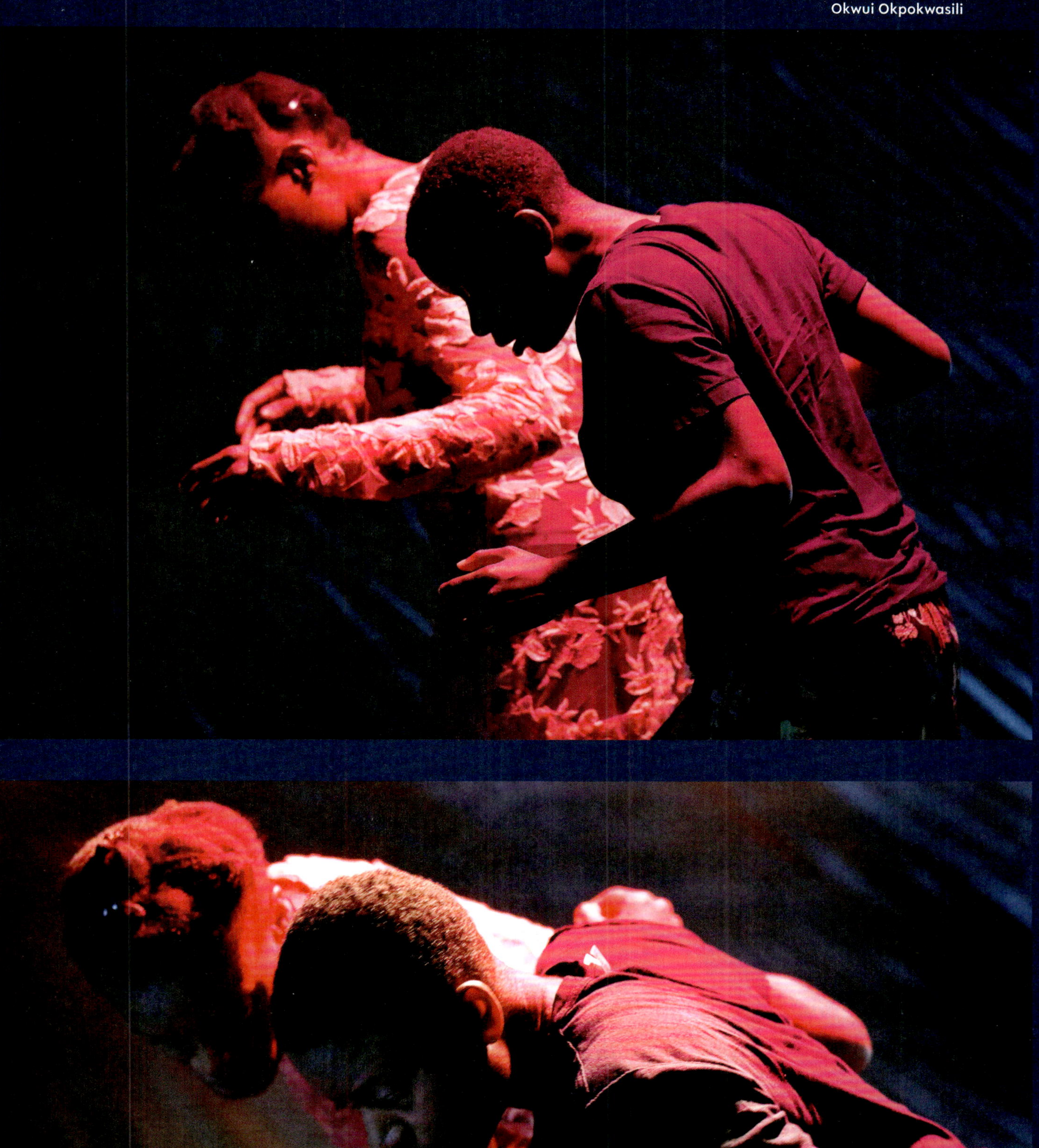

Poor People's TV Room, 2016

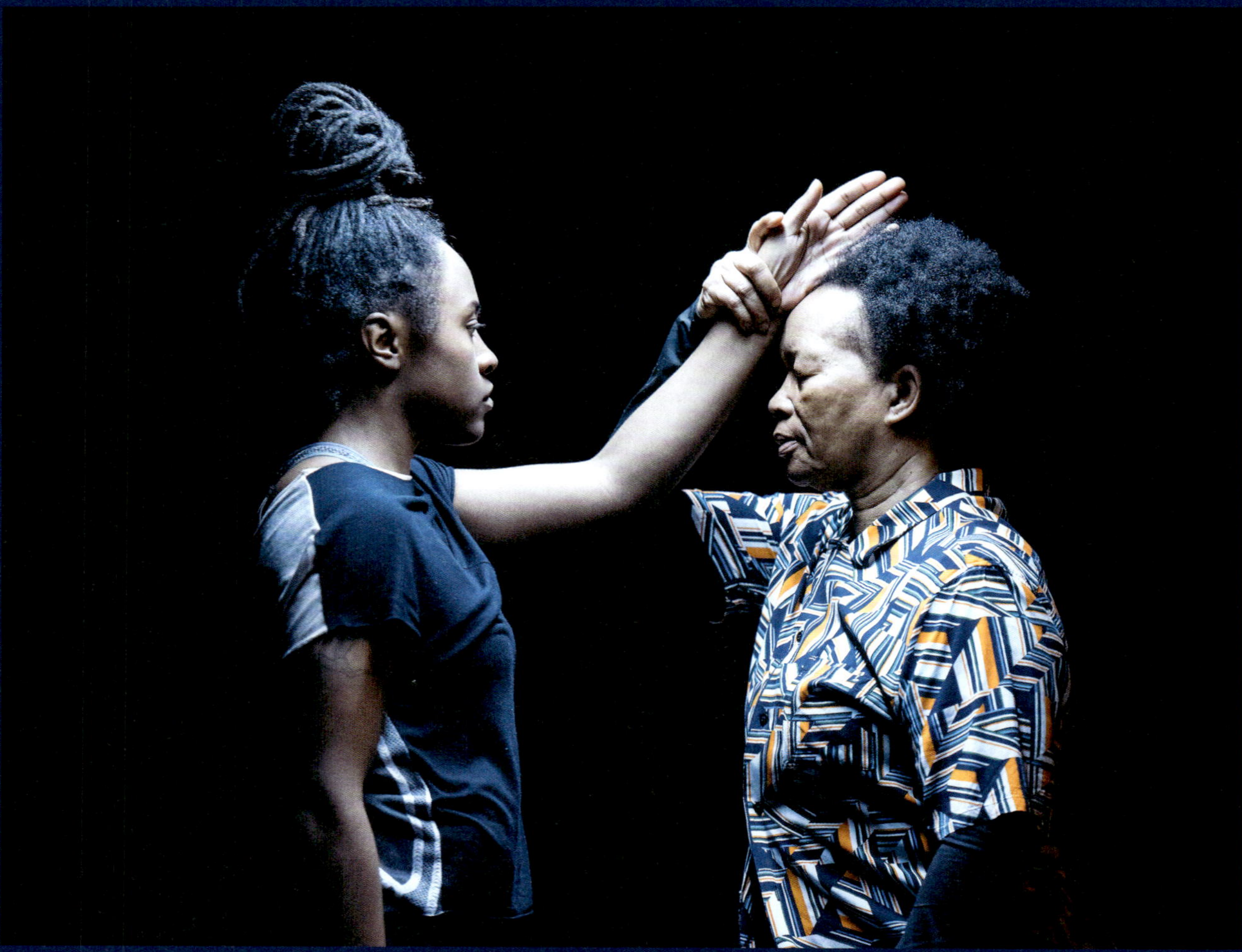

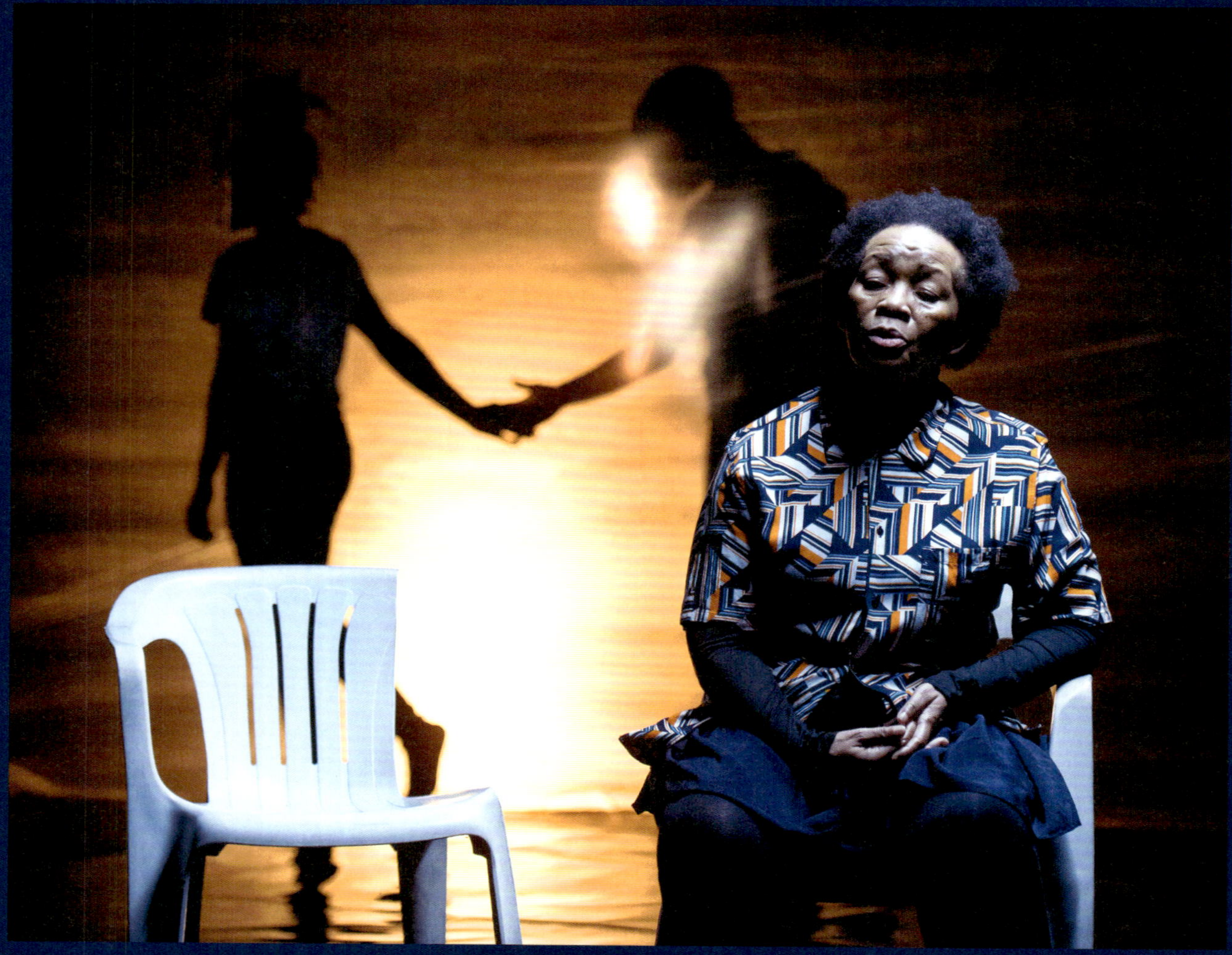

Poor People's TV Room, 2016

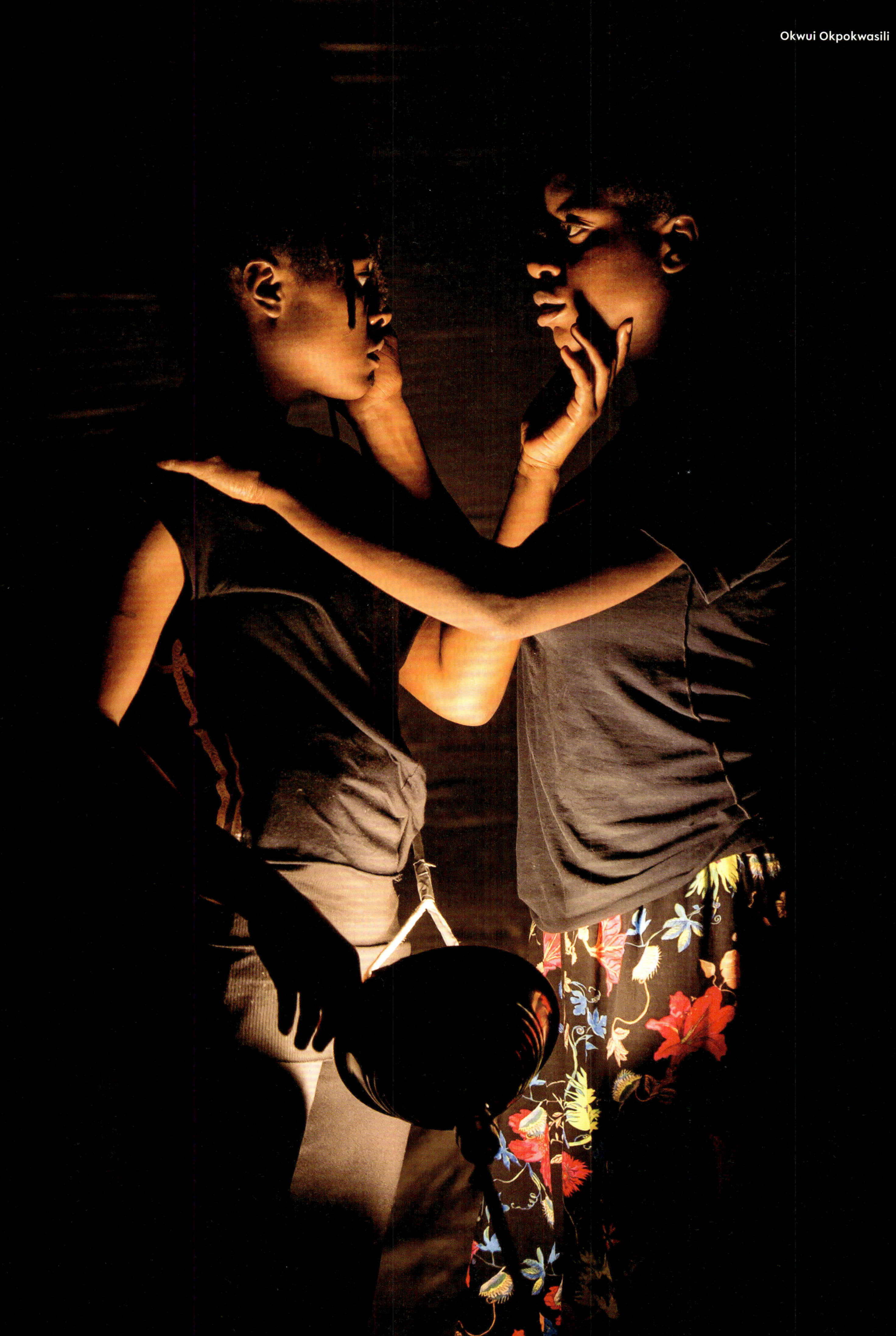

Lara Schnitger

b. 1969, Netherlands. Lives and works in Los Angeles, California.

The Dutch-born, Los Angeles–based artist Lara Schnitger credits her focus on textiles to, among other factors, youthful exposure to the work of Magdalena Abakanowicz, Christo, and Sheila Hicks. Their monumental displays, imbued with various senses of drama and theatricality, resonated with Schnitger's background in the performing arts as well as her attraction to fashion and DIY culture. Beginning with abstract experiments in the 1990s, Schnitger has explored the vast possibilities of textiles through painting, sculpture, installation, and costuming.

Schnitger's works often tell stories, ranging at times to the realms of demons, ghosts, and goddesses. *Leave the World Outside* (2010), for example, creates a mise-en-scène from eight figurative forms that individually resemble gothic butterfly inkblots—variations on a hypersexual Holy Ghost. Based on a banned Charles Baudelaire poem entitled "Damned Women, Delphine and Hippolyta," the installation treats the titular characters' love affair via a pair of sculptures situated at the center of the circle formed by the work overall. As part of a larger installation that transformed New York's SculptureCenter into a medieval piazza, *Leave the World Outside* dealt with themes of metamorphosis, divinity, decay, and sadomasochism.

In other works, Schnitger is more topical, referring to feminist political movements and news related to women's issues by embroidering sloganeering texts onto the works themselves or quoting headlines in the titles. Her textile characters, hoisted up on large wooden dowels, bear pointed monikers like *Slut-stick Souls No Holes* (2015), *Slut-stick No Shave* (2015), and *Slut-stick Boobs Not Bombs* (2017). Such works are exhibited in galleries as static, ghostly sculptures that evoke the absent body their titles reference. But their primary purpose as art objects is to be activated in Schnitger's ongoing project *Suffragette City* (2015–), a traveling hybrid procession-protest that has visited locations including Basel, Berlin, Dresden, New York, Paris, Reims, San Jose, and Washington, DC, for the 2017 Women's March. The project, which draws inspiration from occult rituals, street performances, and protest marches to champion women's rights, streamed through Westwood in Los Angeles as part of the Hammer Museum's Bureau of Feminism initiative in 2016. Performers outfitted in navy blue coveralls, in reference to the cultural iconography of the "Rosie the Riveter" working woman, carried Schnitger's slut-sticks and quilted banners out of the museum space and into the streets. As part of a participatory procession, audience members were encouraged to utilize their bodies and join the performers in the parade as they cast a spell in what would become a magical hybrid of theater, ritual, and protest. By merging women's movements of the past with contemporary ones that focus on an end to victim blaming and slut shaming, *Suffragette City* became an ode to Los Angeles as a city filled with witches, artist-activists, and working women.

Schnitger's work reflects and responds to the spaces she inhabits and the places where she lives, which have included China and Japan as well as the Netherlands and the United States. In the later 1990s, living in Amsterdam, she worked primarily in large fabric installations that required anchoring to the gallery walls, such as *Hornament* (1999) and *Jackson's Nightmare* (1998), which use stockings to create intricate webs throughout the space. After a yearlong stint in Japan, however, where she studied at the Center of Contemporary Art, Kitakyushu, the relative interiority of Japanese society led her to begin creating freestanding sculptures using wooden armatures, which is now signature in her work. "That's when I started making introverted pieces, where the tension would come from the structure inside, instead of from the walls," the artist told *Art in America* magazine in 2006. By making freestanding work, Schnitger centers all dynamics within the sculpture, playing with the multiple valences of interior and exterior. In *Snoop Snap* (2007), for example, the jagged radials of the work's armature are visible beneath the translucent nylon stretched tautly over its wooden bars, its strains akin to the fragility and femininity Schnitger seeks to evoke with her fabric exteriors. The enmeshing of a variety of fabrics and materials, from a cow-print textile to an anonymous collection of furs, conjures up a disembodied femininity in a state of dressing and undressing. *Snoop Snap* functions as an abject representation of womanhood via the fashioned body, ready to explode under its see-through duress.

—Ana Briz

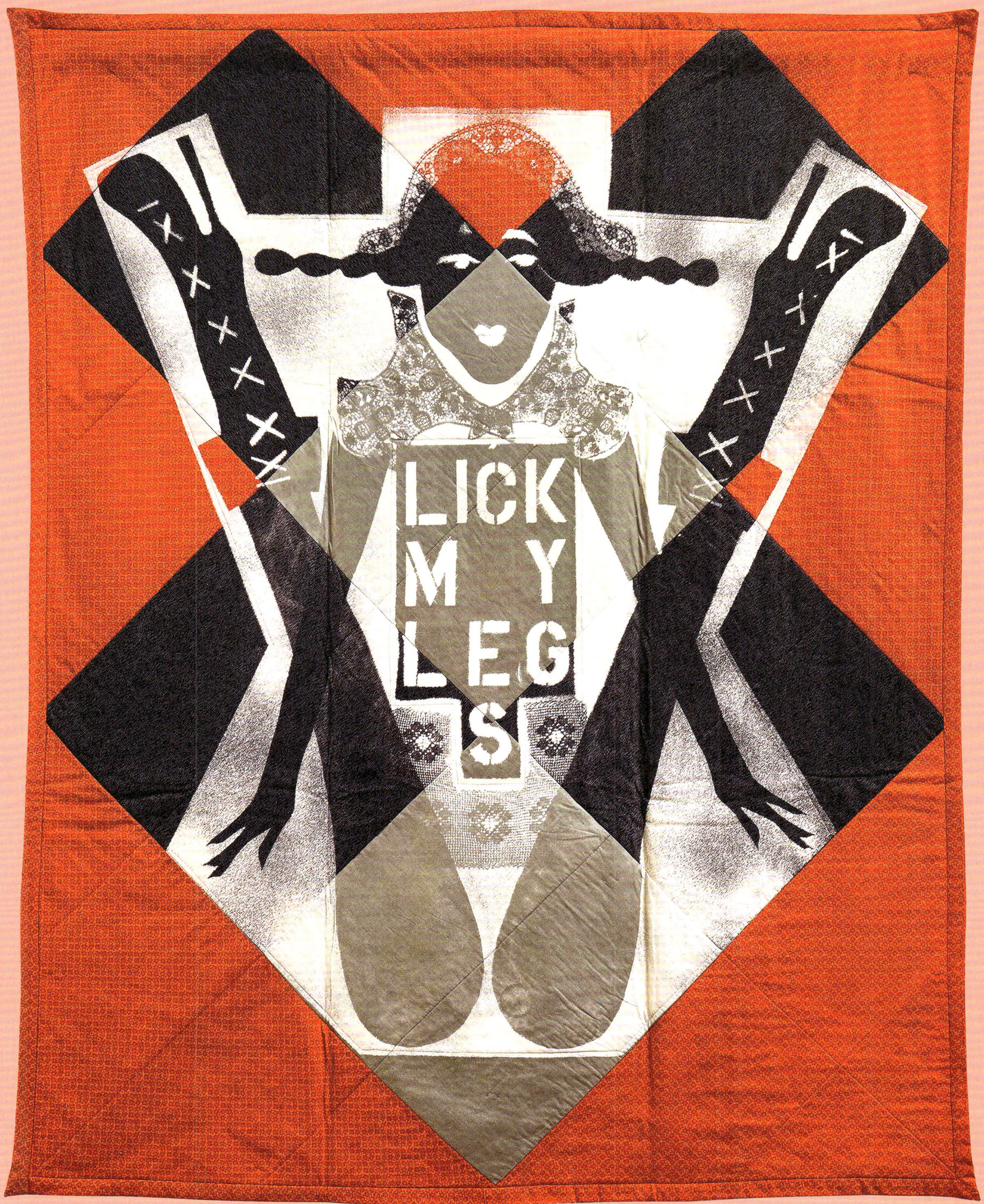

Lick My Legs, 2012

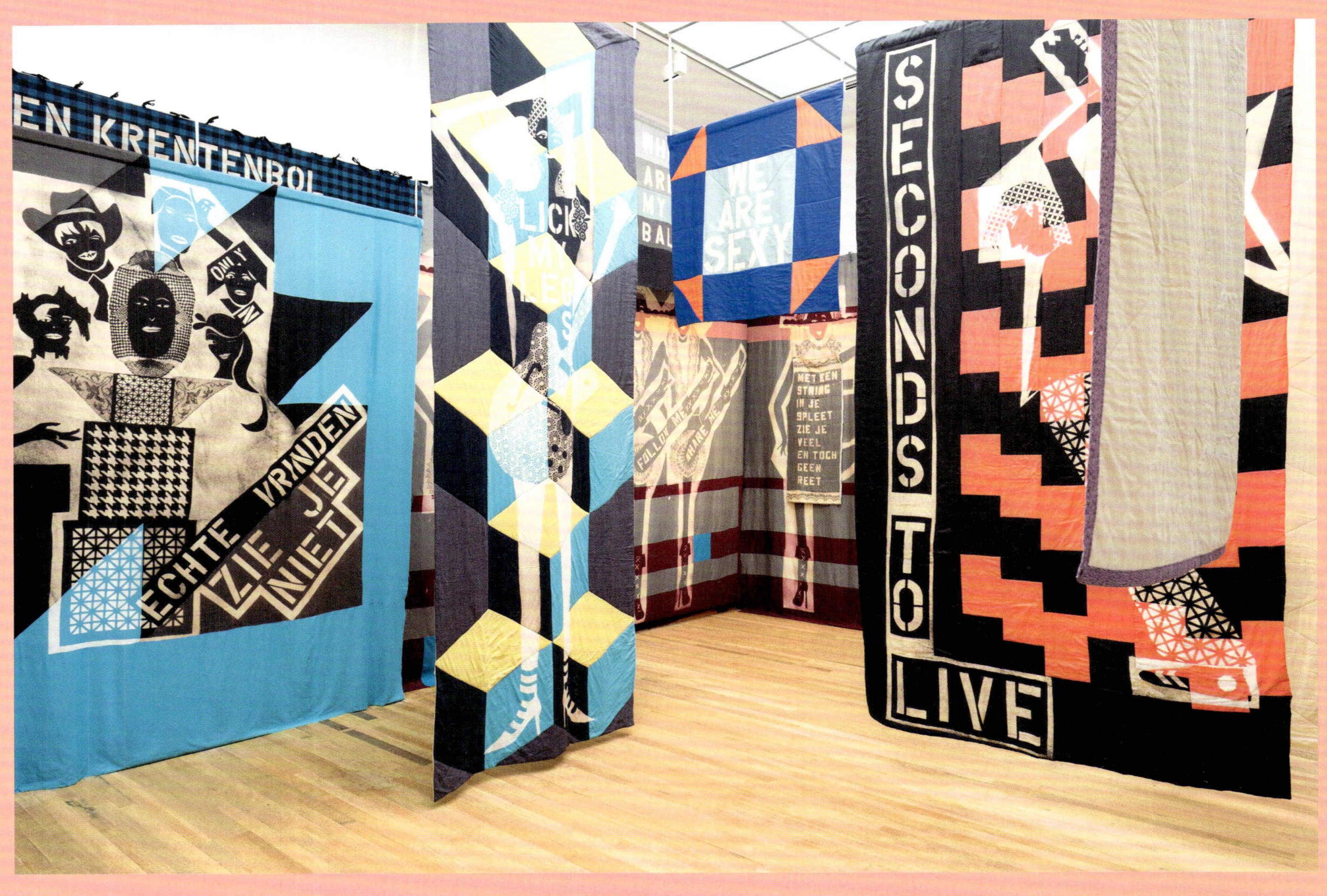

Helper's Little Mother, 2014

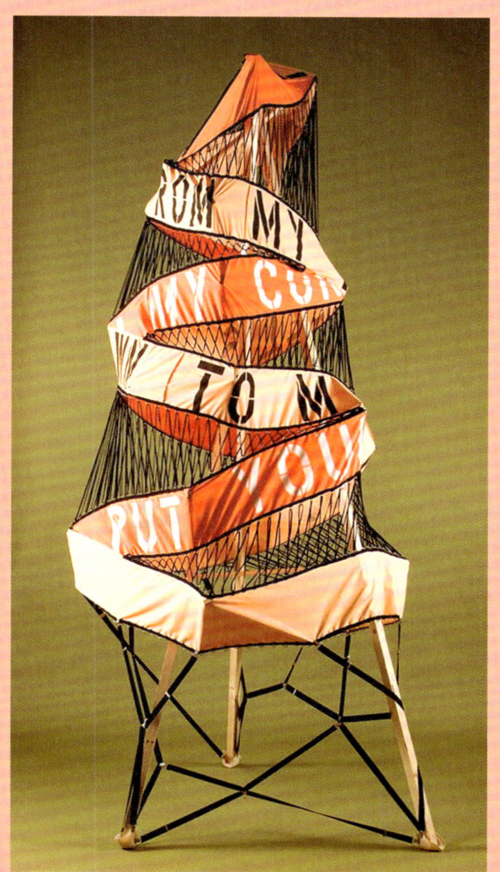
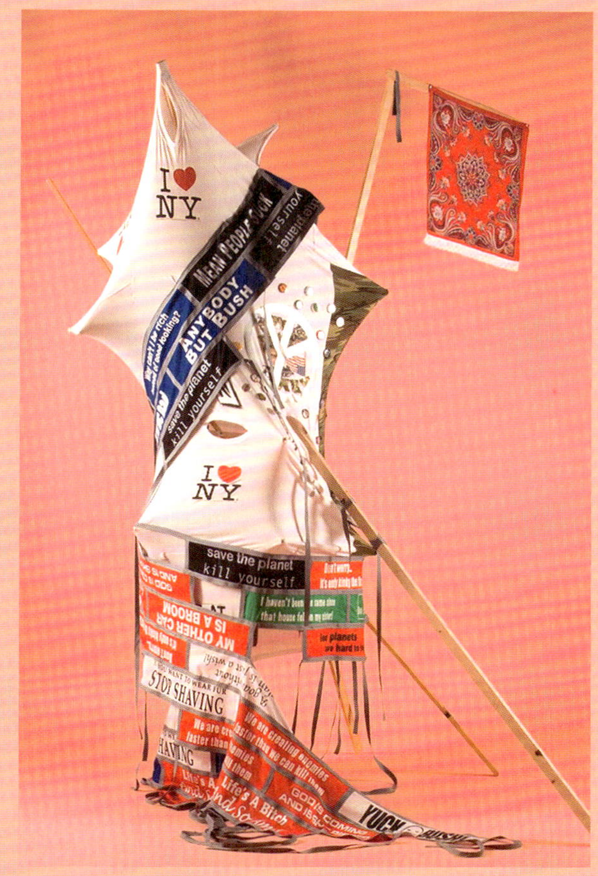
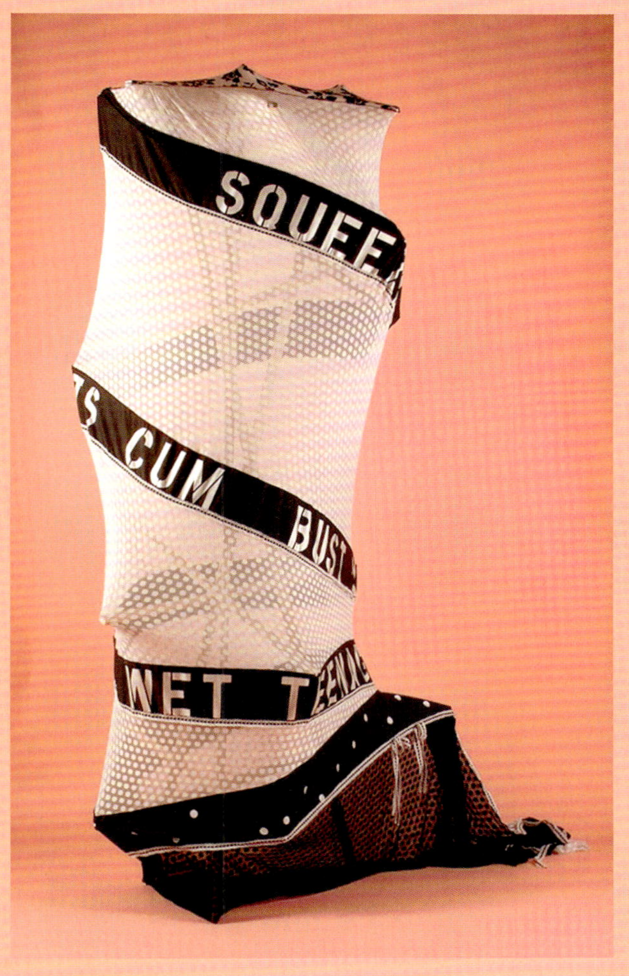
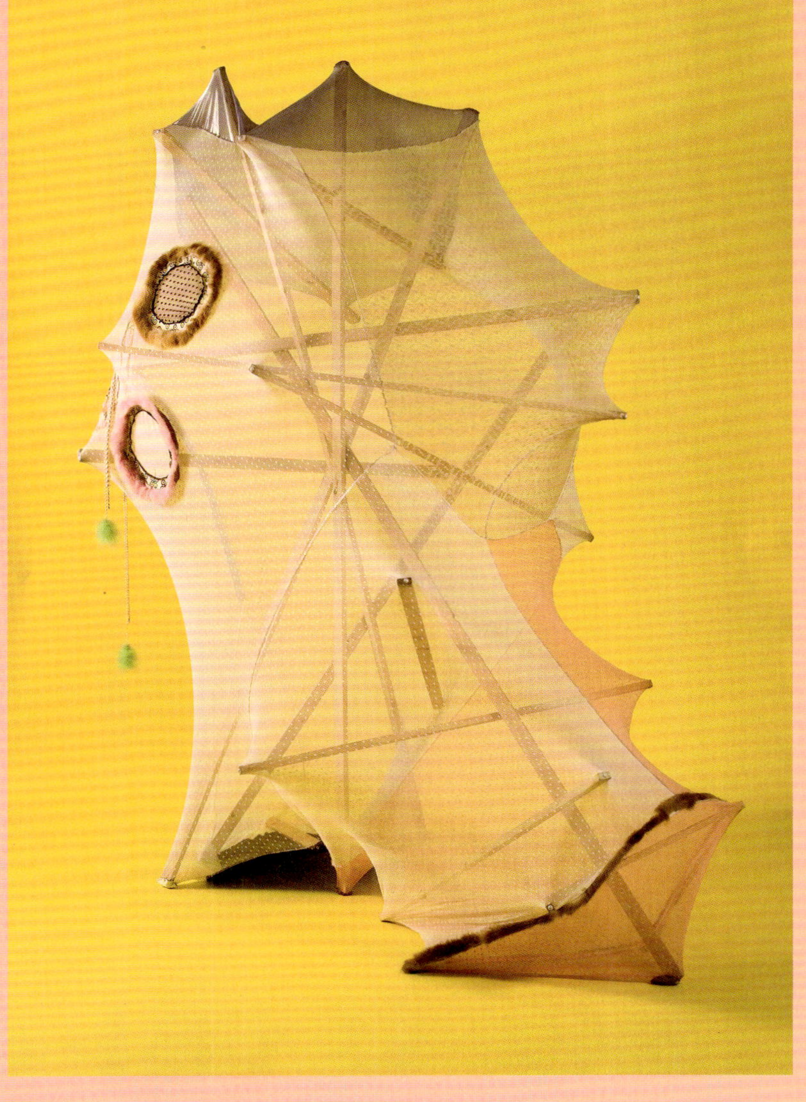

High Heeled Honey, 2005; *Rebel Rouser*, 2005
Dix-huit+, 2005; *Betty Ford*, 2005

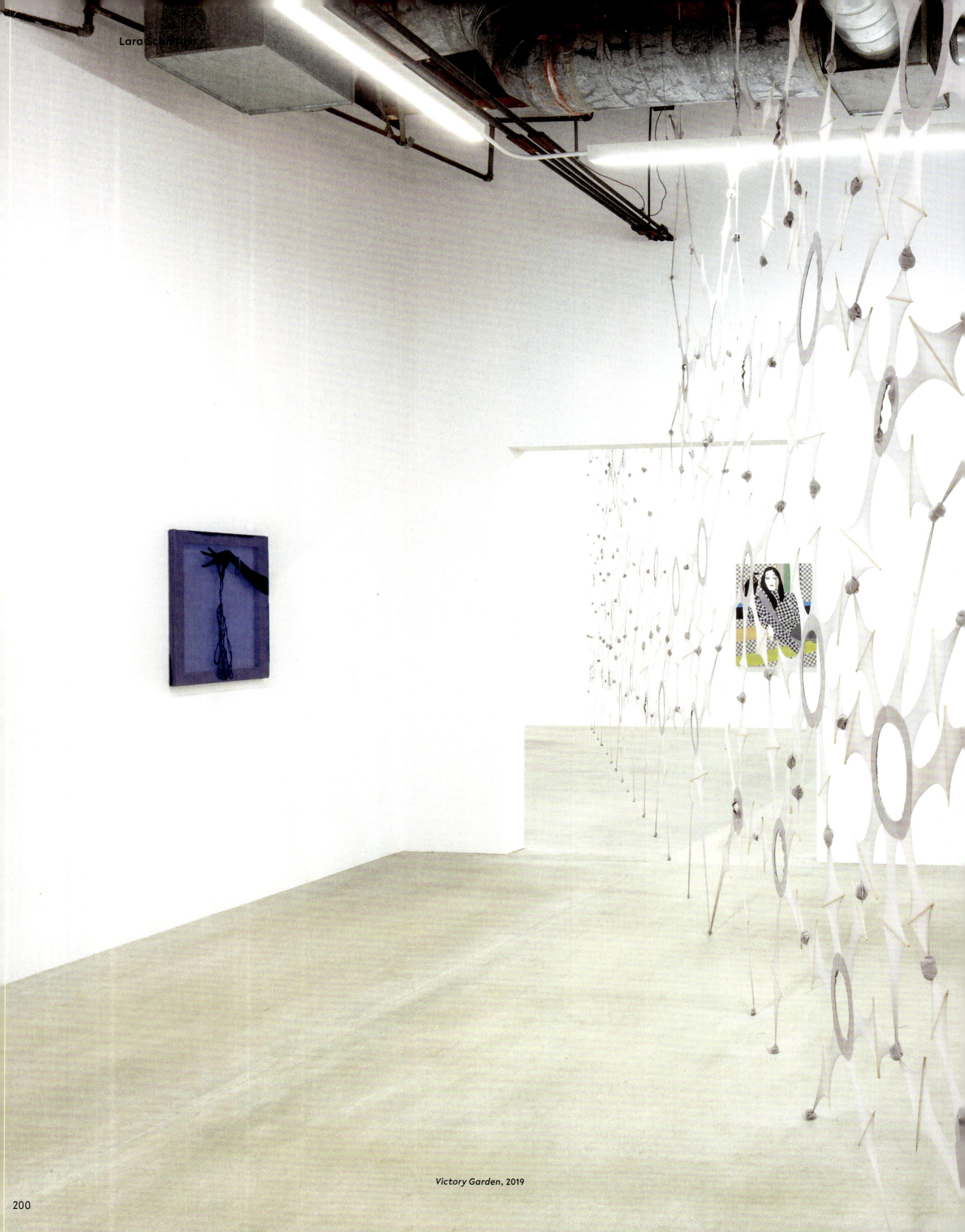

Victory Garden, 2019

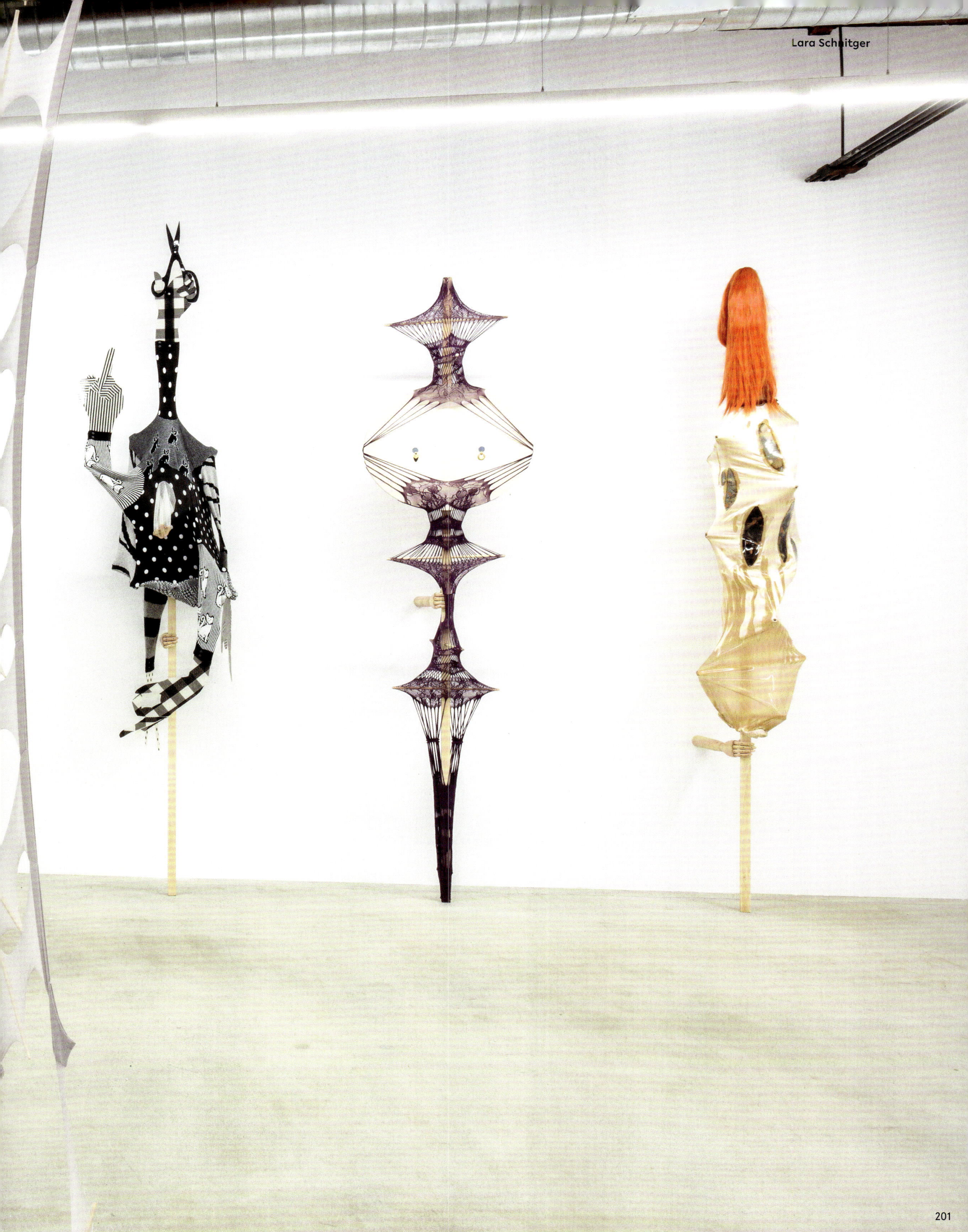

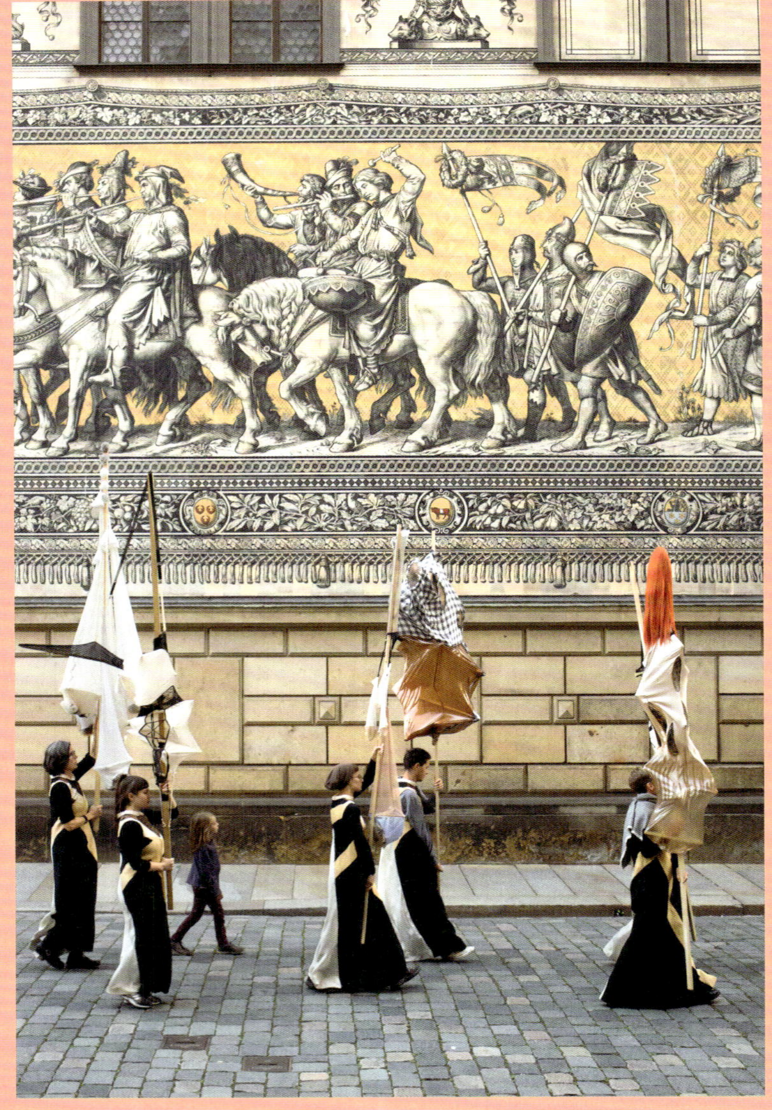

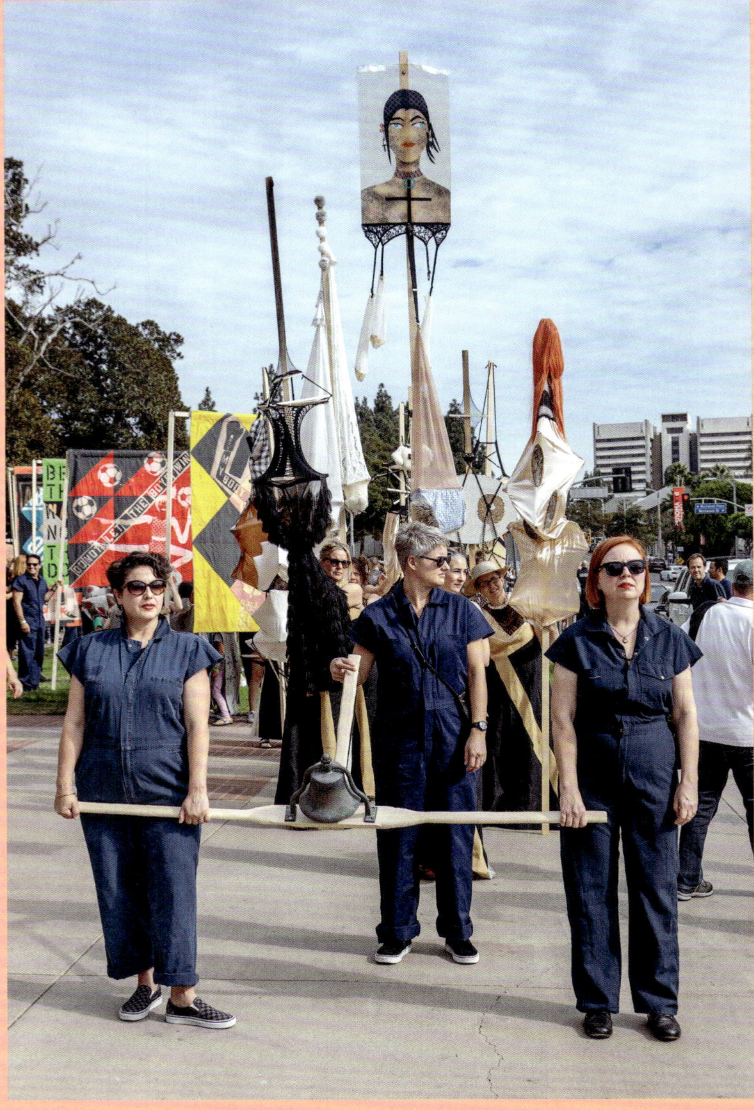

Suffragette City Dresden, 2017; *Suffragette City Los Angeles*, 2016

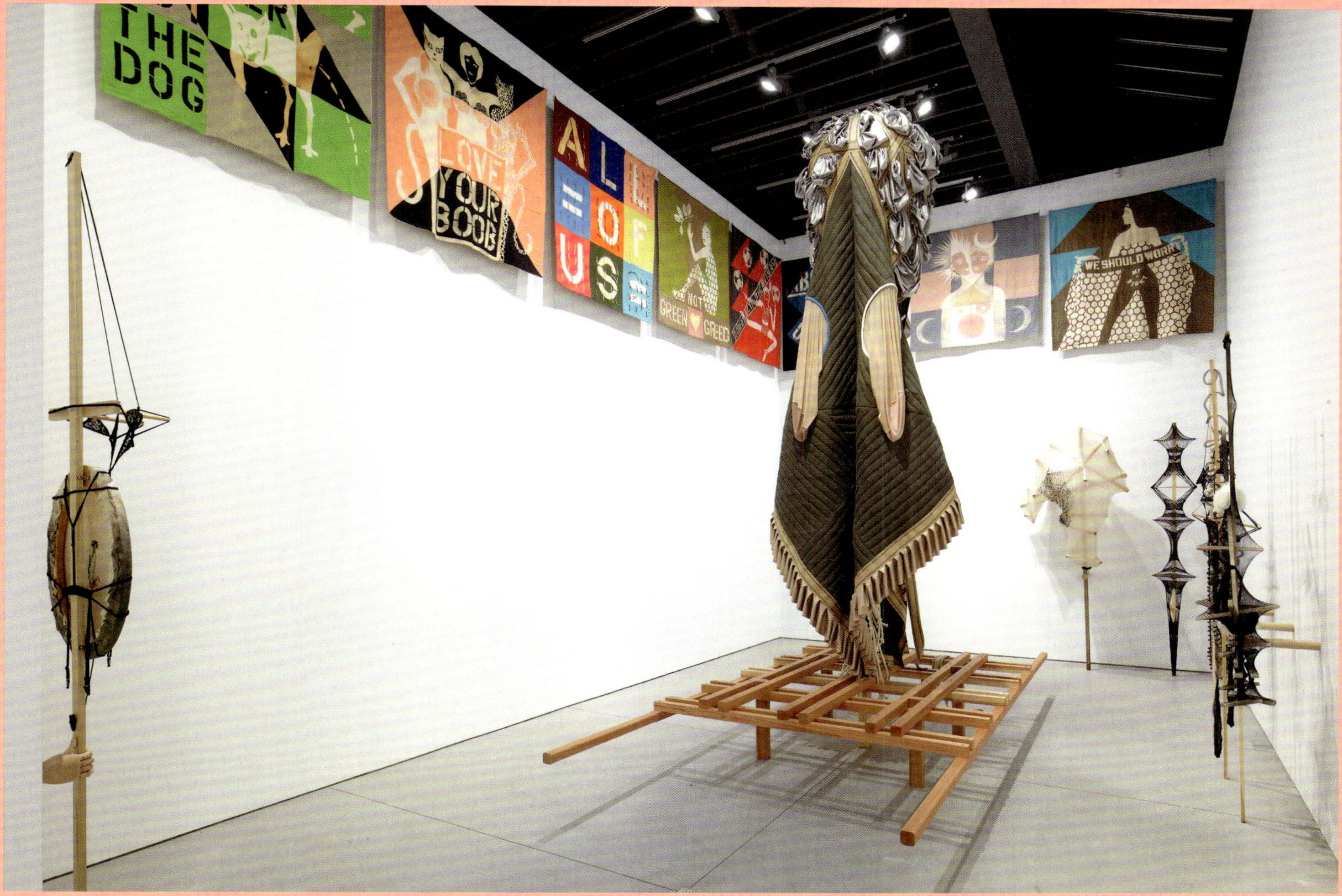

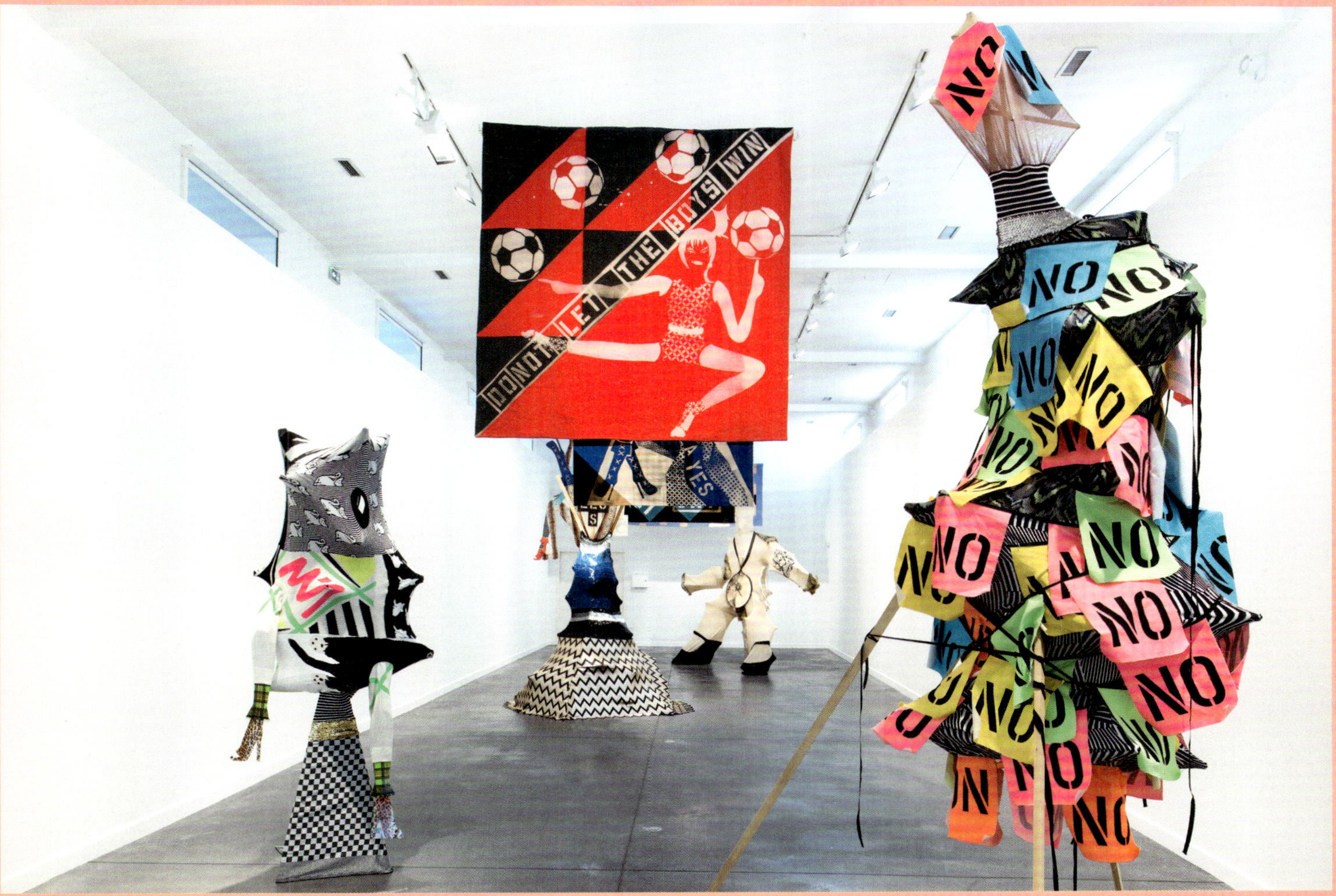

installation view, *Too Nice Too Long*, 2017
installation view, *Suffragette City Reims*, 2015

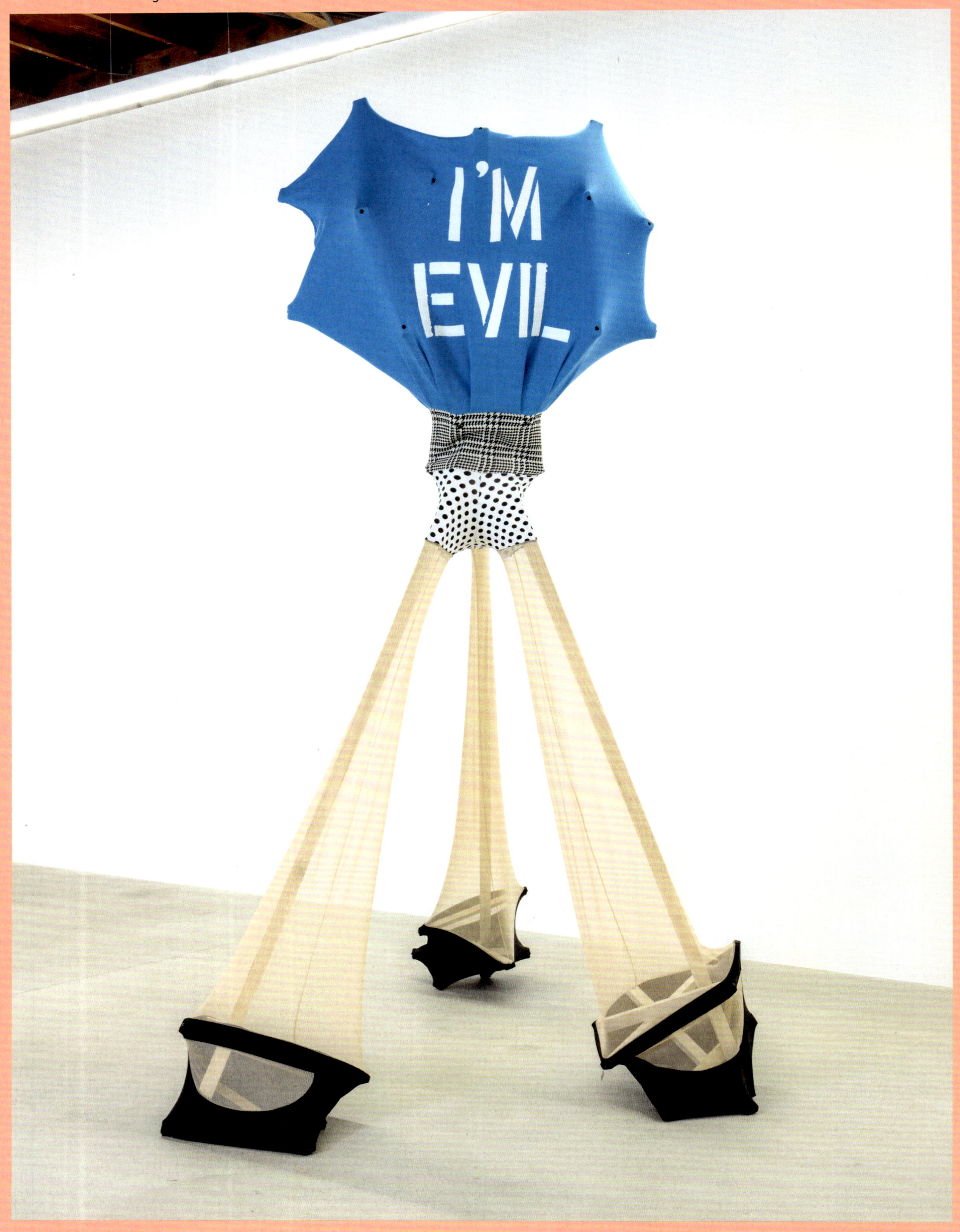

I Am Evil, 2019

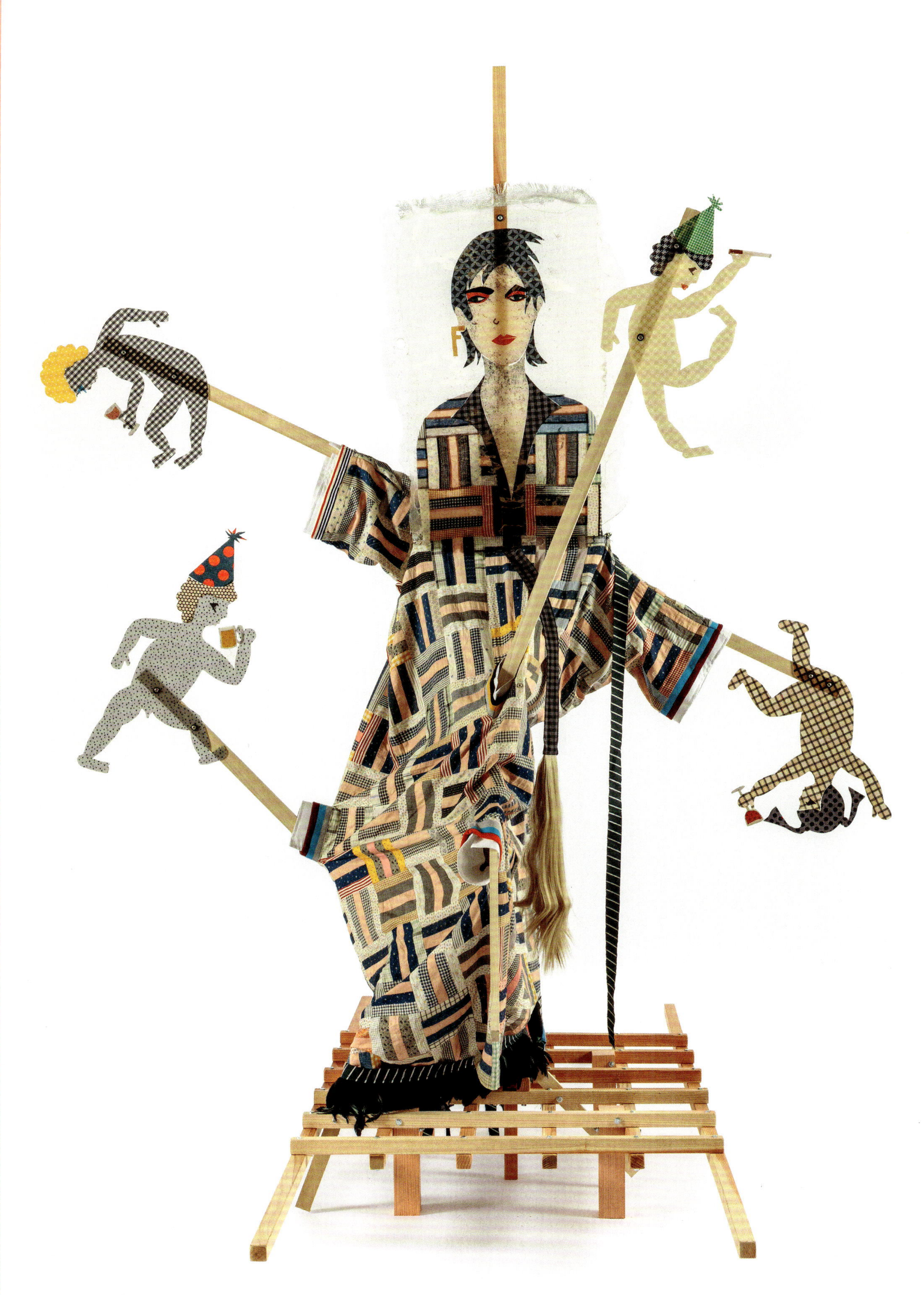

Leto's Party, 2017

Beverly Semmes

b. 1958, United States. Lives and works in New York, New York.

Beverly Semmes is perhaps best known for her early, large-scale installations consisting of oversize handmade dresses mounted directly on the wall. In works like *Red Dress* (1992), scale serves as a metaphor for power, elevating historically undervalued textile and dressmaking traditions to the realm of fine art. Semmes's garments award the female body an undeniable presence, their meters of trailing fabric overwhelming the gallery space and leaving little room for viewers to enter. At the same time, the empty dresses possess a ghostliness, given the absence of real bodies inside them. Their mixing of disparate fashions—in the case of *Red Dress*, the familiar sexy red frock tailored with a more conservative Peter Pan collar and boxy silhouette—speaks to the often-contradictory ways that women's bodies are represented in popular media. Taking up a monumental footprint, the dresses become the uninhabitable husks of a performative gender that lies somewhere between vixen and Barbara Bush.

The female body as a vessel—as an object meant to carry life, or a screen onto which men project both their desires and their hatred—is a trope that Semmes consistently employs in her ceramic and glass sculptures, especially those resembling crude vases, pitchers, and teacups. The tactility of their surfaces, grooved with indentations from Semmes's fingers, viscerally defies a male-dominated tradition of pristine sculpture. The works revel in the pure pleasure of making and physical touch. When overturned or displayed on top of Semmes's textile works, as in *Prairie Dress* (2007), the vessels also speak to the idea of femininity as an uncontainable excess. As fabric spills down the wall and across the gallery floor, the vases are hopeless in their function as agents of control.

Control and contradiction appear as tensions in much of Semmes's most pointed work. For *Witch Hunt*, she presents paintings from her ongoing Feminist Responsibility Project (FRP). The series, begun in 2003 after the artist inherited a stack of old *Penthouse* magazines from a neighbor, consists primarily of pages from vintage porn that Semmes has drawn and painted over in an attempt to obscure (or, in the artist's word, "shield") some of the more lascivious action. Sometimes covering the models' bodies with shapes like those of her vases, Semmes transforms the erotic source material of works like *Piano* (2013) into surreal tableaux of disembodied limbs and biomorphic scrawls. Occasionally she shows the works reversed, so that the bleed-through of ink, glitter, and paint as it appears on the verso of the page becomes the dominant mode of mark making. Like her sculptures and textile work, the Feminist Responsibility Project engages with the erotics of materiality and the politics of sexual freedom while figuring femininity as unmanageable and unfixed. If the defensive impulse of Semmes's gestures reads as somewhat abrasive, it is self-consciously so. In 2011, when she introduced the project at Rowan University Art Gallery in Glassboro, New Jersey, she displayed several magazine drawings along with video, sculpture, and photography, and also presented a performance featuring two women in handmade dresses sitting at a table. Its characters, called the Super Puritan and the Bitch, faced off over an unfinished puzzle formed out of one of Semmes's FRP paintings, *Carwash* (2011). In a contemporary climate where young women are more likely to be accustomed to the sex-positive culture of social media than the antiporn sentiments of the 1970s, the stalemate between the Super Puritan and the Bitch plays out as that eternal conflict between these different strains of first-world feminism.

The complexity of Semmes's feminist action and the sheer undefinability of "feminist responsibility" take precedence in many of the FRP works. Even as their facture attempts to block the viewer's gaze, there are moments where the artist's hand has slipped, letting the barest hint of flesh shine through. In some cases where Semmes has obscured faces and genitals, she emphasizes other elements: navels, cleavage, the pointed heel of a stiletto boot, a ponytail softly trailing down a model's back. Some of the pastel-colored verso images, such as *Blue Arms* (2016), could even be called lovely in their delicate marking. In this tension between Semmes's abstraction and the resilience of the naked figures, ambiguity is the sexiest move of all.

—Vanessa Arizmendi

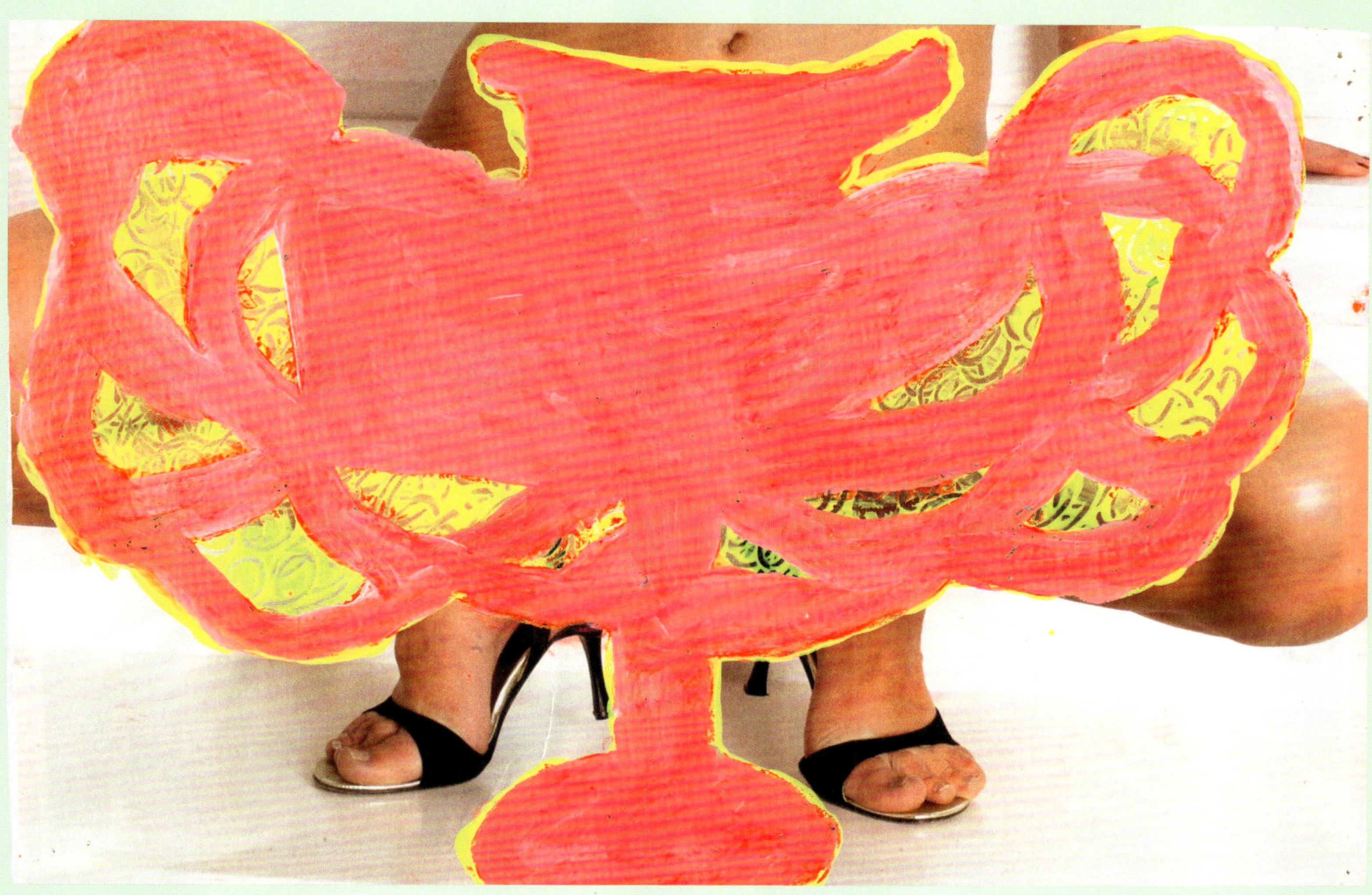

Pink Pot, 2008

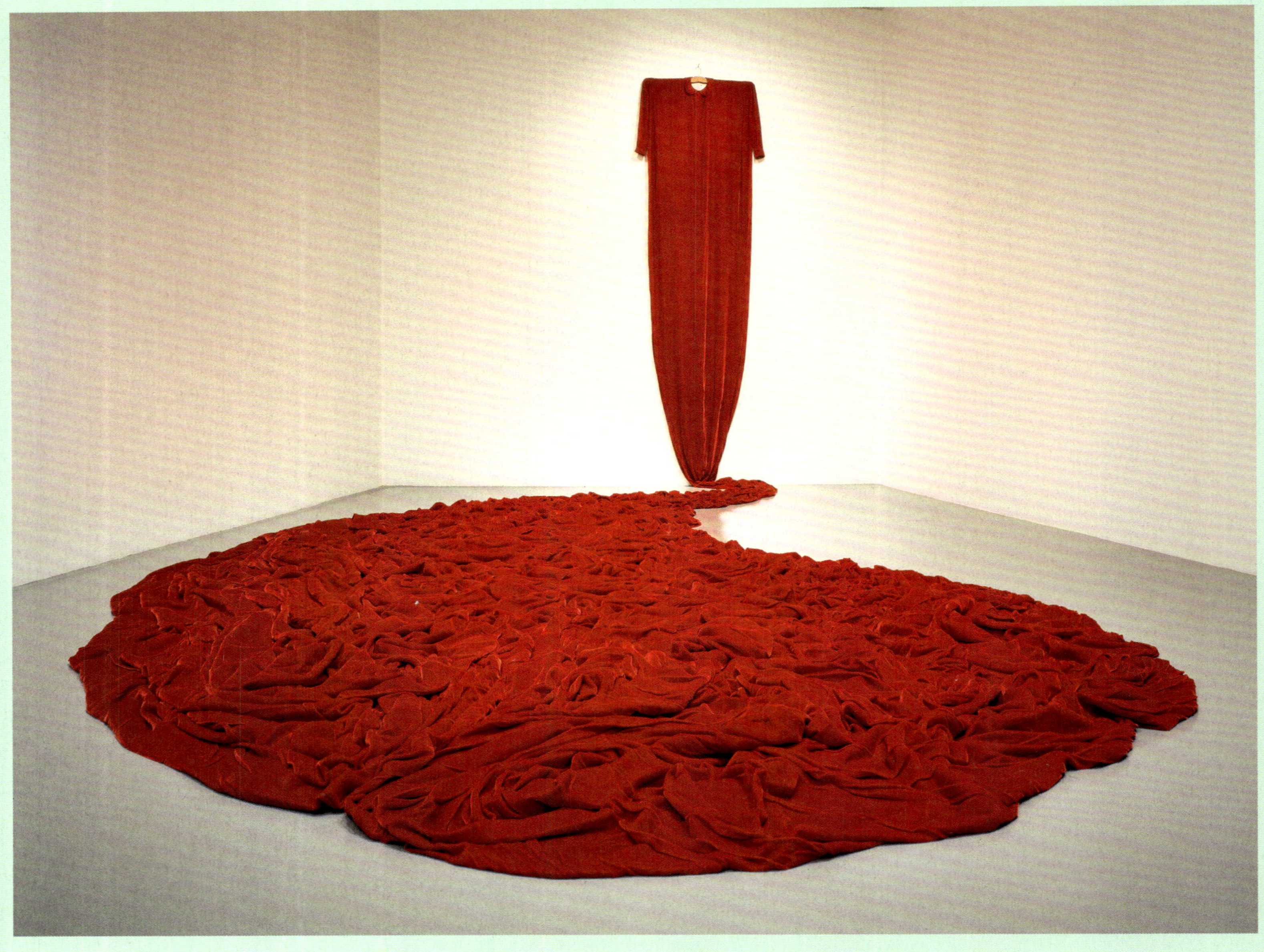

Red Dress, 1992

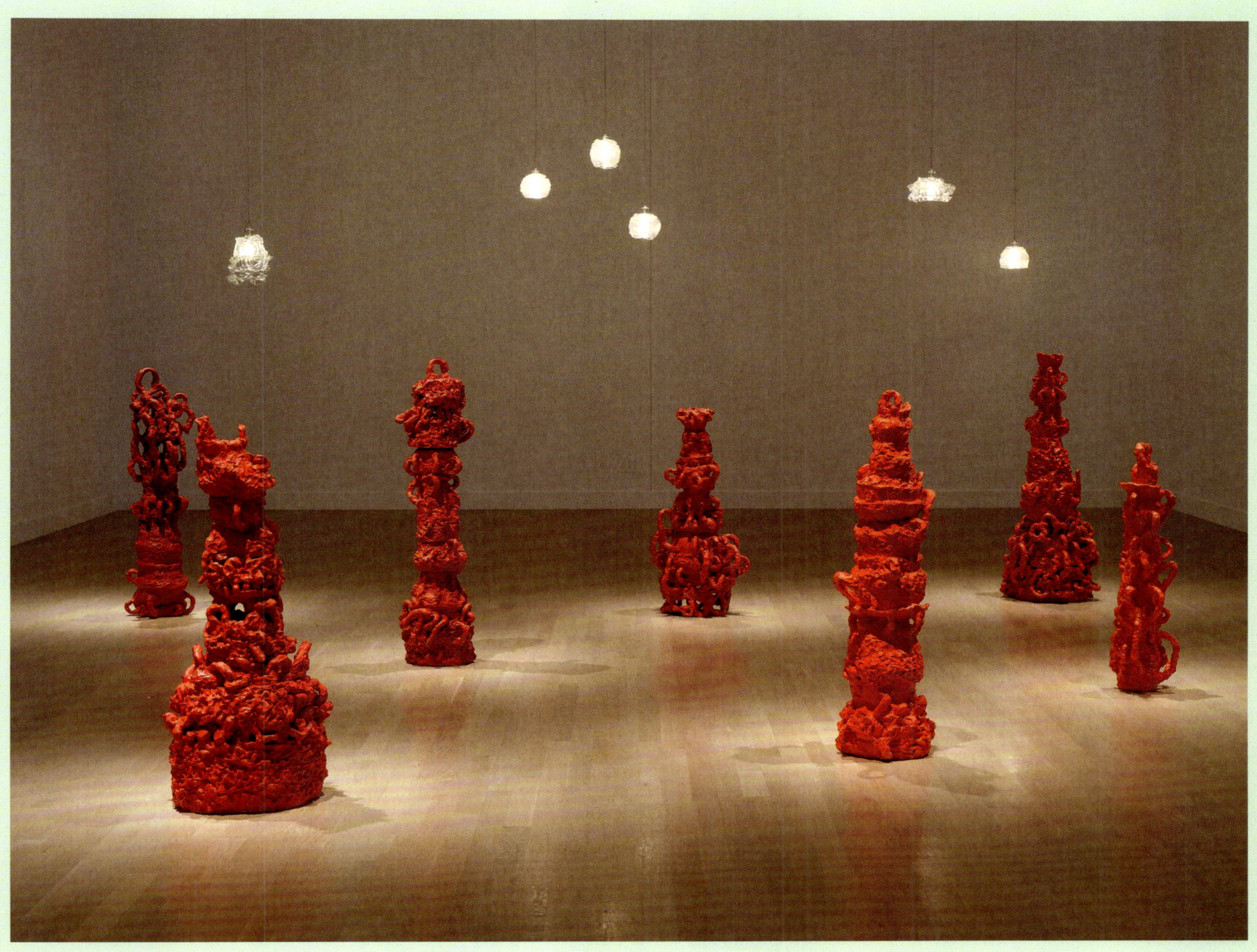

Red Pots, Crystal Chandeliers, 2015

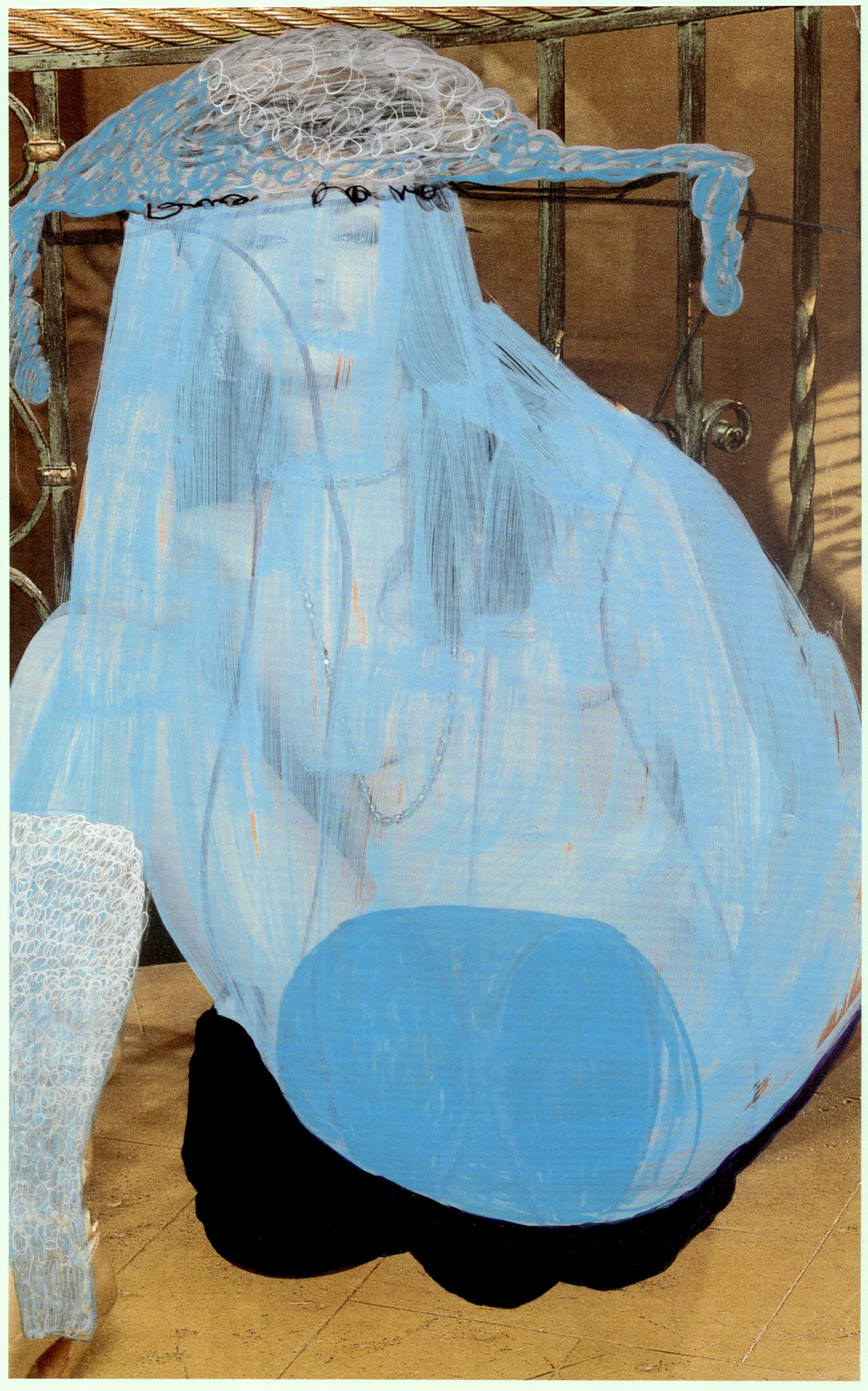

Silver Hat, 2018

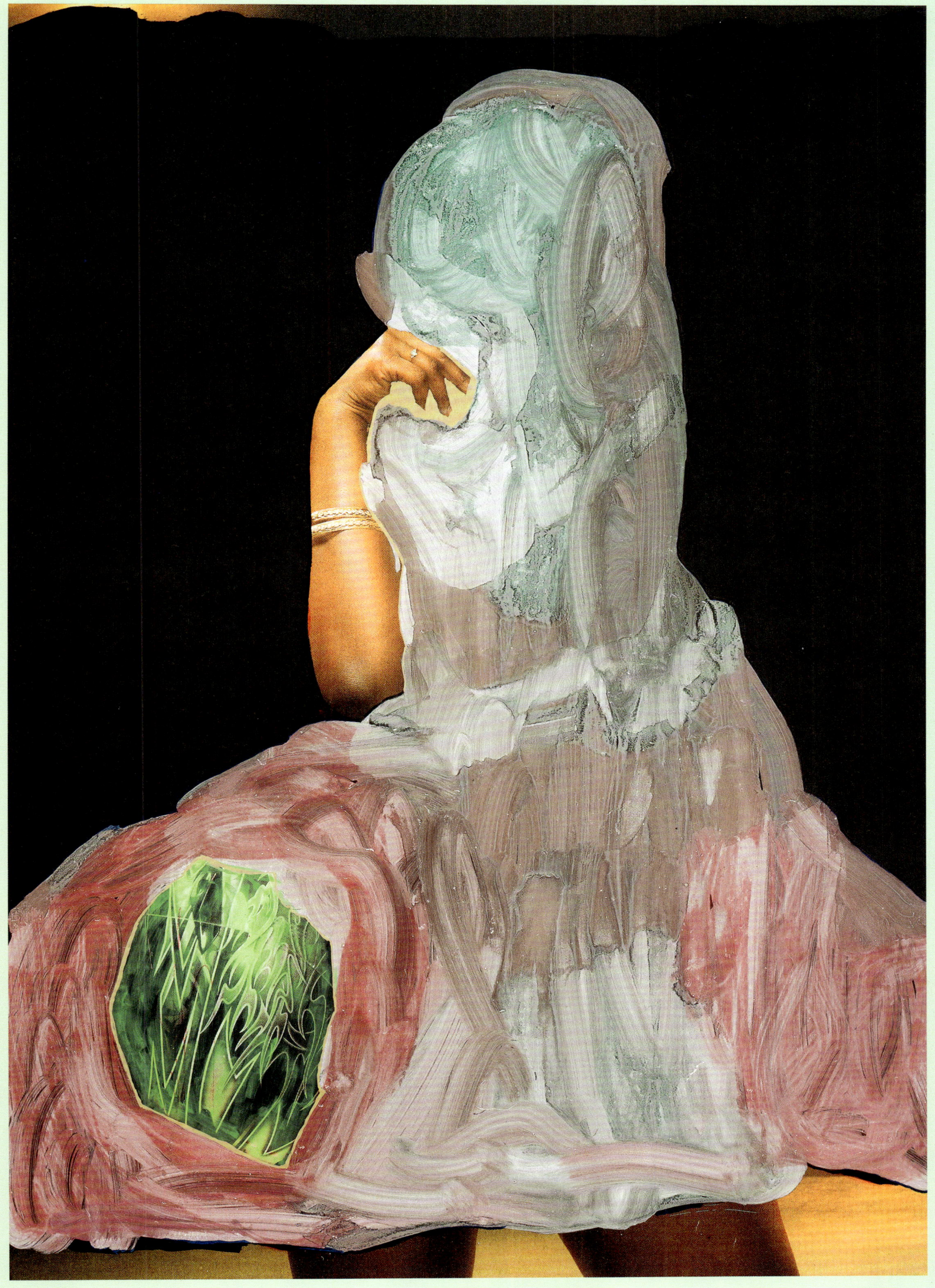

Helmet, 2018

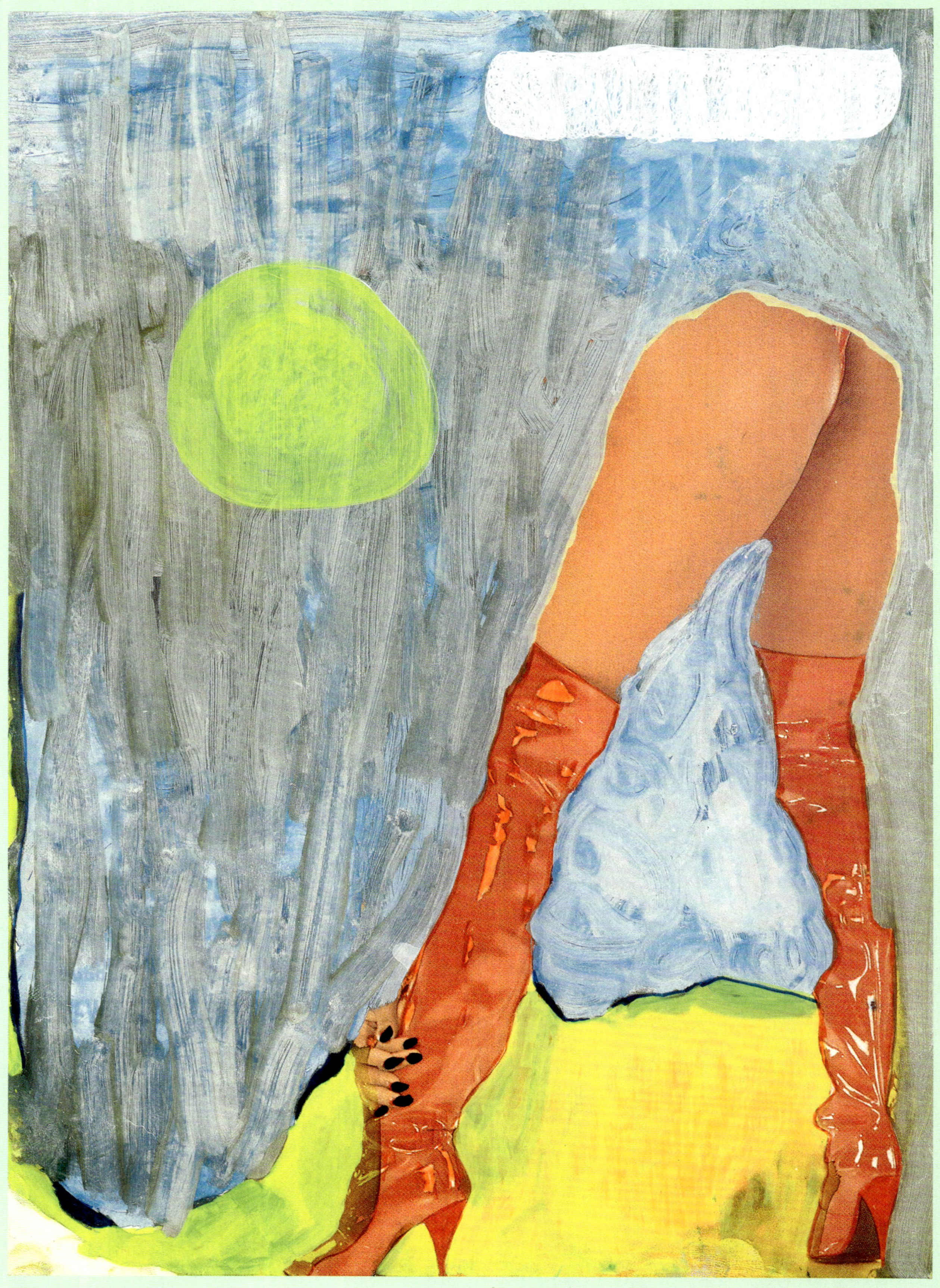

Legs, 2018

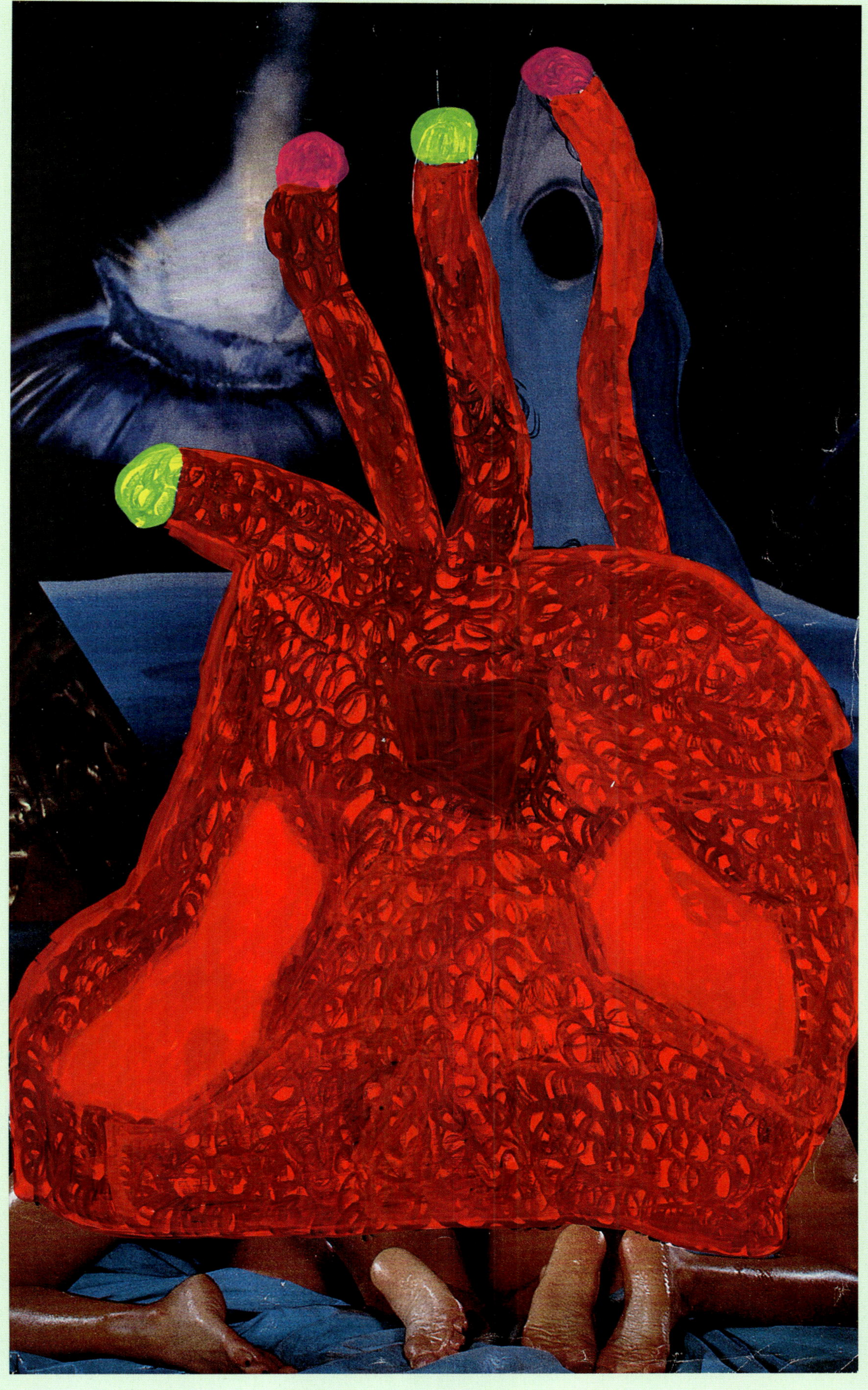

Antenna, 2019

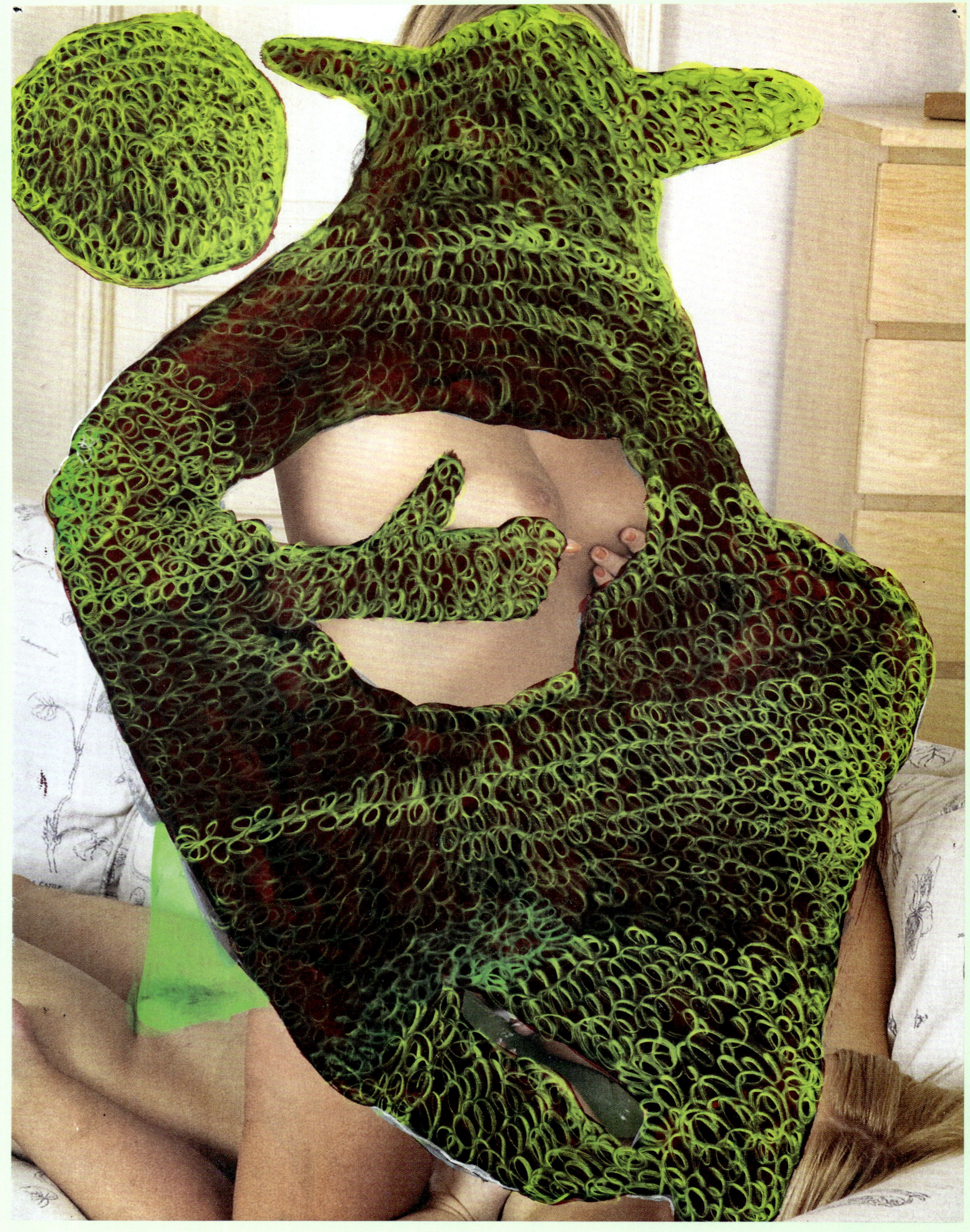

Silver Heart, 2019

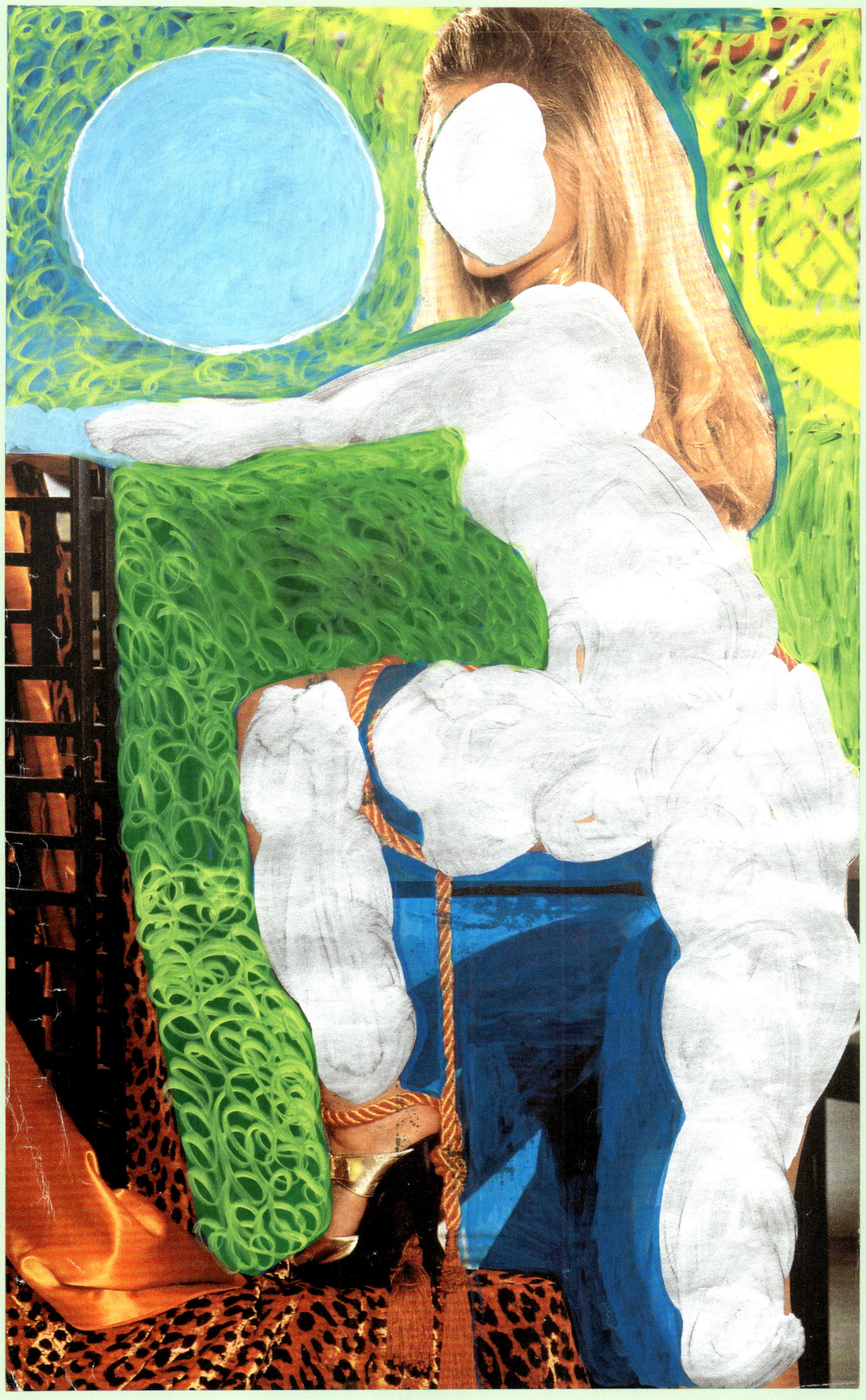

Blue Moon, 2020

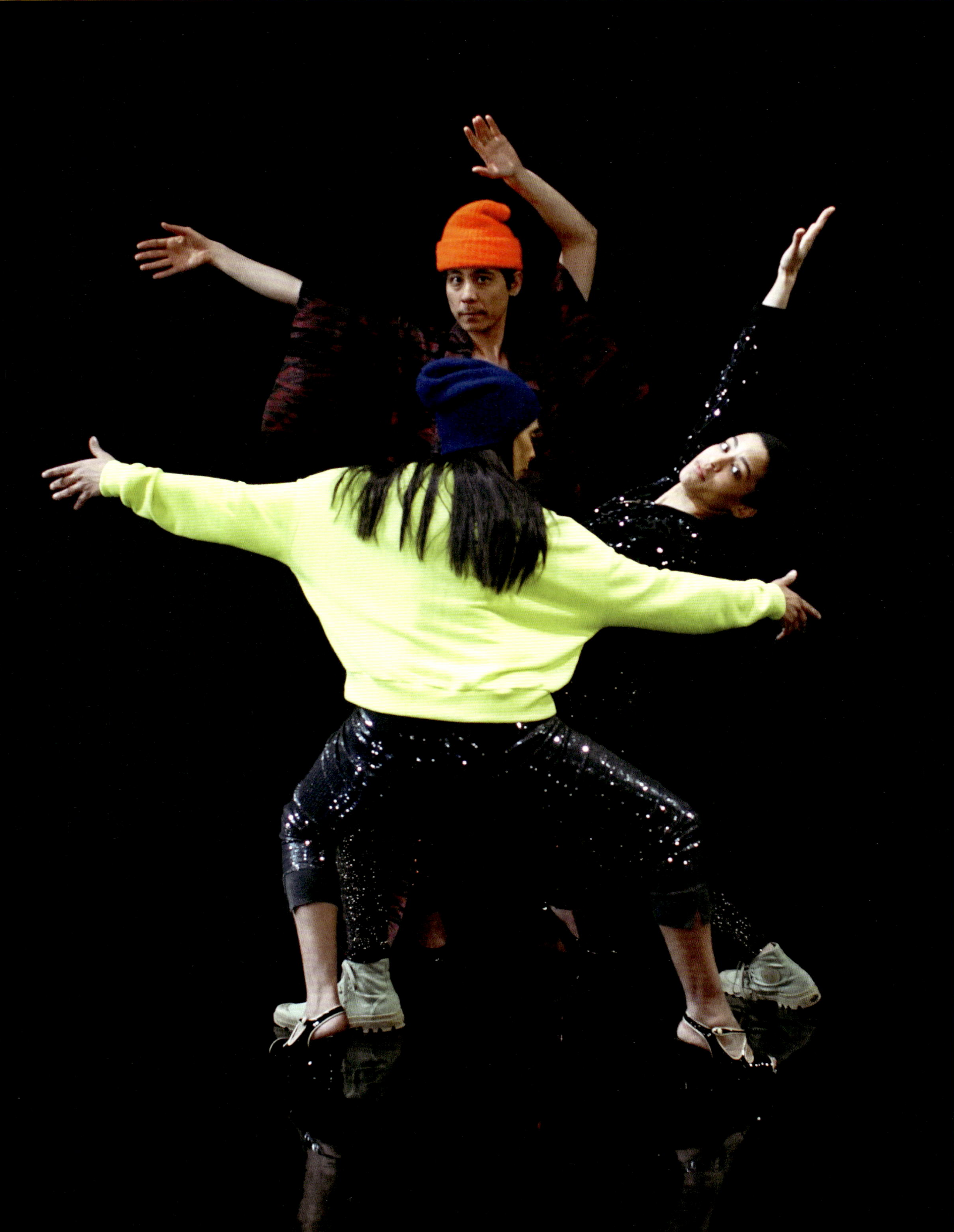

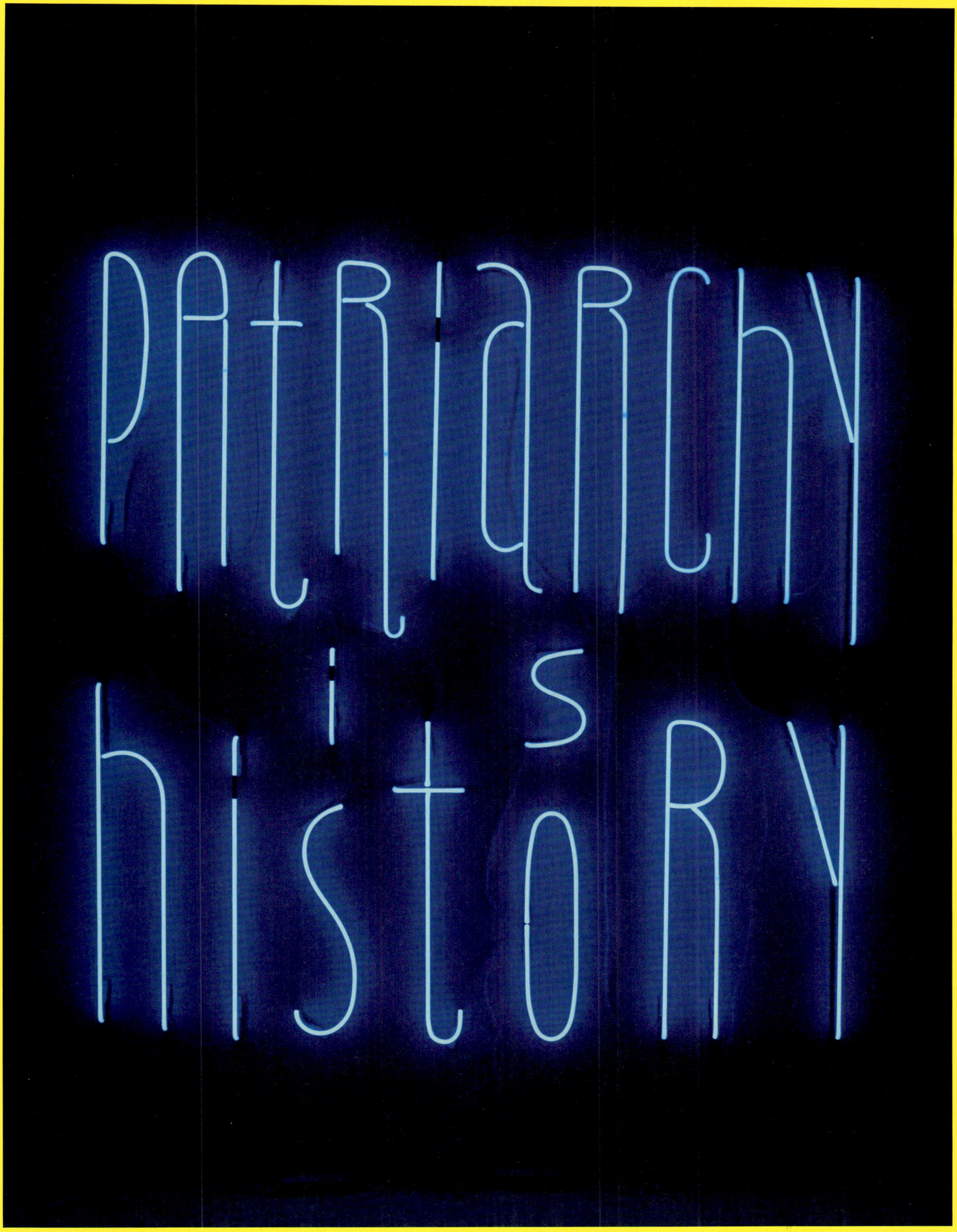

patriarchy is history

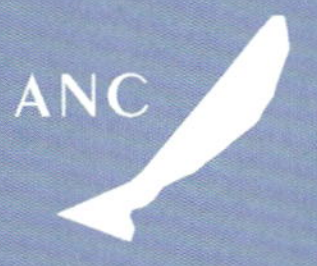
ANC

FRELIMO
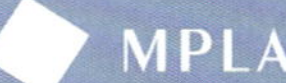
PAIGC

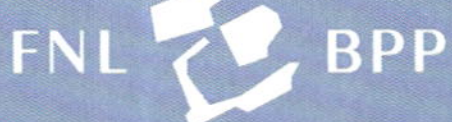
FNL
BPP

MPLA

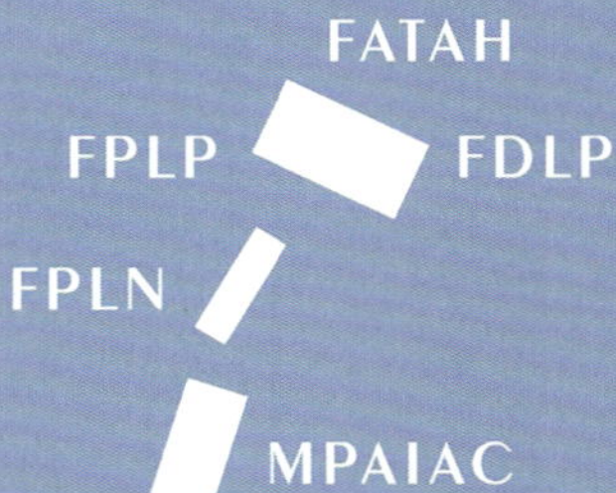
FATAH
FPLP
FDLP
FPLN
MPAIAC

FLE
PFLOAG
FLQ
ZAPU
FLCS
SWAPO

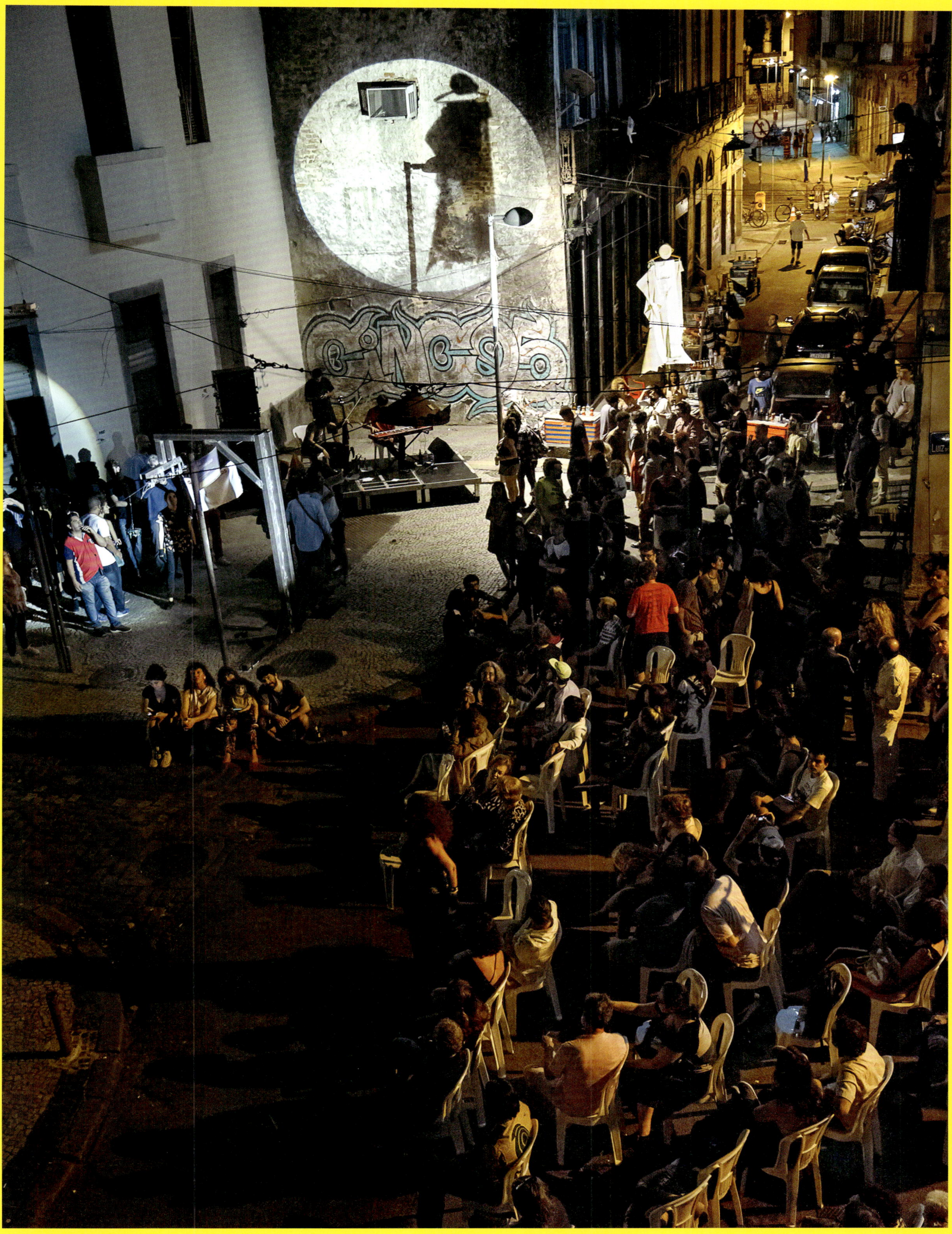

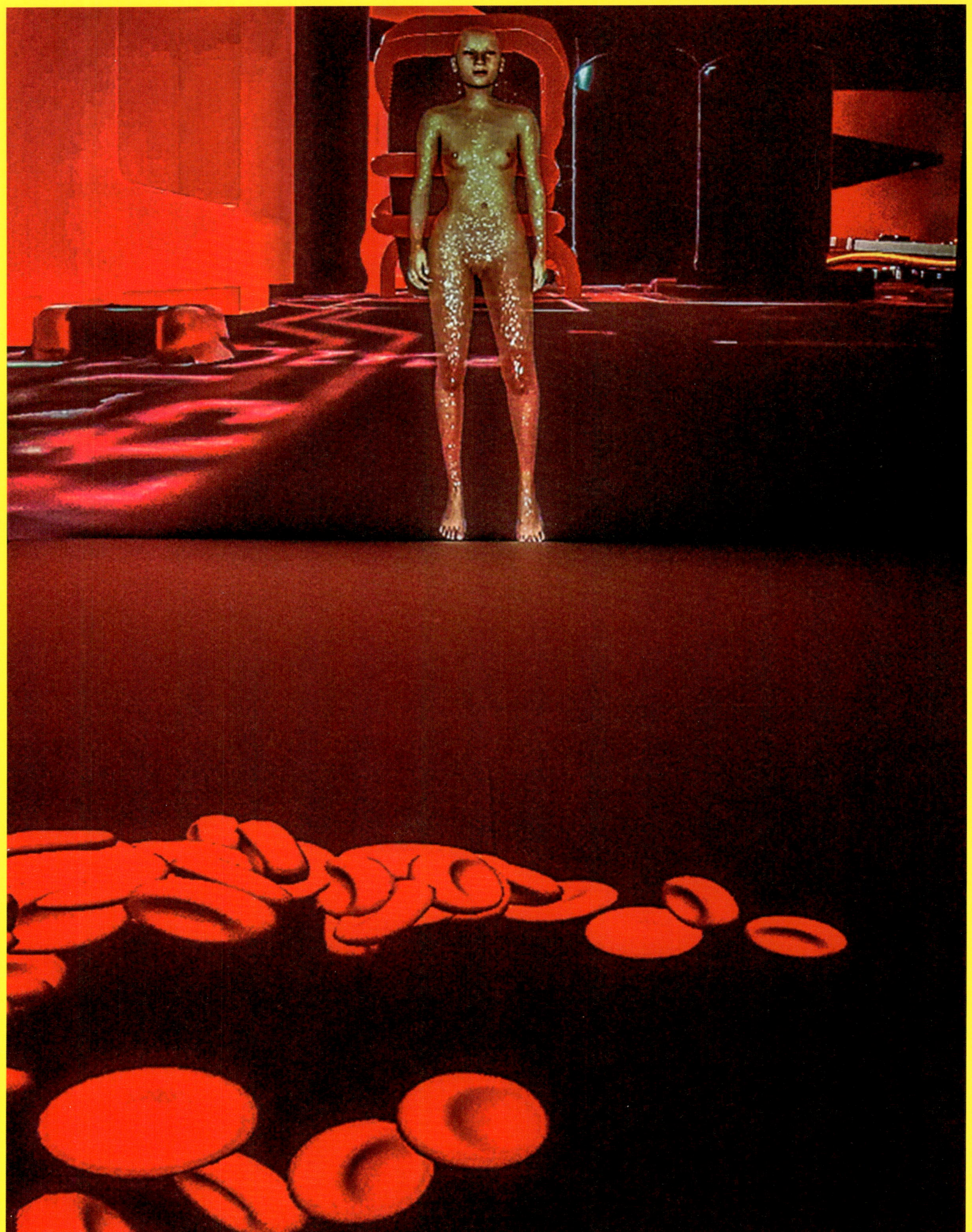

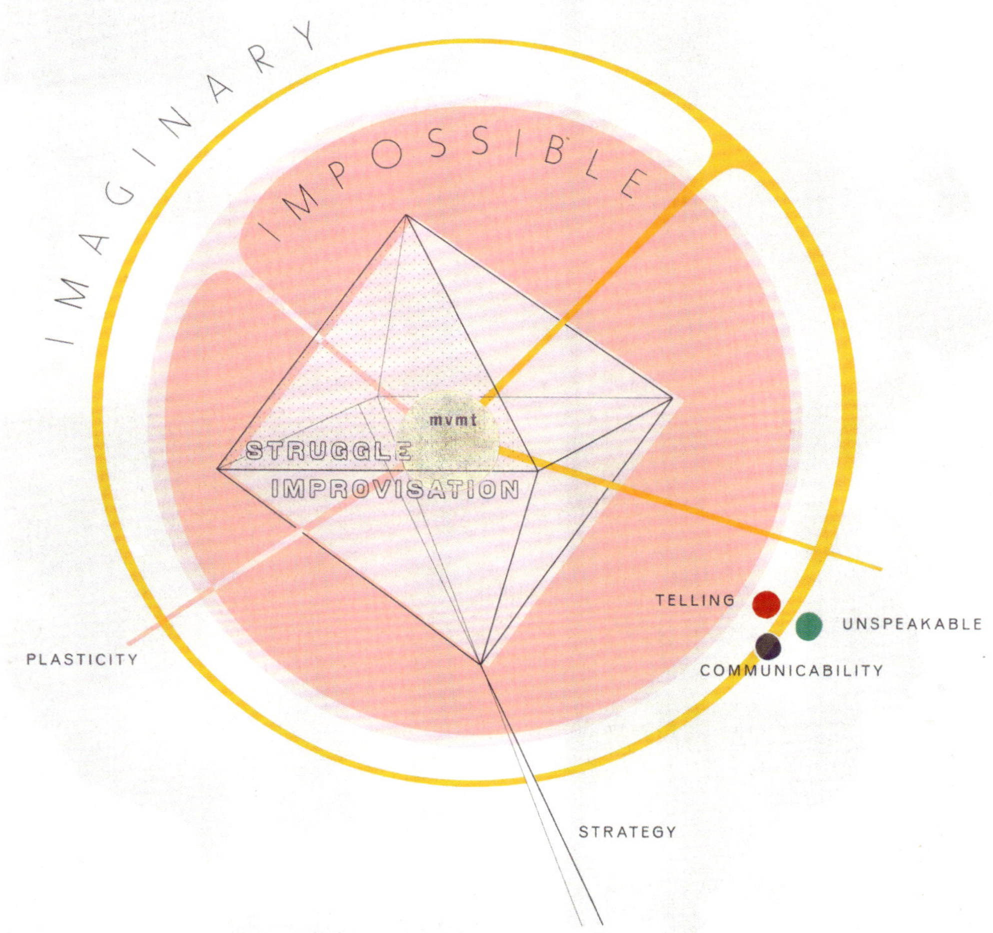

ECSTATIC RESISTANCE

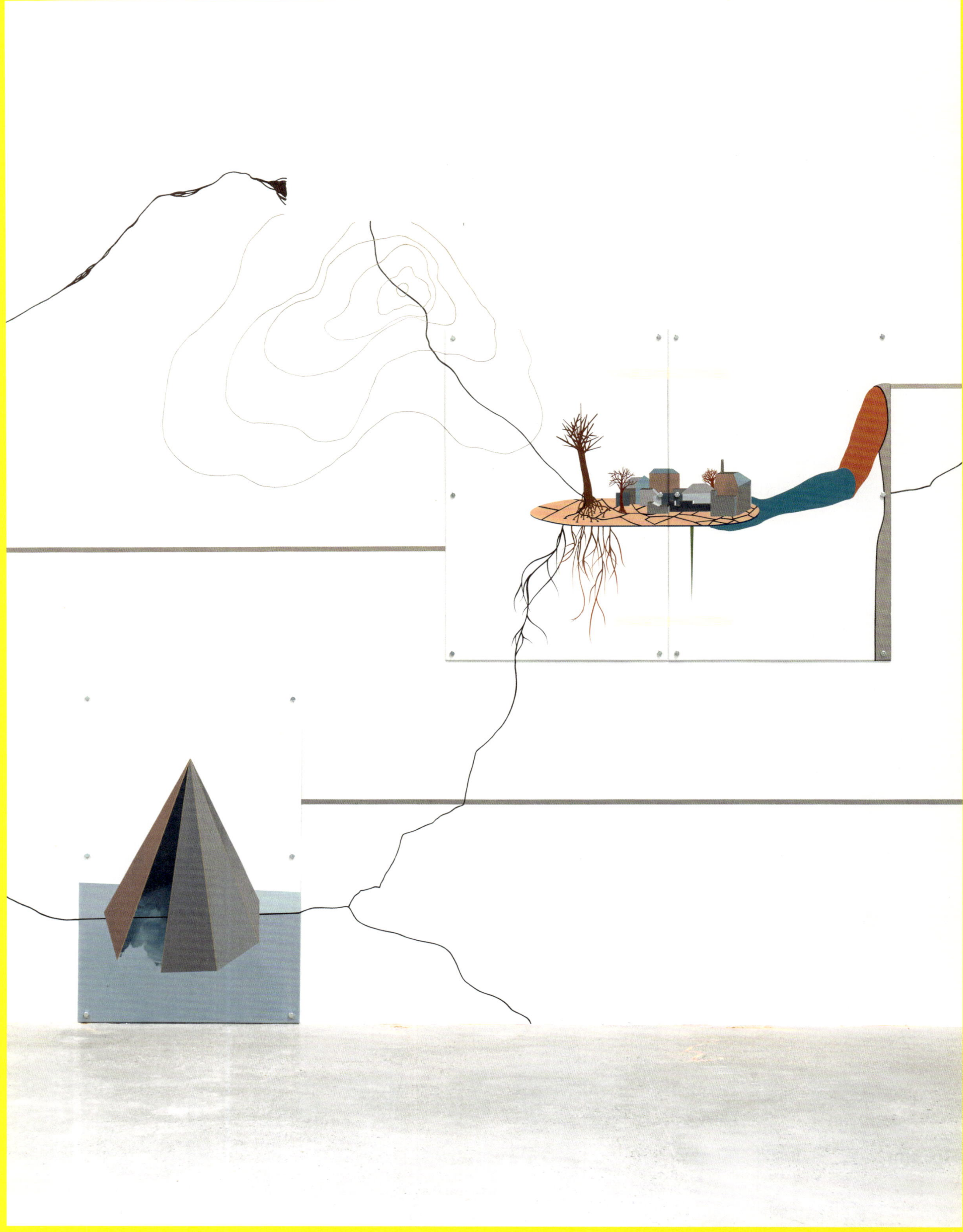

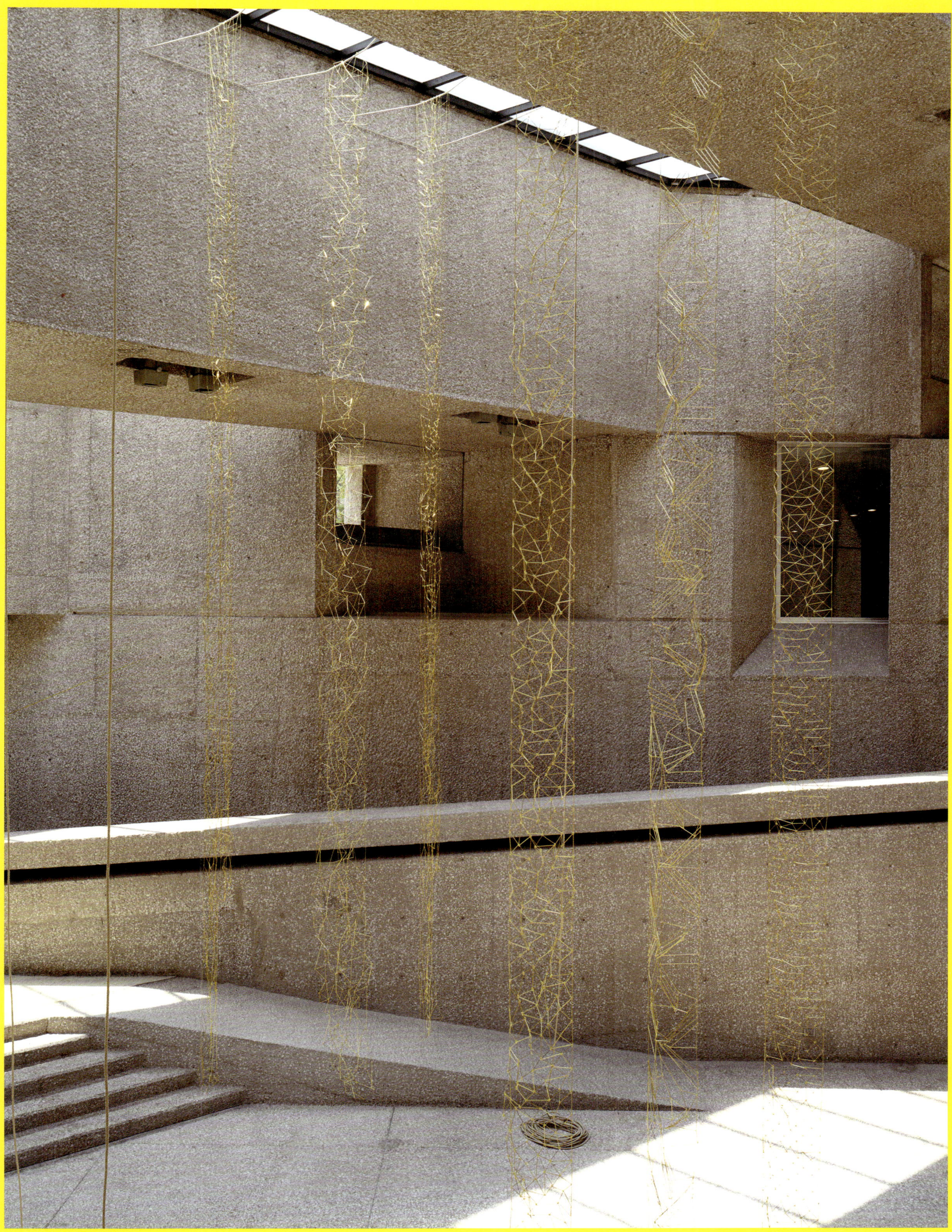

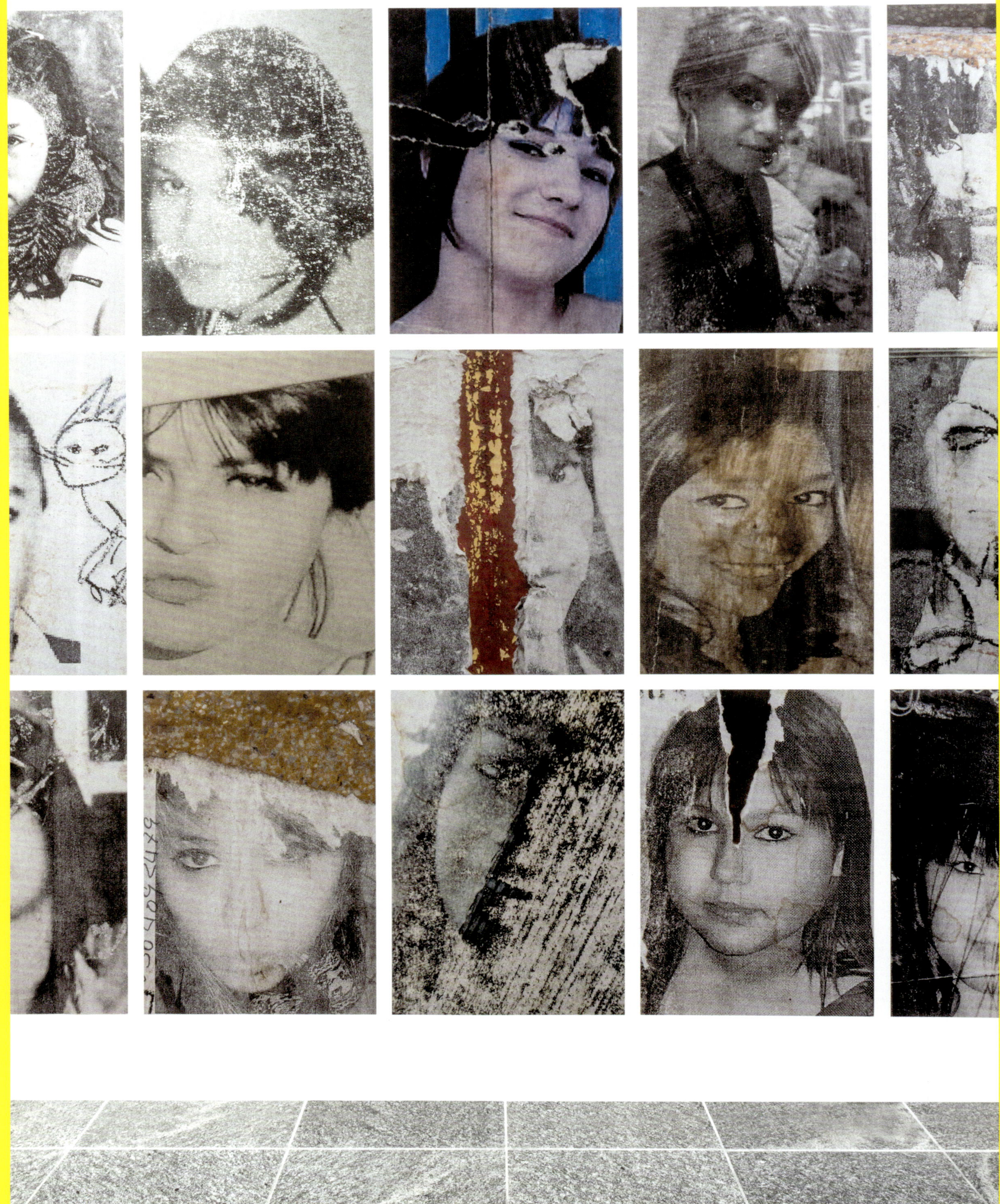